LOCAL POLITICS IN JORDAN AND MOROCCO

Columbia Studies in Middle East Politics

COLUMBIA STUDIES IN MIDDLE EAST POLITICS
Marc Lynch, Series Editor

Columbia Studies in Middle East Politics presents academically rigorous, well-written, relevant, and accessible books on the rapidly transforming politics of the Middle East for an interested academic and policy audience.

Local Politics in Jordan and Morocco

STRATEGIES OF CENTRALIZATION AND DECENTRALIZATION

Janine A. Clark

Columbia University Press
New York

Columbia University Press
Publishers Since 1893
New York   Chichester, West Sussex
cup.columbia.edu
Copyright © 2018 Columbia University Press
All rights reserved

Library of Congress Cataloging-in-Publication Data
Names: Clark, Janine A., author.
Title: Local politics in Jordan and Morocco : strategies of centralization
and decentralization / Janine A. Clark.
Other titles: Columbia studies in Middle East politics.
Description: New York : Columbia University Press, 2018. | Series: Columbia studies
in Middle East politics | Includes bibliographical references and index.
Identifiers: LCCN 2017031563 | ISBN 978-0-231-18358-1 (hardcover : alk. paper) |
ISBN 978-0-231-54501-3 (e-book)
Subjects: LCSH: Municipal government—Jordan. | Decentralization in government—Jordan. |
Jordan—Politics and government. | Municipal government—Morocco. | Decentralization
in government—Morocco. | Morocco—Politics and government.
Classification: LCC JS7503.3.A3 C58 2018 | DDC 320.8095695—dc23
LC record available at https://lccn.loc.gov/2017031563

Columbia University Press books are printed on permanent and durable acid-free paper.
Printed in the United States of America
Cover design: Milenda Nan Ok Lee
Cover image: © istockphoto

To the two Johns in my life

Contents

Acknowledgments

This book was a long time in the making and I owe thanks to the numerous people both at home and abroad who gave me their support, advice, and suggestions throughout the researching and writing process. To everyone, I am deeply indebted. To begin with, this book would not have been possible without the Social Science and Research Council of Canada, which provided the funding for the project. I also owe thanks to my colleagues who helped me in conceptualizing, writing, and revising the research proposal for this project: Jordi Diez, Candace Johnson, and Craig Johnson. Without their help this project never would have materialized. I am particularly grateful to Jordi for his ongoing guidance. I also want to thank my former department chair, Byron Sheldrick, for ensuring that I had the flexibility in my teaching schedule to be able to do the field research.

I owe my deepest thanks to the mayors, municipal councillors, and party leaders, as well as NGO representatives, in all the municipalities I visited throughout Jordan and Morocco. They are the heart and the soul of this book. Research trips took me to parts of Jordan I had never seen before, and to those far from any tourist's list of places to visit. I have to thank all those I met in each of the municipalities for making me fall in love with Jordan all over again. I was overwhelmed with the generosity of everyone I interviewed as they drove me around to some of the stunningly beautiful hidden corners of their municipalities, showed me their development projects, and invited me to their homes for lunch. My same thanks go to all those I met in Morocco for not only going out of their way to facilitate my research but for the warm and truly wonderful introduction they provided me to the country.

I conducted the numerous interviews for this book both on my own and with research assistants. I also had research assistants conduct some of the interviews on my behalf. In Jordan, I especially want to thank Hilda Ayoub and Ola Farawati, each of whom drove with me all over Jordan and joined me in the interviews. Hilda also kindly did some important translations of secondary materials for me. Both played indispensable roles in helping facilitate the interviews, breaking the ice with those we met, and translating some difficult dialects—especially those of some of the other visitors with whom we found ourselves in the mayors' offices (sometimes barging into them), there to complain, for example, about road salting (one citizen was insulted the municipality salted the road in front of his home; he felt it was his own responsibility) or road paving (another citizen demanded that a road be paved precisely because he knew it would lower his brother's home value!). I cannot thank Ola and Hilda enough for all the laughter we had driving long hours and discovering new parts of the country.

Most especially I want to thank Mohammad Yaghi, who conducted interviews on my behalf in Jordan. No doubt his success in all his interviews was due to his patience, kindness, and empathy. I am incredibly grateful for the excellent work he did for me in the field but also for the analysis he provided me of the interviews and for the many discussions we had of my research and of Jordan. Mohammad also conducted a thorough review and analysis of secondary materials in Arabic. His efforts and input were a vital part of this book.

Many others also helped make the interviews possible. Nart Bakir, then at the Ministry for Municipal Affairs, provided me with the ministry's list of municipalities, including telephone numbers. He also kindly engaged in ongoing discussions regarding municipal politics with me. I also would not have started off on a very sound footing if it had not been for Ella Gao and Stephanie Nanes, both of whom were in Amman doing research on local politics during my first field trip. They were extremely generous with their contacts and advice. Ella helped me narrow down which four municipalities I would look at in a more in-depth manner. I also owe thanks to Glen Robinson and Kenneth Ellison; well before I arrived in Jordan, they provided me with a wealth of information on decentralization efforts, municipal strengthening projects, and local contacts.

Others generously and helpfully shared their expertise and time with me in Jordan. I am especially indebted to Myriam Ababsa, Shehada Abu Hdeb, Hussein Abu Rumman, Nidal Adwan, Adnan al-Bakhit, Rami Daher, Mustapha Hamarneh, Hesham Hejaya, Hani Hourani, Mohammad al-Masri, Walid al-Masri, Musa Shtewi, and Tariq Tell. I also cannot forget Omar Abu-Eid, Jamie Allinson, Jocelyn deJong, Joud Khasawneh, Mohammad Kholi, Jihad Mansi, Paul McCarthy, Jamil Nimri, Natasha Shawarib, Mohammad Taamneh, Abdul Razak Tubaishat, and Imam Zaki.

Chris Parker and Jillian Schwedler helped me with the early stages of conceptualizing and formulating my ideas. I also owe thanks to Chris for his encouragement when my energy for fieldwork was flagging. Sylvia Bergh provided an invaluable learning experience at the Twelfth Mediterranean Research Meeting in 2011. Michel Caron, Luna Khirfan, Nadine Kreitmyer, Fuad Malkawi, and Basma Momani provided help along the way. Many thanks also are due to Barbara Porter, Nisreen Abu al-Shaikh, Humi Al-Ayoubi, Sarah Harpending Burgan, Kathy Nimri, Chris Tuttle, and Karen Britt for making my time at the American Center of Oriental Research (ACOR) so enjoyable and productive. The Huneidi and the Abdel Jaber families, Ola's family, and Maya Abu Ayyash were hospitable and wonderful. It is hard to think of Jordan without immediately thinking of them.

This was the first time I conducted field research in Morocco, which was decidedly more difficult (although by no means less enjoyable). While I could fairly easily access all municipalities in Jordan via day trips from Amman (albeit with numerous cellphone calls guiding me along the way), this was not the case in Morocco. Morocco required lengthy stays in hotels as my research assistant, Emanuela Dalmasso, and I toured the country, twice. It was at times, particularly during the winter, grueling. Furthermore, while it was easy to obtain a list of municipalities and their election results from the government's elections website, it was more difficult to ascertain who the mayor was and what the winning coalition was. It often took several telephone calls to the municipal halls and to other sources to determine the mayor and his or her affiliation and to get his or her telephone number. In Morocco, we at times (albeit in a minority of municipalities) also came up against powerful local patrons, including those who had recently been removed from power electorally, who were determined we should conduct brief interviews with supportive participants and leave town quickly. Despite overt threats regarding the consequences of pursuing the research (albeit fairly empty ones) and suggestions that we leave town, we successfully completed all interviews we had planned.

In successfully making my way through all of this, I am deeply indebted to Emanuela Dalmasso. I cannot begin to express how appreciative I am of all Emanuela did during our two lengthy research trips in Morocco. The success of the fieldwork, without a doubt, was due in large part to her organizational skills, her resourcefulness, her diligence and effectiveness as a translator and researcher, and, most importantly, her insightfulness. I also cannot forget her driving skills! Most weeks, Emanuela and I worked seven days per week from early morning to late evening. Thanks to Emanuela we arrived in each municipality fully prepared with all relevant background knowledge and with numerous interviews already set up. As my French was very rusty, Emanuela also acted as translator. Following the interviews, Emanuela's insights were also invaluable. I relied extensively on Emanuela to help me navigate through the complexities of Moroccan politics. Due to her deep knowledge of Morocco, she was able to shed light on references made by an interviewee that I would otherwise not have noticed. Emanuela was able to help me place all that we learned during the interview into a wider context and to provide her own political interpretation, helping my research move forward conceptually and empirically. Just as importantly, she simply kept me going—when I felt too exhausted to continue (and secretly hoped that the interviewee would cancel), Emanuela managed to help me regain my energy and forge ahead. If we worked tremendously long and exhausting hours, it was due to the success of the fieldwork and the important role Emanuela played in that success. I also cannot forget the ongoing discussions we had concerning my research in the years following the fieldwork. None of this would have been possible if Emanuela were not such a lovely person willing to put up with cold weather, sometimes poorly heated accommodations, and my very bad cooking skills! Luckily good restaurants and wine were (almost) always available.

In preparing for my first research trip to Morocco, I was overwhelmed with how supportive and helpful scholars, many of whom I had never met, were in giving me advice and sharing contacts: Ahmed Bendella, Sylvia Bergh, Koenraad Bogaert, Aomar Boum, Donna Lee Bowen, Malika Bouziane, Omar Brousky, Matt Buehler, Myriam Catusse, Francesco Cavatorta, Laryssa Chomiak, Ferdinand Eibl, John Entellis, Eric Fischer,

Cilja Harders, Anya Hoffman, Jerry Lotfus, Francisca Santonja Mayor, Jim Miller, Abdelhay Moudden, Miquel Pellicer, Mark Tessler, Eva Wegner, Greg White, Michael Willis, Amy Young, Sami Zemni, Saloua Zerhouni, and the late Fatema Mernissi.

I would like to give a special thanks to Fatima Akhabbar, Harry Birnholz, Jeff England, Aziz El Maoula El Iraki, Mohamed Madani, Abdelouahad Ourzik, and Mohamed Tamim for facilitating my research once I arrived in Morocco. My helpful research assistant Andrew Watrous set up the initial interviews. Ghassan Wail and Sabrina Belhouari conducted interviews on my behalf after I had left the country. I cannot forget Abdou Berrada, who acted as chauffeur and drove Emanuela and I around the country for our first tour of interviews and also translated during the interviews when the Moroccan dialect was beyond my comprehension skills.

Some of my deepest thanks are reserved for Ellen Lust, who patiently listened to me and gave advice over the phone as I slowly but surely made sense of my research data. Each time she helped move the book project a little forward. Mona Harb, Diane Singerman, and Marc Lynch each read the entire book manuscript and gave invaluable advice that I followed as closely and as best I could. Mona, you may not even remember, but the entire idea for this project stemmed from a suggestion you gave me years ago. Thank you for the much-appreciated long-distance advice. Diane, you have been an inspiration to me since I first started doing field research. Marc, I need to thank you in particular for patiently helping me get through the difficult final versions when I had run out of steam.

Many thanks also to Anne Routon, Miriam Grossman, and Caelyn Cobb at Columbia University Press, to Glenn Perkins for copyediting, and to assistants who helped me with my research, translations, and bibliography, making my workload much lighter and my life much easier: Karry-Ann Cornwall, Nick Hambleton, Alisha Hameed, Basma Abdel Jaber, Nadine Khayat, Nic LaFlamme, Rory Morrison, Kiara Vallier, and especially Pascal Lupien.

Finally, I owe my most profound thanks to my family: my mother, Astrid; grandmother, Martha; and most importantly, my husband, John, who patiently and selflessly put up with my absence and then my presence throughout the researching and writing process. Only with their love, support, and infinite understanding did I finish this book.

Introduction

The headline of a 2013 newspaper article, in reference to the growing importance of municipal issues such as bus fares, green spaces, and garbage collection throughout the Global South, exclaimed, "Suddenly, all politics is municipal" (Saunders 2013). The Arab World is no exception in terms of the challenges facing its municipalities. Municipal service delivery in the Arab World, including the two countries I examine in this book, Morocco and Jordan, suffers from poor performance, coverage gaps, insufficient funding, and ineffective administration (Belghazi, quoted in Harb and Atallah 2015: 5). Jordan's municipal mess became acutely obvious in the 1990s when it was revealed that fewer than 50 percent of municipalities were able to cover even the most basic services. Jordan's municipalities were, and continue to be, struggling under the weight of bloated numbers of municipal employees, whose salaries drain away budgets, leaving no funds to maintain the equipment necessary to collect garbage or salt the roads, for example. Making matters worse is the petty (and not-so-petty) corruption of councillors and employees using public vehicles and gasoline for private use, issuing licenses for illegal building activities, making land deals, and promoting nepotism. Morocco is not much different; local newspapers regularly report that the country's cities are falling apart, as evidenced by their crumbling infrastructure, collapsing buildings, and terrible roads. As in Jordan, Moroccan citizens complain of the lack of repair to municipal street lighting and potholes and of maintenance of green spaces as well as the simple lack of youth centers and cultural centers.

Although they face similar challenges, the two states have taken decidedly different approaches to addressing these issues. Since the 1970s, Morocco has begun a slow, and admittedly limited, process of decentralization, downloading additional responsibilities to municipal councils in order that they, as opposed to central governments deemed out of touch with the local contexts, can better address the needs of their citizens. Toward this end, recent municipal charters have legislated the inclusion of civil society actors into municipal decision-making in order to facilitate local participation, better representation, and, ultimately, improved services and service delivery. In contrast, Jordan has consistently followed a path of greater centralization. It has progressively removed powers and responsibilities from municipal councils. While in the mid-1990s, the central government ordered a report on potential decentralization, it rejected this option in favor of further centralization by amalgamating municipalities in order to reduce waste in the duplication of equipment, for example, and encouraged (and eventually required) municipalities to create development units in order to foster development and employment opportunities. It was not until twenty years later (2015) that Jordan passed its decentralization law; it, too, removed and centralized existing municipal powers. One of the primary questions I ask in this book is why these two states chose these two different options; why do some regimes choose to decentralize and others do not?

The World Bank (WB) and other international financial institutions (IFIs) have been advocating and implementing decentralization reforms throughout the developing world since the 1970s (Cheema and Rondinelli 2007: 8). Situated at the heart of good governance initiatives, decentralization reforms essentially involve the transfer of decision-making powers and resources from central governments to subnational governments such as municipalities. Political decentralization refers to the popular election of local decision makers and representatives and also the incorporation of new mechanisms for citizen participation in local government (Grindle 2007: 7).[1] It is deemed to facilitate the democratic values of public participation, accountability, and transparency in decisions regarding the allocation of public resources, as well as those of equity. Consequently, municipal governments should be able to provide for their constituencies and constituents equally able to pressure their councils to provide for them as effectively as neighboring municipalities do. Decentralization thus promises better and more equitable services via the inclusion of local voices—those of civil society in particular—in the decision-making process. It affects both those who make the decisions and those who benefit from the decisions.

Yet the vast literature on decentralization in the Global South, and particularly in Latin America—where, for the most part, decentralization followed or coincided with a period of democratic transition—has shown decidedly mixed results, with little consensus from country to country or even within countries in terms of governments' responsiveness to decentralization or decentralization's impact (Grindle 2007). Decentralization has been documented to have produced both positive and negative outcomes (Hess 2013: 31)—with scholars finding that many leaders initiate recentralization relatively shortly after introducing decentralization (Dickovick 2011; Eaton 2004). Scholars are challenged to explain why decentralization in the developing world produces both more and less responsive governments, political inclusion, and political stability (Grindle 2007: 3–7).

Nowhere is the resistance to decentralization more evident than in authoritarian regimes. In the words of Landry (2008: 11–12), autocrats "want to achieve growth, but they also want to stay in power, and are therefore keen on developing mechanisms that will presumably allow them to perpetuate their rule. Decentralization is desirable, but it must also be controlled." Indeed, scholars argue that authoritarian rulers largely initiate decentralization as a tool to consolidate political support and stabilize larger regime interests (Craig and Porter 2006: 107). Decentralization reforms have been found to neither challenge existing power structures nor increase local governments' autonomy from central authority (Aggestam et al. 2009: 333). Under the guise of decentralization, authoritarian regimes such as the Kingdom of Morocco and the Hashemite Kingdom of Jordan extend the influence of their dominant political parties, often by creating new layers of local political personnel or countering political threats to the center from ethnically based opposition forces by breaking their regional base into multiple jurisdictions (Romeo 2003: 92). Thus, rather than redistributing power or including new voices, decentralization results in what is commonly known as "elite capture" (Bardhan 2002; Echeverri-Gent 1992; Huque 1986; Johnson, Deshingkar, and Start 2003; Sarker 2003; Slater and Watson 1989; Vengroff and Ben Salem 1992)—the "control, shaping or manipulation of decision-making processes or institutions by elites in ways that serve their self-interests and priorities and typically result in their personal gain at the expense of non-elites and local communities" (Labonte 2011: 91).

It is thus unsurprising that the Middle East and North Africa (MENA) region is one of the most centralized in the world, with few authorities, responsibilities, or resources granted to municipal actors (Siegle and O'Mahoney 2006: 143). Authoritarian regimes, including liberalized or electoral autocracies such as Jordan and Morocco, seek to ensure both that regime supportive elites win municipal elections and that few powers are granted to subnational governments in order that they may selectively grant privileges and resources to shore up regime support. As Harders (2003: 192) states, power structures at the local level not only reflect but also stabilize national political systems. The limited decentralization that has occurred in the region came at a much later date than in most other parts of the Global South (Belghazi 2003; Rosenbaum 2013: 14; Tosun and Yilmaz 2008a, 2008b) and certainly has not entailed the kind of significant developments that occurred elsewhere in the world (Rosenbaum 2013: 14). Moreover, local elected authorities have been kept under central government control through a number of means, particularly via fiscal control (Belghazi 2003; Siegle and O'Mahony 2010: 145).

Yet if both centralization and decentralization are tools by which regimes seek to stabilize their interests—if they are, in other words, both survival tactics—then why choose one and not the other? If, as Hess (2013: 11) states, decentralization is "one of a number of strategies undertaken by autocratic rulers to strengthen their power vis-à-vis potential internal and external opponents," then why do it? Furthermore, if local power structures stabilize national political systems, how is power at the local level reconfigured and what does it mean for regime stability? What opportunities do decentralization reforms offer local elites? Who is empowered at the municipal level and how? Why do some local political elites engage in elite capture and others do not?

The literature on decentralization in authoritarian regimes largely examines the conditions under which authoritarian rulers decentralize, how they maintain political control, and how the institutions of decentralization serve to sustain authoritarianism (see Landry 2008). Hess (2013), for example, persuasively demonstrates how decentralization counterintuitively serves to disperse and thereby limit popular uprisings against authoritarian regimes. However, this literature generally targets the national level of analysis, concentrating on what El-Ghobashy (2008: 1604) refers to as "the ways and means of Goliath's power." Little attention is paid to the responses of local actors and the possible reconfigurations of local power when reforms are initiated from above, creating the false impression that local actors have no agency.

Even the substantial literature—predominantly on Latin America—that examines the persistence of authoritarian enclaves (Cornelius, Eisenstadt, and Hindley 1999; Grindle 2007) and the phenomenon of elite capture (Grindle 2007) neglects local political dynamics. With few exceptions (Bergh 2017), the study of elite capture is dominated by macro-level analyses—examining where and the conditions under which elite capture occurs and not the local political dynamics engendered by decentralization. Analyses of elite capture thus tend to be binary in nature, reduced to whether or not it has occurred and its frequency; how the political processes produced by decentralization at the local level unfold remains underresearched (Kienle 2003b: 10).

As a region, the MENA is repeatedly neglected by comparative studies of decentralization efforts in the developing world (Tosun and Yilmaz 2008a). Comparative studies of decentralization in the MENA states that could reveal variations between or within states are also few in number (ibid.). One notable exception is Harb and Atallah (2015a), who provide an excellent comparative study of decentralization and service delivery in the Arab World, looking specifically at Lebanon, Jordan, Morocco, Yemen, and Tunisia. In each of these countries, they examine the making and politics of decentralization, the legislation and practice of service delivery, and the fiscal structure of decentralization. Missing in the literature, and what this book seeks to provide, are, firstly, answers to why—despite facing similar socioeconomic challenges—some states of the MENA choose to implement decentralization reforms while others do not and, secondly, examples of the local politics of decentralization.

Based on the country case studies of Morocco, which has undertaken the most significant degree of political decentralization in the region thus far, and Jordan, which increasingly centralized from 1955 until 2015, this book examines three interrelated questions: (1) Why do authoritarian regimes choose to either centralize or decentralize? (2) How do local actors, specifically municipal actors, work with and around the opportunities and constraints presented by decentralization reforms? (3) Looking through the lens of elite capture, to what extent does decentralization, as opposed to centralization, have a stabilizing effect for authoritarian regimes? This book thus looks at local political actors as agents of change and from this perspective examines how local elites seize the opportunities that reforms have to offer in order to advance their political agendas and the consequent impact of their actions for local power dynamics and, ultimately, regime stability (Clark 2012: 358).

My argument is threefold. First, I argue that whether or not authoritarian regimes decentralize is determined primarily by their coalition strategies—the strategies regimes use to underpin their rule via societal relations or social contracts (see below). Thus decentralization is a tactic within a larger coalition strategy and, in the case of Morocco, aimed at expanding the monarchy's coalition partners and broadening its base of support. Thus when, following two attempted coups in the 1970s, the Moroccan regime decided to expand its coalition beyond that which it had with the Berber elite, it used decentralization as a lure to secure the entry of the then opposition political parties into the political system and thereby co-opt them. Similarly, in the 2000s, it used decentralization reforms to entice civil society into the fold, where it could appropriate its discourse, essentially "defang" it, and ultimately use it to legitimize monarchical rule. In contrast, in Jordan, where, the regime did not seek to expand its coalition but strategically chose to maintain its "partnership" with the country's tribal elite, the regime had little interest in decentralization and chose to pursue ongoing centralization. Yet, although I argue that coalition strategies provide the incentive to decentralize, the decision to employ decentralization as a tactic also is determined by the institutional strength of the political parties. In Morocco, decentralization would not have been a viable tactic had the political parties not had the institutional structures—the ability to establish branches in municipalities throughout the country—to take advantage of the powers decentralized to the local level. Morocco's political parties thus eagerly embraced decentralization as a means to capture local elites, votes, and resources.

Second, I argue that local political elites do not simply implement decentralization reforms as given; nor is elite capture simply the result of decentralized powers falling into the "wrong hands," as much of the literature (see below) implies. Rather, my examination of municipalities in which elite capture does and does not occur reveals that elite capture (or the lack of it) is a reflection of the opportunities decentralization reforms offer to local actors to pursue their interests. What those opportunities are perceived as being is to a large extent determined by the degree to which their parties lie within the regime's networks of patronage and, as a consequence, the degree to which they are dominated by and rely on patron-clientelism. Morocco's decentralization reforms, specifically the municipal charters, offer regime-supportive parties multiple opportunities to enhance their patron-client ties at the expense of civil society. By establishing civil society organizations (CSOs), for example, municipal councillors act simultaneously as councillors, funders, and CSO representatives, ultimately usurping the decision-making role and funding for civil society. In contrast, the Parti de la Justice et du Développement (PJD, Justice and Development Party), the country's only true opposition party during the period under study, saw a different type of opportunity. Lying outside the regime's networks of patronage and largely rejecting patron-clientelism as a modus operandi, the PJD saw an opportunity to come to power by fulfilling the charters' increased designated role for civil society in municipal decision-making. Local PJD members thus work with and form partnerships with CSO representatives so that they may jointly displace local patrons from power. Thus while in the case of regime-supportive parties, I found that elite capture was the norm and in the case of the PJD it was not, in both cases, the outcome was the result of municipal actors pursuing their political interests.

Finally, the experiences in both Morocco and Jordan show how decentralization reforms consolidate the power of and stabilize authoritarian regimes. As a result of the good governance discourse and initiatives—reinforced by the opposition PJD, which embraces both in order to woo civil society partners—and as a result of the ineptitude and/or corruption of elected officials—both facilitated by the municipal charters—decentralization reforms promote the Moroccan monarch as a political reformer. Furthermore, while privatizing the responsibility for social welfare to municipalities and citizens, good governance and decentralization reforms in Morocco have led to an unofficial recentralization of power: the king or his representatives maintain power through the disaggregated state institutions and "come to the rescue" of the citizens by bestowing the services that their corrupt elected representatives seem unwilling or unable to provide directly to them. This study thus demonstrates how decentralization provides a greater stabilizing function for authoritarian regimes than does centralization, which, as the case of Jordan shows, neither provides the regime with the role of political reformer nor downloads responsibility. Centralization in Jordan has furthermore served to divide and fragment regime-supportive elites.

In sum, this research examines the actual practice of decentralization, rather than the policy of decentralization—which is relatively well documented—at the national and local levels. The book unpacks the panacea of decentralization promoted by international organizations and policy scholars who systematically present it as an ideal policy solution to postcolonial countries' hard journey to democracy. Yet it also considers the mechanisms of authoritarian upgrading, revealing that authoritarian regimes' usurpation of decentralization is less the result of the imposition of Goliath's powers than the reinforcing yet independent actions of national and local actors as they seek to pursue their political interests.

Neoliberalism

I situate this study of decentralization within what Heydemann (2004b) labels third-generation scholarship on economic reform. Within the orthodox political economy literature, third-generation research on the politics of economic reform has taken up the insights of the critical literature on neoliberalism regarding the inherently political nature of economic reforms (Bergh 2012a: 312) and consequently conceptualizes economic policy reform as a political process (Heydemann 2004b: 18). Instead of evaluating the success or failure of reforms, third-generation literature gives more weight, for example, to questions concerning the effects of reregulation in the reorganization of rent seeking. By conceptualizing economic reform in this manner, third-generation literature opens the way to better understanding "how local elites appropriate processes of economic restructuring as an arena of political struggle, both among themselves and with the central government" (Bergh 2012a: 308). It thus also opens the way to a better understanding of the dynamics of elite capture.

The literature on good governance and decentralization tends to be dominated by what Heydemann (2004b: 17) labels "second-generation" work on economic reform, which is marked by a positive view of institutions "along with an appreciation of the link between state capacity and the ability of reformers to construct and consolidate market-supporting institutions." As he states, for this generation of work, the question is not about state withdrawal but about state transformation—reshaping state capacity. In contrast to first-generation literature, which conceptualizes the state as a problem that needs to be overcome by its diminishment (16), second-generation literature sees the need for "new strategies . . . for managing interest groups in ways that prevent some actors from capturing . . . its benefits" (17). The literature on elite capture, for instance, often focuses on the means by which "central intervention" can ensure that local elites are not allowed to exclude the masses of the people from participating in local government (commonly without recognizing "the important role of this same central intervention in cultivating this problematic elite" [Ribot 2002: 48]). An underlying assumption is that elite capture can be eliminated through various forms of regulation or accountability.

Second-generation scholarship thus adheres to a process of reform that is conceptualized in neoliberal terms and to the assumption that strategies can be employed and regulation enacted in order to ensure its successful implementation. Decentralization is understood, more or less, as a one-size-fits-all set of reforms with scholars and policy makers concerned with questions "about how to ensure the 'integrity' of a reform process, about evaluating success or failure by the extent to which interests are kept at arms' length" (Heydemann 2004b: 18). Overlooked is the political. With its focus on how to better implement decentralization (or simply abandon it), second-generation literature largely does not deal with the processes by which local actors adapt to decentralization reforms and use the opportunities the reforms offer to advance their agenda. In other words, it neglects the politics of decentralization at the local level.

The critical literature on neoliberalism has been far more concerned with neoliberalism as an inherently political process. Critical scholarship has sought to understand the "rather blatant disjuncture between the ideology of neoliberalism and its everyday political operations and societal effects" (Brenner and Theodore 2002a: 352). Crucially, as Brenner and Theodore maintain, "the manifold disjunctures that have accompanied the worldwide imposition of neoliberalism—between ideology and practice; doctrine and reality; vision and consequence—are not merely accidental side effects" (353). Neoliberalism, as Peck and Tickell (quoted in ibid.) state, is not a "coherently bounded 'ism' or 'end-state'"; rather, it is a process of "neoliberalization." It is not a "fully actualized policy regime, ideological form, or regulatory framework" that only needs to be adjusted to the circumstances in order to work (353).

Brenner and Theodore (2002a: 362) thus speak of neoliberalism as a process of creative destruction: "the (partial) destruction of extant institutional arrangements and political compromises through market-oriented reform initiatives; and the (tendential) creation of a new infrastructure for market-oriented economic growth, commodification, and the rule of capital." The destructive and creative moments are characterized by what Peck and Tickell (2002: 380) label "roll-back" and "roll-out" neoliberalism, respectively. The moment of destruction can be understood as the dismantling of earlier systems of central government support for municipal activities, the imposition of fiscal austerity measures on municipal governments, and the elimination of public monopolies for the provision of standardized municipal services, such as utilities, sanitation, public safety, and mass transit. While the moment of creation includes, for example, the devolution of new tasks, burdens, and responsibilities to municipalities, the creation of new incentive structures to reward local entrepreneurialism, the creation of new revenue collection districts, the increased reliance of municipalities on local sources of revenue, such as user fees, and the privatization and competitive contracting of municipal services (Brenner and Theodore 2002a: 369–70). Most importantly, the dynamic of creative destruction does not occur "on a blank slate in which the 'old order' is abruptly obliterated and the 'new order' is unfurled as a fully formed totality. Rather it takes place on an aggressively contested institutional landscape" (366). It is an "uneven, multiscalar, multidirectional, and open-ended restructuring process that generates . . . contradictions of its own" (366). As Brenner and Theodore (quoted in Leitner et al. 2007: 5) state, "Neoliberal programs of capitalist restructuring are rarely, if ever, imposed in a pure form, for they are always introduced within politico-institutional contexts that have been molded significantly by earlier regulatory arrangements, institutionalized practices, and political compromises."

In contrast to first- and second-generation work that adheres to neoliberal ideology, according to which "market forces are assumed to operate according to immutable laws no matter where they are 'unleashed'" (Bergh 2012a: 305), third-generation scholarship no longer carries with it the neoliberal assumptions of earlier work (Heydemann 2004b: 18). Integrating the insights of the critical literature, markets are understood as politically constructed and maintained, and reform is understood as a "negotiated process of reregulation that is shaped by the interaction of political and economic interests, including, notably, the interest of incumbents in remaining in power" (18). Similarly, local elites, particularly the local party branches and the councillors in power, do not respond to policies handed down to them from above by simply implementing them; rather, they adapt to them and, in turn, adapt the reforms themselves. It is in this adaptation of decentralization reforms, which lie at the heart of neoliberal reforms, and the political dynamics and contestations they engender that I examine elite capture in this book.

Good Governance, Political Decentralization, and Civil Society

In the fifty years since decentralization was first advocated, a growing number of international and domestic actors have embraced it. Yet within this time period, the concept of decentralization itself has changed. Today, the inclusion of civil society is an integral part of all decentralization reforms. Decentralization involves far more than the devolution of central powers to subnational governments; it includes citizens, commonly via civil society associations, in the decision-making processes of subnational governments. Civil society's inclusion is intended to foster multiple benefits, the most important of which is improved democratic governance. By providing input into decision-making and playing a watchdog role, and consequently ensuring accountability, civil society is seen as a vital player in political decentralization. The avenues by which civil society actors are included may be designed in a myriad of ways; as is the case in Morocco, they are commonly enshrined in municipal charters. By empowering civil society actors, decentralization reforms furthermore have broadened municipal mandates to encompass development goals and initiatives, oftentimes in partnership with civil society actors. Civil society thus becomes an important focus of study for understanding decentralization and elite capture. As I argue throughout this book, civil society has become a significant arena of political contestation under decentralization, with political actors seeking to strategically use civil society's resources, voice, and influence to their political advantage.

Decentralization as an international phenomenon is largely associated with the restructuring, often quite radical, that centralized governments throughout the Global South began undertaking in the 1980s and 1990s, often, but not solely, with the encouragement of the WB and other IFIs.

Decentralization as a policy instrument of development came into focus after World War II, and this period saw some countries decentralize their hierarchical structures (Cheema and Rondinelli 2007: 3). Nevertheless, developmental efforts in the 1950s, 1960s, and 1970s were basically guided by the notion of big government (Sarker 2003: 524). A strong central state was seen as necessary for "late developers" to compete in an international environment dominated by industrialized countries (Hess 2013: 29). Many countries of the Global South pursued large-scale state-led urbanization programs "using the centralized powers of the government to forcefully restructure society and drive it toward rapid industrialization" (29).

By the late 1970s, however, big government was no longer seen as the route to development. Countries of the Global South began embracing decentralization, with the countries of Latin America undergoing the most radical changes as a result of decentralization (Falleti 2010: 6). States have individual and often unique reasons for initiating decentralization, but common international trends may be singled out (Conyers 1983: 99). While there are competing explanations regarding the driving forces behind decentralization (see Grindle 2007: 5–6), as Hess (2013: 30) documents, most explanations for the reforms of the 1980s and 1990s focus on two global trends: (1) the neoliberal move away from state-led developmentalism and toward free-market economics and (2) the transition, particularly in Latin America, from authoritarian to democratic forms of government.

Following the economic setbacks in the 1970s due, for example, to the oil crisis and the failure of import-substitution policies, governments in the Global South began questioning the role of central economic planning and management. The command economy had not produced the hoped-for results; rural poverty increased, and the gap between urban and rural areas grew. Rural development policies became of prime concern as industrialization programs had largely focused on urban areas at the expense of rural areas (Conyers 1983: 99). In response, governments of individual states and international agencies increasingly began viewing decentralization as a means of improving the planning and implementation of national development, particularly rural development. Decentralization was seen as a way of increasing the effectiveness of rural development programs by making them more relevant and responsive to local needs and conditions and allowing greater flexibility in their implementation (99). It also provided for the direct participation of the rural poor in decision-making, an aim influenced by policies such as the "basic needs" approach to development, which regards the right to such participation as a basic human need (100).

At the same time, the Global North was embracing the logic of neoliberalism, which "demanded the dramatic reduction of the state's scope of involvement in society and the economy in order to unleash market forces, and drive countries' economic performance" (Hess 2013: 30). Intellectually grounded in new institutional economics (NIE) and new public management (NPM) (Bergh 2012a: 309), these ideas soon came to underpin the policy prescriptions of what is known as the Washington Consensus: fiscal discipline, public expenditure priorities, the liberalization of trade and direct foreign investment, privatization, and deregulation. Big government was, and continues to be, seen as inefficient, rigid, and unaccountable (Sarker 2003: 526). Downsizing the state and subjecting it to the pressures of the market were to produce more efficient and effective government. The 1980s and 1990s thus witnessed the implementation of structural adjustment programs (SAPs) throughout the Global South. Policy prescriptions included decentralization, which, as Manor (1999: 24) states, was viewed "as a means of linking political demand for services with a requirement that beneficiaries pay for them" and offered the opportunity for central governments to offload obligations to subnational bodies and to facilitate cuts in public expenditure.

The second global trend that helped usher in decentralization was what is commonly labeled as the third wave of democracy: the fall of authoritarian regimes in Latin America in the 1980s and then those of Central and Eastern Europe in the 1990s (Hess 2013: 30). As states throughout Latin America transitioned from military rule to liberal democracy, they sought to develop institutions to gain legitimacy and support for the new and fragile democratic systems (Doner and Hershberg 1999: 66). A wide range of authorities and resources thus were devolved to what were often newly created and elected subnational governments, such as municipalities. Decentralization was understood to stabilize and enhance the quality of nascent democracies; it was also the outcome of growing demands by citizens for political inclusion in transitional polities (Hess 2013: 31). Thus, in one transitional country after another, decentralization soon followed on the heels of democratization.

While most commonly associated with the 1980s and 1990s, decentralization as an important element of both economic and political reform continues unabated. Indeed, in the late 1990s, it became an important element in IFIs' "good governance" agendas (see Craig and Porter 2006). The harsh socioeconomic realities that the early structural adjustment reforms created, and the consequent social and political unrest they engendered, led to the introduction of a "softer, more 'inclusive' neoliberalism" by the WB and other IFIs (Bergh 2012a: 310). As Craig and Porter (2006) document, good governance became a new phase of neoliberal reform. From the 2000s onward, the international development agenda began to consist of three legs—the promotion of economic opportunity through global market integration, the enhancement of social and economic security, and empowerment through innovative governance arrangements for local delivery of health, education, and other poverty-reducing services (4). Capable, corruption-free governance was and is seen as the key "to putting a 'human face' on macroeconomic structural adjustment, enhancing investments in human capital, health and education, working with civil society for better delivery of social services" (6). Good governance is deemed to create "healthier, more educated and engaging citizens able to participate in new market Opportunities" as well as "Security and Empowerment via a new, citizen responsive, capable state" (6).

Thus, the restructured and disaggregated state of the 1980s and early 1990s was "brought back in" as a "capable state"—one that is deemed as necessary to support markets (Craig and Porter 2006: 4). It is therefore an "enabling" state that can support the appropriate legal, financial, and policy institutions in order to ensure more efficient and competitive markets (13). At the same time, the state is no longer regarded as the dominant source of decision-making (Cheema and Rondinelli 2007: 1). Rather, government has come to be understood as "only one, albeit a critically important, governance institution" (2). Among other institutions, civil society emerged as a primary governance institution (Mohan and Stokke 2000: 248).

As the concept of governance began to broaden and become more inclusive, so too did the "thinking about the rationale, objectives, and forms of decentralization" (Cheema and Rondinelli 2007: 6). As Craig and Porter (2006: 6) note, IFIs regarded the decentralized aspects of governance as offering some of the most enticing promises of good governance. The community, the locality, the territories of subnational authorities all came to be seen as the domains where good governance was deemed to offer the most. Here, Craig and Porter explain, "good governance rubrics promised a less corrupt institutional environment for local business, and better access to decentralized service delivery, by responsive agencies held accountable by informed clients" (6).

"Decentralization now encompasses not only the transfer of power, authority, and responsibility within government but also the sharing of authority and resources for shaping public policy within society" (Cheema and Rondinelli 2007: 6). Until the late 1980s, decentralization generally was thought to take three primary forms: deconcentration, delegation, and devolution (3). As Cheema and Rondinelli summarize, deconcentration was the redistribution of administrative responsibilities from central ministries and departments to subnational, such as regional and local, administrative levels by establishing field offices of national departments. Delegation involved the shifting of management authority for specific functions from national governments to semiautonomous or para-statal organizations and state enterprises, regional planning and area development agencies, and multi- and single-purpose public authorities. Devolution was understood as the strengthening of local governments by granting them the authority, responsibility, and resources to provide services and infrastructure, protect public health and safety, and formulate and implement local policies.

While these categories are still used, in the expanded concept of governance of today, decentralization practices are more typically categorized into (at least) four forms: administrative, fiscal, economic, and political (Cheema and Rondinelli 2007: 6–7). Administrative decentralization "includes deconcentration of central government structures and bureaucracies, delegation of central government authority and responsibility to semiautonomous agents of the state, and decentralized cooperation of government agencies performing similar functions through 'twinning' arrangement across national borders" (6–7). Fiscal decentralization includes "the means and mechanisms for fiscal cooperation in sharing public revenues among all levels of government; for fiscal delegation in public revenue raising and expenditure allocation; and for fiscal autonomy for state, regional, or local governments" (7). Economic decentralization includes market liberalization, deregulation, privatization of state enterprises, and public-private partnerships (7). Finally, political decentralization, with which this book is concerned, includes

> organizations and procedures for increasing citizen participation in selecting political representatives and in making public policy; changes

in the structure of the government through devolution of powers and authority to local units of government; power-sharing institutions within the state through federalism, constitutional federation, or autonomous regions; and institutions and procedures allowing freedom of association and participation of civil society organizations in public decisionmaking, in providing social beneficial services, and in mobilizing social and financial resources to influence political decisionmaking (7).[2]

As Cheema and Rondinelli (2007) summarize, in this broadened conceptualization of governance, political decentralization is promoted as a means of increasing the capacity of local governments, the private sector, and civil society organizations to extend services to a larger number of people. It is further understood as a way to grant political representation to a diverse variety of political ethnic, religious, and cultural groups without destabilizing the state. It is deemed to foster more creative and innovative responses to public needs, to address regional imbalances, to empower communities, and to mobilize private resources for investment. Finally, decentralization is now also seen by many "as an instrument for building institutional capacity within local governments and CSOs to achieve UN Millennium Development Goals and improve chances of successfully implementing policies for the poor that depend on local communities to take ownership of poverty-alleviation programs" (7).

Consequently, decentralization is understood as involving far more than the transfer of authority and resources to local-level governments. Rather, it (theoretically) includes the devolution of authorities and resources as well as the broadening of municipal government mandates to encompass development goals and the empowerment of civil society and civil society's inclusion in planning and decision-making at the municipal level. According to the logic of decentralization, municipal governments make more informed decisions and are more accountable to their populations than central governments due to their proximity to the people they are serving. The impetus for municipal governments to make the best use of their "local knowledge" and engage in responsive decision-making comes from elections—the opportunity for people to vote elected representatives out of office if they are found wanting (Sadanandan 2012: 211). By making government more accountable and providing enhanced opportunities for citizen participation in public life, decentralization is deemed to improve democratic governance (Selee 2011: 1).

Decentralization reforms position civil society activists at the center of reform, making them also central to the political contestations that local-level reforms have engendered. As noted above, economic reforms are shaped by the interaction of political and economic interests, including the interest of incumbents in remaining in power and of political challengers hoping to gain power. The political dynamics of elite capture thus are increasingly played out via civil society as political actors "negotiate" the new powers and resources granted to civil society actors. As I demonstrate in chapters 5 and 6, both regime-supportive parties and the PJD have sought to exploit civil society and its newfound role and resources in the charter to further their respective political goals. While the regime supporters have appropriated these roles and resources for themselves and the PJD has essentially joined forces with civil society, both parties have done so in order to capture political power.

To Decentralize or Not Decentralize?

Despite the wave of decentralization that has swept the Global South, decentralization remains a puzzling phenomenon (Eaton 2004: 6–7). As Eaton asks, why would politicians at the center surrender power? Decentralization transfers authority and resources to subnational actors; consequently, the very politicians who have the most to lose—those at the center—control the decision to decentralize. Decentralization divides and fragments rather than concentrates power (14). Answering this question has occupied much of the research on the subject of decentralization in the Global South (see Dickovick 2011; Grindle 2000; Manor 1999; O'Neill 2003, 2005). While the policy makers of numerous democratic and authoritarian, federal and unitary, states have chosen to proactively decentralize, many have also recentralized and successfully wrestled authority and resources back from subnational actors. Scholars thus have questioned why national actors would decentralize, why they have decentralized to different degrees, and how they have managed to get away with recentralization. This book, specifically chapters 1 to 3, begins with this fundamental puzzle: why, during the time period under study, did Morocco decentralize while Jordan did not? The answer to this question lies primarily in coalition incentives and disincentives.

The question of why states decentralize is particularly relevant in electoral autocracies such as Jordan and Morocco where what Eaton, Kaiser, and Smoke (2010) call "institutional incentives" act as strong *disincentives* to decentralization. They argue that there are four broad categories of explanations, or what they call incentives, for why states decentralize and for the type and extent of decentralization states choose: electoral incentives, partisan incentives, coalition incentives, and institutional incentives (13–33). While the first two respectively look to the balance of power between political parties and internal party structures / interparty competition in the decision to decentralize, the third, coalition incentives, looks at societal actors, in particular at the societal relations or social contracts that underpin the regime's rule to explain states' stances vis-à-vis decentralization. Institutional incentives concern the formal and informal institutions that incentivize or disincentivize decentralizing. In the Global South in particular, informal institutional incentives, such as clientelism, play a paramount role in decisions regarding decentralization (24).[3] As Eaton, Kaiser, and Smoke state, in authoritarian regimes many governing officials "are in their positions precisely because they have mastered the art of clientelistic exchange, regularly securing political support for local brokers in exchange for appointments to government jobs (patronage) and other government largesse, which these local brokers can in turn exchange for political support at still more local levels" (24). Decentralization directly challenges institutions such as clientelism by relocating decisions about revenue distribution and public expenditures. In more centralized systems, decentralization threatens national politicians' ability to claim credit for the benefits they deliver. With decentralization, local-level governments—empowered with greater resources and decision-making capabilities—can effectively displace their national patrons. In Jordan, for example, as I demonstrate in chapters 1 and 2, tribal elites and the country's Transjordanian population in general benefit from a dense network of patron–clientelism (to no small extent fostered by electoral laws put into place by the regime; see chapters 2 and 4) that spans from members of parliament (MPs) to ministers, civil servants, mayors, business leaders, and citizens alike, all along tribal lines. In this context of tribally based clientelism, decentralization of powers and responsibilities to municipal governments would not only mean the loss of power and influence of ministers and MPs but the breakdown of the institution of patron-clientelism by which Jordan's tribal elite and Transjordanians are privileged and through which, in return, the monarchy retains its primary base of support (see below).

The key to understanding why Morocco decentralized while Jordan did not lies in their coalition strategies. While decentralization is premised on the ability of both regimes to continue to be able manipulate electoral outcomes to the benefit of pro-regime independents and parties, the Moroccan and Jordanian regimes' respective decisions whether or not to decentralize are primarily driven by "coalition incentives"—the degree to which decentralization would act to facilitate the regime's decision to expand or maintain its coalition partners. Seen in this light, the 1976 municipal charter in Morocco must be understood in context of the regime's decision to broaden its coalition and bring new political actors into a partnership: decentralization reforms acted as a tactic to lure new actors into the coalition.

The research on what Eaton, Kaiser, and Smoke (2010) call coalition incentives views the threats to national leaders' survival as the most important determinant in decisions to decentralize or not. "In evaluating decentralization reforms, politicians consider how proposed changes are likely to affect the coalitions that support them and/or the opposition coalitions with which they are embattled. All political incumbents—regardless of whether they are operating in democratic or authoritarian contexts or in relatively stable or highly unstable environments—are engaged in the construction and maintenance of support coalitions" (25). Particularly in ethnically divided societies, Eaton, Kaiser and Smoke explain, national politicians tend to privilege concerns about the likely impact of decentralization on the ethnic coalition that brought them to power and/or sustain their rule (28). Consequently, the decision to decentralize has far less to do with service delivery or administrative efficiency than it does with the "negotiation of interethnic coalitions" (28; see also Falleti 2010).

Centralization thus enables the Jordanian regime to selectively privilege its coalition partner—the tribal elite and the Transjordanian population in general—with economic development and socioeconomic benefits, to name just two examples, while balancing security concerns. Jordan's tribal elite played a pivotal role in both state- and nation-building in Jordan. It is no exaggeration to say that the state-building project could not have been completed without the support of the tribes. The tribal elite that emerged from the state-building process grew to become an important economic and political pillar of support for the monarchy, with the monarchy increasingly dependent on it following successive waves of Palestinian refugees entering Jordan as a result of the wars with Israel. We thus see increasing centralization throughout the late twentieth century as the regime repeatedly sought to "invest" in its coalition with the Transjordanian tribes by granting them, for example, privileged positions in the army, in order to strengthen its partnership in the wake of successive political and socioeconomic crises. Consequently, following the alleged attempted coup of the 1950s (see chapter 1), the monarchy bestowed increasing patronage on the army, rebuilding and cementing its partnership with the tribal elite who dominated it. Even with the imposition of Jordan's SAP, Transjordanians, while also feeling the pinch, directly and indirectly continued to benefit from privileges not granted to the country's Palestinian population.

Centralization in Morocco similarly enabled the monarchy to privilege the Berber elite. In Morocco, the monarchy forged a "coalition" with the Berber elite in order to counterbalance the parties of the former nationalist movement, the Istiqlal (Independence) Party in particular, in the postindependence struggle over the distribution of power. Much like in Jordan, a Berber elite soon dominated the government and state institutions, especially the army.

The primary incentive for the Moroccan monarchy's decision to decentralize lies in the change in its coalition strategy following the two attempted coups of the 1970s (see chapter 1). After the second coup attempt, the monarchy sought to broaden its coalition to include the (then) opposition parties of the former nationalist movements. In 2003 and 2009, the monarchy similarly sought to co-opt and integrate the country's new civil society activists into the political system. In both cases, decentralization reforms functioned as important tactics to accomplish the regime's goals. In the 1970s, the regime used the 1976 municipal charter as bait to entice the opposition parties into electoral participation, and eventually into the government. The 1976 charter offered local elites the opportunity to have greater decision-making powers over issues that concerned their interests and, in turn, offered political parties the ability to capture these elites and their resources and votes. The regime thus used decentralization to bring the then opposition parties into the political system, secure their support through patronage, and ultimately legitimize the monarchy and the political system via the parties' embrace of a system that grants powers to the institution of the monarchy at the expense of institutions of elected representatives of the citizenry. With the 2003 and 2009 charters, the regime repeated this same strategy of broadening its support base by including the country's new civil society elite—itself partially created as a result of the regime's turn to good governance—into municipal decision-making under the guise of devolving power. In both cases, decentralization was a tactic to co-opt new coalition partners.

However, while coalition incentives were the driving reason for decentralization in Morocco, they were not the only consideration. I argue in chapter 3 that "partisan incentives"—specifically the institutional strength of political parties—offer insights into why the Moroccan regime viewed decentralization as advantageous and opposition parties "took the bait." As Eaton, Kaiser, and Smoke (2010: 18) explain, intra-party and inter-party incentives also shape decisions to decentralize; how a political party is structured and how it competes with other parties for power can uncover sources of support for and opposition to decentralization. Researchers look at the fragmentation (the number of parties), polarization (the degree of ideological distance between them), and institutionalization (the degree to which parties exist as organizations separate from their leaders) of the party system in determining decentralization. Each of these dimensions can shape decentralization.

With Moroccan political parties having more institutionalized structures than those in Jordan, they are able to take advantage of decentralization and expand their networks of patron-clientelism. Political parties in both countries are weak, revolving around their respective leaders and held together by patron-client ties as opposed to ideological leanings. Yet there are important differences between the two. The main political parties in Morocco have relatively long histories and large networks of associated organizations and trade unions. Furthermore, while they may be top-heavy, they have institutional structures at the national, regional, and local levels. With decentralization, they could establish branches almost anywhere in the country and bring local elites and their votes (clients) and resources into the party. The parties thus were attracted to decentralization by the real prospect of greater political and material benefits. This was and is not the case in Jordan. With the exception of the Islamic Action Front (IAF), Jordan's political parties are small, commanding relatively few seats in parliament; even the IAF holds a relatively small share. The majority of candidates for parliamentary elections run as independents (or as a list of independents), their loyalties rooted in tribal and family allegiances. Jordan's tribal

MPs furthermore overwhelmingly rely on promises of service delivery to secure votes from their fellow tribe members. Yet to deliver on these promises, MPs must create and maintain networks of patron-clientelism with those who have decision-making powers over these services—namely, but not strictly, (appointed) ministers. As tribally based independents, MPs have no institutionalized structures to speak of and, should they try, would solicit few votes outside their tribe or clan. Without any institutionalized party structure with which to enter local elections and take advantage of any expanded municipal powers, Jordan's MPs consequently would receive no benefits from decentralization. Whereas decentralization extended the patron-client networks of regime-supportive political parties in Morocco, it would have undermined the networks of *wasta*, or connections, on which regime-supportive MPs, ministers and many citizens in Jordan rely.

Finally, the case of Morocco indicates that in electoral autocracies, decentralization is premised upon the continuation of the regime's ability to ensure electoral outcomes in the favor of coalition partners. As noted above, some of the most groundbreaking research on why national actors choose to decentralize has been conducted on what Eaton, Kaiser, and Smoke (2010: 19) call "electoral incentives." In her influential work, O'Neill, for instance, argues that decentralization occurs when national parties believe that subnational offices will be important to them in the future (see also O'Neill 2003). As Eaton, Kaiser, and Smoke (2010: 15) state: "When national parties calculate that their electoral fortunes are more promising at the subnational level, and consequently that holding subnational offices will be important to them in the future, they are more likely to support decentralization to make these offices more powerful." Building on O'Neill, Eaton (2004) points to the military-led regimes of Chile and Uruguay and argues that a broader set of motivations and strategic calculations drive national politicians in authoritarian regimes to endorse decentralization. Rather than the fear of losing national office, he argues it was "the calculation that decentralization would augment their power at the center by delivering disproportionate benefits to their own parties relative to the opposition" that drove national politicians to endorse decentralization (19). In the southern cone of Latin America, it was only after eliminating electoral threats from subnational officials that the military governments respectively adopted policies that substantially expanded the authority of subnational governments (Eaton, Kaiser, and Smoke 2010: 16).

While maintaining a façade of multipartyism and free and fair elections, both "centralized" Jordan and "decentralized" Morocco use a variety of tactics ranging from gerrymandering electoral districts to manipulating voting procedures to ensure the electoral success of the political representatives of their coalition partners, at least in key districts. In this regard, "electoral incentives" cannot be said to act as "incentives" that spur regimes to decentralize, yet electoral outcomes are fundamental to a regime's calculations. Decentralization is premised on the continuation of means by which election outcomes are determined in the coalition partners', and therefore the regime's, favor.

Elite Capture

In many cases the decision to decentralize becomes far less puzzling when decentralizing policies in individual states are examined more closely—legislation to "decentralize" may in fact preserve national policy makers' abilities to control subnational actors even after revenues and expenditures are transferred or, alternatively, after political authority but without fiscal authority or additional revenues is transferred (Eaton 2004: 7). As Harb and Atallah (2015b) observe of the MENA region, states pursue decentralization in response to IFI pressures and internal realities that municipalities are inadequately serving their citizens, yet, at the same time, they are wary of relinquishing power and subvert the very reforms they advocate. In his study of China, where authorities initiated economic decentralization—and, consequently, the empowerment of local officials—in order to foster economic development, Landry (2008) demonstrates how the Chinese Communist Party's (CCP) personnel management system is a key factor in explaining China's enduring authoritarianism. Using data collected at the municipal, county, and village level, Landry details how the promotion mechanisms for local cadres have allowed the CCP to reward officials for the development of their localities without weakening political control. Thus, in Conyer's (1983: 106) words, one of the problems identified in the decentralization literature is that decentralized powers go to the "wrong" people—central government appointees and local elites—so there is no meaningful increase in the participation of the mass of the people.[4] In authoritarian regimes, where "central intervention" plays a pivotal role in cultivating local elites and ensuring elite capture (Ribot 2002: 48), scholars have documented how central governments often play an important role in cultivating elite capture (46).

Yet strictly focusing on how authoritarian regimes seek to ensure elite capture risks neglecting how local elites respond to decentralization reforms—in other words, their agency. Chapters 5 and 6 question why and how local elites respond to decentralization reforms in practice and examine the processes of elite capture. My analysis reveals that elite capture is not the result of decentralized powers going to the wrong people or the lack of it as a result of powers going to the right people. Rather, in their efforts to maintain or gain electoral power (and the perks that go with it), local elites strategically exploit decentralization to their political advantage. Local actors, all local actors, seize the opportunities the reforms have to offer in order to advance their political agendas. Thus, in Morocco, pro-regime parties have used the decision-making powers and resources the charters offer civil society to expand their patron-client ties and thereby maintain their hold on power at the expense of civil society. Standing on the outside of the neo-patrimonial networks of patronage, the opposition PJD strategically has taken advantage of a very different set of opportunities that the reforms furnished. It created partnerships or coalitions with civil society activists to electorally defeat long-established pro-regime patrons. In both cases, municipal actors utilized these opportunities legally and in accordance with the charters.

To a large extent, scholars have not looked at the process by which elite capture occurs. As Fjeldstad (2003) documents in her review of the literature on decentralization and corruption, including elite capture, "a major share of the empirical research on the issue in both economics and political science are cross-country regression analysis. These aggregate studies naturally lend themselves to study macro-determinant and effects of corruption (and vice versa)."[5] The bulk of the literature on decentralization tends to examine the presence of elite capture, whether or not it has occurred, but not the processes by which it occurs.[6] Research that is not based on statistical analysis, Fjeldstad (2003) continues, appears to be based on personal opinion alone. This study reveals complex dynamics at work at the local level and, most importantly, the agency of local actors who adapt to reforms and, in the process, adapt the reforms themselves.

To be sure, there is a substantial portion of the literature on decentralization, much of it in states undergoing or those that have undergone

democratic transition, that is concerned with the local dynamics that produce elite capture. In her study of Mexico, Grindle (2007: 8) notes the
survival of authoritarian enclaves where local elites captured the elections
and/or where local elites continue to inequitably benefit from decentralization. Bardhan (2002: 192) identifies the same problem and in a series of
articles argues that while local governments may have better local information and accountability pressure, they are also more vulnerable to capture
by local elites, who will then receive a disproportionate share of spending on
public goods. Similarly, Bergh (2017), in her meticulous study of decentralization and participatory development projects in rural Morocco, traces
how the functions and benefits that the 2002 municipal charter devolved
to the local level were captured by the existing elite and used to strengthen
patronage networks.

Analyses point to the fact that decentralized political systems are more
prone to corruption, including elite capture, because there simply are
more opportunities for it (Fjeldstad 2003). As Prud'homme (1995: 211)
explicates, there are several reasons why this may be so. First, local officials usually have more discretionary powers than national decision makers.
Second, local bureaucrats and politicians are more likely to be subject to
pressing demands from local interest groups in matters such as taxation
(Fjeldstad 2003). Bardhan (2002: 194) concurs that while central governments also are subject to capture, at the local level "collusions may be
easier to organize and enforce in small proximate groups involving officials, politicians, contractors and interest groups; risks of being caught and
reported are easier to manage, and the multiplex interlocking social and
economic relationships among local influential people may act as formidable barriers to entry into these cozy rental havens." Accountability mechanisms, he continues, also "are often absent or highly ineffective at the local
level" (195). Other researchers note that decentralized political systems are
more prone to corruption because the potential corrupter needs only to
influence a segment of the government and, as Fjeldstad (2003) summarizes, because there are fewer centralized forces and agencies to enforce
honesty. Other scholars support this finding.

Operating on the assumption of corruption, most analyses, in seeking
to explain why elite capture occurs, point to the policy-institutional environment with the implicit and often explicit assumption that the right mix
of institutions will eliminate elite capture. Based on their review of the
literature, Johnson, Deshingkar, and Start (2003: 1), for example, find that

elite capture is predominantly attributed to the lack of mechanisms to ensure accountability. A significant number of studies thus point to the need for increased central government monitoring over local governments (Bardhan 2002; Crook and Manor 1998; Tendler and Freedheim 1994). Scholars similarly attribute elite capture to flaws in institutional design whereby local elites operate with minimal internal or external controls, monitoring mechanisms, or oversight (Labonte 2011: 95). Others point to the low threat of sanction, producing rather than preventing opportunism (94–95; see also Wong 2010). The research on elite capture thus tends to provide analysis concerning the implementation of decentralization— institutional structures, legislation, finances, and human resources—and the outcomes (whether or not elite capture has occurred); the politics that lies in between—the agency and processes on which I shine light in this book—tends to be ignored (see Labonte 2011: 104–12; Vengroff and Ben Salem 1992; Yilmaz and Venugopal 2013).

Critics of the institutional approach argue that it overlooks the complexities and resilience of power relations operating within local communities (Labonte 2011: 95). The literature on decentralized antipoverty programs—for which community members participate in the selection or targeting of beneficiaries and in benefit delivery—tends to look more closely at the politico–socio–economic context within which elite capture occurs.[7] It consequently examines a much broader range of conditions under which elite capture takes place, with a shared consensus of the close association between elite capture and inequality (see Conning and Kevane 2002; Galasso and Ravallion 2005; Mansuri and Rao 2004). Pan and Christiaensen (2012: 1620), for example, find several factors to explain the high likelihood of elite capture, including local power structures, levels of awareness, income level and poverty, community homogeneity, program design features and official eligibility criteria, and whether the program concerns the distribution of public or private goods. Conning and Kevane (2002: 384) similarly note the potentially rigid rank-based hierarchical structure that governs people's lives. Yet these studies continue to discount the agency of local actors—an agency that I argue lies at the heart of elite responses to decentralization reforms.

Prud'homme (1995: 208), a former consultant to the World Bank, was one of the first to argue that the logic of decentralization does not hold water—it assumes the people "vote with their feet," yet this is commonly not the case, as local politicians often have no campaign or mandate of which to speak. Yet Prud'homme, too, denies local actors agency and focuses instead on the institutions of patronage in which they operate. Similarly, other scholars argue that the logic that underlies the presumed positive political results of decentralization falsely assumes that local politicians' accountability and responsiveness to voters is based on programmatic appeals and policy achievements; overlooked is the fact that patronage is regularly used to mobilize voters.

While studies have shown, and this study confirms, that decentralization has empowered local politicians to engage in patronage politics (Sadanandan 2012), I argue that local actors respond to decentralization reforms according to how the charters can best serve their interests to maintain or gain political power. Whether local actors subvert decentralization reforms or in fact uphold them by honoring, for example, the commitment, in the case of Morocco, to include civil society in the making of municipality's local development plans, is determined by the degree to which those reforms serve their interests. For pro-regime elites, decentralization reforms offer legally sanctioned opportunities by which they can capture additional power and resources and ultimately strengthen or even expand their networks of patron-clientelism. Their ability to do so is facilitated by the vague and overlapping jurisdictions of responsibility that the charter does little to clarify. Municipal councillors, for example, establish nongovernmental organizations and, as NGO heads, apply to the municipal council for funding, judge which NGOs receive funding, and (unsurprisingly) are granted funding from the municipality. In the process, citizen participation, as well as any improvement in service delivery, is subverted. The issue is less that newly devolved powers went to the "wrong people" but that all local actors respond to decentralization reforms in terms of the opportunities that best serve their interests. In the case of Morocco's "palace parties" and "loyal opposition parties," this means exploiting the reforms to enlarge the patron-cliental networks that bring them to power.

Indeed, within the literature on economic reform in the MENA, studies have demonstrated that local actors adapt to and use reforms as a political strategy.[8] Menza (2012) and Clark (2012) examine how local elites adapt to and adapt the neoliberal reforms to local dynamics and agendas in Egypt and Jordan, respectively. Menza, examining the popular quarter of Misr Al Qadima in Cairo, Egypt, traces the rise of lesser notables—real estate contractors, workshop owners, and wholesale-retail merchants—as a result of SAPs. He examines how these notables invest in building their status not only by forging socioeconomic links with their neighborhoods (by donating to charitable organizations, for example) but also by establishing patron-client relations with state officials. Shedding "light on some of the practical manifestations regarding the effects of neoliberal policies on urban popular quarters," Menza (2012: 325) demonstrates how the lesser notables act as intermediaries between the state and the population, resolving disputes, facilitating services, and finding jobs. He goes on to point out the difficulty the state will have from divorcing itself from the patron-client networks of the lesser notables—including Islamists and Islamist charities. In earlier work (Clark 2012), I examine the case of municipal strengthening and poverty alleviation programs in Jordan (see also chapter 4 of this book). Central to these projects is the strengthening of municipalities' local development departments and the introduction of public-private partnerships (PPPs). I show how the PPP projects built as a result of the programs—projects ranging from olive oil factories to gas stations to multipurpose halls—soon became tools or prizes in the local patron-client systems.

Yet decentralization reforms offered a different set of opportunities for Morocco's opposition party, the PJD, which, at least during the period under study, had few or no clientelistic ties to the center to benefit politically. The PJD has taken advantage of the new decision-making roles assigned to civil society in the 2009 municipal charter. By becoming more active within civil society and working with civil society activists, the PJD has been able to gain the support of the population, forge coalition agreements with civil society activists, and ultimately come to power electorally. Based on the trust it gained by working in and with civil society activists, the PJD entered electoral lists and coalitions with CSO activists to remove established patrons from power. The charter enabled the PJD to essentially use civil society activists in its attempts to ascend to power: its partnerships were based on the understanding that if elected to power, it would fulfill the charter by prioritizing civil society's concerns and integrating civil society activists in municipal decision-making.

Elite capture is the outcome of local actors pursuing their interests. In this regard, its absence is not the result of the right mix of institutions and accountability. Nor does it derive from democratically minded actors seeking change. Rather it too is the outcome of complex local forces in which participatory goals of decentralization coincide with the strategic needs of local actors. What determines whether or not elite capture occurs is the parties' relationship to the regime and, based on that, how it can best utilize decentralization reforms to access or maintain political power.

Regime Stability

Viewed through the lens of elite capture, to what extent does decentralization serve to stabilize or destabilize authoritarian regimes? Chapters 4, 5, and 6 directly question whether, given that centralization and decentralization are both strategies intended to ensure the endurance of authoritarianism, decentralization makes a difference. I argue that as a tactic of authoritarian regime stabilization, decentralization is more stabilizing than centralization in the long run. Decentralization enables authoritarian regimes to promote themselves as political reformers while undermining elected representatives and justifying the reassertion of state powers as a result of those representatives' ineptitude and corruption. Indeed, after having presumably granted elected officials the means by which to better serve their constituents, decentralization effectively allows the Moroccan monarch to come to the rescue of citizens by directly providing hospitals, streets, sewage, and other services that elected officials could not or would not.

My research confirms studies elsewhere in the Global South and in the MENA that economic reform has not resulted in the lessening of central state control. The small but burgeoning literature on neoliberal economic reforms in the MENA region reveals an array of reforms, most commonly privatization reforms, but little accompanying political reform.[9] Indeed, the maintenance of the central state and a loss of accountability (a "bypassing of traditional checks and balances") are two of the most common themes highlighted by authors examining the privatization of municipal services in the MENA region (Kadirbeyoğlu and Sümer 2012). Writing about Cairo under Mubarak, Ben Nefissa (2009) notes the reinforcement and increasing powers of presidentially appointed governors—overriding the powers of civil servants and ministries representing the public sector at the local level—as a result of economic reform. Instead of instating genuine decentralization, the Egyptian regime abandoned and suppressed participation and decentralization while making attempts at "hypercontrolled planning for a few select areas" and encouraging "informal, irrational decentralization" elsewhere (189). Thus Ben Nefissa (2009: 190) concurs with Hibou (1999b) and other analysts that neoliberalism has not entailed a loss of state control "but rather a transformation of the ways in which it intervenes and exercises power with increased exclusions and irrationality." It does so, she continues, at reduced cost but also with reduced accountability and reduced democracy. Similarly, Saadi (2012), writing from an insider's perspective, having been an elected member of the Casablanca municipal council (2003–2009), also expresses concern over the local council's loss of accountability as a result of privatization. He notes the persistence of central control that serves to marginalize the local council and points to the unbalanced power relationship between the delegating authority (the council) "with limited resources and contested political legitimacy" and the private operator, in this case a "multinational corporation operating in several countries—with a global economic scope, control over technology and considerable expertise in dealing with local municipalities" (387). As a consequence, the municipality was highly limited, if not marginalized, in its ability to raise issues of concern to Casablanca's citizens in the review and renewal of the contract for water provision.

In Morocco, decentralization has led to the empowerment of the countries' appointed governors but not to the loss of central state power. While central powers may have shifted to new decision makers, they have not lessened. Indeed, as a result of the establishment of new institutions of neoliberal economic reform, they have increased. Hence, despite its bottom-up structure of decision-making, the National Initiative for Human Development (INDH)—the largest state initiative in Morocco to combat poverty—concentrates power in the hands of state-appointed officials at the top. Approximately half of the INDH projects fall under its *transversal*, or cross-cutting, program, which is based, in keeping with the spirit of good governance, on calls for proposals from civil society. Technically, the process begins at the bottom with local-level CSO leaders representing the interests of the population, yet the lower-level committees, which are presumably intended to have the greatest say in which CSO projects get funded, are regularly bypassed as officials at the top have the final, and sometimes the only, say. Moreover, the INDH allows the state to extend its control into new areas as it not only co-opts and appropriates civil society's discourse for its own purposes but also ensures that only those CSOs with politically acceptable agendas receive funding. Tracing how the INDH depoliticizes civil society actors, Bergh (2012b: 415) and Bono (2010) agree that "political" associations are not deemed to be "good development actors" and do not receive INDH funding. The INDH creates a direct link to CSOs granting the state a substantial role in their affairs. More to the point, it encourages and fosters technocratic CSOs that focus on particular projects and not on the political structures that underlie the country's socio-economic challenges.

Examining Morocco's good governance reforms, several scholars note the reorganization and extension of state power under the guise of greater participation of civil society in the initiation and implementation of development projects. Zemni and Bogaert (2011: 412) note that both INDH and Villes sans Bidonvilles (Cities Without Slums) programs, while bringing civil society voices into the decision-making and implementation processes, remain top-down in their approach. Berriane (2010: 107) concurs, arguing that

> even if the State seems to be disengaging itself from some of its core duties (education, poverty reduction, etc.) when integrating private actors into the implementation of public policies, it does not, in fact, lose much of its control. If the State seems to be disengaging itself from certain public policies . . . leaving the space for private actors such as NGOs to take over its duties, the State is actually . . . integrating and co-opting these same actors into the state system. . . . Not only does the State not lose control through this process but . . . it actually redeploys itself through different means, thus gaining even more control.

Indeed, Morocco's privatization and technocratization of social welfare in the form of its good governance initiatives such as the INDH further work to the benefit of central state powers by shifting the responsibility for social welfare to societal groups. Ben Nefissa (2009: 190–92) documents the same dynamic in Cairo, where new state policies give infrastructure or services to working-class neighborhoods only when they can raise money on their own to pay for them. In one neighborhood, "self-help" initiatives financed the post office, police station, medical centers, youth clubs, Qur'an study groups, public squares, gardens, and buildings for the local district offices. NGOs and other associations thus become codependent with administrative and state structures, eventually propping them up and lessening their financial and public responsibilities.

Most importantly, economic reforms and decentralization have enabled the Moroccan monarchy to promote itself as a political reformer and service provider at the expense of elected officials. It is in this capacity that decentralization helps stabilize authoritarian regimes in ways centralization cannot and does not. While municipal councils presumably have been empowered, via decentralization, to better provide services with the aid of civil society, the charters provide multiple opportunities for elite capture and all but ensure it. The enhanced opportunities for patron-clientelism as a result of the charter (which I argue in chapter 5 are not accidental) have meant that poor service delivery in Morocco continues to be the norm. Elected officials thus are discredited, leaving the king, by way of an equalization program or the INDH, to address the needs of frustrated citizens, thereby enhancing the legitimacy of the monarchy at the expense of elected officials, and directly provide the infrastructure or service that elected officials could not or would not. Thus the monarchy, having devolved power to elected officials is still, in the end, the body that best takes care of its citizens.

While good governance and decentralization have enabled the Moroccan monarch to present himself as a political reformer and, simultaneously, to maintain the system of neopatrimonialism, centralization in Jordan provided neither of these functions during the period under study. Indeed, in the context of shrinking state resources, centralization proved to fragment pro-regime elites as they competed for access to patronage. As poor service delivery continued, the monarchy was not able to present itself as reformist. Any patronage or projects, such as schools, the monarch presented directly to the population were seen as unequal and ad hoc, thus furthering discontent.

Methodology

I chose the cases of Morocco and Jordan for this study based on the fundamental puzzle that the two states pose: why would two relatively similar regimes adopt different policies vis-à-vis decentralization? Both countries are monarchies with elected parliaments and municipal councils—they are, in other words, electoral authoritarian regimes or electoral autocracies—and both have been praised by the WB for undertaking the most far-reaching reform of public-sector employment in the MENA region (Baylouny

2010: 56; Harrigan and El-Said 2009a: 159). Both regimes were forced to implement SAPs in response to their respective economic crises and the consequent social dislocation and political discontent they engendered. Both regimes moreover initiated political liberalization measures to counter the growing economic frustrations. Finally, both looked at decentralization to ease the economic burden on the central state and the economic inequalities facing their respective populations. Yet Morocco has undertaken the most significant degree of political decentralization in the MENA region thus far. While the central state retains significant control, since the issuing of the 1976 municipal charter, municipal governments have progressively gained decision-making power regarding the development of and the provision of services to their municipalities. Conversely, from 1955, when Jordan promulgated its first postindependence municipal law, until 2015, when it passed a decentralization law, Jordan effectively removed powers from municipal councils. Indeed, its so-called decentralization law does the same. While the two cases of this book are monarchies, the insights provided by them are relevant for nonmonarchical authoritarian regimes elsewhere. Neither the strategies of state control deployed vis-à-vis the administrative or elected bodies nor the patron-client ties that sustain the two authoritarian regimes are unique to monarchies (Albrecht and Schlumberger 2004).

The cases of Morocco and Jordan thus offer a means to compare decentralization using a most-similar-systems design. Furthermore, by studying the two trajectories that Morocco and Jordan have followed, I was able to examine decentralization from three different methodological perspectives. The first is a study across time, examining the progressive evolution of decentralization within Morocco and the local dynamics it has engendered. The second is a comparative study of municipalities in Morocco and Jordan, contrasting and highlighting the markedly different nature of local responses and dynamics as result of the two regimes' adoption of different strategies of state control. Finally, the third is a within-case comparison of municipalities within Morocco, questioning why elite capture occurs in most but not all cases.

This book examines Morocco and Jordan from the time of the passing of their first municipal laws (1960 in Morocco and 1877 in Jordan) until 2015. The bulk of the analysis, however, focuses on the municipal councils elected to power in 2007 in Jordan and in 2009 in Morocco. Morocco's 2009 councils were the last to be elected while the Islamist PJD was undisputedly considered the country's only opposition party. Following

2011 and the writing of a new (post–Arab Spring) constitution in Morocco, the PJD entered into government for the first time, and its leader, Abdelilah Benkirane, became prime minister (PM). Since 2011, it is questionable whether the PJD may still be called an opposition party, for many analysts now consider it as having joined the ranks of Morocco's other co-opted "opposition" parties (see chapter 3). By focusing primarily on the municipal councils elected prior to this change of events, I was able to compare Morocco's pro-regime parties with the opposition PJD in order to examine how the two types of parties responded to decentralization. As I demonstrate in chapters 5 and 6, this difference helps us to explain why elite capture does not occur in some cases. In the case of Jordan, the 2007 council was the last to serve a full term prior to 2015. In 2011, the central government dissolved all councils and replaced them with appointed councils; new elections were not held until 2013.

I undertook the majority of the field research for the study between 2010 and 2012. In Jordan, I conducted the field research in 2010 and 2011. I then supplemented these interviews with secondary materials collected both in and outside of Jordan between 2008 and 2015. I conducted my fieldwork in Jordan in two phases. The first involved a qualitative survey of twenty-two municipalities located in all regions of the country. I conducted interviews with representatives in all concerned ministries, mayors, councillors, international and domestic civil society representatives, and representatives of international aid agencies. The second phase involved more in-depth interviews in four of the twenty-two municipalities. I based my selection of the four municipalities on the following criteria: a municipality in which an influential tribe dominated; a municipality with a relatively powerless tribe; a municipality with a large Palestinian population; and a "mixed" municipality that cannot be said to be dominated by any tribe. In addition, I also ensured that there was variation among the municipalities according to governorate and municipal size. In the end, I chose the following municipalities: a municipality dominated by an influential tribe, the Naimat, in the governorate of Ma'an in the south; a municipality dominated by a large tribe but one not well represented in positions of power, the Bani Hassan, in the governorate of al-Zarqa', close to the capital, Amman; a municipality with a large Palestinian population in the governorate of Jerash, also relatively close to Amman; and a tribally mixed municipality in the northern governorate of Irbid.

I conducted the bulk of the fieldwork in Morocco 2011 and 2012; it similarly entailed a survey of municipalities followed by more in-depth research in a selected number of the municipalities. Morocco has a significantly larger number of municipalities spread out over a far greater territorial expanse, so it was considerably more challenging than in Jordan to visit a representative sample of municipalities. Due to this logistical reason and the existence of a far greater amount of secondary literature, much of which was based on impressive fieldwork (Bergh 2007; Catusse with Cattedra and Idrissi-Janati 2007; Catusse and Zaki 2010; Pellicer and Wegner 2015; Wegner 2011), I decided to conduct a relatively small yet in-depth survey of municipalities and to rely more heavily on secondary sources. Keeping regional variation and variation in the size of municipalities in consideration, I conducted a qualitative survey of eight municipalities located in the provinces of Chefchaouen, Errachidia, El Jadida, Ifrane, Kenitra, Khemisset, Khenifra, and Tiznit.[10] I included both urban (Chefchaouen, Ifrane, Kenitra, Khemisset, Khenifra, Tiznit) and rural municipalities (Errachidia, El Jadida) in the survey, yet I intentionally biased the survey toward urban municipalities for two reasons. Urban and rural municipalities have different electoral systems, proportional representation in the case of the former and a first-past-the-post system in the case of the latter. The first-past-the-post system in rural municipalities is a candidate-centric system that is biased toward the reelection of incumbents—the majority of whom are pro-regime local notables. Party politics—the competition and election of parties as well as coalition building—tends to be limited to urban municipalities. Urban municipalities thus represent a better case in which to examine the impact of decentralization reforms on the electoral strategies on pro-regime and on opposition parties. Furthermore, while the majority of Morocco's municipalities are designated as rural, many of them do in fact have populations above the threshold of 35,000 that supposedly determines the designation of municipalities, and many more are on their way, through population pressure, to becoming urban municipalities.

As in the case of Jordan, I conducted my field research in Morocco in two phases, During the first phase (2011), I conducted qualitative interviews with central authorities, the Ministry of Interior in particular, and their representatives; representatives of international aid agencies; international and national civil society representatives in the capital, Rabat; and former and current mayors and councillors, as well as civil society representatives in the eight abovementioned municipalities. In the second phase (2012), I conducted more in-depth interviews in the municipalities located in Chefchaouen, Errachidia, Kenitra, Khemisset, and, to a lesser degree, Tiznit. I chose these municipalities in order to better understand the dynamics of elite capture. The research municipalities in Chefchaouen, Errachidia, and Kenitra are all cases in which the PJD came to power in 2009 and elite capture did not occur.[11] The remaining two municipalities are both examples of elite capture. Comparing these five municipalities in a more in-depth manner enabled me to better understand why elite capture does and does not occur, and specifically the significance of opposition party politics for elite capture.[12]

I did not include either capital, Amman and Rabat, and in Morocco I also did not include any of the largest cities. In Jordan, the municipality of Greater Amman (GAM) is under the prime minister's office and not the Ministry of Municipal Affairs, it furthermore has different legislation that applies uniquely to it. For this and other reasons, such as funding, GAM cannot be said to be representative of the country's other municipalities. In Morocco, all major cities are divided into *arrondissements*, or boroughs, each with its own elected council; the amalgamated city then has a supra-council comprising representatives from the other councils. The larger cities thus also entail political dynamics not representative of the vast majority of municipalities in Morocco. The complexity of the municipal system in Morocco's major cities furthermore would have made the impact of decentralization on agents much more difficult to ascertain.

The book is divided into six chapters followed by a conclusion. Chapters 1 through 3 examine the first question of this book: why Morocco chose to decentralization while Jordan did not. In chapters 4 through 6, I tackle the second and third questions: how municipal actors work with and around the opportunities and constraints presented by decentralization reforms, and the extent to which decentralization, as opposed to centralization, stabilizes authoritarian regimes.

CHAPTER I

Coalition Building and the Social Relations
That Support Authoritarian Regimes

Any discussion of decentralization in the Arab World—particularly the question of why Morocco has taken steps toward political decentralization while Jordan has not—must go back to the colonial period. For it is in the political history of the British colonial authority, in the case of Jordan, and the French, in the case of Morocco, that we find the roots of the centralized state structures and the relationships of monarchical social control that guided their differing decisions. Both the British and the French built on existing structural and political foundations and completed the centralization projects begun by the ruling dynasties—the Ottomans and the Alawites, respectively. The social contracts created during this process—in Jordan, what Tell calls the Hashemite Compact with Transjordanian tribes,[1] and in Morocco, the French creation of and alliances with the rural Berber nobility—were then expanded by the post-independence regimes in order to consolidate monarchical rule. In Jordan, the monarchy's coalition—to use Eaton, Kaiser, and Smoke's terminology (see introduction)—with the tribes enabled it to weather the tide of Arab nationalism, the influx of Palestinian refugees, and the political and economic instability that followed the successive waves of refugees. In Morocco, the monarchy's coalition with the Berber elite significantly contributed to its effort to weaken the Istiqlal Party (Independence Party), the party with which it had fought against the French for independence and the only real challenger to the monarchy's hold on power after independence. Indeed, until the early 1970s, Jordan and Morocco followed remarkably similar patterns—despite significant differences in the type and nature of colonial rule. Yet, while the Jordanian monarchy maintained its coalition with the tribal elite even after the rise of national-ist currents and an alleged coup plot within the Transjordanian-dominated army, the Moroccan monarchy, following the attempted coups of 1971 and 1972, lessened its reliance on its coalition with the Berber elite and, armed with phosphate-related rents, undertook sweeping redistribution policies in order to broaden its base of support. It is during this time period—the early 1970s—that the coalition strategies of the two monarchies began to diverge. The monarchs' decisions whether or not to decentralize were out-comes of these different coalition strategies.

Following the attempted coups in Morocco, the monarchy sought to consolidate power by broadening its coalition and including the Istiqlal as a partner. Rather than privileging and essentially manipulating Berber-based political parties in order to weaken the opposition parties of the former nationalist movement, the monarchy turned to the nationalist par-ties themselves, and to Istiqlal in particular, to co-opt and thereby neutral-ize them by bringing them into the political system. In this context, there were important incentives for the monarchy to embark on some degree of decentralization. The monarchy was able to use the 1976 Municipal Char-ter to entice the opposition parties back into electoral participation and eventually into the government itself. For their part, Morocco's opposition parties willingly took the bait (see chapter 3); they were attracted by the possibility of establishing party branches and capturing local elites and their resources in municipalities throughout the country, and they consequently viewed decentralization as an important opportunity. The 2002 and 2009 charters were to play the same "enticement function," albeit with different and new coalition partners.

In Jordan, by contrast, following the alleged coup attempt, the monarchy turned to the country's tribal elite—the segment of society with which the British and the monarchy historically had been coalition partners. Tribal shaykhs had played a key role in state-building in Jordan, and continued to be an important feature of both the state and society post-independence. With the rise of nationalist (antimonarchical) parties in the 1950s and the alleged attempted coup, the relatively young monarchy in Jordan faced a very different constellation of forces from those encountered by the Moroc-can monarchy. On the one hand, there was the pivotal role the tribes played historically, and continued to play in redistributing royal patronage. On the other hand, there were the growing numbers of Palestinians who had entered Jordan following the wars with Israel and whom the monarchy presumed to have loyalties lying outside of Jordan. The monarchy thus sought to strengthen its coalition with the tribal elite and attempted to woo back the Transjordanians who had been enticed by pan-Arab nationalism. It continued to do so after each successive crisis the regime faced. The monarchy's deepening dependence on the tribes and, conversely, of the tribes upon the monarchy would serve as a disincentive to any reform measures that would lessen the tribal elites' control on power. By devolving power away from the center—where tribal elites hold their status and ability to direct services and resources to their tribes—decentralization posed a threat both to the tribal elite and, in turn, the monarchy.

State-Building in Jordan

The centrality of the Bedouin tribes to the state-building process in Jordan cannot be overstated. Building on Ottoman practices and those of the Arab government's short-lived rule, the British colonial powers bound the country's Bedouin tribes to the rudimentary state, offering them key roles in the army in particular, in exchange for loyalty. The Bedouin-dominated Arab Legion, especially its Desert Force, enabled Britain to bring the desert regions under the control of the state and secure the country's borders; it also transformed the role of the tribal shaykhs and tied their interests to those of the state. Even as the state consolidated and took over many of the roles previously held by tribes, the government ruled through the tribal shaykhs and the latter retained an important—albeit changing—political leadership role. By the time of independence, the tribal shaykhs had become important political (and economic) players, representing their tribes and acting as conduits for channeling and allocating resources and services from the state to their people. They had, in other words, developed an important stake in the future of the monarchy.

The British mandate of Transjordan was created as a result of the capitulation and subsequent demise of the Ottoman Empire in October 1918, marking the end of World War I. Shortly thereafter, Allied and Arab forces entered Damascus, where Sharif Faysal bin Husayn, the leader of the 1916 Arab Revolt against the Ottomans—his father, Sharif Husayn ibn Ali, had committed his men to the revolt in exchange for the British promise of the creation of an Arab state when the war was over—established an Arab Administration as part of the Occupied Enemy Territory Administrations East. The administration extended over what was to become Transjordan. Faysal's rule, however, was short lived. The San Remo Resolution of April 25, 1920, granted the mandate of Greater Syria to the French, and Faysal's forces were expelled from the country in July 1920. Palestine and the land east of the Jordan River formed a single mandate under the authority of the British. This, too, was not to last long. In 1921, the British unilaterally divided the territory into two mandates, separated by the Jordan River. The lands east of the Jordan River became the emirate of Transjordan.

Although the Arab government under Faysal had reactivated the defunct Ottoman institutions (see below), its jurisdiction over Transjordan had been negligible. During World War I, the Ottomans, Hashemites, British, and French all had courted the tribes for support in exchange for "guns, gold, and grain" (Alon 2005: 218; Tell 2000). Following the war, Faysal's government continued the Ottoman policy of granting subsidies and bestowing honorary titles in order to secure the allegiance and loyalty of key shaykhs. Faysal also integrated some of them into his administration. In exchange, the tribes were able to diversify their sources of income, enhance their leadership positions within their chieftaincies, and maintain independence and autonomy. However, when Britain withdrew its troops and halved its financial support for Faysal in 1919, this system became increasingly untenable. In the context of an uncertain political future, the lengthy absence of Faysal as he engaged in negotiations in Europe over the future of the promised Arab state, his government's inability to subsidize local leaders, and the French encouragement of discord between the shaykhs and the Arab government (largely through various forms of payment), the government's influence in Transjordan quickly evaporated; the vacuum that emerged was filled by local elites (Alon 2007: 15–16).

At the beginning of the mandate, nearly the entire population of Transjordan was organized along tribal lines, with the tribe serving as the main source of solidarity, structuring all political, economic, and social relations and providing security. This applied not only to the nomadic and seminomadic tribes of the area but also to the settled populations in villages and towns (Alon 2005: 213; Tell 2013: 31). Transjordan comprised several tribal units or chieftaincies, each operating independently. These included the

Huwaytat confederacies in the south, a tribal alliance under the Majali tribe in the al-Karak region, and the tribal chieftaincies led by the Bani Sakhr and the 'Adwan in central Transjordan. In the north, every district or group of villages functioned as an independent tribal alliance under the leadership of a shaykh or za'im (leader) (Alon 2005: 216–17).

Balancing their primary aim of protecting their larger trade interests (predominantly in Palestine and Iraq) and their obligation to prepare the mandate for independence, after the collapse of Faysal's government, the British sought an "inexpensive solution" according to which the area east of the Jordan River would remain in the British sphere (Tell 2000: 50, 2013: 57). In August 1920, a day after Faysal's departure for Europe, the British convened a meeting with local elites and informed them that Transjordan would be placed under a British mandate but that the inhabitants would form their own regional governments with administrative apparatuses in the districts of al-Karak, Salt, and Ajloun. However, the regional governments succumbed to tribal divisions and tensions and were unable to perform their tasks (Jureidini and McLaurin 1984: 11; Massad 2001: 103; Tell 2000: 50–51, 2013: 56–58). A new solution, that of possible indirect British rule with an "Arab veneer," opened up when, in November 1920, Abdullah bin Husayn, the younger brother of Faysal, arrived in Ma'an with several hundred fighters intent on ousting the French from Greater Syria and restoring Hashemite control (Tell 2013: 61). Abdullah eventually met with Churchill in Jerusalem (March 1920), where the two came to an agreement (originally for a six-month trial period) according to which the British would create the emirate of Transjordan, led by a government headed by Abdullah but under the direction of the British resident. Abdullah was to maintain peace with Syria and Palestine and keep Transjordan as free as possible from nationalist agitations (see below). In return, Abdullah received a monthly subsidy and an understanding that Britain would promote, when possible, his candidature for the Syrian throne. The precise borders of Transjordan were not clear; however, Transjordan was conceived as lying south of Syria, west of Iraq, east of Palestine, and north of the Arabian Peninsula.

When the emirate was established, its rulers faced a formidable challenge, for the inhabitants could resist state policies at will (Alon 2005: 218). Two systems of government emerged in the early years of the emirate. Based on the reactivation of the three Ottoman administrative provinces (liwa'), the newly formed Arab government (backed up by the Royal Air Force, RAF), controlled the settled population.[2] As part of the larger Tanzimat project of centralizing and standardizing the empire, the Ottomans had issued the Vilayet Law of 1864, which had created a "unified and nested hierarchy of provincial offices with their corresponding administrative divisions" (Reimer 2005: 191).[3] This was followed, in 1877, by a provincial municipality code (see chapter 2). Jordan's first municipal (*baladiyya*) administration was created in Irbid in 1881,[4] followed by Salt (c. 1888), al-Karak (c. 1894), Ma'an (c. 1898), al-Husn (c. 1908), al-Tafilah (before 1909), and Madaba (c. 1912) (Reimer 2005: 194). The municipality of Amman, today's capital, was established in 1909 (Ababsa 2015: 12). By 1920, the number of municipalities had grown to eleven (Ahmaro 2014: 67), although some municipalities were established, then periodically closed or dissolved, and later reestablished (Reimer 2005). Under the new Arab government, the Ottoman municipal system was further expanded into new areas as part of the state-building project.

In contrast, nomadic and seminomadic tribes were under the personal authority of Abdullah and enjoyed almost complete autonomy. In April 1921, along with the ministerial administration and basic laws, the new government created the Tribal Administration Department with the positions of tribal administration representative and deputy representative. Concerned primarily with expanding his reign into Syria, Abdullah took little interest in the daily administration of the country or the strengthening of the central government, leaving these matters to the discretion of his ministers. Abdullah looked after the tribes through his cousin, confidante, and representative of the Tribal Administration, Shakir ibn Zayd, and cultivated the shaykhs' support and cooperation by "securing the tribes extensive autonomy from the government, offering presents, transferring plots of state land to private owners, and exempting certain tribes from the obligation to pay taxes" (Alon 2005: 219).

By 1924, however, Abdullah faced deteriorating relations with his government and a tribal opposition that included two tribal rebellions and ultimately paved the way for a more interventionist system of colonial rule (Alon 2005: 220). While the far more serious of the two, in 1923, was successfully put down by the British, the revolt triggered a debate in Jerusalem and eventually London as to the nature of the Transjordanian state (now technically a constitutional monarchy, according to the wording of the declaration that created Transjordan as a separate entity from Palestine) and the role of Abdullah in it. The rebellions of 1921 and 1923 were largely triggered by Abdullah's policy of granting of subsidies, land grants, and tax exemptions to the Bani Sakhr in order to gain their support in confronting the Wahabi Brotherhood (Ikhwan) incursions from south of Transjordan (in what is now known as Saudi Arabia). In the context of the central government's improved control over semi-settled and settled areas, and consequently its ability to collect taxes (and back taxes), the Bani Sakhr's exemption from tax payment and the consequent need for the government to tax other communities more in order to make up the difference provoked the resentment of the settled tribes, particularly the al-Balqa' alliance, headed by the 'Adwan. When the 'Adwan marched on Amman, their show of strength soon expanded to include large segments of society when what came to be known as the al-Balqa' movement—a group of educated Transjordanians—supported them and elevated the "localised tribal affair to a general popular protest against the foreign Arab government, an outcry for a complete reform of the Emirate" (Alon 2007: 54). While Abdullah initially took a conciliatory approach and the government tendered its resignation, events escalated as tribes throughout the country formed into opposing alliances. In September 1923, the 'Adwan launched a revolt. RAF planes and the Reserve Force (see below) suppressed the revolt (and protected Abdullah). Approximately one year later, in August 1924, the British presented Abdullah with an ultimatum "to reform his administration and accept British supervision or to give up his throne" (Alon 2007: 59).

From that point onward, Britain began to more forcefully impose its vision of a Western-style state on Transjordan (Alon 2007: 60). The British commenced a concerted state-building project, one that would entail the transfer of what had historically been tribal responsibilities and functions to the state. They abolished the position of the deputy representative of the Tribal Administration Department (1923), the Tribal Administration Department (1924), and the position of tribal representative (1926). Shortly thereafter, they established the elected Legislative Council.[5] Having reformed the central administration, the British, under the command of Lt. Col. Frederick Peake, sought to strengthen the armed forces to ensure that the Arab government could rule the country without fear of intervention from tribal chiefs (Massad 2001: 106). Toward this end, all police and military forces were merged with the Reserve Force (created with the establishment of the emirate with Abdullah as commander-in-chief), renamed the Arab Legion (al-Jaysh al-'Arabi, the Arab Army, in Arabic). Following the poor performance of the Arab Legion in repelling Ikhwan raiders, the British reduced the legion in size and responsibilities and, in 1926, created the Trans-Jordan Frontier Force (TJFF), under the command of the Royal Air Force.

With Ibn Saud's increasing military victories, the British reorganized Transjordan's armed forces once again—under the new leadership of Capt. John Glubb. Peake had predominantly recruited from the Palestine gendarmerie and had deliberately staffed the TJFF with non-Transjordanians (see Massad 2001: 108). Yet the "alien" composition of the TJFF had garnered little local support (Tell 2013: 76). Even with the aid of 'Abdullah and Shakir, and with RAF aerial support, it was unable to put a stop to cross-border raiding. Consequently, the British dispatched Glubb to Transjordan from Iraq, where he had been tasked with pacifying the Bedouins, in order that he essentially replicate his success in Transjordan. Glubb established the Desert Patrol (Quwwat al-Badiyah), a new elite force within the Arab Legion made up entirely of Bedouins recruited from the nomadic and seminomadic tribes (Lewis 1987: 44; Massad 2001: 105; Vatiliotis 1967: 72).[6] By the late 1940s, the renamed Desert Mechanized Force had eliminated the raiding and had established an international reputation as a highly effective British mercenary force.

Under Glubb, the Bedouin Desert Force played a crucial role both in Transjordan's state- and nation-building. It helped bring the desert areas under state control and slowly shift loyalties to the incipient nation-state. According to Massad (2001: 110–11):

> By incorporating the Bedouins into the . . . state apparatus . . . , Glubb ensured that not only would their internecine and international raiding be stopped, but also their group loyalty would be transferred to the nation-state, guaranteeing that the Bedouins would protect that state against all threats, especially so due to their contempt for city-folk from which anti-state threats might arise. Also, due to their kinship ties across the new national borders and their tribal affiliation, the Bedouins were seen as a threat to the nation-state. Nationalizing them, therefore, through territorialization, was part of nation-building.

Glubb's ability to recruit tribes that had been "implacable foes of ordered government" (Bocco and Tell 1994: 108) must be understood in light of his policy of "humane imperialism," according to which the forces had both a military and a welfare purpose (Tell 2013: 87–88). The poverty of the Bedouin—in no small part due to imperial policy—imbued Glubb's approach with a social dimension that entailed employment and subsidies to tribal shaykhs and the application of tribal law wherever possible. As Bocco and Tell (1994: 120) state: "These elements were underpinned by a kind of hearts and minds policy designed to prevent the hunger of the tribes leading to the recrudescence of raiding, and to stymie Ibn Saud's attempt to gain influence among them." To a large extent, Glubb followed Abdullah's precedent of cultivating close relationships with the shaykhs, offering them economic assistance and giving their sons priority in recruitment to the army (Alon 2007: 226).[7] Subsidies were provided to shaykhs to encourage their cooperation in the control of raiding. The forces also recruited heavily from the poorest of Bedouin tribes. In addition, soldiers' pay was such that it could sustain several families. Public works formed another type of employment for the Bedouin—again with heavy recruitment from among the poorest. Glubb also engaged the forces in the supervision of tax collection to ensure a fair distribution of revenues.

Shaykhs were further integrated into the state when they became recipients of state salaries. Glubb's humane imperialism was paralleled by the work of, and his eventual usurpation of, the powers of the Tribal Control Board (TCB), established in 1929. The TCB was established as the cornerstone of a more interventionist policy of British involvement in the everyday control of the tribes. The TCB dealt with all issues within the jurisdiction of the tribal courts, controlled nomads' movements and determined the locations in which they could camp, and investigated raids or breaches of the peace in which nomads were involved. Glubb worked closely with the shaykhs in the daily policing of the desert and the settlement of disputes as part of the TCB's work and saw the shaykhs' traditional judicial role as a vital means by which to enhance their cooperation with and their integration into the government. In the words of Glubb: "The tribal shaikh . . . constitutes a danger, so long as he possesses influence with the people, but enjoys no share in the government. It is therefore important to associate the shaikhs with the government in every way possible. To employ these shaikhs to assist in the work and the administration of justice is the wisest of policies" (Alon 2007: 99).

The 1936 Bedouin Control Law and Tribal Courts Law (by 1936, Glubb had wrestled control of the powers of the TCB from Abdullah and the board) were the ultimate manifestation of this philosophy (Alon 2007: 100). The legislation introduced legal procedures that resembled the traditional tribal system. Cases were tried exclusively by tribal chiefs who followed customary law. However, the Arab Legion, not the tribes as historically had been the case, was responsible for facilitating the hearing and for executing the verdict.

By the mid- to late-1930s, the overall process of state formation in Transjordan had reached a "critical mass," with the central government having expanded its functions and tightened its control over the population (Alon 2005: 227). State agencies were increasingly taking over the role of the tribes, but tribal organization, identity, and ethos remained a dominant feature of society. Abdullah continued to play a crucial role in facilitating the state's rule in nomadic and seminomadic areas, where he maintained a "chieftaincy-like political system based on close personal relations, an open-door policy, mediation . . . and, when possible, conciliation" (228). Time and again, Britain availed itself of Abdullah's sway over the tribal leaders (228). The relative weakness of the central government (by the end of the mandate, the state apparatus still could be described as rudimentary at best), combined with the small number of British personnel, made it necessary to control the population via their local leaders while, at the same time, gradually limiting their autonomy (221).

Thus, despite the beginning of the disintegration of tribal confederacies as the state was gradually taking over some of the roles of the tribes and the increasing attempts from within the confederacies to challenge shaykhs' leadership positions, on the eve of independence in 1946, many shaykhs had managed to retain, if not strengthen, their ascendance within their tribes. As Alon (2005: 228) elaborates: "The government ruled through the shaykhs, not in place of them, and continued to delegate responsibility for maintaining law and order, tax collection, dispute settlement, and distributing state largesse. Shaykhs remained the main link between the central government and the population, maintaining and even increasing their status as important political actors even as the powers of central government increased." Yet their legitimacy now increasingly derived from their status as the exclusive representative of their tribes vis-à-vis the central government and less so, as had been the case previously, from the recognition of their moral authority by fellow tribesmen (231). They thus became a "framework for channelling and allocating resources and services originating from the central government" (234).

The government's land reform program had been central to this transformation of the role of the shaykhs. Implemented in 1927, the goals of the program had been to increase agricultural production and tax revenues and thereby reduce Transjordan's dependence on British subsidies. However, land reform unintentionally had worked to the favor of large landowning shaykhs by securing their preexisting rights of landownership and helping them to increase their holdings. When the economy improved in the late 1930s and 1940s and land prices soared, landowning shaykhs who had been able to borrow money against the land or to purchase more land became rich (Alon 2007: 127–28; Fischbach 1994: 105–7). Many shaykhs relocated their center of activity to Amman, the capital, and began acting as mediators between their people and the various government departments. The tribal shaykh thus came to be the point of access linking the state to its people and vice versa. In this capacity, many shaykhs succeeded not only in preserving their leadership roles but also in keeping their leadership positions within their immediate families following the end of the mandate.

By the time of independence, tribal shaykhs were important political and economic actors, fully "entwined in the state structure and identified with its interests" (Alon 2005: 231). A new order, a "Hashemite compact," had been forged that bound rural Transjordanian tribes to the regime during the British mandate and linked the monarchy with the tribes. The monarchy's rule was buoyed by both tribal structures and identity. This identification of state interests with tribal interests would deepen in years to come.

Independence and the Consolidation of Monarchical Rule

The monarchy's coalition with the tribal elite was to be tested shortly after Jordan's independence. At that time, a nationalist movement inspired by the rise of Jamal Abdel Nasser and Pan-Arabism, following the 1952 coup in Egypt, developed as a result of the growing public discontent with the ongoing presence of the British, the 1948 war with Israel, the arrival of thousands of Palestinian refugees and economic crisis, and Glubb's perceived military restraint in the ongoing border war with Israel. These events and frustrations were to contribute, broadly speaking, to interrelated growing political trends within the Arab Legion and within society at large, and these trends would challenge the very existence of the monarchical state. In 1957, the monarchy demanded the resignation of the nationalist prime minister (PM) sparking massive public demonstrations and an alleged attempted coup within the military. After armed forces loyal to the regime successfully put down the coup, the king turned to those he perceived to be the most important pillar of monarchical support. With the nationalist movement having recruited from both Palestinians and Transjordanians, the monarchy turned to the Transjordanians in order to win them back and secure their loyalties.[8]

Following independence, the new Hashemite Kingdom of Jordan passed its first constitution (published as law in 1947 and ratified in 1952), creating a bicameral parliament with an appointed upper house (the senate, *majlis al-a'yan*) and an elected lower house (the chamber of deputies or *al-majlis al-nawwab*).[9] To a large extent, however, little had changed. Power remained firmly in the hands of the monarch and his appointed ministers. British influence in the kingdom furthermore remained "virtually intact" (Tell 2013: 115). The Anglo-Jordanian Treaty was revised to give Jordan legal sovereignty; however, Jordan's defense and finances remained under British control. Glubb continued to head the Arab Legion.

The 1948 war with Israel, however, was to have a profound effect on Jordan. Paraphrasing Jureidini and McLaurin (1984: 16), it is safe to say that no other event in Jordan's history has been nearly as profound in its impact on Jordanian life as the influx of Palestinians resulting from the wars with Israel. The 1948 war with Israel brought 70,000 Palestinians fleeing to Jordan at a time when Jordan's population was approximately 440,000. Two years later, King Abdullah annexed the West Bank and extended citizenship to the Palestinians living there as well as to the 1948 refugees now settled in Jordan. By the mid-1950s, therefore, 790,000 Palestinians had been granted Jordanian citizenship (Brand 1995: 47). In response to the annexation of the West Bank and the revelation of Abdullah's peace negotiations with Israel and, more generally, to the direction of the kingdom under continued British influence, public resentment toward the monarchy began to develop shortly after the 1948 war. By the mid-1950s—inspired by events in Egypt—an alliance of opposition parties, the Jordanian National Movement (JNM, al-Harakat al-Wataniyyah al-Urduniyyah), supported by "the street" had formed in the name of Pan-Arabism, leading to riots and demonstrations against the British connections to the regime in Amman, Irbid, Salt, and the towns of the West Bank. By 1956, the National Socialist Party (NSP) and the Ba'ath Party had gained relatively large followings; this included elements within the legion, within which the growing anticolonial and anti-British sentiments in the country reinforced brewing discontent. Legion officers resented the control of the establishment by foreign senior officers. (Glubb had faced a shortage of officers as the legion expanded rapidly at the beginning of World War II and again in 1948, and he consequently recruited many British officers to take command of the Arab army.) Junior officers, in particular, were frustrated by what they perceived to be the slow pace at which the "Arabization" of the army was occurring through promotion. At stake, as Vatiliotis (1967: 110) observes, was the fundamental question of whether Jordan should exist as a nation-state at all or whether it should be part of a larger Arab sovereign entity—as both the NSP and the Ba'athists argued. Central to these competing visions was, of course, the future role of the monarchy.

When Jordan's potential entry into the Baghdad Pact triggered widespread riots in 1955 and 1956, King Hussein (Abdullah's grandson and, in 1952, successor) dismissed Glubb, effectively ending Britain's role in the country and the region.[10] Glubb's ouster made the JNM a powerful national political player. In 1956, the nationalist parties of the JNM won a massive electoral victory, and Sulayman al-Nabulsi, head of the NSP, was appointed PM. Within six months of the elections, King Hussein was in a battle with the JNM—"a battle essentially fought over two opposing images of the future of Jordan" (Anderson 2005: 177). The JNM favored a state ruled by representative government and economically, militarily, and politically united with Egypt and Syria. Al-Nabulsi's government consequently moved Jordan to the left and toward Egypt; signed the Arab Solidarity Agreement with Egypt, Syria, and Saudi Arabia; and terminated the Anglo-Jordanian Treaty. In opposition to these efforts, the king and his aides sought to improve relations with the United States and attempted to prevent the nationalist government in its efforts to move the country to the left. When Prime Minister al-Nabulsi announced that Jordan would exchange diplomatic representation with the Soviet Union (shortly thereafter, he also announced his desire to take steps in preparation for amalgamation with Egypt and Syria), the king demanded his resignation (Anderson 2005: 182).

Al-Nabulsi's resignation provoked a huge public uprising. Yet the nationalists were disunited; more importantly, "they underestimated the political power of the conservatives" (Aruri 1972: 140). Despite massive public support for the nationalists, tribal support for the monarchy remained significant within the military due in no small part to reaction against the series of "antinationalist" purges in the bureaucracy and army and by nationalists speaking freely of a Jordan Republic, as if the king had abdicated. The commander of the armed forces and one of the leaders of what are now referred to as the Free Officers (the largely better-educated members of the officer class who were resentful of seconded British officers and inspired by the example of Nasser), Ali Abu Nuwwar, was among those who spoke openly of a Jordan Republic. When an uprising occurred at the army camp of al-Zarqa', the monarchy accused Abu Nuwwar, a non-Bedouin Transjordanian, of attempting a military coup.[11] According to Tell (2013: 121), Abu Nuwwar and "other would-be coup-makers were foiled with relative ease. A deep-seated loyalty to the monarchy became apparent whenever conflicts came out into the open and involved non-commissioned officers and the rank and file."

With the help of its new and generous patron, the United States, Hussein was able to extend royal patronage, concentrate power in the hands of the monarchy, and ultimately crush the JNM.[12] Taking advantage of 1957 Eisenhower Doctrine, King Hussein and his men incarcerated or exiled the leading figures of the JNM and imposed martial law (spearheaded by a royal secret police that would eventually be institutionalized in 1964 as the General Intelligence Department).[13] Martial law banned all political parties, imposed strict censorship over the media, and purged the bureaucracy of Palestinians deemed insufficiently loyal to the regime (Boulby 1999: 21; Schwedler 2006: 43).

However, the king focused his greatest attention on the rank and file of the army, the monarchy's real source of power. Following the elimination of the JNM, the king set about expanding the monarchy's historical coalition with the tribes. In Tell's words, "the basic elements of the 'Hashemite compact' forged in Mandatory times was reproduced on an expanded scale, one that held villagers as well as the Bedouin in economic thrall to 'direct entitlements' disbursed by the state and a militarized welfare system that fell under the sway of the Palace in 1957" (2013: 114–15). Above all, by widening the ambit of army employment, the king cemented the sources of the regime's power and rebuilt the social foundations of Hashemite rule among the villagers and Bedouin of the East Bank. With the ousting of Glubb, the king gained access to Arab Legion funds, and he used those resources to expand the Jordanian Arab Army from 23,825 in April 1956 to 36,455 in May 1960 (120). Military service offered good pay, as well as medical and school benefits, for the now "Arabized" army. With the integration of the National Guard (heavily recruited from the West Bank) into the army in 1956, these benefits spread to many Palestinians as well. By the end of the 1950s, the military had grown to become the largest employer, after agriculture, of village workers (Baylouny 2010: 53), with the government spending more revenue on the Jordanian Arab Army than it was collecting on an annual basis (Tell 2013: 123).

Jordanization

Within a relatively short period of time, following the arrival of new waves of Palestinian refugees as a result of the 1967 war and the rise of the Palestine Liberation Organization (PLO) and its guerrilla activities within Jordan, Hussein was to target these recruitment strategies and rewards more narrowly toward Transjordanians, and key tribes in particular, and to selectively recruit them into all institutions of the state as he had done with the army. By the mid-1970s, a process of "Jordanization" had replaced any of the regime's original and relatively brief attempts to integrate the Palestinians. The Jordanization program reinvigorated tribal ties and bound the tribes even more closely to the regime, as jobs in the state became sine qua non of what it meant to be a Jordanian. In the face of a population increasingly divided between Jordanians of Jordanian descent (Transjordanians) and Jordanians of Palestinian descent, and with growing Transjordanian sensitivities to the Palestinian population, the monarchy chose to deepen its historical coalition.

The annexation of the West Bank in 1948 had necessitated a policy that would integrate the two peoples on either side of the Jordan River. This had involved the "remodelling the bases of identification with the state in a way that would, if not blur the distinctions, at least lead to acceptance of the monarchy" (Brand 1995: 50).[14] The result was an attempt to create a hybrid Jordanian identity for the two communities, one that would focus on the monarchy in general and the king in particular as the central symbol of Jordan. Palestinians and Transjordanians were understood as "two branches of the same family" (51–52).

The 1967 war with Israel, however, put an end to the regime's attempts at a hybrid identity. The influx of more than 250,000 additional Palestinian refugees as a consequence of that war (Brand 1995: 52–53)—less than twenty years after the first wave of Palestinians—led to a heightened sensitivity on behalf of Transjordanians to Israeli claims of "Jordan is

Palestine" and, as Brand (52–53) states, undoubtedly fueled resentments in general. These resentments only increased with the escalation of Palestinian guerrilla activities, including the PLO launching attacks on Israel from Jordan.[15] Already facing a loss of sovereignty over parts of the country in and around refugee camps to guerrilla fighters, when the Marxist Popular Front for the Liberation of Palestine had hijacked three airplanes, in September 1970, King Hussein commanded the Jordanian army to rid Jordan of the guerrillas and restore order. Black September, the ten-day carnage that ensued, during which the Jordanian military directed all its available forces against the Palestinian presence in the country, left more than 3,000 Palestinians—both guerrillas and civilians—dead (Cleveland 2000: 353). In the rift that was to emerge between Palestinians (the "West Bankers") and the Transjordanians (the "East Bankers"), Transjordanians began viewing the Palestinians "as guests whose presence in the army, security and public sector represented a threat to Jordanian national identity" (Harrigan and El-Said 2009b: 41). From the Transjordanian perspective, "the Palestinians were not just ungrateful for the refuge that Jordan had provided them, they were also traitors, real or potential" (Brand 1995: 53).

As Massad (2001: 13) states, much of the country's elite, including the Palestinian elite, backed the regime; the Jordanian army included Palestinians; and, conversely, the Palestinian guerrillas included Transjordanians. Nevertheless, the 1970 clashes ushered in a trend that saw the emergence of a policy by which the regime preferentially recruited Transjordanians into the civil service, paralleling their already privileged positions within the army. The "Jordanization" campaign prioritized Transjordanians and dramatically minimized the power of the (Palestinian-dominated) merchant class and the presence of Palestinians in the civil service and the military. The regime purged many Palestinian bureaucrats and officers (as well as some Transjordanians) from their positions in the bureaucracy and army and co-opted leading members of loyal Transjordanian families into influential positions in the cabinet, civil administration, army, and security. At the same time, "discriminatory policies against Palestinian-Jordanians (constituting more than half the population) became increasingly institutionalized: there was less government representation, less employment in the public sector, fewer academic opportunities, and less access to public funds" (Massad 2001: 13–14). The result was that, between 1961 and 1975, the Transjordanian-dominated military experienced a threefold expansion.

One-fourth of the domestic labor force was in the security services by 1975. Similarly, by 1985, the number of employees in the civil service (not including the military) also had tripled (Baylouny 2010: 53). By 1986, more than half the entire labor force worked for the state in some capacity (Brynen 1992: 81).

Those who were co-opted into the influential state positions (with, as Harrigan and El-Said [2009b: 42] note, little regard for merit or competence) in turn co-opted their family members, relatives, and close friends. The process of Jordanization was deepened as jobs were increasingly won based on *wasta* (mediation or connections) as civil servants were hired merely for being "sons of the nation" (*ibn al balad*)—in other words, for being Transjordanians.[16] In this manner, tribal and regional ties were revitalized; as a consequence, public institutions soon came to constitute different groups and power centers—northerners, southerners, Christians, or al-Saltiyya (people from Salt) (42).

Whether, as Brand (1995: 53) states, the regime designed "Jordanization" to "placate Transjordanians, punish Palestinians, improve security, or some combination of the three," a division of labor based on ethnic lines—with Transjordanians in the public sector and Palestinians in the private sector—was firmly established by the end of the 1970s.[17] Employment within the state not only provided a steady income but access to social security, health care, emergency loans, and inexpensive consumer goods. When Jordan's public social insurance system was introduced in the late 1970s, it was contingent on employment—specifically employment in the state—and not citizenship. Thus, much like the labor market, Jordan's welfare regime also was effectively split by national origin. State welfare was furnished completely for Transjordanians, partially for Transjordanian Christians and other minorities considered regime supporters (who received limited access to government jobs), and marginally for Palestinians, who were generally employed in the private sector (Baylouny 2010: 51–54). Military personnel and their families also were eligible for state-subsidized housing and (essentially free) university education (through a quota system). At retirement (with most retiring at the age of thirty), military officers could receive their pension even if they secured new employment (54). It is little wonder that in 1983, the state's health and education spending amounted to $163 per person—more than four times the average among developing countries (US$39) (54; Brynen 1992: 81; World Bank 1984: 150).[18]

Thus, as it had done in the past, the monarchy secured its rule through the country's Transjordanians, in particular the tribal elite. More than ever, regime patronage flowed through tribal lines. By focusing its recruitment strategies and rewards on Transjordanians, the regime forged the growing expectation of and identification of Transjordanians with service in the civilian and military state apparatus. There is no question, as Brand (1995: 48) states, that while not all Transjordanians belonged to the favored tribes, "a central part of what it meant for many Transjordanians to be 'Jordanian' was associated with employment by the state, especially in security services or the military."

Rentierism and the 1989 Riots

The Jordanization project and the vast resources it entailed were largely funded by external rents, the majority of which were a consequence of the oil boom in the Gulf in the 1970s. When international oil prices dropped in the 1980s, Jordan was faced with a crippling debt, and the degree to which the Transjordanians were dependent on the state became clear. When Jordan was forced to turn to the International Monetary Fund (IMF) and implement economic reform that made deep cuts to state expenditures, including hires, the Transjordanians, the segment of Jordanian society most privileged by the successive kings and on whom the regime relied (and continues to rely) for support, were the first to be hurt, and the first to respond. In 1989, riots broke out in Transjordanian-dominated cities throughout the country.

As discussed above, Jordan has been characterized by aspects of rentierism from its very beginning. The British granted subsidies to the crown, civil administration, the Arab Legion, and King Abdullah (Brynen 1992: 78). Following independence, Jordan continued to rely heavily on foreign aid with, for example, foreign grants—primarily American—accounting for 58 percent of all government revenues between 1967 and 1972 (78). External rents have been so important to Jordan's existence that Brand (1994: 277) argues that the country's foreign policy can be said historically to have been guided by "budget security"—the state's or leadership's drive to ensure the financial flows necessary for its survival. Most scholars agree. Rents enabled the monarchy to provide the abovementioned types of neo-patrimonial political and economic privileges to regime-loyal tribes and other communities while allowing them to essentially avoid any substantial tax burden. The large state sector—fueled by rents—furthermore allowed the regime to co-opt traditional notables, emerging bourgeois, and professional elites alike into positions of state authority. Rentierism, in turn, enabled these groups to engage in domestic rent-seeking. Opportunities for nepotism were valuable rewards, allowing elites to distribute neopatrimonial benefits of their own to members of their extended families and other constituencies (Brynen 1992: 81). Rentierism moreover allowed the government both to intensify its Import Substitution Industrialization (ISI) by implementing high tariff and no-tariff barriers (combined with financial incentives) to protect and diversify local industry (Harrigan and El-Said 2009a: 77) and to simultaneously offer financial and other incentives to local industrialists in order to further encourage private sector development (Brynen 1992: 81). As a consequence, a whole array of (predominantly Palestinian) entrepreneurs flourished with the encouragement—passive or active—of the state.

Yet it was the rents that Jordan accrued as a consequence of its exportation of skilled and semiskilled workers to the oil-rich Arab Gulf states in the post-1973 oil boom era that had the most profound effect on the shape of its economy (Brynen 1992: 79: Harrigan and El-Said 2009a: 76). The oil boom in the Gulf brought high levels of Arab trade, including tariffs and taxes, and (petrodollar) aid to Jordan. By the early 1980s, almost one-third of the country's labor force was working in the Gulf, remitting an annual average of US$918 million between the mid-1970s and mid-1980s (Harrigan and El-Said 2009a: 76). Workers remittances reached a peak of approximately 475 million JD (US$1.2 billion) by 1984, an amount equivalent to more than a quarter of GDP (Brynen 1992: 79).

When international oil prices collapsed in the late 1980s, Jordan was not spared from the regional economic slowdown.[19] The government's response in its efforts to maintain economic rewards to the tribal elite only worsened the slowdown. The regime faced shrinking resources, dwindling reserves, and a growing debt, as laborers returned from the Gulf (35,000 expatriates returned in 1987 alone) (Brynen 1992: 88); foreign remittances dried up, regional trade decreased, aid promises went unfulfilled, and the currency devaluated as a result of the kingdom's 1988 administrative detachment from the West Bank (Baylouny 2010: 55). With unemployment on the rise and the Jordanian dinar experiencing sharp declines, in November 1988, the government put emergency controls on a wide range of luxury imports and restricted foreign-currency transactions.[20] In February 1989, it used its martial-law powers to close down all of Jordan's private money changers in an effort to stabilize the value of the dinar (Brynen 1992: 88).

Despite declining revenues, the regime was reluctant to reduce overall state expenditures; to do so would have entailed the withdrawal of the economic rewards that sustained Jordanian neo-patrimonialism (Brynen 1992: 86).[21] The monarchy avoided austerity measures and instead borrowed international funds; when it did make cuts, they were generally at targeted planned development investments as opposed to current expenditures (such as general administration, defense, or social welfare) as the latter supported key elites and important constituencies or had come to be seen as essential parts of the social contract associated with rentierism (87).

By 1989, Jordan's external debt had grown to 245.2 percent of the GDP (Knowles 2005: 120). In comparison, the external debt as a percentage of GDP by region during the same year was: 20.152 percent for the Middle East; 20.928 percent for the Middle East, North Africa, Afghanistan, and Pakistan; 42.332 percent for sub-Saharan Africa; and 29.786 percent for the emerging and developing economies.[22] In spring 1989, the regime had no choice but to turn to the IMF—seeking $275 million in standby credits and assistance in rescheduling its foreign debts—and began implementing IMF loan conditions (Brynen 1992: 89; Harrigan and El-Said 2009a: 79). The reforms were directed toward the liberalization of the economy and its integration into international markets and included the removal of state subsidies, the privatization of public sector investments, and cuts in state employment.[23]

The reforms threatened to hurt the Transjordanians the most, for they had the greatest stake in state employment and benefits. In 1989, triggered by fuel increases, riots erupted in Ma'an and other Transjordanian towns, including al-Karak, al-Tafilah, and, later, Salt. While the cutback of subsidies on foods, electricity, water, and petroleum as a result of the economic restructuring affected the entire population and the riots eventually spread throughout the country, the Palestinians refrained from rioting (Lust-Okar 2004: 169). The violence occurred in the king's traditional stronghold, among the Transjordanians in the south. It was clear "that their concern was not only the increasingly autocratic style of the . . . government but also (and more fundamentally) their growing inability to extract jobs, development funds, subsidies and other economic resources from the state—resources that were, in turn, critical elements in the neo-patrimonial maintenance of their own positions and constituencies at home" (Brynen 1992: 89).[24]

It was little wonder that the riots had a geographic dimension. With Transjordanians and Palestinians occupying different labor markets, a near dichotomy of employment opportunities characterized (and continues to do so) rural and urban regions of the country. Inhabiting the rural northern and southern regions, the latter home to Ma'an, al-Karak, and al-Tafilah, Transjordanians primarily worked in the state and army; 90 percent, 92 percent, and 99.5 percent of the domestic labor force of these three cities respectively worked in the public sector in 1989 (Baylouny 2010: 81). In contrast, Palestinians lived in the central, urbanized area of the country, where the bulk of private employment and industry was concentrated. In the central cities of Amman, al-Zarqa', and al-Balqa', the percentage of the domestic labor force working in the public sector ranged between 56 and 58 percent (80). The overcentralization of the state and the Jordanization program had contributed to a system in which the Transjordanians, who represented the backbone of the monarchy, composed some of the poorest segments of the population and/or were living in some of the poorest regions of the country.

With his coalition threatened, King Hussein's response to the riots was swift, initiating political liberalization as a release valve to let off any economic (and therefore political) frustrations. In 1989, he reinstated parliamentary elections, the clear objective of which "was to provide political dissent—present and future—with an outlet for legal expression as a means of preventing both further violence and the emergence of an organized opposition front that favoured radical confrontation with the regime" (Schwedler 2006: 50). In 1992, the government legalized political parties (twenty-two quickly registered, as candidates no longer had to run as independents), issued new press and publications laws, and eased other restrictions banning political activism.[25]

Despite these reforms, the king maintained vast powers, and political power remained highly centralized. Indeed, the king did not call for or implement any form of decentralization of central powers. Yet in addition to the pressures from above (see chapter 2), pressures for political decentralization also had been building from below since the 1970s. Shortly after the Jordanization program, Transjordanians had begun calling for an increase in the powers of local governments as a solution to geographic imbalance (Transjordanians, who worked in the state, inhabiting the poorer, rural areas and Palestinians, who dominated the private sector, living in Amman, the city with the greatest wealth and services). The networks of wasta that had developed over time had contributed to a system whereby wasta determined who received municipal services and who did not. By the 1990s, the municipal system was bankrupt, with 51 percent of municipalities not offering services of any kind (Center for Strategic Studies 2004: 17). Yet while demanding reform, the tribes were also the greatest "disincentive" to decentralization reforms, as the latter would entail a loss of their political power, privileges, and ability to redistribute jobs, services, and other resources to their constituencies (see chapter 2). Quite simply, decentralization reforms would negatively affect their ability to be important access points for wasta. The tribes therefore would increasingly become part of the problem. When repeatedly faced with this dilemma— the catch-22 whereby the Transjordanians both suffered from the lack of reform and at the same time were poised to lose power and privileges should there be reform—the monarchy would choose to maintain the coalition and resist decentralization.

Morocco

The early history of today's Jordan is marked by its process of state-building, an important aspect of which was the incorporation of many of the functions historically performed by the tribes under the purview of the state. Despite this process of consolidation and centralization, however, the tribal shaykhs maintained an important role acting as mediators and access points between themselves and the government and state; more often than not, they performed this role in the stead of representatives of political parties (although political parties including tribal shaykhs but devoid of any real platform or ideology would also develop). Jordan thus began independence with weak state and party structures. This was not the case in Morocco, which began its independence with a highly centralized, strong state and a history of established political parties. Much as the British had done in Jordan, the French in Morocco expanded the existing state into areas previously beyond the sultan's control. The postcolonial regime inherited the networks of alliances and control established by the French and, building on them, created a coalition with the rural Berber nobility—much as the monarchy in Jordan had done with the tribes—in order to entrench its rule and ensure its survival. Most importantly, the monarchy would use the Berber elite to weaken the parties of the nationalist movement, and the Istiqlal Party in particular, in the power struggle over the nature of the future political system and the distribution of power during the years following independence (1956).

Yet the similarities between Jordan and Morocco vis-à-vis their coalition strategies were largely to end in the 1970s. In response to two failed coup attempts in the early 1970s, the Moroccan monarchy changed its coalition strategy when it reached out to new elites. The monarchy now strove to woo the nationalist parties in order to ultimately bring them into the government and co-opt them. The monarchy thus embarked on a two-pronged strategy of gaining popular support through, on the one hand, its "Moroccanization" and social welfare programs and the 1975 Green March and, on the other hand, gaining the cooperation and participation of the opposition parties by offering them formal and informal incentives to engage in the writing of a new constitution and to enter the 1977 elections. Both of these prongs were financed through phosphate-generated rents. Within this context, the monarchy would use the 1976 charter as a means to accomplish its change in coalition partners by enticing the nationalists into the system (see chapter 3).

The Alawite Dynasty and the French Protectorate

In Morocco, the regime is often equated with the *makhzen*, a word that literally means "warehouse" and historically referred to the place where the sultan's taxes were stored prior to the establishment of the French protectorate in 1912. The term was used to denote the royal family, the royal court, and the feudalistic state. Today, it continues to refer to the central power or, as El Amrani (2009: 304) refers to it, the "economic-security nexus." That nexus includes the king, the most important political actor, as well as high-level civil servants, large economic and landholding interests, businessmen, and politicians. Yet the makhzen is far more than just the king or the state. It includes formal and informal networks of domination emanating from the king—who stands at the apex of a ruling elite made up of members from the country's most prominent families—throughout politics, the military, and business (Claisse 1987: 34–37). From this apex, power is exercised through a system of patronage and clientelism. It is little wonder that Hibou refers to the makhzen as "omnipresent and omniscient" (quoted in Hoffman 2013: 159).

That the makhzen's influence has expanded over time reflects the monarchy's historical efforts to entrench and protect its own political position vis-à-vis the country's political parties. Morocco began its independence with a "highly efficient, highly centralised and . . . highly powerful state apparatus" (Willis 2012: 34). The post-independence regime enjoyed far greater control over its territory and population than in Jordan or even than had been exercised during the precolonial period in Morocco, when large parts of the country fell under Bled as-Siba, or the land of dissidence (see below), and operated independently of the central government. During the colonial period, the French consolidated the existing state structures, leaving the postcolonial regime greater political authority than any regime prior to it. Yet the colonial period also witnessed the rise of a strong nationalist movement. While the monarchy and the nationalist movement had worked together in their efforts to rid Morocco of the French, in the postcolonial era, the two were to compete over different visions and political control of Morocco.

When the French protectorate began in Morocco in 1912, the monarchy had already been in existence for several hundred years. As Morocco did not fall under Ottoman rule, the Alawite dynasty has been largely uninterrupted since in the seventeenth century when it was founded. The first Alawite dynasty continued and strengthened the model of religious caliphate that had begun during the Saadian dynasty (1510–1659) that preceded it. Thus, the early Alawite rulers laid stress on their Sharifian descent from the Prophet Muhammad and their commitment to enforce Islam. Even today, the king claims his legitimacy based on his genealogical descent from the Prophet and from the fact that he is also the caliph—the legitimate successor to the Prophet's secular and religious authority (Joffé 1988: 201). Since independence, successive constitutions furthermore have enshrined the role and legitimacy of the king in the political process (see below).

Although European powers had attempted to establish control over what is now Morocco as early as the fifteenth and sixteenth centuries, it was not until nineteenth that they were successful. The protectorate lasted forty-four years (1912–1944), during which time France was able to take effective control of Morocco through its increasing influence over its finances and economies (facilitated by Morocco's mushrooming debts to France and other European states) (Willis 2012: 19). The French—heavily influenced by Morocco's first French *résident général*, Marshall Louis-Huberet-Gonzales Lyautey—made the decision to retain the existing political structures and rulers and to rule indirectly through them. Although the sultan was "obliged to do the bidding of the local French *Résident Général*," he maintained his position (20). A central part of this approach was the pacification of the rural areas and their incorporation into the state, a feat with which the precolonial regimes had struggled. By successfully bringing the rural areas and the Berber tribes that lived there under control of the central political authority, the French not only largely preserved but also strengthened Morocco's traditional social and political institutions.

Revolts against French colonial rule began in Morocco's rural areas and spread to its cities and town. While the French colonial authorities had successfully pacified the tribes of the rural and mountainous regions of the French protectorate, the northern region of the Spanish protectorate began experiencing serious uprisings in the 1920s.[26] In response, the French brought their military weight to crush the revolt and its attempts to create an independent state in 1926. The decisive defeat of these attempts at armed resistance to colonial rule gave way to more politicized forms of opposition in the 1920s and 1930s (Willis 2012: 24). From that point onward, new oppositional groups and associations emerged in the country's urban centers.

The emergence of these groups and associations can be attributed to a variety of factors—including European economic and demographic decline as a result of World War II and the rise of the American discourse of self-determination. However, just as in Jordan (albeit at a later period in time), the influence of new socialist and nationalist ideologies also played a significant role. Primarily based in the cities of Fès and Rabat, nationalist groups began forming among various elite circles in the 1920s. While the groups in Fès referred to religion and were more traditional and conservative than the groups from Rabat, which were more European in outlook and ideology (as many of their leaders had been educated in France and elsewhere in Europe), by the early 1930s, the two had managed to form a single organization, the Kutla al-Amal al-Watani (National Action Bloc, NAC) (Willis 2012: 25–26).

By 1944, the NAC had transformed itself into a political party, the Istiqlal, demanding the end of colonial rule and the establishment of a representative government. While mainly found within elite urban circles, the Istiqlal soon established a support base outside of its elite origins and within a broader cross-section of Moroccans, particularly among urban workers. Beginning in the late 1940s, it began engaging in direct confrontations with the colonial authorities. By the 1950s, these confrontations were violent; the first outbreak of armed violence began with sporadic guerrilla attacks in the countryside that then were augmented by more coordinated activity in the towns and cities. When France decided to exile the sultan as a result of his increasing cooperation with the Istiqlal and his reluctance to kowtow to the French authorities, it effectively unified the opposition—the palace and Istiqlal—behind a widespread popular anger. Shortly thereafter, the French negotiated an end to the protectorate. The leaders of the nationalist movement who had played a crucial role in forging a national consciousness and mobilizing the population against the colonial presence were poised to play—and expected to play—central roles in the post-independence politics (Willis 2012: 34).

Rural-Based Notables and the Consolidation of the Monarchy

Colonial rule bequeathed important legacies to the post-independence regime. The monarchy was able to make use of the comprehensive central administrative control and the attendant infrastructure that the French had established throughout the country. It also adapted many of the tactics the French had employed to subdue the tribal areas and consolidate its rule. Much as the French had created and used the rural-based Berber elites, or notables, to expand and strengthen the state, the monarch turned to the same Berber groups to weaken the Istiqlal in its power struggle with the party after 1956. Thus, in the early post-independence period, the monarchy forged a coalition with the Berber elite and, in the name of multipartyism, created Berber-based political parties to counter the Istiqlal and to bolster the monarchy. Monarchical dominance could not have been achieved without the creation of "palace" or "administrative parties" such as the Berber-dominated Mouvement Populaire (Popular Movement, PMP), the rotation of the political parties the monarchy favored and disfavored in and out of parliament, and the intentional splintering of the nationalist parties.

As Willis (2012: 43–44) states, immediately following independence, Moroccans began to witness the "creeping control of the system by the palace." The monarchy had worked closely with the nationalist movement, represented by the Istiqlal, during the struggle for independence; however, following independence, the two differed regarding independent Morocco's power-sharing and political arrangements. While King Mohammed V (1909–1961) envisioned a return to precolonial status quo, according to which the monarchy had near absolute power, the Istiqlal sought a constitutional monarchy, with the monarchy having largely symbolic powers. Between 1956 and the promulgation of Morocco's first constitution (1962), the two were engaged in an intense competition for power. Indeed, the struggle between the king and the Istiqlal was predominantly responsible for the seven-year delay of the first post-independence constitution and a wait of eight years before elections were held (Storm 2007: 34).

The outcome of this power struggle was reflected in the constitution. The political parties demanded that the 1962 constitution have some democratic elements. It enshrined multipartyism and guaranteed participation by the full citizenry. However, the constitution gave the king wide-ranging legislative and executive powers, including the authority to appoint and terminate government ministers, dissolve parliament, declare a state of emergency, and rule by decree (Storm 2007: 22). Most importantly, it deemed the person of the king inviolable and made the ministers answerable to the palace rather than to parliament (Willis 2012: 69).

The 1960s saw the monarchy not only further entrench its dominance but also "increasingly personalize political power in the personage of the king" (Storm 2007: 54). Coming to power in 1961, Hassan II assumed for himself an array of positions, serving as PM (as his father, Mohammed V, had done beginning in 1960) and taking control of the ministerial portfolios of interior, defense, and agriculture. By the time of the writing and adoption of the 1962 constitution, Hassan II held absolute power. He moreover further institutionalized the enormous powers of patronage developed by his father and assumed the authority to appoint all meaningful positions of power and responsibility in the kingdom, including in the government, police, and army (Willis 2012: 54).

Hassan II's usurpation of power at the expense of parliament was complete by the mid-1960s, when he declared a state of emergency and ruled by personal decree for five years. Unable to control a critical parliament, more than 50 percent of whose seats were held by opposition party members, he resorted to repression and had members of the Union Nationale des Forces Populaires (UNFP, the National Union of Popular Forces) and the Moroccan Communist Party (PCM) arrested, accusing them of plotting to assassinate him (Storm 2007: 23, 25). Extra-parliamentary groups, such as the National Union of Moroccan Students, soon called for complete resistance against the system (Sater 2010: 34). When residents of the country's growing *bidonvilles* (shantytowns)—inhabited largely by rural migrants who had left for the cities due to the growing economic crisis in the rural areas—joined these groups, events culminated in riots in Casablanca in 1965 (Storm 2007: 25). Hassan II called in the army to quell the riots and dissolved parliament.

The end of the state of emergency was marked by the monarchy's announcement of constitutional amendments, to be approved by popular referendum, in preparation for new elections, the first in seven years. Morocco's second constitution (1970), however, simply consecrated the practice of the state of emergency (Willis 2012: 69). It further diminished the powers of parliament and the government vis-à-vis the monarchy. A new title was added to the king, Amir al-Mu'minin (Commander of the Faithful), making him the "supreme representative of the Nation." The title of Amir al-Mu'minin had been used for the sultan beginning in the twelfth century and refers to the Sharifian status of the royal family—descendants of the Prophet Muhammad. While Islam had always been the main source of legitimacy of the Moroccan monarchy, Hassan II consciously emphasized the religious authority in order to establish a link with pious ordinary Moroccans and thereby further strengthen his hand in dealing with the elites (56). Most importantly, he retained the act of *bay'a*, an oath of allegiance to the king.[27] As Sater (2010: 6) explains, the bay'a confers legitimacy on the king's title Amir Al Mu'minin, making him effectively stand above the constitution and the division of state powers into legislative, executive, and judicial institutions. In 1979, the state published the official interpretation of the bay'a; it confers divine powers on the king as the "holder of the legitimate authority of God's shadow on earth and his secular arm in the world" (Claisse 1987: 38; Sater 2010: 6).

The constitution furthermore stated that the king's domains were to be established by personal decrees (*dahirs*) and therefore not by the constitution. Members of parliament (MPs) could now be prosecuted for not showing due respect for the king, the Muslim faith, or the monarchical system even when expressing those opinions as part of their parliamentary functions. In addition, the constitution reduced the parliament from a bicameral house to a unicameral house with two modes of selection—direct for one-third and indirect for two-thirds—thus strengthening indirectly elected councillors at the expense of directed elected representatives. These adjustments, both in the number of houses and in the mode of selection, were an attempt to create a pro-regime government at the beginning of each parliament in order to counterbalance the parties of the nationalist movement (Al-Mossadeq 1987: 70). Years later, the same type of "adjustments" were to be made at the municipal level to ensure the victory of pro-regime rural elites in local elections (see chapters 3 and 5).

In the years following independence, the creation of political structures that supported and reflected the "almost untrammeled monarchical power" (Willis 2012: 68) could not have been achieved without the monarchy's use of tactical measures such as the creation of pro-regime elites and political parties and, consequently, the manipulation of parliament. Both Mohammed V and Hassan II used patronage to ensure the support of elites and created what are often referred to as "palace" or "royal" or "administrative" political parties to ensure that no political party (loyal or opposition) became powerful enough to be perceived as a threat to the monarchy. The most important of these in the monarchy's struggle versus the Istiqlal was the Berber elite.

As discussed above, prior to the establishment of the protectorate, the kingdom of Morocco had been under the authority of the sultan and his makhzen administration. The Arab and Berber tribes that populated the kingdom were ruled by a hierarchy of agents of authority (*agents d'autorité*), with *pashas* governing the cities, *qaids* supervising the tribes or fractions thereof in the countryside (qaids presided over tribal *jama'as*, tribal councils of elders), and *khalifas* (deputies of the qaids), shaykhs, and *muqaddim* (at the clan level and the village level respectively) assisting the qaid (Bergh 2007: 83). Bled al-Makhzen (land of the makhzen, where taxes were paid) comprised the predominantly Arab populated plains of the kingdom; its ruling elite was predominantly urban and composed of bourgeois families active in trading and crafts (Fès, Tétouan, Meknès, Salé), the *makhzenian* families, dependents of the Royal House, and *chorfa*, descendants of the prophet (Bennani-Chraïbi 2009a: 205–219, 2009b). Bled as-Siba (land of dissidence, where the sultan's power could not reach and consequently taxes were not paid) is the name given to those areas of the kingdom that periodically rejected the centralizing authority of the makhzen—the mainly mountainous Berber territories, the leaders of which were predominantly tribal.

The French authorities not only maintained and strengthened the makhzenian structure but also imposed French supervisory agents at every level. They furthermore brought Bled as-Siba under the authority of the makhzen by creating a class of rural elites and making them agents within the system (such as shaykhs, muqadims, and qaids). As Liddell (2010: 316) notes, the French saw the necessity of having the population perceive the indigenous intermediaries as legitimate and consequently sought to win the allegiance of Moroccan notables. Understanding that Morocco's rural elites lacked the wealth and education of their urban counterparts, the French augmented their property holdings and anchored their influence through symbols of prestige such as education in new elite schools, thereby cultivating a new class of rural, predominantly Berber, elites. The French created a military college in Meknès for Berbers for a career in the French army, as well as a system of schools for the sons of Berber notables; the best students would then go to a French college in Azrou (Waterbury 1970: 113). Much like the tribal elite in Jordan, Berbers became mediators. Their new status and survival were predicated on their role as intermediary between their various clientele groups and the goods and favors coming from the central bureaucracy. After independence, Morocco's urban and rural elites took over the pivotal positions in the state left by the French.

King Mohammed V sought to leverage this rural-based notable in order to weaken the urban-based nationalists (Liddell 2010: 316). As the symbol of national resistance and independence, the monarchy was extremely popular after independence. However, its support was not institutionalized, particularly not in comparison to the Istiqlal, which had an established structure of cells and militants (Willis 2012: 44). The monarchy thus set about creating its own networks of supporters and allies to counter those already possessed by the Istiqlal. It turned to those in Morocco who either felt they had been sidelined by the Istiqlal or had some degree of antipathy to it: the Berber elite. The monarchy took advantage of the Berber groups' resentment of the urban notables, particularly of the urban elites from Fès who made up a significant portion of the Istiqlal leadership.[28] These urbanites largely shunned Berber groups both on account of their own middle-class biases but also because the Berber notables had collaborated with the French colonial administration (44). The monarchy thus reversed its pre-independence alliance, established a multiparty system, and promoted the rural notables as "defenders of the throne" (Bennani-Chraïbi 2008).

Among other measures, the monarchy secured the support of the rural elites by rejecting pressures for large-scale land reform and redistribution and by introducing protectionist barriers; it further appealed to both rural and urban elites by allowing them to acquire the lands abandoned by the departing Europeans (Willis 2012: 233–34). Support for the agricultural sector thus was not an economic issue but a system by which the patron state protected elite farmers (Harrigan and El-Said 2009b: 113). In fact, in its efforts to protect and preserve its key allies among the rural nobility, the monarchy did not undertake any real efforts at development and land reform (other than small-scale technical reforms) in rural Morocco. Taxation, industrialization, and other reform projects were either blocked or simply not pursued. This was to damage long-term rural development in the kingdom, exacerbate differences with urban areas, and ultimately lead to the massive rural-urban migration that contributed to the political unrest that would follow in the decades to come (see below) (Willis 2012: 77–78).

The "organizational bulwark" used by the monarchy against the Istiqlal in the early post-independence years included the PMP, the Parti Democratique de l'Independence (PDI, Democratic Party of Independence), and other predominantly—albeit not strictly—Berber-based groupings that over time would become the basis of royalist governments (Willis 2012: 45). Angered by the Istiqlal's attempts to take over local administration in rural areas following independence, several rural leaders had created the PMP to coordinate resistance to the Istiqlal's incursions. Blocking all attempts by the Istiqlal to dissolve the Berber-based PMP, the monarchy shattered the Istiqlal's hopes of being the single ruling party and granted the PMP legal recognition as a political party in 1959 (44).

To be sure, as part of its struggle for power against the Istiqlal, the monarchy fostered divisions within the Istiqlal. The party suffered from deep internal splits between its right and left wings (Storm 2007: 14). The king encouraged the activities of the PDI, which had split from the Istiqlal in 1946 and which the Istiqlal sought to exclude from the post-independence political scene. The king also played an important role in the UNFP's schism from the Istiqlal in 1959 (Willis 2012: 45).[29]

The 1960 municipal and communal elections were the last step in the administration's concerted action to reestablish relations and secure its coalition with the rural notables.[30] As Hammoudi (1977: 31) states, "This is the only way one can interpret a type of administrative organization in which both the sheikh, at the tribal level, and the *moqaddem*, at the village level, were chosen within the local groups and their prerogatives enhanced. It amounted to rebuilding a network through direct administrative channels."[31] Post-independence, the regime "Moroccanized" and expanded the preexisting centralized administrative system much as the French colonial powers previously had. A single chain of command was established from the Ministry of Interior downward to the appointed muqaddim at the village level into the tribal areas now organized as municipalities (Bergh 2007: 86). To staff the administrative structure, the monarchy recruited from the closed circles of elites—those who had lost the social positions they had held under the French colonial powers and the large landowners who needed administrative access to protect their property (89). The makhzenian system was maintained through the tight monitoring of the elected councils by the (unelected) representatives of the central authorities, the limited fiscal resources granted to the municipalities, and the heavily circumscribed decision-making authorities. The new parties that were opposed to the nationalist movement, the Istiqlal and the UNFP, were also given various "advantages" in the voting procedures (Hammoudi 1977: 31).

The Turning Point: The Attempted Coups of the Early 1970s

The 1971 and 1972 attempted coups—both from within the army—marked a significant turning point in the monarchy's coalition strategy. Following independence, the monarchy also had secured its coalition with the Berber elite by recruiting the latter to the military. In May 1956, the king had created the Forces Armées Royales (FAR, Royal Armed Forces), with the monarch as the supreme commander and the crown prince as chief of staff. The king chose the bulk of the officer corps from Berber families as they provided the perfect counterweight to the overwhelmingly urban and Arab nationalists of the Istiqlal (Willis 2012: 83). In the years prior to the attempted coups (and particularly during the country's state of emergency following the 1965 riots), the king had increased his reliance on the army, which played a bigger and bigger role as senior officers, benefiting from patron-client ties, were appointed to positions of authority throughout the Moroccan state and society (Sater 2010: 34). Yet although both coups were unsuccessful, they caused the king to reverse his coalition strategy and follow a two-track approach of, on the one hand, reaching out to the nationalist parties and, on the other hand, wooing the population with populist measures. With the Berber elite perceived as a less reliable coalition partner, the monarchy turned to these parties with the aim of bringing them into the political system. The monarchy thus embarked on a new and expanded coalition strategy, one that marked a significant divergence from that of the Jordanian monarchy's. It also paid off. By 1977 the king had secured a new base of support, and the nationalist parties, including the Istiqlal, were fully co-opted. The key to his success would be the 1976 municipal charter (see chapter 3).

In 1971, a group of rebel, largely junior, military leaders attacked the Skhirat palace during the king's birthday reception at which several hundred of the country's senior government members, military officers, and other members of the elite were present. Within a few hours, loyal military troops were able to put down the coup, arresting or killing its leaders. On August 16, 1972, a similar set of officers initiated a second attempted coup against the king—this time they were led by Mohamed Oufkir, the defense minister and the chief of staff tasked with reorganizing the military and safeguarding the king following the 1971 attempted coup (Willis 2012: 91). Four F-5 military jets intercepted and attacked the king's personal airliner; although the royal airplane was damaged, the king landed and escaped unharmed.

The reasons for both coups are relatively unclear. The 1971 rebel officers seem to have been provoked by the widespread and endemic corruption within the government and the royal family (Willis 2012: 90). Sater (2010: 36) argues that the leaders of both coups were motivated by the pervasive corruption and by the rigging of the constitutional referendums of 1970 and 1972. While the leaders of the second coup are also thought by many to have been prompted by corruption, others argue that Oufkir, the most powerful man in the country after the king himself, was suspicious that the king intended to kill him because he had accumulated significant power and was privy to a vast amount of information and so attempted to act first (91).[32] Storm (2007: 32) points to the fact that the king had slowly begun to alienate himself from the hardline members of the army with his efforts—albeit highly limited—to draft a more democratic constitution and hold parliamentary elections.[33] The coups may have been caused by the threat of power-sharing and the potential loss of patronage to the military.

Whatever the motivations, "the coups prompted Hassan to expand dialogue and contact with the political parties, whom he had effectively ignored since the suspension of parliament in 1965, in an attempt to recruit allies and widen the base of support for the regime" (Willis 2012: 92). The king thus "readjusted" his alliance with the military (and enhanced the powers of the Ministry of the Interior in its place) and attempted to lure the opposition (nationalist) parties back into the political system by easing repressive measures. At the same time (and much like the king of Jordan following the alleged coup in 1956), Hassan sought to win over the population at large and undertook a massive economic and bureaucratic expansion program.

That the state was able to pursue a two-track approach of populism while ensuring the privileges to key elites was made possible by a massive boom in international phosphate prices in the mid-1970s. From the autumn of 1973 to January 1974, international prices for phosphates rose from $14 to $42 per ton; in 1975, they rose to $68 (Denoeux and Maghraoui 1998: 56). With production and commercialization of phosphates controlled by a state-owned monopoly, all additional revenues went into state coffers.

As part of the king's efforts to secure support, Morocco pursued high protectionist barriers, overvalued its exchange rate to stimulate domestic industrialization, and invested heavily in irrigation, the phosphate sector, and infrastructure (Harrigan and El-Said 2009a: 149). It also began the nationalization of colonial lands and the Moroccanization of the industrial and service sector. The state thus reclaimed foreign-owned land and embarked on an agrarian land redistribution program. Similarly, the "Moroccanization laws"—a series of statutes that required that all foreign-owned enterprises be at least 51 percent Moroccan-owned—entailed the transfer of the majority ownership of previously French-owned companies to Moroccans (Cammett 2004: 252–53; Willis 2012: 234). All of these measures served to secure the political support of the nationalist parties and to open up huge new sources of patronage for the monarchy to distribute, and thereby recruit and retain allies (Willis 2012: 234). Support for the monarchy was further solidified through the appointment of members of families with extensive economic interests to key administrative positions and of major industrialists and bankers to high-ranking government posts. As Cammett (2004: 250) states, "dense networks of public officials and private interests arose, blurring the lines between business and government and establishing an entrenched set of state and societal interests benefiting from protective trade policies."

At the same time, the monarchy also began to follow more populist distributive policies designed to promote social welfare. The government increased public sector and public enterprise investment, public sector employment, and civil servants' wages, and it introduced basic food subsidies and producer subsidies. From 1970 to 1983, the state "was a 'cash cow' for the notables, politicians and bureaucrats providing all kinds of rents via tax breaks, tariff protection, licenses and so on, and a 'wet nurse' to the majority by providing subsidised goods, price controls and assistance to peasants during frequent periods of drought" (Ali quoted in Harrigan and El-Said 2009a: 149–50).

Buoyed by external rents, the king also embarked on the Western Sahara campaign in order to reestablish and reinvigorate political consensus with the parties. In 1975, 350,000 unarmed Moroccans marched into what is now internationally referred to as the Western Sahara to reassert Morocco's historic ties to the territory following the departure of the Spanish colonial powers. With Spain's departure in 1975, Morocco became embroiled in an ongoing territorial dispute against the Polisario Front, the independence movement of the Western Sahara (created in 1973 with the original goal of ending Spanish occupation and financed by Algeria). Referred to as the Green March, the 1975 campaign successfully united all groups and parties of differing political stripes, including the Istiqlal, around the nationalistic goal of reclaiming the Western Sahara (Bergh 2007: 93; Storm 2007: 38–40; Willis 2012: 126). Consequently, constitutional questions regarding power sharing were temporarily forgotten or shelved for a later date.

The monarchy's tactics worked. In 1977, the al-Koutla al-Watanniyya (National Bloc, formed by the Istiqlal and the UNFP in response to the 1970 constitution and its strengthening of the monarchy at the expense of parliament) was essentially co-opted into the system. Riding on a wave of political (and economic) support, the king announced that elections would be held in 1977. Although the 1972 constitution (which maintained the unicameral house and had done little to make elections more free and fair) remained in place, the Istiqlal and the Union Socialiste des Forces Populaires (USFP, Socialist Union of Popular Forces, a splinter party from the UNFP that soon eclipsed it) both participated in the 1976 municipal elections and the 1977 national elections. The 1976 municipal charter was the bait that ultimately lured them to enter the elections (see chapter 3).

When King Hassan II invited the Istiqlal and the USFP, along with loyalist MPs, to form a government following the 1977 elections, the Istiqlal accepted. Thus, by 1977, the king had fully secured the new coalition; and the opposition parties were far more silent and far less oppositional. According to Willis (2012: 127): "The re-entry of the National Bloc parties into the formal political system, essentially on the palace's terms, signaled the beginning of a new phase in Moroccan party politics that would persist for the next two decades. This saw the opposition parties participate in elections and institutions but accept—albeit not without protest—a heavily circumscribed role in parliament and local government. Irregular elections produced significant and clearly manufactured royalist 'majorities,' often for equally manufactured newly formed parties." After 1977, the king's religious and constitutional powers were increasingly accepted (Sater 2010: 48).

In an effort to further weaken the nationalist parties, King Hassan II encouraged the creation of additional loyalist political parties, such as the Rassemblement National des Indépendants (RNI, National Rally of Indepdendents) and the Union Constitutionnel (UC, established in 1983 to appeal to the expanding younger generation of urban Moroccans who, until this point, were uninvolved in politics) (Claisse 1987: 45; Willis 2012: 127). He also aggressively pursued a divide-and-rule policy by which "marginalized and excluded political currents faced severe repression whereas mainstream political parties sought a place in the state's constitutional 'consensus'" (Sater 2010: 49). The end result was that whereas, previously, groups suffering from repression would have found vocal allies in the political parties and parliament, this was now no longer the case (49–50). In addition to the shrinking proportion of seats in parliament they commanded, there was increasingly less difference between the co-opted "opposition" parties and the palace parties.

Morocco's SAPs and the Bread Riots

As in Jordan, the Moroccan monarchy's coalition strategies were made possible by external rents—in this case generated by phosphate sales—that enabled it to sustain its patronage of the rural Berber notables and, later, to undertake massive redistribution policies and eventually cement its popularity (and thereby weaken that of the opposition parties) with the 1975 Green March. In 1976, however, phosphate prices collapsed. In the context of the consequent public deficit of nearly 20 percent of GDP, as public spending was not decreased accordingly, an increase in international oil prices in 1979, and drought and social unrest, the government aborted two early attempts at economic reform and continued to buy political support by increasing public sector wages, the minimum wage, and food subsidies (Harrigan and El-Said 2009a: 150–51). With the foreign debt standing at 84 percent of GDP by 1983 (Sater 2010: 123), Morocco was one of the most indebted countries in the world, and the government was forced to seek emergency financial assistance.[34] Similar to Jordan, the SAP that was imposed soon triggered riots—in Morocco, it was among the country's poor, in the shantytowns of its largest cities. Hassan II introduced political liberalization in response to the riots. As Denoeux and Maghraoui (1998: 77) state, Hassan II "seems to have realized that he must nurture a political climate and ruling strategies that are better adapted to the changing political and socio-economic realities of Morocco." Moroccan society simply had become too complex and politicized for the king to ignore public sentiment.

In 1983, Morocco negotiated one of the first SAPs in the MENA region with the IMF and the World Bank. In the words of Denoeux and Maghraoui (quoted in Sater 2007: 84), with the introduction of the SAP, "new concepts such as 'individual initiative,' 'economic efficiency,' 'competitiveness,' 'austerity,' and 'productivity' entered the arena of public debate" as Morocco began the process of reforming its public finances, monetary policy, and external trade arrangements, as well as the state's role in each. Morocco liberalized its exchange rate policy, depreciated the dirham, and encouraged foreign imports; at the same time, it reduced price controls and subsidies on basic necessities—much like Jordan would do in 1989. Ten years later, it followed these steps by reorganizing the banking sector and the stock exchange. In 1989, it designated 112 public enterprises, among them, "the jewels of the public sector," for privatization (Catusse 2009b: 190).[35] As Catusse (192) documents, taking into consideration the financial holdings of these companies in other companies, they represented 40 percent of the state's portfolio in 1989 and included the country's big cement, steel, petrol, phosphate, and mining industries; four of the main banks; insurance companies; finance companies; and service companies, as well as public services such as post and telecommunications, transport, abattoirs, water, and electricity companies. Morocco furthermore joined the General Agreement on Trades and Tariffs (GATT), which later became the World Trade Organization (WTO) in 1987; signed a partnership agreement with the European Union (EU) in 1996 (paving the way for a free-trade areas between Morocco and the EU), and signed a free-trade agreement with the United States in 2004.

The reorientation of the economy, the lessening of job opportunities in the public sector, and the reduction of food subsidies had a substantial impact on the lower middle classes and the poor. Real wages declined, and unemployment substantially increased as a result of the economic reforms. One of the gravest consequences of the SAP was the steep rise in the number of squatters and of bidonvilles in and around urban centers. Morocco increasingly began to witness the poor turning to the streets or to the "boats of death," bound for Europe in search of a better life (D. Maghraoui 2008: 197). To be sure, the widespread disparities between rich and poor had been evident prior to the economic reforms.[36] As Catusse (2009b: 201) notes, prior to the SAP, Morocco had been particularly modest in terms of providing social security for its citizens. State social policy in terms of expenditures on education, health, and infrastructure furthermore displayed a strong urban bias (Harrigan and El-Said 2009b: 114). The SAP thus exacerbated the effect of an already inadequate state social security system (see chapter 3).

As a consequence, there was a significant acceleration of rural-urban migration and an explosion in urban squatters and shantytowns in the 1980s. These shantytowns were to be at the core of popular uprisings, often referred to as the "IMF riots" or the "bread riots" in 1981, 1984, and 1990 (Catusse 2009b: 199).[37] The most serious of these took place in 1984 when rioting spread to approximately fifty cities. The security forces took almost three weeks to restore order and killed approximately 100 people in the process (Lust-Okar 2004: 163; Sater 2010: 60).

Similar to King Hussein in Jordan, King Hassan II responded to the riots with a series of measures designed to introduce a limited degree of political reform. These granted the parliament limited additional powers, eased restrictions on political parties and civil society, and displayed a greater respect for human rights. The monarchy thus increasingly began to portray itself as a political reformer—albeit with the aim of co-opting civil society actors. The monarchy was seeking to create a new civil society elite through its reforms, an elite that it was then to harness and co-opt for purposes of legitimation (see chapter 3).

Conclusion

The early history of the two monarchies reveals important differences that would have an impact on their respective coalition strategies and, as a consequence, their decisions to decentralize or not in the years to come. The nature of the relationships of the two monarchies with their respective post-independence coalition partners—in particular, the role the latter played in securing the institution of the monarchy—was fundamentally different. In Jordan, the "Hashemite Compact" arose out the crucial role that the tribes played in the creation of the state and the country's national identity. In the early years of the state, both the British and the monarchy needed the Bedouin-based army to help consolidate the country's borders, particularly in the south, and to bring the Bedouin tribes under the centralized administration of the new state. A tribal elite soon developed with both political and economic power, one that bound the tribes to the monarchy both through its identification with the monarchy and the networks of wasta that had developed between the shaykhs and their tribes. When the monarchy faced successive political and economic challenges, including the rise of Arab nationalism and an alleged coup attempt in the 1950s, the monarchy had few options but to turn to the coalition partner that had secured its rule from the beginning of the monarchy's creation. The need to strengthen its historic coalition with the Transjordanian population and the tribal elite was all the more pressing given the growing numbers of Palestinians—whose loyalties were perceived to lie elsewhere and who were increasingly resented by the Transjordanian population.

This stands in contrast to the Moroccan monarchy's early coalitions—with the Istiqlal prior to independence and with the Berber elite post-independence. While the Istiqlal had played an important role in ousting the French and the Berber elite in preserving the role of the monarch as more than a mere figurehead, neither coalition had the historical depth of the tribal elite in Jordan; nor had they played such an integral role in either state- or nation-building. To be sure, the Berber elite had played a role in bringing Bled as-Siba under the auspices of the state, and in this sense they strengthened the monarchy in areas it had not controlled before. Yet the monarchy as an institution had existed for several hundred years prior to the arrival of the French or the creation of a Berber elite. The Berber elite had played an important role in the monarchy's competition with the parties of the former nationalist movement; however, it was not integral to either state- or nation-building to the same extent as the tribes in Jordan. These differences between the two monarchies go a long way toward explaining why the Jordanian monarchy consistently has chosen to maintain is coalition strategy whereas in Morocco, following the two attempted coups in the 1970s, the monarchy sought to broaden its base of support to include a new coalition partner.

Within this context, decentralization in Morocco—in the form of the 1976 municipal charter—was a tactic used to entice new coalition partners, the Istiqlal and other parties of the former nationalist movement, into elections and eventually into the government. Indeed, it was partially as a result of the success of the 1976 municipal charter as a tool to entice and co-opt the opposition that the opposition parties were discredited and that the multiparty system no longer served to legitimize the monarchy. By the 1990s, the monarchy needed to "reattach" the growing middle class in Moroccan society that was increasingly "unattached" to the regime; it thus turned to civil society as a new coalition partner. As in 1976, both the 2002 and 2009 charters were promulgated in an effort to promote the monarch as a political reformer and secure the "partnership" of the country's new civil society elite to the regime by granting it new decision-making powers.

Yet other determinants that were to influence both monarchies in their decisions whether or not to decentralize were also established during the pre- and post-independence periods. In Morocco, the monarchy relied heavily on the institution of the parliament, and the multiparty system in particular, in securing its dominance. The regime created or supported the creation of "palace" or "administrative" parties, such as the PMP, to weaken the Istiqlal and ensure that pro-regime parties dominated the parliament and government. The multiplicity of pro-regime parties also guaranteed that those parties remained weak and posed no threat to the regime. Political parties and the institution of parliament became important vehicles through which neo-patrimonial benefits were distributed. As I discuss in depth in chapter 3, while political parties, including the Istiqlal, were top-heavy, devoid of any real platform, and permeated by interlinking chains of patrons and clients tied to the regime, they had institutional structures with party branches. The comparison of Morocco and Jordan indicates that party institutionalization cannot be overlooked as a factor determining decentralization. The institutionalization of Morocco's parties—at least relative to Jordan—enabled the parties to benefit from decentralization and the empowerment of municipal councils in 1976. The parties, including the Istiqlal, were tempted by and took advantage of local elites (patrons), their votes (clients), and resources by bringing them into their parties in 1976. They could not have done so had they not been sufficiently institutionalized and had relevant structures in place.

In Jordan, by contrast, the tribal structure was the primary vehicle by which the monarchy bound Transjordanians to the regime; this was increasingly the case following the imposition of martial law. Jordan's parliament continues to be dominated by tribal independents or parties that compete for votes based on the services, resources, and jobs they can provide to their tribal constituencies. The result has not only been the creation of vast networks of wasta but the continuous revitalization of tribalism and the weakening of ideologically based political parties. These factors were to present strong disincentives to decentralization. Political decentralization devolves powers away from the country's ministers and undermines MPs' networks of wasta with which they provide these services. Without institutionalized party structures, Jordan's tribal candidates cannot take advantage of any devolved powers to the municipalities outside of their immediate tribes or clans; the regime's coalition partner stands only to lose power and privileges with political decentralization. Thus, despite pressures to decentralize, the regime would increasingly centralize.

CHAPTER II

Centralization and "Decentralization" in Jordan

In 2005, King Abdullah II announced the National Agenda—a frame-work for reform that put decentralization front and center in public debate. Outlining the agenda's new approach to political participation, the king argued that political development should start at the grassroots level and then move up to decision-making centers, not vice versa. The kingdom's twelve governorates would be reduced to three or four regions, each with a directly elected local assembly and directly elected municipal councils. Taking over responsibilities of central decision makers, less aware of the interests and needs of each region, the new assemblies would have greater fiscal authority and the ability to make decisions over "public facilities, investment priorities, expenditures on capital and services projects, and in overseeing the performance of official bodies in all areas" (Satloff 2005). The king's 2005 speech was the first time that decentralization entered public debate to any significant extent; however, it was not the first time the issue of decentralization, specifically administrative decentraliza-tion, had been raised and rejected in Jordan. Since the early 1970s, there had been economic and political pressures to rectify the growing imbal-ance in wealth and services between urban and rural municipalities. Yet, during the sixty-odd years prior to the speech, Jordan had steadily removed powers from municipal governments. Even when the extent of Jordan's municipal crisis was revealed in the 1990s—with fewer than 50 percent of municipalities able to cover their employees' salaries and provide basic services—and foreign donors became engaged in municipal-strengthening projects (see chapter 4), the regime continued to centralize and implemented a program of amalgamation to save costs. In fact, when Jordan finally implemented so-called decentralization in 2015, the reforms removed powers from municipalities, transferring them "upward" to the new executive councils at the governorate level. In the choice between centralization or decentralization, the monarchy in Jordan clearly has chosen the former.

At the heart of the regime's ongoing pursuit of centralization, including the distribution of resources and taxes, lies what Ababsa (2015) calls the regime's "balancing act": its attempt to favor the supporters of the regime, the Transjordanians, who inhabit the impoverished rural areas, while controlling the political expression of the Palestinians, who are residents of the large cities, and, increasingly after 1989, the Islamic Action Front (IAF), which finds its primary stronghold in Palestinian-dominated areas.[1] Centralization is thus a tactic of the regime's coalition strategy. With the Palestinians not only constituting a demographic threat but also wielding economic strength, the Transjordanian-Palestinian rift threatens the kingdom's internal stability (Reiter in Gabbay 2014: 5). The regime consequently has pursued policies that maintain the centralized nature of the system while balancing security concerns with selective economic development and socioeconomic benefits directed at Transjordanian-dominated governorates and municipalities. To assuage Transjordanians' concerns regarding the concentration of government resources in (Palestinian-dominated) Amman to the perceived discrimination of the tribes in the rural areas, the regime has created new subnational bodies and directed funds and patronage to them. It has also kept municipal councils weak and devoid of any real authority or responsibilities. An overview of the history of Jordan's municipal laws and amendments reveals that the regime has consistently clawed back municipal powers and responsibilities and centralized them in the hands of ministers. At the same time, it has not only implemented an electoral system biased toward tribal candidates and against political parties, the IAF in particular, but also directed municipal funding overwhelmingly toward Transjordanian-dominated municipalities.

Confronted with international and domestic pressures for political reform beginning in the 1990s, municipalities facing a crisis of service delivery, and the failure of economic reforms, amalgamation in particular, the monarchy was forced to consider decentralization as a political and economic solution to the municipal crisis in 2005. To a large extent, the municipal crisis had been caused—and continues to be—by the networks of *wasta* (see chapter 1) in which municipal councils were embedded and by which municipal services were distributed. The regime's preferential treatment of Transjordanians by ensuring that the electoral laws favor tribal independents over ideologically based parties has meant that members of parliament (MPs) are elected by promising services they can deliver to their constituents. In this regard, they not only compete with mayors for the role of service providers but create vast networks of patron-clientelism with ministers, university presidents, and business leaders, to name just a few, in order to secure and provide services, employment, and resources for those who voted for them. Consequently, wasta has contributed significantly to the unequal, unfair, and inadequate service delivery in Jordan's municipalities; municipalities with mayors with better wasta to the center receive more or better (or both) services. Yet while contributing to the municipal crisis, wasta is also the reason why Jordan's Transjordanian elite has resisted decentralization. Not only would political decentralization entail a direct loss of power for Jordan's tribal elite as a result of the potential transfer of decision-making authority and responsibilities from Amman to the governorates or municipalities, but, by putting service delivery (back) in the hands of the municipalities, it also would undermine the system of wasta on which not just MPs but many Transjordanians rely.

As I discuss in chapter 3, a further disincentive to political decentralization lies in the simple fact that, in contrast to Moroccan MPs, Jordan's MPs overwhelmingly do not belong to political parties and, as such, cannot take advantage of any expanded municipal powers or resources as a result of political decentralization via municipal elections. Because Jordan's MPs commonly run as independents or as part of a loose party of tribal figures and gain their votes from their tribes, they largely can only run where their immediate tribe or clan is located. The one party that does have the capability to establish branches beyond a small handful of electoral districts, and the party the regime has sought to keep from power, is the Islamic Action Front.[2]

Facing a catch-22 in which the monarchy's coalition partners, the Transjordanians, inhabit the regions most in need of reform of the country's hyper-centralized system yet stand to lose the most from reform, the monarchy has chosen a path to decentralization that, similar to other reform initiatives, lies within the framework of the monarchy's historic concern to maintain the ethnic and political balance in Jordan and of the tribal elite's resistance to losing its privileges and wasta. Consequently, in its pursuit of the "right decentralization formula" following the 2005 announcement—one that would address economic reform while not altering the ethno-political balance or the regime's ability to maintain it—the regime repeatedly shelved, postponed, and amended decentralization before a plan eventually was passed in 2015. In the end, the (administrative) decentralization law it did pass further centralized municipal powers.

Political Liberalization

As discussed in chapter 1, in 1989, King Hussein introduced a series of political reforms in response to the economic hardships as a consequence of the country's structural adjustment program (SAP).[3] Yet within a relatively short period of time, it became abundantly clear that the reforms ultimately were meant to defuse political dissent without substantially altering the balance of power—either in terms of the monarchy's power, as noted in the preceding chapter, or in terms of the privileged position of the Transjordanians. By the mid-1990s, the door to Jordan's political opening clearly was closing, with most analysts considering the amendments to the 1993 electoral laws instituted in the lead-up to the 1993 elections and Jordan's signing of the peace accord with Israel in 1994 as marking the end of political liberalization under King Hussein. By the late 1990s, opposition parties and Transjordanian-dominated pro-regime elites and parties were both coordinating protests to condemn the 1993 amendment and normalization of relations with Israel. The joint opposition, however, masked the continuing deep divide between Transjordanians and Palestinian-Jordanians and the resurfacing of tensions between the two over the rights of Palestinians in Jordan. For Transjordanians, the accord reignited fears regarding what they perceived to be the real or potential erosion of their privileged position within Jordan. In response, the king established the beginnings of a reform agenda that was ultimately to take the shape of the National Agenda and would emphasize decentralization.

The year 1989 witnessed the ushering in of a variety of political reforms, allowing for greater freedom of speech, press, and association and for elections to be held. While political parties remained banned for the 1989 elections (with candidates running as independents), they were legalized in 1992 and over twenty parties ran in the 1993 parliamentary elections.

However, there can be no doubt that the regime's primary concern embarking on political liberalization and going into the 1989 parliamentary elections was to ensure the continued political dominance of tribal candidates. According to the minister of the interior at the time, the objective was to produce a "fair system" but one "within the context of this concern" (Mufti quoted in Schwedler 2006: 50). Consequently, a system of proportional representation was only briefly considered in 1989, as it likely would have produced a Palestinian majority within the assembly (50). A block voting system, whereby voters had as many votes as there were seats to be filled within the district, was adopted. Yet the seats of the electoral districts were distributed disproportionately; while the Transjordanian-dominated town of al-Karak was allotted approximately one seat for every 10,000 people, all of greater Amman, where Palestinians are concentrated, was allotted one seat for every 25,000 people (50).[4]

The block voting system—which encourages the creation of strong party organizations—brought the Islamist bloc (composed predominantly of Muslim Brothers running as independents, see below) 40 percent of the elected eighty-seat Lower House, a significant victory, in the 1989 elections.[5] Following the legalization of political parties, the Muslim Brotherhood (MB) together with other Islamists formed one of the country's first political parties, the IAF. Consequently, in 1993, King Hussein faced the strong possibility of the Islamists again winning a substantial number of seats in the upcoming elections—or at least enough to potentially derail or delay any proposed legislation. With the warming of relations between Jordan, the United States, and Israel and the signing of a peace accord with Israel on the horizon—initiatives that were bound to incur domestic resistance, particularly from the Islamists—the king issued a temporary amendment to the electoral law. The aim of the amendment was evident: to ensure that tribal MPs loyal to the king would be brought to power in the 1993 elections in order to secure the passage of the future peace treaty within parliament.[6]

The 1993 electoral law introduced the "one person, one vote" electoral system, which granted each voter one vote regardless of the number of seats allotted to his or her district. It consequently forced voters to choose between tribal loyalties and ideologically based parties, such as the IAF. Given that tribal loyalties are strong in Jordan, largely because most social, economic, and political objectives are achieved through traditional patronage and kinship relations, the amendment had a powerful impact on electoral outcomes by putting political parties at a clear disadvantage. The 1993 electoral law furthermore maintained the gerrymandered electoral districts from 1989. The parliamentary elections thus were biased against political parties, as opposed to independent tribal candidates loyal to the regime, and against urban areas.

The 1993 law played an important part in fueling the massive protests of the 1990s (see below). The IAF and other opposition parties demanded a repeal of the one-person-one-vote law, including its gerrymandered districts, and ultimately boycotted the 1997 elections.[7] Yet the tensions between the Islamists and the monarchy were a relatively new phenomenon; they also were not unrelated to the divide between Transjordanians and Palestinians. Established and registered as a legal charitable society in 1945 (under the patronage of Abdullah I), the MB had had a relatively long history of legal political activism prior to 1989.[8] While its early focus was on religious education, it became more politicized following the 1948 war and began calling for the implementation of Islamic law (*shari'a*) and the establishment of an Islamic order.[9] Yet it was allowed to continue operating and in 1953 was redesignated as a "general and comprehensive Islamic committee" and allowed to be politically active. It thus participated in the 1956 parliamentary elections that brought the Jordanian Nationalist Movement (see chapter 1) to power, winning four out of forty seats (Abu Rumman 2007: 18). Quite simply, the regime saw the growth of the MB as a means by which it could undermine the rise, and later the popularity, of pan-Arab nationalism.[10] Consequently, the MB was even allowed to operate during marital law while other groups and parties had been banned and driven underground.

In return for its protected status, the MB supported the monarchy politically; it by-and-large refrained from criticizing the political structure or the legitimacy of the monarchy itself. The monarchy rewarded MB leaders for their loyalty and cooperation with positions in various governments. In recognition of the MB's loyalty during Jordan's 1970–1971 civil war, King Hussein made Izhaq Farhan, a prominent MB member, the minister of education for five consecutive cabinets (1970 to 1974). He was furthermore minister of *Awqaf* in 1972 for approximately one year (Bar 1998: 32; Hourani et al. 1993: 3–14; Wiktorowicz 2001: 95–101).[11]

Relations between the MB and the regime were to become strained beginning in the mid-1980s, and most especially after 1989 when the MB took a leadership role in the protests against the peace accord with Israel.

While the MB had had relatively little mass following in the 1950s and 1960s, its popularity rose significantly in the 1970s and 1980s. With funds from the Gulf, it had been able to expand its charitable activities; it further-more began actively participating in student unions and professional asso-ciations (from where it would eventually spearhead the "anti-normalization" protests of the 1990s, see below). When the MB began organizing strikes against tuition increases on university campuses, its relationship with the regime began to sour.[12]

Yet it cannot be ignored that the rise of the MB in political and social popularity and its tensions with the regime also had much to do with its Palestinian bias. While the MB had both Palestinian and Transjordanian leadership and support, it was considered a Palestinian organization. Follow-ing Black September and the expulsion of Palestinian fighters to Lebanon in 1970, the MB had filled the vacuum and made significant gains in recruitment within the camps and among Palestinians at large (Abu Rum-man 2007: 20). In this regard, the 1993 law was not only an effort to ensure the electoral victories of tribal candidates at the expense of ideologically-based political parties; it was also an effort to curtail Palestinians' electoral gains.

The 1994 peace accord with Israel—whose passage the 1993 electoral law was designed to ensure—was to trigger debates similar to those seen following Black September and again in 1988, with Jordan's judicial and administrative disengagement from the West Bank, over the political rights and civil status of the Palestinian-Jordanians. As Nevo (2003: 199) argues, the peace accord once again unleashed the debate over the future identity of Jordan, and over the place of the Palestinians in that future. The issue took on an even greater intensity as a result of the 1990–1991 Gulf War and the return of over 200,000 Palestinians, which aroused fears among the Transjordanians that demographic changes favoring Palestinians would lead to the loss of their tribal elite's power (Reiter 2004: 73). A growing group of Transjordanian nationalists viewed the peace process and the events leading up to it as an opportunity to reorga-nize the internal Jordanian structure and to stipulate that political rights and Jordanian citizenship would accrue only to those Palestinians who "accept the current order of the Hashemite monarchy and the role of the Army, and remain loyal to the regime and the state even in the cases of a possible clash between Jordan and the future Filastin (the Palestinian state)" (73).

By spring of 1997, the "anti-normalization" movement (opposed to normalization of relations with Israel, beginning with the peace accord) was protesting in the streets. Originally led by the Islamists, the movement now garnered support from the full political spectrum, including prominent pro-regime—Transjordanian—figures; new organizations based on alliances between parties, associations, and personalities hitherto political opponents formed. Both sides feared that the accord would hinder, if not preclude, the creation of a Palestinian state and were concerned about the resulting possible effects of such an outcome on the two communities in Jordan itself. Transjordanians worried that the Palestinian-Jordanians would settle permanently in Jordan and that frustrated Palestinians from the West Bank and Gaza would relocate to Jordan, increasing their numerical strength. Most importantly, they were concerned that the Palestinians would gain full citizenship rights at the expense of the Transjordanians and their historically exclusive privileges. Palestinians questioned how much they would see their rights translate into practice and how they would be expected to fit into a Transjordanian conception of national identity. When the economic development promised as a result of peace did not materialize, the opposition was able to link the country's growing economic crisis with the "unnatural peace with Israel" (Kornbluth 2002: 94). Thus when riots broke out in Transjordanian-dominated Ma'an and al-Karak in June 1996 and again in February 1998 following the implementation of IMF austerity measures, they reflected (as they had in 1989) far more than a protest against rising costs.

By the autumn of 2000, Jordan was experiencing some of the largest and most violent demonstrations since the onset of political liberalization in 1989. In November 2000, after the outbreak of the al-Aqsa intifada and the election of right-wing Ariel Sharon in Israel, the Anti-Normalization Committee of Jordan's Professional Syndicates Association posted the names of "normalizers" (those who engage in relations with Israel) to be blacklisted from their professions and all economic dealings. In February 2001, it posted a second list that included the chief of the Royal Court and a former royal adviser.[13] With increasing political violence repeatedly fueled by external events, King Abdullah II suspended parliament after its session expired later that year and postponed the November 2001 elections. Elections were not held again until June 2003.

It was during this suspension of parliament that the king made decentralization part of his reform agenda. In an effort to gain control of the political situation and to ensure continued support of Transjordanians, Abdullah II proposed a series of top-down political reforms. The first of these was the Jordan First (al-Urdun al-Awalan) campaign of 2002. The campaign was an effort to define a new social contract among Jordanians, and it laid out the king's political, social, and economic vision for Jordan.[14] The monarchy thus attempted to rebuild national unity on "one Jordanian 'family' and one nationality in the kingdom" (Ryan 2010: 10) and to refocus the political agenda on domestic issues (as opposed to events in the Occupied Territories or Palestinian identity or Palestinian refugees setting the domestic agenda). Paraphrasing Köprülü (2009: 75), Jordan First aimed to make Jordanian identity more Jordanized, less Palestinianized, and less Arabized. The campaign thus implicitly demanded that Palestinians living in Jordan choose either to be full Jordanian citizens or assume the Palestinian national identity (75).[15]

The king appointed a National Committee to work out the Jordan First initiative; the committee then drew up the National Agenda and categorized reform into three main areas: political, administrative, and social. Amid growing international and domestic consternation, the king launched the National Agenda—"touted as major political and administrative reform" (Satloff 2005)—in February 2005.

Jordan's SAP and the Monarchy's Coalition with the Tribal Elite

The post-1989 period also had witnessed (what presumably were) deep economic restructuring and privatization reforms according to the IMF-imposed SAP—reforms that threatened to hurt Jordan's Transjordanian population the most. Yet after approximately fifteen years of economic reform (and protests against it), surprisingly little had changed. The state-society ties and the forms of patronage that were rooted in the formation of the state remained the same; while their details may have altered, their basic logic had not. The monarchy had maintained its essential coalition with the Transjordanian elite even if this coalition was now somewhat less lucrative for many Transjordanians. In fact, in the wake of the protests, Jordan's predominantly Transjordanian elites in the bureaucracy, in business, and in the military saw their privileges either unaffected or enhanced. With privatization, the Transjordanian elite had not lost its positions of power in the public sector, nor had the Palestinians, who had dominated the private sector, gained political influence. While the monarchy was committed to the path of neoliberalism and privatization, it was a path that took the concerns of the Transjordanian bureaucratic elite into consideration—elites who quite naturally resisted changes to their privileges and patronage. This was the same "path" the monarchy would follow when it pursued decentralization in the years to come. Alongside the privatization program, the state thus continued to have a large role in economic planning (Ryan 2010: 14). It also continued to assert this role by offering Transjordanians employment in the military and other socioeconomic benefits. What it could not do, it downloaded to royal NGOs (RONGOs, see below), which similarly sought to counterbalance the often harsh consequences of the SAP on Transjordanians, and systematically at the expense of Palestinians. All aspects of the regime's economic reform policies thus served to protect the historic privileging of the Transjordanian population and, most particularly, the power of its tribal elite.

As stated in chapter 1, Jordan first embarked on its program of state-led modernization, including industrialization, in the 1950s. The Jordan Cement Factory Company, the extension of the Jordan Phosphate Company, the Jordan Petroleum Refinery Company, and the Jordan Vegetable Oil Industries Company were established in the 1950s; all were based on public-private partnerships. The nationalist bureaucrats who initiated the program did so with the cooperation of a "small group of wealthy Jordanian merchants and some additional Palestinian businessmen" (Wils 2004: 140). With time, the bureaucrats had established themselves as a new segment of Jordanian elite, and the merchants with whom they had develop strong ties also benefited. Most importantly, this group of businessmen remained largely Transjordanian and repeatedly capitalized on their relations with the high-level bureaucrats to keep out other competition and to defend their privileges, including access to information as well as import licenses. By 1989, this business elite had made increasing use of personal relations to not only the state administration but also to the palace (142, 143–44).

These close relations explain in part why sensitive reforms such as the reorganization of public administration and the privatization of public companies were repeatedly postponed. Quite simply, the "palace elite had to strike a balance between consideration of regime survival and commitments to international financial agencies" (Wils 2004: 146). Indeed, Reiter (2004: 75) notes that the government actually postponed the privatization of state-run companies for fear that the only buyers would be Palestinians who would acquire total control of the Jordanian economy and thereby accumulate sufficient political leverage to change the character of the regime and deprive the ethnic Jordanians of their relative advantage.

To be sure, as Ryan (2010: 14) points out, King Abdullah's economic reforms created "a constituency of like-minded elites who share his enthusiasm for neoliberal solutions to Jordan's development." This has been reflected in the king's political appointments, with the top cabinet posts going to technocratic elites with experience in Jordan's industrial and trade zones. In 1999, Abdullah II established the Economic Consultative Council, which acts as a type of shadow government for economic affairs. The prominence of private sector representatives on the council—with seven of its twenty members being Palestinian—attests to the ongoing rise of the Palestinian economic elite (Reiter 2004: 86–87).

However, using formal negotiations and informal rent-seeking, Transjordanian elites have been able to protect their privileges and manipulate reform policies. Confronted with privatization, Jordan's rentier elites increased their economic base by acquiring the privatized companies (Knowles 2005: 143). Senior bureaucrats tried to avoid, postpone, or cushion serious policy measures; they were joined by the business elites who sought to maintain their ties with the bureaucratic elite, and therefore their exclusivity (Wils 2004: 154). The "palace elite," Wils (155) furthermore notes, additionally privileged political allies and other influential groups by granting them rent-seeking opportunities related to privatization and politically risky undertakings, such as doing business with Israel.

In fact, by 1998 no major public companies had actually been privatized. After 1998, when privatization began, the state continued to equivocate on a wholehearted commitment to the process, citing job losses and the question of security. Many Jordanians feared that the uncontrolled opening of the economy to foreign investment could lead to an Israeli takeover of vital assets, such as the phosphate industry (Knowles 2005: 155). By the end of 2002, the Jordan Investment Corporation (JIC), established to attract private investment, had divested shares in forty-nine public companies. However, this has not resulted in a strong market economy. As Knowles (185) explains, first of all, many of the divestments have been to the Social Security Corporation (SSC, legally and administratively independent of the state), whose board of directors is chaired by the minister of labor and dominated by state officials. The second dominant reason is that the JIC has continued to invest in new projects in partnership with the private sector. Finally, the Transjordanian-dominated parliament managed to have a "golden clause" inserted into the privatization law according to which the government can veto any company policy that it deems against "national interest," which included the loss of significant jobs.

The end result is that the state has retained a significant role in the economy—albeit a less direct one—and both the state and the rentier elite continue to be able to rent-seek. Transjordanian elites continue to circulate, by appointment, between government posts and positions in public sector companies, and the public sector continues to outweigh the private sector (Ryan 2010: 14). While the number of public companies has been on the decline as a result of privatization, the remaining government-owned companies are the backbone of Jordan's economy and they overbalance the economic value of Palestinian-owned private companies (Reiter 2004: 77–78). Securing their nominations via their close relations to the prime minister (PM), the boards of trustees for the five top public companies thus look like a Jordanian who's-who (80, 81). Furthermore, between one-third and two-thirds of all workers in Jordan continued to be on the state's payroll (Sharp 2015). Of these workers, 75 percent were estimated to be Transjordanian.

Thus, it is unsurprising that in the midst of the economic slowdown of the 1990s, the only sectors to grow were the military and security services (Baylouny 2008: 301). In the wake of the 1989 protests, the monarchy almost immediately turned to its historical base of support. As it had always done, the monarchy sought to reestablish and deepen its ties to the military. By 1998, largely as a result of subcontracting and new economic enterprises, not only had the military budget increased (equaling one-quarter of the total government budget), but military employment had reached 10 percent of the labor force in general, and as high as 20 percent in rural areas (Baylouny 2010: 57–58). In 1992, almost immediately after economic reform began, military conscription was eliminated, thus "allowing for the possibility of East Banker or Jordanian domination of the army once again" (Baylouny 2008: 301).

Throughout the 1990s, the regime funneled its social largesse to the military. As Baylouny (2008: 303) documents, social welfare for military personnel and their families included scholarships reserved for personnel and their dependents, free medical care, and military cooperatives stores selling goods at preferential prices. All of these were enhanced following the

SAP. Just as importantly, less direct avenues of privilege also benefited Transjordanians in the military. For example, Transjordanians, particularly those in the military, began to receive special access to public universities via a quota system. Following 1989, the regime began establishing public universities in Transjordanian-dominated rural areas such as al-Karak, al-Mafraq, al-Tafilah, and Ma'an; leaving the much more expensive private universities to serve the urban, Palestinian-dominated areas (Reiter 2002: 143). Up to 60 percent of the students accepted for admission into public universities in the 1990s entered via these *mukrumat malakiyya* (privileges of the king) (151). The categories of these privileges or quotas all indirectly targeted Transjordanians.[16] The largest quota category receiving the king's privileges was the army and security (143).[17]

The regime maintained its strong commitment not only to the military and security forces but to the public sector and to the poorer elements among the country's rural Transjordanian citizens (Bertelsmann Stiftung 2014: 15). While the public sector increasingly began to cooperate with the private sector, primarily NGOs, in providing much of its social welfare (15), the state did not lose its role in social welfare provision, and certainly not its ability to direct social welfare to select groups of Transjordanians. Moreover, where the state was unable to play a role, the royal family stepped up to the plate.

Jordan's public sector shrunk in size following 1989 and continues to do so. Yet via Jordan's social insurance program, under the SSC, public sector employees continue to benefit from social welfare provision to which those working in the private sector have little access.[18] Furthermore, while neo-liberalism has resulted in the marketization and NGO-ization of public services, the state also has maintained its ability to direct these services to its "preferred clients" through public-private partnerships (PPPs). Many of these are initiatives of the king. In 2008, for example, the king launched an initiative entitled Decent Housing for Decent Living. The program is run through the government agency, the Housing and Urban Development Corporation, but construction costs are primarily financed by the private sector. As Bouziane (2010: 40) points out, through programs such as Decent Housing, funds can be directed to Transjordanian areas; this program provides housing or plots of land to low- and limited-income Jordanians such as civil servants, military personnel, and civil and military retirees.

Furthermore, most PPPs are in fact with RONGOs—royal NGOs established by individual members of the extended royal family (Bertelsmann Stiftung 2014: 15; Lenner 2013).[19] The state relies increasingly on

RONGOs to implement its programs. Thus, where the state has withdrawn, the royal family, through RONGOs, has moved in. RONGOs are another avenue by which Transjordanians are privileged. As Boerwinkel (2011: 14) states when discussing the Jordanian Hashemite Fund for Human Development (JOHUD), the largest NGO in Jordan: "It is obvious that their choice of projects—they fund local NGOs—indirectly perpetuates the regime's powerbase. This royal NGO mainly focuses on projects in the countryside, covering villages with Transjordan populations, often Bedouin. Not coincidently, these are the regime's main pillars of support."

RONGOs such as the Jordan River Foundation, established by Queen Rania, are deeply involved in poverty reduction. The core of the country's social protection system is provided by the National Aid Fund (NAF), established in 1986. It provides cash transfers on a recurring or occasional basis to vulnerable groups; it also offers health insurance cards and vocational training programs. As Jordan has reduced its general (non-targeted) subsidies, the NAF cash transfers have taken on increasing importance. Beginning in 2004, the NAF cash transfers, as well as the other aspects of the Social Productivity Programme of which the NAF is now part, such as income-generating and productivity-enhancing projects, began to be explicitly targeted at the country's newly designated "poverty pockets" (Lenner 2013). Poverty pockets are subdistricts where more than 25 percent of the population is classified as poor using a percent incidence of poverty (UNDP 2013: 26). Poverty pockets consequently identify areas with high incidence of poverty rather than areas with high total numbers of the poor (37). This has resulted in large amounts of poverty-reduction programming being targeted at predominantly *rural* areas. However, if one looks at the locations of the largest numbers of poor households, using incidence of poverty, the vast majority of Jordan's poor live in the urban areas of Amman, al-Zarqa', and Irbid. These areas, however, are not classified a poverty pockets. Furthermore, the percentage of Palestinians among the urban poor is much higher than among the rural poor. Jordan's rural areas are, as discussed in chapter 1, overwhelmingly Transjordanian.

To be sure, Jordan's SAP hurt Transjordanians—who dominate the public sector—more than Palestinians, who dominate the private sector. While the SAP inflicted a heavy toll on Jordanians of all origins, with poverty reaching 20 percent of the population in 1991 and rising to 30 percent by 2000, a significant amount of poverty was among the working poor, about half of whom were in the state's employ (Baylouny 2008: 295). The highest rates of poverty were in al-Mafraq and al-Karak, followed by al-Balqa', Irbid, al-Tafilah, and Ma'an. The same distribution held for those families in absolute or abject poverty (296). Ma'an and al-Karak also saw the highest proportion of income spent on food and drink—over 55 percent (297–98). Yet poor Transjordanians have benefited from initiatives from which poor Palestinians are excluded (Bertelsmann Stiftung 2014: 15). Despite severe yet undesignated poverty pockets within Palestinian-dominated Amman, only poor rural Transjordanians benefit from infrastructure programs, productivity-enhancing measures, monthly cash assistance, health cards, free schools meals, and winter coats for children, as well as benefits and pay raises for government employees (15; Lenner 2013).

What increasingly emerged therefore, following the imposition of the SAP, was a system whereby Transjordanians benefited through jobs and programs to which Palestinians—who make up anywhere from 43 percent to two-thirds of the population (Zahran 2012: 3)—had no access. Much of this is done via quotas, which are justified with numbers that privilege Transjordanians. It is a system of patronage under the guise of affirmative action, poverty reduction, and NGOs. And, chapter 4 shows, it is a system on which the Transjordanian-dominated municipalities rely heavily.

With the SAP, Jordan thus continued to have a highly centralized political and economic system, one that not only maintained Transjordanian political and economic dominance but also continued to implement policies that favored Transjordanians. Economic reforms were delayed or implemented to ensure state—in other words, Transjordanian—control over the economy. Sectors in which Transjordanians are disproportionately employed, such as the military, continued to grow even as the economy was shrinking. Social welfare continued to be linked to public employment. Even where the state downloaded responsibilities and entered PPPs, these commonly were with royal institutions targeting those who are considered the bedrock of regime support.

The Creation of Governorates and Development Groups

The systematic favoring of Transjordanians is reflected in Jordan's centralized administrative structure and in the creation and location of its territorial units, their powers, and their funding. Under its highly centralized system, the regime has designed many of the country's governorates and other regional bodies, such as regional development bodies, to address the growth in size and wealth of Palestinian-dominated Amman. They thus were created with political, as opposed to the proclaimed economic, objectives: to address Transjordanian concerns over the growing numbers and concentration of Palestinians and the perceived imbalance in resources and services between rural Transjordanian-dominated regions and urban Palestinian-dominated ones.

Jordan's administrative system is marked first and foremost by the fact that it is not only centralized but hyper-centralized. All governorates fall under the jurisdiction of the Ministry of the Interior (MoI). Governors are appointed by the king and act as agents on behalf of the MoI in Amman. Most decisions continue to be made in Amman, not by the governors in the governorates. In Jordan's hyper-centralized system, governors have relatively few powers. Indeed, in 2005 when the king announced the National Agenda, the system was still so centralized that Jreisat's words—speaking of the administration in the 1980s—still held true: regarding the "excessive control tendencies at the Cabinet and the prime minister levels . . . [p]olicy matters, allocation of resources, and even senior personnel matters are routinely referred to the prime minister . . . for action" (1989: 100).

Broadly speaking, governors play two roles. The first, and by far most important, is a security function. The governor is responsible for all security, law, and public order in his governorate (there has never been a female governor). Before 2015, it was only in this area of security that the governor could be said to have had any executive authority. The second function is to foster socioeconomic development in their governorates. In 2001, governors were tasked with creating a favorable investment environment. And in 2008 they were additionally charged with supervising the municipalities' local development units (LDUs, see chapter 4)—a role that previously had been under the Ministry of Municipal Affairs (MoMA).[20] However, until 2015, the role governors played vis-à-vis socioeconomic development was primarily one of planning and coordinating the activities of the various sectoral ministries in their respective governorates. They played no role in the implementation of a policy or industry. Indeed, the system was so centralized that governors, for all intents and purposes, had no budget to speak of with which to implement anything; this was the job of the sectoral line ministries. Their financial autonomy was limited to 100,000 JD

(US$142,000); the rest was determined in Amman or had to be approved by Amman (Ababsa 2015).

Until 2015, every governor had two councils that supported him; the governor chaired them both. The first was the Executive Council, which included the local directors of the various sectoral line ministries. As a European Union (n.d.) study points out, while called an Executive Council, the council had no executive powers; its role was to coordinate the line ministries. The second council was the Consultative Council—an appointed body of MPs, mayors, and heads of civil society organizations. Again, the EU study points out that while this council, by its composition, appeared to represent some form of local participation, the council was not elected and was only accountable to the appointing body, the MoI.

While governorates fall under the MoI, municipalities fall under the MoMA (with the exception of Greater Amman Municipality [GAM], which comes directly under the PM's office, see below) and technically do not report to the MoI. However, as governors are responsible for all security, law, public order, and (as of 2008) the LDUs, the MoMA's approval of a municipal development project, for example, must run by the governor's desk. Municipalities must also directly receive permission from the governor for all issues related to security, including the hosting of a lecture. The sectoral ministries, such as the Ministries of Health, Education, and the like, are all represented within the governorates by regional agents (directors). Directors' powers are also very weak as they, too, essentially implement decisions made in Amman. Little has changed today.

At the governorate level, the system therefore is composed of a series of vertical independent "silos," each representing one of the sectoral line ministries and receiving orders and budgets from Amman (European Union n.d.: 11–12). Within each silo, resources flow down from Amman to the directorates in the governorates, to the districts, and finally to the municipalities. At least until 2015, citizens had no input. Cutting across the vertical silos are the MoMA, the MoI, and the Ministry of Planning and International Cooperation (MoPIC); each plays, to a greater or lesser degree, some sort of coordinating role across the "silo-ed" line ministries. MoPIC is responsible for socioeconomic planning and development (including for sectors) at the national level. The MoI, as noted above, is in charge of security but also plays a role in socioeconomic development across the governorates. MoMA is responsible for all municipalities and, through their LDUs (see chapter 4), plays a similar development role across municipalities.

The administrative structure over which governors (presumably) preside originally was established during the latter years of the Ottoman Empire and the early years of the British mandate period (Doan 1991: 177). Under the Ottomans, the boundaries of the administrative structures were created to ensure the peaceful passage of the annual pilgrimage. With the fall of the Ottoman Empire and the severing of the former administrative and economic ties to Damascus, the British essentially relied on the administrative hierarchy the Ottomans had used. The country was divided into five governorates (*muhafaz*, singular)—Irbid, al-Balqa', al-Karak, Amman, and Ma'an—which were subdivided into districts (*liwa*), subdistricts (*qada'*), and *nahia* (178). With independence in 1946, Jordan maintained the five governorates; when Jordan annexed the West Bank in 1948, the kingdom was divided into two governorates (Amman and Jerusalem) with eight districts (and the desert administration). In 1965, it was reorganized again, and the six districts became governorates. Three of these were lost to Israel in 1967, leaving Jordan with the governorates of al-Balqa', al-Karak, Irbid, Ma'an, and Amman.

Since 1967, Jordan has created several regional bodies and governorates. This process has been marked by two noticeable trends: (1) the ongoing centralization of powers and (2) efforts to rectify the growing regional and ethnic imbalance in resources and services. With the influx of large numbers of Palestinian refugees in 1948 and 1967, Jordan's urban structure became extremely taxed as most refugees settled in the larger urban centers (Doan 1991: 179). The growing imbalance in Jordan's population distribution was then exacerbated by ongoing migration of Palestinians to Jordan and, later, by Palestinians returning as a result of the first Gulf War. Amman exploded from a city of 20,000 in 1921 to 812,513 in 1985 (179). One-half of the country's population (3 million at the time) lived in the governorate of Amman in 1985. These numbers stood in tremendous contrast to al-Zarqa', the second-largest city at the time, with a population of 274,972, and to Ma'an, the capital city of the governorate of Ma'an, with a population of only 13,474 (179).

Following the 1970s economic boom, "a warning note was sounded about the rapid growth of Amman," as Amman was increasingly absorbing the lion's share not only of Jordan's population but also of its resources

(Doan and Adas 2001: 276). Estimates suggested that Palestinians made up 75–80 percent of Amman's population and a substantial percentage of the nearby city of al-Zarqa' (Doan 1991: 179). While administrative reform had been on the agenda since the 1960s, only when confronted by growing Transjordanian resentment over the concentration of national resources in an Amman increasingly dominated by Palestinians, did the regime begin to consider administrative decentralization (179; Doan and Adas 2001: 276). Of concern was less hyper-centralization than hyper-centralization at the expense of Transjordanians. The regime thus sought to reorganize its spatial administration and create new subnational bodies to address Transjordanian concerns—bodies that attempted to address regional inequalities without lessening any centralized control. The political motives of these new bodies were not only reflected in their locations and numbers but in the fact that some of them were simply economically unviable. In other words, they were created as acts of patronage and would require relying on forms of patronage.

In the late 1970s, the cabinet began holding its meetings in all the governorate capitals. As Gubser (1983: 114) observes, the purpose of the roving cabinet was to demonstrate the government's interest in regional development and to counterbalance the bias toward Amman. The government began increasingly talking about "regionalization" with the PM stating that the goal of regionalization was "to give power back to the regional centres and the provinces, to give more power to the mayors and governors, and to allow the local communities everywhere to develop and run their own affairs" (114). The mechanism for this new local participation was to be local institutions and large regional councils composed of mayors, village council heads, and civic leaders; the latter would have authority over regional socioeconomic issues. In fact, the government at the time declared it "unhealthy for the government to take a patronizing attitude to the people and to treat them as if they were only objects of service, not participants in the development process" (114).

The first efforts at addressing Jordan's imbalance in economic development was the creation of new regional development groups or bodies. Yet the regional development groups represented a further centralization of decision-making powers as they removed decision-making authority from the municipalities and placed them under new unaccountable bodies—bodies that were directly under the appointed PM. They were initiatives to deal with socioeconomic problems—and thereby hopefully some of the regional resentment—without altering the centralized locus of power and decision-making. The epitome of the regional development groups had long existed. The Jordan Valley Commission had been created in 1972 after the influx of Palestinian refugees in 1967. In 1977, the commission was transformed into the Jordan Valley Association (JVA), a quasi-independent authority tasked with establishing effective agricultural and development policies for the region. The JVA took control of the newly built and foreign-funded irrigation facilities in the valley and was given expanded powers.[21] After 1988, it came under the Authority of Water and Irrigation. The JVA council is appointed directly by the cabinet. Although a new regional body was created, it in effect removed decision-making rights and responsibilities from the municipalities. Its master plans override any projects initiated by the municipalities that fall within its territory. Moreover, it has not empowered the residents who fall within its jurisdiction in any manner—they have no input into any JVA decisions (Doan and Adas 2001: 277). As Gubser (1983: 115) writes of the creation of the JVA, "people were considered primarily as 'objects' . . . of manpower plans and services."

Loosely modeled on the JVA, the Aqaba Regional Authority (ARA) was created in 1983 (with its operations beginning in 1984). The ARA was accorded a special status and given the responsibility for developing the region economically and socially. The ARA (transformed into the Aqaba Social Economic Zone Authority, ASEZA, in 2001) also did not fall under the jurisdiction of the governorate. Rather, the ARA/ASEZA has financial and administrative autonomy and also is directly linked to the PM's office (Doan and Adas 2001: 277). Aqaba no longer has a municipal administration; all functions have been delegated to the ASEZA (Ababsa 2015).

In 1984, the king created the Royal Commission for Administrative Development. The administrative problems constraining effective public administration in Jordan were then reflected in the Hashemite Kingdom of Jordan's Five-Year Plan. Doan (1991: 180) summarizes three main problem areas with the spatial structure of the regions: jurisdictional, economic, and social. As a result of the rapid growth and arbitrary establishment of administrative boundaries during colonial times, there were jurisdictional irregularities at the regional and subregional levels. The distinctions between the various levels of the administrative system were unclear. Economically, the variation in governorate size also presented a problem. Most importantly, as Doan (180) states, the existing regions did not always reflect the tribal nature of the rural population in which local perceptions of the "common" interest were often based on tribal affiliation rather than spatial location. This represented a particularly pressing problem for political decision-makers. . . . Political tension was increasing over the administrative distribution of resources, particularly among tribes in peripheral areas that were an essential part of Hussayn's ruling coalition. . . . Because the existing regions were not contiguous with tribal areas, some groups felt their needs were not being adequately addressed and that they were being administratively dominated by larger, more powerful regions.

The government thus redrew the regional and subregional boundaries to establish more legitimate regional authorities at the local level. As Doan (1991: 181) states, by restructuring regions, decision makers hoped to "appease local communities and create acceptable units which would no longer be dominated by the more developed regions." Amman was restructured and GAM created. Balancing the need to address the concerns of the country's Transjordanians with the security concerns regarding large numbers of Palestinians in the capital city, the regime amalgamated several municipalities and village councils surrounding Amman under the GAM umbrella in 1985.[22] The "Amman Region" created in 1963 had been a vague concept in terms of its borders and administration (Malkawi 2002). Most importantly, it had fallen under the same legislation as all other municipalities. This was to change with the creation of GAM. While the official reason for the GAM amalgamation was to better coordinate the decisions made by the multiple municipal councils in and around the capital, GAM lacked any real autonomy. It was to report directly to the PM's office, not the MoMA.[23] Furthermore, unlike all other municipalities today, only half of its council is elected; the PM's office appointed half of the councillors plus the mayor. As Ababsa (2015) notes, it was no coincidence that the government singled out Amman, with its large concentrations of poor, many of them Palestinian, and placed it under the authority of the PM.

The government also created three new governorates: al-Zarqa', al-Mafraq, and al-Tafilah (Ababsa 2015). These were formed by removing territory (and populations) from the governorates of Amman, Irbid, and al-Karak, respectively, to counterbalance the weight of these three cities where Palestinian refugees were concentrated and to create employment (for Transjordanians) in the police and administration (ibid.; Doan 1991: 181). The government divided the original governorate of Amman into two: Amman (population 1 million) and the new al-Zarqa' (population 425,000). It also divided Irbid into two governorates: Irbid (632,000) and the newly created al-Mafraq (93,000). Al-Karak was divided into the governorates of al-Karak (112,000) and the newly created al-Tafilah (37,000). As Ababsa (2015) notes, the new governorates clearly reflected political considerations more than economic ones. Quite simply, some tribes felt that their needs were being neglected and that they were being administratively dominated by larger, more powerful regions (Doan 1991: 180). These units were designed to assuage the concerns of Transjordanians—the new governorates' lack of economic viability (supposedly the reason for their creation) underscores this. While al-Zarqa', a dense urban area capable of attracting industrial and service investments, had the potential to be a viable economic hub, the same could not be said for al-Mafraq and most certainly not for al-Tafilah. Al-Mafraq and al-Tafilah were created to assuage Transjordanian anger and nothing else, for both governorates were economically unviable. From their inception, these governorates were vehicles of patronage. The small population base of al-Tafilah and the extremely low population densities of al-Mafraq and Ma'an made the ability of the new structures to support wider development questionable (182). Their economic unviability was exacerbated by the lack of smaller towns and cities. Of the three new governorates, only al-Zarqa' had a system of "urban poles" capable of supporting development. al-Tafilah, in particular, with no more than four localities of over 2,000 inhabitants and only 6.5 percent of its business firms engaged in manufacturing in 1985 (compared to 10 percent in al-Mafraq and 16 percent in al-Zarqa'), "absolutely needed private and public investment" (182). With the private sector making up only a small portion of the economic activities of both al-Mafraq and al-Tafilah, the figures for these two governorates "suggest that no amount of administrative restructuring will have much effect on regional development without substantial investments from outside the area" (182).

The Clawback of Municipal Responsibilities

An overview of Jordan's municipal territories, laws, elections, and funding similarly reveals the regime's overriding commitment to its coalition

with the country's Transjordanian population. The government's centralization of municipal powers extends well beyond the regional development
groups; since independence, there has been an ongoing clawback of powers from municipalities to the central government. Since independence,
Jordan has only had four municipalities laws (1955, 2007, 2011, and 2015)—a
surprisingly small number given the significant demographic changes the
country has experienced. Between 1955 and 2007, and particularly after
1989 and the subsequent lifting of martial law, municipalities lost the majority of their responsibilities; furthermore, many of those responsibilities
legally designated to municipalities are, in practice, under the purview of
various ministries. While the central government has consistently justified
the ongoing clawback with an economic rationale (most commonly, the
lack of qualifications and expertise at the local level), much like the creation of the abovementioned governorates, this clawback is directly related
to the country's geographic and ethic division of labor. The regime consistently has sought the centralization it requires to ensure ongoing patronage of rural-based Transjordanian municipalities while controlling for the
rise to power of Islamists and limiting the powers of municipalities.

As discussed in chapter 1, the Ottoman parliament enacted its first
municipal code in 1877; mandate Jordan's first municipal code (1925) followed the 1877 code closely. The 1877 code consisted of sixty-seven articles prescribing "a long list of duties for the new municipalities—opening
of new streets, the paving and widening of old ones, illuminating public
walkways, improving sanitation, controlling and improving the circulation of traffic, removing refuse, designating areas for burials, licensing and
inspecting construction and demolitions, and ensuring the availability of
potable water to urban residents" (Reimer 2005: 191–92).[24] During the
post–Ottoman period, municipalities played an important role in the state-
building policies—they were an important part of the "shift from tribe to
town as the locus of political control in Transjordan" (206). Thus, once
Abdullah's government had established a degree of control over the territory, it sought to extend municipal government into new areas. The failure of municipalities to perform their duties and to undertake any public
works projects resulted in the promulgation of two new municipal codes,
in 1938 and 1939, that respectively reduced the representative character
and fiscal prerogatives of municipal councils (193).[25] The two new codes
sought to create a more centralized administration. While the centrally
managed reform was a sign of the growing sophistication and power of

the government in Amman, the new legal provisions for the *baladiyya*s severely compromised local self-government (207).

With independence, the government recommitted itself, both in terms of discourse and laws, to policies of local participation and decentralization. It issued its first comprehensive law regarding local administration, the Law for the Administration of Villages, in 1954; the Law of Municipalities No. 29 of 1955 was issued shortly thereafter. With the 1955 law, a Department for Municipal and Rural Affairs was created within the MoI (itself established in 1921) to deal with all municipal affairs. In 1965, an independent Ministry for Municipal and Rural Affairs was formed.[26] The 1955 law gave the MoI extensive control over municipalities and local governments. Moreover, the law did not clearly designate the roles of municipalities and those of the central government via the appointed governors. While it defined a municipality as a financially independent local institution (World Bank 2005a: 7), it "*clearly* [did not] provide the municipalities with the requisite autonomy to allow for the creation of policy responses, which would, as a result, allow municipalities to effectively respond to unique local requirements" (*Policy Paper* n.d.).[27] Yet the 1955 law granted municipal councils thirty-nine responsibilities, including service provision (educational, health, leisure, water, electrical, transportation, and communication services); administrative responsibilities (such as the planning and maintenance of public and private areas belonging to the municipality); inspection responsibilities (in the areas of building, trading, service, and leisure activities); financial responsibilities (such as the collection of land taxes and fees for building permits); and legal responsibilities (Ababsa 2015; Center for Strategic Studies 2004: 17–21).

Despite the massive changes in population size and demographics, Jordan did not issue a new municipalities law until 2007; by that point, thirteen of the thirty-nine original functions had been commandeered by the central government (Hayajneh 2008; *Policy Paper* n.d.). Others were technically in the law as municipal functions but only de jure, not de facto. In contrast to much of the Global South, including Morocco, where governments have decentralized in the contexts of their SAPs, Jordan centralized. Via repeated amendments to the 1955 law, the government used its powers to claw back municipal responsibilities. This process sped up after the financial crisis further intensified in the 1990s.[28] In the context of the protests that were building against the 1993 elections law for parliament and the peace accord, as well as other measures put into place in the lead-up to the country's first municipal elections (1995) following the 1989 political opening, the government amended the municipal law and removed many of the municipalities' responsibilities, redistributing them to the central ministries (Hayajneh 2008; World Bank 1995). The government also dissolved all elected councils and appointed caretaker municipal governments to oversee preparation for the upcoming municipal elections; it also disbanded eight local councils (World Bank 1995).[29] As a World Bank (1995) study states: "The driving force behind the municipalities draft law appears to be an intent to alter local political forces, in part to overcome changes in the political balance caused by refuge [sic] camps and other economic/demographic restructuring that has occurred. Decisions on the most efficient means for delivering government services do not appear to have been a major issue in the discussions." More evidence of this assessment is the fact that three months prior to the elections, the cabinet appointed city managers for all of Jordan's major cities and towns—sixteen in total (NDI 1995: 7). The managers remained after the elections to presumably help reduce the new mayors' workloads. Yet the authority of these managers in relation to that of the mayors was not made explicit; in many cases, appointed managers and not mayors were soon running the municipalities.[30]

The 2007 law designated twenty-six fields of responsibility to municipalities, yet even in regard to these fields, their role remained severely restricted. Many of the services continue to be administered by public service companies or the private sector (Hayajneh 2008). Despite their designation as municipal responsibilities, water, electricity, sewerage, gas, education, health, social action, and housing are entirely outside the scope of municipalities (ibid.; World Bank 2005b: 13). According to the 2007 law, the MoI is responsible for fire protection, policing, and security; the Ministry of Education for primary education (both construction and management of schools); the Ministry of Water and Irrigation for water and sewerage services; the Ministry of Health for all hospitals and medical centers; the Ministry of Public Construction for all public buildings; and the Ministry of Transportation for all bus services.[31] Electricity is delivered by the Jordanian Electricity Authority. In addition, various ministries have jurisdiction over municipal properties. The Ministry of Tourism controls all tourist sites; it determines, develops, and manages tourist sites and collects the entrance fees. Thus the castles in al-Karak and Ajloun or the Roman ruins in Jerash are under the authority of the Ministry of

Tourism, with none of these municipalities having a say in how these sites are run; nor do they receive any revenues from them, yet they must service them.[32] Central ministries can also locate public utilities, such as electricity-generating industries, in rural municipalities without requiring municipal approval. Moreover, national utilities are exempt from all local taxes. Even in areas where the municipalities have retained a role for themselves, such as urban planning, their lack of technical and financial capabilities means that in practice the activity is done at the central level. Plans are "made to be approved" by the municipal council (Ababsa 2015; World Bank 2005b: 13). Any modifications to a plan require central government approval—a long and arduous procedure as a result of the high centralized nature of the system. As a World Bank study points out, many of these services, particularly fire protection, water and sewage, and transportation, are commonly provided by municipal governments around the world (Morocco included) (World Bank 1995).[33] To put it in perspective, it would be as if the FBI were in charge of firefighting in every locality throughout the United States. Jordan's hyper-centralization surpasses most countries in the world.

Both the 2007 and the 2011 laws continued to list fewer responsibilities than the 1955 law, and to list responsibilities over which municipalities actually do not have full (or, in some jurisdictions, even partial) control (Ababsa 2015). They did not give municipalities the authority or right to provide input into the policy formulation and decisions regarding services provided by central agencies, nor did they grant them the autonomy to formulate policies adapted to the needs of their individual municipalities. Municipalities furthermore continued not to be consulted by the agencies providing basic "municipal" services. Real authority remained in the hands of the central government, namely the Council of Ministers, the MoMA, and the MoI via the governor.[34]

The changing municipal election laws shed light on the politics dictating these shrinking municipal responsibilities. The regime has historically manipulated municipal election laws with the aim of ensuring that successful candidates are supportive of the monarchy (or at least could not cause trouble). As Ababsa (2015) states, each municipal election has been accompanied by a reform of electoral law in favor of tribal assemblies that support the regime and that limit Islamic opposition—the only opposition that can mount a significant electoral threat and one that, as discussed above, has a substantial Palestinian contingent. The regime thus has consistently sought to ensure the electoral success of Transjordanian candidates and to depoliticize the municipal councils they head.

Unlike at the parliamentary level, Jordan's municipalities continued to have elections throughout martial law (Ababsa 2015). However, they were held on an irregular basis and at different times—municipalities did not have their elections on the same day. Furthermore, no parties were allowed, and it was illegal for candidates to have any ideological basis to their platforms. Finally, the MoI could appoint a mayor in place of elections and commonly did so, particularly in Palestinian-dominated municipalities. Until 1989, for example, the government consistently appointed mayors and council members for Ruseifa, a Palestinian municipality close to Amman (Razzaz 1991: 206).

Following the country's political opening, the government revised the municipal election law and made several changes to it in preparation for the 1995 elections, when political parties were allowed to present candidates for the first time since 1957. Mayors and councillors were allowed to be directly elected, whereas previously only the council had been directly elected while the mayor had been indirectly elected by the elected local councils. The only exception was Amman where, as noted earlier, half of the council was to be elected and the rest, including the mayor, appointed.

However, following the strong showing of Islamists in the 1999 municipal elections, the government changed the electoral system again. The new law in preparation for the 2001 municipal elections mimicked the electoral procedures of Amman and applied it to all municipalities. The 2001 elections saw the mayors and half of all the municipal councils appointed by the central government while the voting public elected only half of the municipal council (Ababsa 2015). The government justified the loss of autonomy by arguing that it ensured that qualified people are in charge of municipal affairs (and, indeed, municipal engineers and planners echoed the need for competent personnel and not just representatives of circumscribed tribal interests to sit on municipal councils). However, the changes "were also especially motivated by the concern of the Government of keeping the political scene under control, particularly in a context marked by an upraise [sic] in the popularity of the Islamic party which gained control of several municipalities during the last local elections. It was also a question of keeping a certain 'balance' threatened in certain cities by the demographic weight and political growth of the populations of Palestinian origin" (World Bank 2005b: 7).

In July 2007, under the pressure of much public outcry against the electoral law (supported by a General Accounting Bureau report stating that the appointment of mayors and councilpersons had not improved the financial situation of the municipalities) and amid popular protests against the improper disposal of public land to international investors in Amman, the government reverted the municipal electoral law to the previous system (Ababsa 2015).[35] However, the redemocratization of the law came hand-in-hand with more overt and systematic attempts to manipulate the election outcomes.[36] The 2007 elections were marked by vote buying, ballot stuffing, and the transfer of voter registrations from one district to another. The authorities were accused of using army personnel to weigh the electoral odds of pro-government candidates by busing plainclothes soldiers from polling station to polling station (in 2007, military voting was allowed for the first time). Calling foul play, the IAF withdrew its candidates from the election at the last moment; for similar reasons, it boycotted the 2013 municipal elections.[37] As expected, tribal independents won overwhelmingly in both elections.

The "concern for political and demographic 'balance' . . . [also] underlies the principle of 'management' based on the territorial delimitation of municipalities and the amendment of the Law which authorizes the Government to subdivide the communal territories in zones and to determine which for each one of them the number of councilors to elect" (World Bank 2005b: 7). Indeed, Hourani et al. (2010: 41) found no uniform or proclaimed standards by which the electoral districts are determined—either with respect to the number of inhabitants or the number of representatives for each district. This results in huge discrepancies in the number of electoral districts and the distribution of seats. Their conclusion was that boundary delimitation is subject to various random standards: the number of inhabitants; the administrative divisions adopted by central government; the rural versus urban nature of the area; the demographic nature; and tribal distribution.

If we look at the four cases Hourani et al. study, this last criteria, tribal distribution—or, more accurately, the distribution of Transjordanians and Palestinians—appears to weigh heavily. In Rusaifa, Greater Ma'an, Greater al-Mafraq, and Greater Jerash, they found that while Ma'an, al-Mafraq, and Jerash have approximately the same population (ranging from about 40,000 to 60,000), Rusaifa has a significantly larger population. It is a Palestinian-dominated municipality with a population of approximately 280,000. Yet if we look at electoral districts, we find that Rusaifa has five districts and a total of fourteen seats, Greater Ma'an has one district but twelve seats, Greater al-Mafraq has five districts and twelve seats, and Greater Jerash has three districts and ten seats.[38] Thus the smallest municipality—the Transjordanian-dominated Greater al-Mafraq—elects the same number of councillors as the largest municipality, Palestinian-dominated Rusaifa, despite that the population of Rusaifa is more than four times greater. As chapter 4 details, in Jordan's patronage- and wasta-based system, the number of elected representatives determines how many people (and which people) get services.

Municipal Funding

The regime's political objectives are perhaps most clearly displayed in the amount and direction of municipal funding. In terms of public spending, the 2010 budget for all governorates represented approximately 34 percent of total spending, much of which is devoted to security measures. The municipal budget, on the other hand, accounted for less than 3 percent of the total (European Union n.d.: 13). While the municipal slice has increased slightly in the last few years, it remains well below the 25–30 percent of many other developing countries. Jordan's municipal governments continue to be responsible for one of the lowest shares of total government expenditures in the world—a clear sign, several sources note, of the high degree of the country's centralization (World Bank 1995). There also is a significant difference between expenditures on Amman and those on all other municipalities. GAM's share of total expenditures was 88.79 million JD in 2003. This amounted to 1.27 percent of the GDP, approximately 47.32 JD per capita (World Bank 2005b: 17). At the same time, the total expenditures on all other municipalities combined amounted to 85.69 million JD—2.56 percent of total public expenditures and only 1.23 percent of GDP. The total spent on all municipalities, with the exclusion of GAM, amounted to only 23.81 million JD, significantly less than what was being spent on GAM alone (17). Finally, there are significant differences between municipalities, including between the administrative centers of governorate municipalities. We see a deliberate bias toward municipalities dominated by Transjordanians, a select few in particular, and largely against those municipalities with large Palestinian populations.

As Ababsa (2015) delineates, municipalities have three income sources. The largest, accounting for 57 percent of their revenue (2004), is state transfers based on a tax of 8 percent on refined petroleum products and 40 percent on the sale of vehicles and traffic violations. The second is derived from a variety of property taxes, construction permits, and commercial leases. The third is the Cities and Villages Development Bank (CVDB), a governmental bank created in 1985 and administrated by the MoMA. Municipalities may borrow money from the CVDB. These loans are calculated (theoretically) according to the size of the municipalities, their administrative rank, and their income-generation contribution. Municipalities also receive various contribution and grants from a variety of public and, sometimes, private sources.

A close look at the fuel tax transfer between 1995 and 2000 reveals that the distribution is not related to any formula regarding size or population. In theory, the transfer formula favors small municipalities with a population of fewer than 20,000 inhabitants (World Bank 2005b: 28). In practice, however, the World Bank found that the transfers go to the municipalities that house the administrative centers of the governorates. Al-Karak had a transfer amount three times higher than what its shares should be. Jerash and al-Mafraq had transfers up to five and six times higher than the maximum number of shares they should have received. Madaba's transfers were approximately two times what it should have received (28). Furthermore, there is a clear disparity between governorates with the municipalities in the governorates of al-Mafraq and al-Karak—both of which are dominated by Transjordanians—receiving six times the share of al-Zarqa' and Irbid—both of which have large Palestinian populations (28). After 2001, with the amalgamation of municipalities (see below and chapter 4), lip service to the distribution formula was abandoned entirely, and it became even more evident that certain municipalities and governorates are favored at the expense of others (29).

Rather than being guided by poverty or unemployment rates, the transfers reinforce the existing socioeconomic inequality. As pointed out by a World Bank (2005b: 31) study, the gap between al-Zarqa' and al-Karak constitutes the most significant example. While the governorate of al-Zarqa' is characterized by one of the highest rates of poverty (22 percent) and by the lowest level of real consumption per capita in Jordan, it also is the most underprivileged in terms of the distribution of governmental transfers. Al-Karak, which is the most favored by the distribution system, has one the lowest rates of poverty (12.2 percent) in the kingdom and the highest level of real consumption per capita outside of Amman. Yet, having stated this, these numbers "fluctuate wildly," so much so that the World Bank describes the government allocation of resources to municipalities as "as much unstable, unforeseen and chaotic as it is uneven and inequitable" (32–33). Keep in mind that the fuel tax transfer is the most important source of income for municipalities.

If we look at property taxes as an example of the second category of revenues we see a similar picture (World Bank 2005b: 20–21). Technically, property tax (a land and building tax) is not a transfer, it is a local tax. However, with the exception of Amman, Irbid, and al-Zarqa', which collect their own taxes, the tax on property is collected by the central government and transferred back to the municipalities after a deduction of approximately 10 percent for overhead (20). The tax rate is determined and fixed in Amman based on a formula that theoretically is consistent throughout the country. Leaving aside the issues of collection, in particular the role that favoritism and clientelism play in the undervaluation or reduction of the amount of tax to be paid, there is a strong interannual variation of the total amount and of the per capita amount of this tax (22). The World Bank report notes, with the exception of those municipalities that collect their own local taxes, "an astonishing and almost chaotic variation" (22) in the tax on property recorded from one year to another. It also details the significant discrepancy between municipalities. While the World Bank report stops shy of stating that the government uses some sort of distributive policy that is influenced by political considerations, it is clear that the property tax "transfer" reflects the same trends as the fuel tax transfer (23).

The same bias can be said to occur in terms of grants and contributions—overwhelmingly from the public sector but occasionally from the private sector—that municipalities receive (World Bank 2005b: 68). Grants and contribution constitute an important part of the total revenues of the municipalities of the administrative centers of the governorates. Despite that grants and contributions are transferred in an "informal way," and that their distribution is not the result of centralized decision (but rather the result of various initiatives and requests), the World Bank found a strong correlation between fuel tax transfers and grants to municipalities. Here also the governmental transfers of funds to the municipalities reveal an evident favoritism of Transjordanian-dominated municipalities. As the World Bank report scathingly stated, the distribution of rents was not based on any formal and explicit rule but follows "'institutional clientelism' that is based on an unequal distribution of 'social and institutional capital' of mayors and cities, that is to say of their networks of influence and support in the spheres of the administration and the central authority" (71).

Examining an eight-year period of grant and contributions transfers (1995–2003), the report found that 27 percent of total grants and contributions went to al-Karak (World Bank 2005b: 69). In fact, the difference between al-Karak and the other administrative centers of governorates is such that that World Bank found it "difficult to represent them all within the same frame or to use the same scale for their graphic representation!" (69). The transfers to the other municipalities pale in comparison. The municipalities that are in a relatively favored position are Ajloun, Salt, Jerash, and al-Tafilah. At the lowest end of the scale are al-Zarqa' and Irbid. While al-Karak received a total of 78 JD in grants and contributions per person, al-Zarqa' and Irbid received grants and contributions amounting to 4.4 and 3.8 JD, respectively, for the same eight-year period (70).

The greatest expenditures on municipalities go, of course, to GAM, which, for reasons already noted, is not included in the transfers discussed above. GAM is the capital and Jordan's center of finance and investment, and it is home to just shy of 50 percent of the country's inhabitants. Yet it is important to note that GAM's budget is not spread evenly within its borders. There is clearly an East and a West Amman, with a growing disparity between the two (Ababsa 2011: 207; Alfdeilat 2014). For obvious political reasons, statistics only differentiate Jordanians from foreigners and not between citizens (Ababsa 2011: 212); however, East Amman comprises the informal housing communities developed near the Palestinian camps of Wahdat and Jabal Hussein (207). East Amman is where GAM's poor live and, as noted above, where the majority Jordan's poor—along with the Palestinian-dominated municipalities of Russeifa and al-Zarqa'—are located (225). The two Ammans "reflect types of activity, degrees of citizenship (between Transjordanians, Jordanians of Palestinians origin who receive services and aid from [the United Nations Relief and Works Agency] and refugees holding only travel documents)" (207). As numerous studies make clear, it is West Amman that has overwhelmingly benefited from GAM's massive development projects of the last few years, not the poor, mostly Palestinian, residents of East Amman.

Wasta and Jordan's Municipal Crisis

The regime's attempts to balance the regional and ethnic disparities between urban, Palestinian and rural, Transjordanian governorates and municipalities while at the same time controlling the political expression of Palestinians, and particularly the IAF, is reflected in the country's territorial units, responsibilities, electoral laws, and municipal taxation and funding. Yet despite the regime's efforts to ensure the economic viability of rural municipalities, centralization and its privileging of Transjordanians resulted in a municipal crisis—most particularly in the Transjordanian-dominated municipalities—that became abundantly evident in the 1990s. Service delivery in Jordan's municipalities is inadequate, uneven, and unfair—with significant discrepancies both between and within municipalities according to ethnicity, tribe, and even clan. Beyond the insufficient and unequal distribution of funds, these inequalities and ultimately the country's municipal crisis can be attributed to the system of wasta that has developed both as a result of the centralization of political power and the 1993 electoral law. The 1993 law not only affected who won seats in parliament—tribal independents and tribally based parties loyal to the regime—but the nature of political competition. By stacking the deck in favor of pro-regime tribal candidates, the 1993 law revitalized tribalism with voting and parliament revolving around tribally based patronage and not policy; candidates tend to be more successful when they eschew ideology and policies (see Jaber 1998). Candidates thus run on the basis of tribal support and their ability to distribute state resources to their constituents, and voters elect those they feel can best deliver jobs, services, and resources: tribal candidates with good wasta. MPs thus have created dense networks of wasta with ministers, public sector officials, business leaders, and the like in order to be able to deliver on their campaign promises. With decisions regarding municipal service delivery largely made in Amman, mayors also are entangled in the networks of wasta that emanate from the capital. They use wasta to secure services, employment, and resources; importantly, these services are commonly only provided to those who voted for them—members of their tribe or clan; those who did not vote for them receive their services later, or sometimes not at all. Wasta not only exacerbates the inequality of service distribution but, in many cases, contributes to municipal bankruptcy.

As discussed above, the 1993 law weakened Jordan's already weak political parties, suffering from a lack of institutionalization as well as agendas, programs, and plans. While the nationalist and leftist parties such as the Ba'ath Party and the Communist Party had been able mobilize the streets in large numbers in the 1950s, martial law and other repressive measures aimed at curbing their popularity and influence have had their effect. With political liberalization, these parties continued to struggle as the IAF gained in prominence; no doubt partially due to the MB's place of privilege under martial law. Consequently, with the exception of the IAF, by 2005, Jordan's parties were small and weak, suffering from internal divisions born of personalistic or ideological clashes and/or weak and divided leaderships that often led to their ultimately splintering.[39] Just as importantly, the so-called ideological labels of parties were relatively meaningless and the majority of parties did not have specific platforms.

The impact of the electoral law was immediately apparent in the 1993 elections. Only 18 percent of the 534 candidates were affiliated with a political party, and only 11 percent explicitly so (Lucas 2005: 58); candidates running on party labels won only 38.75 percent of the seats. This trend did not improve over the following years (Lust-Okar 2006: 461).[40] In 2003, political parties were still only winning 30 percent of the seats, or thirty-three seats in an enlarged house. However, of those thirty-three seats, eleven were won by the National Constitutional Party, a pro-regime, tribally based party (Hourani, Abu Rumman, and Kamel 2004: 115).[41] As Droz-Vincent (2011: 120) reports, even those candidates who claim to be independent of family or tribal connections at the very minimum use their kinship ties as sources of support, or they at least exploit the discursive theme of kinship and tribalism. Little has changed with successive reforms of the elections laws (see below).

Jordan's MPs thus run predominantly as independents, based on their tribal ties and, importantly, their ability to deliver goods and services. In response to the 1993 law, tribes or clans put forward candidates who had the best abilities to access resources from the executive authorities. Rather than policy, Jordan's parliamentarians are focused on service delivery—so much so that a Friedrich-Ebert-Stiftung report questions whether Jordan's parliament can be considered a parliament or a municipal council (Hussainy 2014: 6). The report (6) quotes the results of an Identity Center survey according to which 34 percent of voters cast their votes for candidates capable of providing services. Parliamentarians thus are not engaged in their assigned tasks: legislation, oversight, and representation. This "lopsided" system has its consequences, one of which is the reinforcement of favoritism and nepotism. As the study (7) states: "Understandably, the candidate or the deputy would be careful to offer the service to that social group, which he or she deems a source of potential votes, to the detriment of other groups in the electoral district . . . creat[ing] more sensitivities and tension among the different groups."

As I discuss in greater detail in chapter 4, MPs create and nurture ties of wasta in order to provide jobs, services, and resources to their tribes and to secure their votes. Once elected, they continue to develop and foster these ties of wasta to fulfill their constituents' demands. MPs create large networks of wasta with ministers—who are appointed in Jordan and most commonly of Transjordanian descent—and other public and private figures who have resources and their own wasta in order to get roads paved, establish hospitals, or provide university scholarships or jobs in the municipalities within their districts. They are, in other words, reliant on a system in which central and not local powers make the decisions. Centralization thus pits MPs in competition with municipal mayors for the distribution of services, with MPs having a significant advantage. It also means that mayors commonly use wasta to access resources in Amman and distribute them to those who voted for them. Given that voting typically falls along tribal/clan lines, services go to the tribe or clan of the mayor, but not others.[42] It is little wonder that tribal figures in rural areas often negotiate among themselves to put forward the best possible candidate (see chapter 4). National politics, tribal politics, local issues, and local demands are all intimately connected, as families or coalitions of families (tribal clans) select candidates in primaries well before the official election day and (tribal) politics is revitalized (Droz-Vincent 2011: 120).

The one-person-one-vote law was used in the 2003, 2007, and 2010 legislative elections, each time bringing predominantly pro-regime tribal candidates to power (Ryan 2004: 58).[43] Even after the law was eliminated, in 2012, political parties continued to be weak and marginalized. In preparation for the 2013 elections, the one-person-one-vote law was replaced by a mixed electoral system whereby voters cast two votes in the 2013 elections, one for a candidate in their district and one for a party list at the national level.[44] However, as an Identity Center report notes, the 2013 law simply reinforced the existing "patron-client relationship that emerged during the rentier era of Jordan's political history" (*Map of*

Political Parties n.d.: 22).[45] As the report deftly states: "No longer able to directly disseminate patronage to ensure the continued support of its key constituencies, as it did before political liberalization in the 1980s, the state now uses elections to indirectly provide benefits to its pillars of support. . . . [E]lectoral victories (and the material perks that follow them) continue to be served to state loyalists, and political parties maintain their marginal importance" (23). The same can be said of the 2016 elections law.[46]

It is within this context—of inadequate municipal funding, the regime's privileging of Transjordanian-dominated municipalities, and the tribal elite's embeddedness in dense networks of wasta—that Jordan's municipal crisis and its ongoing centralization must be understood. By 1995 the country's municipalities—numbering 259—were in an administrative and financial crisis, yet this crisis was largely overshadowed by the protests of the 1990s. Municipal problems, including the abysmal service delivery (see chapter 4), were not new but until then had repeatedly been bandaged over the years by loans to municipal government from the government's CVDB. Using these loans, the government had repeatedly forgiven municipal government debts. With the SAP, this became increasingly difficult to do, and most municipalities were massively in debt and suffering from an absence of organizational structure, a lack of planning and programming, a shortage of qualified employees, an inflation of the number of employees, and a dearth of basic equipment. (Center for Strategic Studies 2004: 17). According to one MoMA study conducted in the 1990s, the number of municipal employees (many of whom were "wasta hires," see chapter 4) at the time totaled 16,000, amounting to approximately one employee for every 368 citizens. The average municipality was spending approximately 43 percent of its expenditures on salaries (25). Consequently, the same study found that only 49 percent of municipalities were able to cover their employees' salaries and were providing basic services. Thirty-two percent could only cover a part of the salaries and were not offering any kind of services. And 19 percent could not cover any of the salaries and were not offering any kind of services (17). Thus 51 percent of municipalities were not providing any services to their populations. Furthermore, those services being provided were done so on a selective basis—to those who voted for the mayor. Most disconcertingly for the regime (yet unsurprising), the crisis was most acute in the (Transjordanian-dominated) peripheries and less so in well-funded (Palestinian-dominated) GAM.

Amalgamation

In response to the crisis, the regime implemented two changes: the creation of LDUs beginning in 1993 (see chapter 4) and a policy of municipal amalgamation. It also requested the assistance of the United Nations Development Programme (UNDP) in the formulation of a comprehensive report for administrative decentralization.[47] The regime chose to shelve decentralization in preference for the amendments to the municipal code and amalgamation—in other words, greater centralization. Yet amalgamation did little to improve the municipal crisis.

The government presented a draft law for amalgamation to parliament in 1993 and ratified it in 1994; the amalgamation, or "fusion" of municipalities, occurred over a two-month period in 2001. Amalgamation was seen as an important step in raising the level of capabilities of the municipalities—larger municipalities would presumably be more efficient in providing for the needs of their constituents. The large number of relatively small municipalities was directly related to the tribally based system of patronage and wasta. Between 1979 and 1989, the number of municipalities had nearly doubled, from 90 to 173; it then jumped again to 214 in 1994 (World Bank 1995). During this time, many village councils (a "village" had a population of under 2,500, but this administrative category was eliminated in 2001 as part of the amalgamation effort) applied to become municipalities and thereby receive a larger portion of the centrally shared taxes and the right to have an elected, as opposed to an appointed, council. One of the stipulations, according to the 1955 Law of Municipalities, was that a municipality have a minimum of 2,000 inhabitants. Yet the World Bank (ibid.) notes that a significant number of municipalities were found to have populations of under 3,000, and some were as small as 417 inhabitants! While the World Bank study draws no conclusions from these numbers, the data strongly indicate political interference (cabinet makes the final decision regarding the designation of a municipality) to please individual clans by granting them their own municipality. With each clan having its own mayor, clans would have more access to wasta, and therefore to services, employment, and resources.[48]

In 2001, amalgamation reduced the number of municipalities from 328 to 99, and then to 93. Municipalities were amalgamated based on their proximity and their similarity to each other, with the end goals being elimination of the duplication of services, cost savings, and, to a much lesser extent, strengthening municipal voices (assuming that larger municipalities would carry more weight). Cost, however, was the most important factor in the decision to amalgamate (Fox and Gurley 2006: 6). Technical managers (usually engineers) also were appointed by the central authority to the municipal governments, usually to head the newly created LDUs or some form of investment committee.

Yet amalgamation produced mixed results at best. With fewer mayors, and consequently fewer tribes or clans with access to wasta, amalgamation simply increased the competition between tribes or clans for mayoral positions. In many municipalities, amalgamation worsened inter- and intra-municipal inequality (see chapter 4). By 2005, with the promulgation of the National Agenda, it was clear that increased centralization in the form of amalgamation was not the solution for the problems facing municipalities.

Jordan's So-Called Decentralization

Driven first and foremost by the country's economic crisis, and under increasing pressure to offer political reform, the king announced the National Agenda in 2005. Several proposals for decentralization were put forward that were then either withdrawn or postponed. Each shared similar features—that limited powers be devolved to the governorate level and that the central authorities retain the ability to appoint all or a portion of any new councils at the governorate level. The regime sought not only to protect the powers (and wasta) of the tribal elite but also to ensure that no formula would allow the Islamists to gain power at the municipal level; this meant that any decentralization would be solely at the governorate level and that municipalities would not only lose powers but come under the increasing control of appointed executive directors.

Following his 2005 speech, the king appointed a Royal Commission of the Regions in order to turn his speech into action. The commission, seemingly in order to assuage Transjordanian concerns over any potential loss of power that decentralization could entail, had a strong Transjordanian flavor—of the twelve members on the committee, the majority were conservative-minded old guards, and only two were of Palestinian origin (Wikileaks 2005). The "regions" plan that eventually emerged combined the existing twelve governorates into three "development areas," or regions

(North, Center, and South), each of which would have its own capital and elected assembly, the purpose of which would be to manage services and to develop policies to attract business (Ababsa 2015).[49]

The plan was met with fierce criticism from government circles, political parties, and the media. Most importantly, the plan triggered many of the same debates and rifts as in the 1990s. With few details of the plan provided, both Transjordanians and Palestinians feared the possibility that the three regions would be joined by a fourth region: the West Bank.[50] Transjordanians foresaw a possible implementation of the "Jordan Option"— often touted by Israel's right wing—whereby a future Palestinian state would be part of a confederation with Jordan. Palestinians were angered by the possibility that the regions plan would potentially deprive them of a viable and independent state. Transjordanians feared possible changes to the electoral law in light of any regional elections; this, they worried, could allow urban Palestinian Jordanians to exert greater influence than their more rural Transjordanian counterparts (*Policy Paper* n.d.). Just as importantly, Transjordanians objected to the location of the capitals of the regions—which tribes would benefit from having a regional capital city and all the resources (and attendant wasta) that customarily are accrued to a capital city and which would be, in comparison, discriminated against.

Jordan's political (tribal) elite furthermore criticized the plan's potential to transfer primary responsibility for many areas of planning, spending, and service delivery from Amman to the regions.[51] They worried the plan "could translate into a huge shift of influence over jobs and money from politicians and bureaucrats in the capital to local officials in the provinces" (Satloff 2005).[52] Indeed, the plan threatened to change not only the balance between Transjordanians and Palestinians but also the lopsided nature of the competition between MPs and mayors. It would undermine the very system of wasta the tribal elite rely on.

Facing intense resistance the relatively vague regions plan effectively disappeared.[53] Yet, as Satloff (2005) observes, having promised real change, the regime's credibility was now at stake. Abdullah's six years on the throne had been marked by dozens of royal decrees but little real reform or parliamentary involvement (ibid.).[54] The regime had justified the latter as a response to "the barrenness of parliamentary life, in which ideological parties are weak, personality cliques are powerful, and a blocking coalition of Islamists and tribal conservatives regularly found common ground in opposing some of the government's more progressive reforms" (ibid.).

Indeed, in presenting the decentralization initiative, the king claimed to hope that it would improve the work and quality of the national parliament by removing parliamentarians' responsibilities to manage local constituents' needs and allow truly national parties to flourish. Yet while the king was under pressure to do more than merely reshuffle the cabinet, the palace would be unlikely to press forward with a plan that could turn its most loyal supporters into aggrieved critics (ibid.). Nor would it pass a law that would enable the Islamists to dominate power.

At the behest of the king, the government reexamined the 2005 plan in 2007 and 2008.[55] In 2009, the minister of planning created an Inter-Ministerial Committee on Decentralization with support from the UNDP. While the committee's goal was to give mayors greater opportunities to express their respective communities' needs and visions by increasing their engagement within the existing centralized system (thus incorporating them upward, as opposed to decentralizing competencies downward), this strategy was considered too risky for the (Transjordanian-dominated) central government: "in order to control the tribes and to prevent Islamists from assuming a powerful base in Municipalities, reform was proposed only at the Governorate level" (Hallaj et al. 2015). In 2009, the PM created the Technical Working Group on Decentralization, the task of which was to develop a Decentralization Strategic Framework (Ababsa 2015).[56] The 2010 draft plan kept Jordan's twelve governorates and was to incorporate all elected mayors in governorates into a Governorate Council of Municipalities (ibid.).[57] While not all details of the plan were made clear, municipalities would be under greater central supervision and gain no additional responsibilities.

Much like the previous plan, the 2010 plan's vagueness (albeit less so) fueled concerns of the jurisdiction, authority, and regional divisions and prevented the plan's implementation (*Policy Paper* n.d.).[58] Once again, the government failed to reach a consensus regarding concrete steps for the plan's implementation.

With the 2011 Arab Spring, decentralization was one among many reforms to be put back on the agenda. Jordan's Arab Spring began with protests against the rise of commodity prices and unemployment in the southern Transjordanian municipality of Thieban but soon spread all over the country and evolved into demands for democratic reform. Jordan's protestors did not demand a change of regime as the Tunisian and Egyptian protesters had, but they did insist on constitutional reforms limiting the king's authorities—particularly his prerogatives to appoint and dismiss the government, dissolve the parliament, and appoint deputies to the Upper House of parliament. More disconcerting for the regime was that, as in the 1990s, the protests received broad public support, both ethnically and geographically (Yaghi and Clark 2014: 236). Economic and political pressures to decentralize were soon exacerbated by arrival of large numbers of Syrian refugees beginning in 2011 and the economic stress their numbers put on Jordan's municipal services and resources (see Hallaj et al. 2015).[59] During the Arab Spring protests, Jordan's municipalities also erupted into protests. Led by smaller tribes and clans—those who had lost their ability to access wasta in the new and larger post-amalgamation councils—the protesters demanded better municipal services and the redrawing of municipal boundaries—the reversal of amalgamation (see chapter 4).

In 2015, Jordan passed its first comprehensive decentralization law and a new municipalities law, along with two other governance laws (Day 2015; see also "Jordanian Parliament" 2015). Unsurprisingly, the two laws do not download many powers to municipal councils and their mayors; any downloaded powers have gone to the governors and, at the municipal level, to appointed executive directors who have gained powers and responsibilities at the expense of elected mayors and councillors. The decentralization and municipalities laws established two additional elected bodies—a local council and a governorate council—the latter being elected but still led by the governor appointed by the PM. Each governorate now has an appointed governor, an appointed executive council, and an elected governorate council. The responsibilities of the governor include the execution of all general policies of the state, the supervision of development plans and services throughout the governorate, and security (the governor may also request the deployment of the armed forces). The appointed executive councils include the heads of the respective governorates' subdistricts, the general directors of ministries in the governorate, directors of development zones and industrial zones, and a maximum of three executive directors (nominated by the MoMA) from the municipalities. No elected representatives from the municipal or local councils are on the executive council.[60] Furthermore, 25 percent of the elected governorate council is appointed by the PM (upon nomination by the MoI). The regime thus retains its ability to privilege pro-regime loyalists through patronage.

Each municipality continues to be run by an elected mayor and municipal council; however, the municipal council members represent the heads of the new elected (and smaller) local councils. Local councils are made up of a head and a council; the head of the council is the one who receives the largest number of votes.[61] Municipal and local councils generally share the same authorities; however, those of the local council are weaker than those of the municipal council. Broadly speaking, the role of the local councils is to implement the decisions of the municipal council and make recommendations to the municipal council; in addition, local councils distribute licenses for activities such as owning and raising livestock. Thus, while a municipal council has the power to create gardens, yards, and parks, the local council can only recommend establishing them; and while the municipal council can establish sport clubs and cultural centers, and local council may only monitor them.

Citizens now vote for local councils that have reduced powers from the former municipal councils. Furthermore, the new municipal councils also have reduced powers. All municipalities continue to have executive directors appointed by the MoMA based on a nomination from the municipal council. While the MoMA argues that municipalities now have greater power ("Almasry" 2015), Jordan's new laws increase centralization, turning the elected council members into employees for the government appointed members. Real authority is vested in the appointed executive director, who has greater authority than the elected mayor.[62] The executive director ensures the performance of the municipality's administrative staff, prepares the agenda for council meetings, determines the annual budget and sends it to the mayor, supervises the municipal income and orders expenditures, and implements municipal council decisions. While executive directors theoretically are to represent the municipalities in the executive council at the level of the governorate, in practice there is now a clear chain of command from the appointed governor and executive council down to the elected council members of the municipalities, who in essence no longer have the power to make strategic plans ("Laws of Decentralization" 2015).[63]

With Jordan's so-called decentralization law, the regime has continued to resist downloading powers to a free election market in which Palestinians, particularly Islamists, may win. Indeed, "the extent to which the polarization between Palestinian-Jordanians and native Jordanians continues to dominate the nature of public debate and political reform" (Köprülü 2014a: 318) is clearly demonstrated by the special status still granted to GAM. The municipal council of Palestinian-dominated Amman continues to be under the authority of the PM's council and not the MoMA; the PM's council appoints its mayor and 25 percent of its council members.

Much like the Jordanian monarchy's other post-2011 reform initiatives, decentralization must be understood as one more "imitative institution" (Albrecht and Schlumberger 2004). While it may imitate decentralization by creating a new elected council at the governorate level, it effectively centralizes the powers of municipal authorities. The monarchy in Jordan has followed a path keeping the concerns of those in the central government in mind: seeking economic reform while limiting political decentralization and any loss of power and privileges to the Transjordanian elite. Thus with the powers of the Transjordanian elite protected, decentralization successfully passed in 2015. Political decentralization would have entailed not only a direct loss of power for Jordan's appointed ministers but an indirect loss of power for Jordan's (predominantly, Transjordanian) MPs who obtain their votes via wasta-secured services to their constituents. In the (unfair) competition between parliamentarians and municipal mayors and councillors in providing services, centralization benefits ministers and MPs.

Conclusion

In contrast to Morocco, Jordan's coalition strategy has entailed a tactic of centralization—one that privileges Transjordanians and prioritizes their concerns. Administratively, it has resulted in the regime's creation of unviable territories, the inadequate and unequal distribution of resources and funding, electoral laws designed to ensure Transjordanian dominance, the concentration of real decision-making powers in Amman, and the depoliticization of local councils by placing them under the authority of state-appointed managers. In an effort to rectify the imbalance in the relationship between "the geographic and political center" (the city of Amman and the political regime) and "the geographic and human peripheries (the countryside and the badia)" (Al-Shalabi and Ali 2013: 84), the regime has consistently sought to bestow patronage on the country's Transjordanian-dominated rural municipalities at the expense of its Palestinian-dominated urban municipalities; at the same time, it has justified the imposition of appointed city managers or executive directors who oversee elected mayors and councillors in terms of economic rationale and reforms. The end result has been the removal of powers from municipalities and the erosion of democracy—this includes the so-called decentralization law of 2015.

Political decentralization would not only entail the downloading of ministerial powers away from Amman to the municipalities but the unraveling of the networks of wasta that provide Transjordanians with services, goods, and employment; it would, in other words, undermine the institutional clientelism that privileges Transjordanians over Palestinians. Since Jordan's MPs run based on their tribal or clan ties, they furthermore would not be able to take advantage of any decentralized powers to municipalities. As I argue in chapter 3, without any viable institutional structure with which to open cells in a significant number of municipalities, Jordan's MPs could not garner votes outside their tribes or clans. Consequently, they would not be able to take advantage of any new municipal powers. This, too, stands in contrast to Morocco's MPs, who run on a party basis and have the institutional structure to capture local elites and their votes and absorb them into their parties in municipalities throughout the country.

Jordan's ongoing centralization and the electoral laws furthermore mean that its municipalities are embedded in and reliant on networks of wasta, according to which few mayors and councillors are elected according to merit and few "municipal" services are distributed equally to all municipal citizens. Wasta thus significantly exacerbates the biased and limited funding that municipalities receive from the center. In a context of limited economic resources, wasta pits tribes versus tribes and clans versus clans as their representatives seek to access wasta. As a consequence, municipal mayors and councillors work on behalf of those who voted for them, not others. In the long-term, as I argue in chapter 4, this is having a destabilizing effect on the regime's bedrock of support.

CHAPTER III

Decentralization, Co-optation, and Regime Legitimation in Morocco

Centralization and decentralization are both strategies designed to deal with regime maintenance and survival (Nellis quoted in Bergh 2007: 93). Although the Jordanian and the Moroccan regimes both considered decentralization as a potential means to address both economic and political grievances, only Morocco implemented a process of decentralization—albeit a controlled and limited process, and one entirely on the regime's terms. Decentralization in Morocco has been introduced in four phases: (1) from 1960, with the first municipal elections and the first Municipal Charter, to 1976 and the issuing of the second Municipal Charter; (2) from 1976 to 2002, when the third Municipal Charter was issued; (3) from 2002 to 2009 and the issuing of the fourth Municipal Charter; and (4) from 2009 to the present. Each new charter devolved slightly greater executive powers to the municipal councils.[1] Furthermore, the 2002 and 2009 charters increasingly reflected the monarchy's proclaimed focus on good governance and on consulting civil society actors in local development. The 1976 charter expanded municipal budgets and granted municipal *présidents* (mayors are referred to as presidents rather than *maires* in Moroccan French) greater responsibilities vis-à-vis the budget and the administration. The 2002 charter further enlarged the president's sphere of control and the provision of most services under the purview of municipal councils. Municipal councils also were charged with promoting the creation of civil society organizations (CSOs) to encourage local development.

This emphasis on local development was then enshrined in the 2009 charter, which requires all municipalities to establish consultative councils made up of members of local associations and civil society and, based on their feedback, to create a *plan communal de développement* (PCD, local development plan).

In order to understand why one monarchy chose centralization and the other decentralization, Morocco's charters must be placed within the context of the regime's strategy—initiated in 1972—of expanding its coalition by integrating and co-opting the opposition (as discussed in chapter 1). Each charter was a means by which the regime sought to bring political and social elites into the political system, to bolster its legitimacy by portraying itself as a political reformer, and, as discussed in chapter 5, to effectively place the onus of the ongoing economic crises on the so-called empowered elected municipal councillors. Whereas the 1976 charter was promulgated with an eye toward seducing the opposition parties into the government, the 2002 and 2009 charters sought to bring the country's growing number of civil society activists into the political system.

The charters thus indicate the monarchy's efforts at regime legitimation. Coming on the heels of two failed coups, the 1976 charter reflects the monarchy's need to expand its coalition beyond the Berber elite. Its primary purpose was to entice the opposition parties to end their boycott of the political system and to participate in the 1976 municipal elections and the 1977 parliamentary elections. That the opposition parties were successfully lured by the 1976 charter had much to do with their own institutional strength. The parties saw decentralization as an opportunity to expand their bases. They were keen to take advantage of local polls and resources and, relatively speaking—certainly in comparison to Jordan's political parties—they had the institutional structure to do so. Rather than competing with presidents, mayors, or councillors for votes, as in Jordan, opposition parties at the national level were able to establish local branches throughout the country's municipalities and to attract the support of local elites, their resources, and their clients.

Both the 2002 and the 2009 charters reflect the monarchy's need to establish new social relations in order to legitimate its rule. By the end of the 1990s, the opposition parties had been essentially discredited. Following their entry into the political system in the 1970s, they had moved increasingly closer to the regime, largely to avoid losing any of the gains they perceived themselves as making. When the Istiqlal accepted the office of prime minister in 1997, there was little left to distinguish it from palace or administrative parties. With political parties increasingly lacking credibility or legitimacy, the monarchy reached out to civil society—activists who had gained prominence as a result of the king's good governance agenda—for a new expanded coalition. The 2009 charter can be seen, as the 1976 charter before it, as bait—this time to lure the civil society activists armed with technocratic solutions to municipalities' political problems into the political system.

Political Liberalization in the 1990s: The Palace and the Opposition Parties Get Closer

As in Jordan, following the imposition of its structural adjustment program (SAP), Morocco also witnessed a degree of political liberalization in the late 1980s and the 1990s. Morocco's political opening—including freedoms of expression and association—was driven by a variety of socioeconomic changes, only some of which were related to the economic restructuring as a result of the SAP (Denoeux and Maghraoui 1998: 76). The most important of these changes was the country's rapid urbanization and the consequent rise of an educated urban middle class.[2] As this group became an important socioeconomic player, the monarchy, to ensure some form of attachment to these new and important social forces, had to seek out new social relations (Layachi 1998b: 27). The 1990s consequently saw an increase in political liberties, but with the intent of integrating these new social forces and co-opting them into the regime. Morocco's political liberalization thus is more accurately labeled co-optation under the guise of political liberalization and democratization. The co-optive nature of Morocco's political liberalization was clearly reflected in the monarchy's overtures to the opposition parties in the form of *alternance* (the "rotation" of prime ministers with the opposition parties being allowed to head the ruling coalitions in government and hold the position of prime minister for the first time). That the monarchy reached out to the opposition parties, and that the latter accepted their overtures, was less a sign of the country's growing democratization process than a continuation of the process of co-optation begun in the 1970s. Indeed, throughout the 1980s and 1990s, the opposition parties moved closer and closer to the regime—both as a result of the expanded coalition and, just as importantly, as a consequence of what Lust-Okar (2004, 2005) calls the "divided structure of contestation" (see below) that the regime simultaneously put into place. As she persuasively argues, the divided structure of contestation created a dynamic by which the opposition parties were increasingly less willing to be "oppositional," quite simply for fear of being excluded from the political system, or even from all political activities. The parties' eventual acceptance of alternance was a final blow, rendering any distinction between palace or administrative parties and opposition parties essentially meaningless.

Following the economic crisis of the 1980s, King Hassan II began to accommodate some of the more pressing political demands being made on the regime (Denoeux and Maghraoui 1998: 69). To be sure, Hassan introduced limited change in very specific areas rather than a sustained process of democratic transformation (Ottaway and Riley 2006: 3). However, a variety of reforms were made, including greater respect for human rights, a limited increase in parliamentary powers, greater opportunities for political participation by parties and civil society, and some efforts at reducing corruption. The mid-1980s had witnessed the emergence of publications demanding that the largely taboo issues of social and political reform be placed on the public agenda (Sater 2002b: 106–8). As part of this new (albeit incipient) intellectual climate, there had been growing criticisms of the public authorities and their role in the human rights abuses under King Hassan II.[3] Consequently, many of the king's initiatives in the 1990s were directed toward human rights. In 1990, he created the Advisory Council for Human Rights (Conseil Consultatif des Droits de l'Homme, CCDH) and, in 1993, the Ministry of Human Rights, to which one of the founding members of the Moroccan Organization for Human Rights (Organisation Marocaines des Droits Humains, OMDH), established in 1988, was appointed. The 1992 constitution further proclaimed Morocco's commitment to international human rights.

Yet it was Hassan's decision to reach out to political parties that had the greatest political significance during this period of reform. Beginning in the early 1990s, Hassan began involving all political parties more directly in the discussion of a new electoral law and of electoral procedures. He allowed moderate Islamists to run for the first time in the 1997 elections, although only under the banner of an already existing "party of the administration" (see below). Most importantly, he sought several times to reconcile with the (reestablished) Koutla al-Demouqratiyya (Democratic Bloc) and further integrate the opposition parties into political life, specifically by bringing them into the government in the form of alternance.[4]

Through official speeches, the king proposed the offer of alternance three times in the 1990s to the Koutla. That the Koutla eventually accepted it in 1997 had much to do with the fact that it had been outmaneuvered by the monarchy; equally, however, it was also due to the fact that the opposition parties were significantly less oppositional than they had been in 1977. Following the coup attempts in 1971 and 1972, and the monarchy's seeming realization that ruling alone had become both too costly in terms of popular support and too difficult, as the military proved beyond its control (Storm 2007: 36), the king expanded his strategic coalition and allowed moderate parties into the system while other parties and groups were not permitted to function. A divided "structure of contestation'" thus was put into place whereby a clear line of demarcation was drawn between an expanded, "constructive" opposition—those working within the bounds of the regime—and an opposition not permitted by the palace to operate (Lust-Okar 2005: 59). Islamist groups in particular were considered to be "excluded" and had the choice of conducting activities illegally, and suffering the consequences, or agreeing to the monarchy's rules of the game, including a political system decidedly in its favor. As a result of the divided structure of contestation, the opposition parties were caught between their fear of losing the privileges they had gained from being "included" and their fear that those groups excluded from the political system (e.g., the Islamists) could exploit social, economic, and political discontent to cause serious regime instability (5).

The opposition parties exhibited growing wariness of calling for any political actions, such as strikes, in the early and mid-1980s. A 1981 strike led by the Confédération Démocratique du Travail (CDT, Democratic Confederation of Labor) had left numerous people dead, and the police arrested thousands (Lust-Okar 2005: 130). And in January 1984, violent demonstrations and protests had broken out across the country, with 100 people killed. In contrast to the 1981 strike, the CDT had not called for the 1984 protests, nor had any other union or opposition party. Caught between their desire to hold on to some of their recent political gains (the opposition had recently joined in the government in preparation for new elections with an opposition leader assuming the portfolio of minister of state [131]) and their fear of a similar violent outcome as in 1981, the opposition parties chose to make "angry statements against the adjustment policy and denounce rising prices, but . . . not to mobilize a general strike" (131). As Lust-Okar explains, the opposition parties were in a difficult position. While they wanted to mobilize the masses against the price increases, they saw the upcoming elections as an opportunity to gain influence and did not want to lose it by confronting the king. In choosing sides between the radical (excluded) Islamist opposition that was taking advantage of the population's massive frustration and instigating the riots against the regime and the monarchy, the "included" opposition picked the latter (131).

When the palace initiated alternance as part of the political liberalization of the 1990s, the opposition parties moved even closer to the palace. The new Koutla was significantly larger than the Koutla al-Wataniyya of the 1970s (see chapter 1) and included the Istiqlal, Union Nationale des Forces Populaires (UNFP, the National Union of Popular Forces), Union Socialiste des Forces Populaires (USFP, Socialist Union of Popular Forces), the Partie du Progrès et du Socialisme (PPS, Progress and Socialism Party), Organisation de l'Action Démocratique et Populaire (OADP, Organization of Popular Democratic Action), the CDT, and the Union Générale des Travailleurs du Maroc (UGTM, General Union of Moroccan Workers) (Storm 2007: 55). Although the opposition parties had entered the government in 1977, following the 1983 municipal elections and the 1984 parliamentary elections (when it became clear that they had been outmaneuvered by the king), they refused to take part in the formation of the subsequent government.[5] By 1987, any remaining semblance of national unity came to an end as a referendum on the Sahara was in the offing and issues of institutional reform took center stage. The opposition again focused on democratization, with party members arguing "that it was necessary for the opposition parties to rehabilitate—to join forces and become a credible alternative as during the early 1970s" (45–47, 50).

When the palace first initiated alternance in response to the uncontrollable strike violence in Fez in 1990 and invited the Koutla to join the government's coalition of parties, the Koutla declined, both as a statement against the lack of acceptable political reform and out of the fear "that it was a trap that would simply co-opt and de-fang their criticism of the regime" (Willis 2012: 141). However, the palace's overtures resulted in a form of dialogue (albeit a predominantly one-sided one) between the monarchy and the Koutla. The talks with (or "to") the Koutla centered on constitutional reforms (in 1992 and in 1996), general liberties and freedoms, governmental accountability, and free and transparent elections (Zemni and Bogaert 2006: 105).

Refusing to participate in the government based on the argument that participation was pointless until the constitution was revised to limit the king's powers and grant more authority to the government and parliament (Ottaway and Riley 2006: 6), the Koutla boycotted the 1992 constitutional referendum. However, in 1996, the king ordered another constitutional revision, effectively hijacking the Koutla's demands and taking control over the reform process (Zemni and Bogaert 2006: 106). The 1996 constitutional reform reinstated the second (indirectly elected) chamber of parliament that the Koutla had been demanding, yet the prerogatives of the first (directly elected) chamber were curtailed because the reinstated second chamber was granted relatively equivalent legislative prerogatives. Despite the loss of the directly elected representatives, the opposition parties no longer had strong grounds to reject the constitution. The Koutla consequently accepted the 1996 constitution and participated in the 1997 elections.

The Koutla's participation in the 1997 elections reflected the reality that the opposition parties were no longer as oppositional as they had once been and, as Zemni and Bogaert (2006: 106) state, that they understood that the only way to really participate in the system was to acknowledge that the king held all the major political playing cards. Following the elections, for the first time, the king broke from precedent and linked his choice of prime minister to election results; a coalition government under the opposition leader Abderrahman Youssoufi, a longtime opponent of the regime (imprisoned twice and then exiled for fifteen years) and leader of the USFP, was formed (D. Maghraoui 2008: 196). Within the opposition parties, the final decision whether or not to join the government was hotly debated—whether it was a historic opportunity for the opposition or an attempt by the *makhzen* to co-opt the Koutla (Willis 2002: 6). In the end, the opposition parties chose to accept alternance. Finding itself in a paradoxical situation whereby the king was now suddenly using the same democratic rhetoric as the Koutla had been for decades, the Koutla had no choice but to join.

While alternance appeared to signal that the king was open to the democratic process, neither had royal power been limited nor had the balance between the palace and elected officials changed. More importantly, as Ottaway and Riley (2006: 6) state, the king had engineered alternance:

It was not imposed on him by an overwhelming electoral victory of the Kutla parties, which had won only 102 of 325 parliamentary seats. As a result, the Youssoufi government had little power, leaving the king once again the arbiter of Moroccan politics. The government's parliamentary majority in the lower house was small, and the indirectly elected upper house was in the hands of conservatives. The king maintained control over major policy issues, for example, imposing the neoliberal economic policies prescribed by the International Monetary Fund and the World Bank on the left-leaning USFP.

The Youssoufi government was able to achieve little while in power—what it did accomplish did not meet the expectations of the population (Storm 2007: 123). The king prevented some of the democratic reforms the government wished to see; others were not supported by elements within the fragmented parliament that proportional-representation electoral systems often create. The result was a weak and fragmented representative government that came across as a less viable option to the executive monarchy—a perception in which the king played no small role (127).

By the time of Hassan's death, any semblance of a real opposition party for all intents and purposes no longer existed. As Willis (2002: 6) states, the move by the Koutla parties

> from the ranks of the opposition into the Government . . . muddied the established Moroccan political scene that had long been characterized by governments dominated by pro-palace parties and technocrats and with an opposition composed of the Istiqlal and the leftist parties. Not only did the political terms "opposition" and "government" now become confused, but in the view of several dissident voices within the Kutla and beyond, it also confused the nature and purpose of the Kutla which had been founded on the very notion of "opposition."

What now defined opposition parties was less their ideologies than the fact that they were—and continue to be—"to varying degrees—opposed to the existing system and power structures and seek to change them" (3). Alternance had reduced any remaining differences between the palace or administrative parties and the opposition parties to insignificance.

The 1976 Charter

The discrediting of the country's political parties with alternance in the 1990s was a continuation of the regime's strategy of co-opting opposition parties that began in the 1970s—a strategy in which the 1976 charter played no small part. Tightly controlled by the central state (indeed, it is only on the premise of state control, as Landry [2008: 11–12] observes, that decentralization is initiated in authoritarian regimes), decentralization offered the monarchy a means to entice the opposition parties into participating in the political system, to integrate the Western Sahara, and to address the country's growing socioeconomic needs. The monarchy thus used the 1976 charter to tempt the opposition parties into a coalition. The parties, including the opposition parties, also had incentives for supporting decentralization in 1976. The institutional strength of the parties—certainly compared to Jordan—enabled them to establish branches in municipalities throughout the country and to take advantage of the new powers bestowed to the municipal level. In fact, they were eager to take advantage not only of the new responsibilities but, importantly, of the local patrons and their clients and resources these new responsibilities would attract. As a consequence, decentralization also served to integrate local notables into the political system.

To a significant degree, the 1976 charter was issued as bait to lure the opposition parties to end their fifteen-year boycott (see chapter 1) and run in the urban municipalities and rural communes in the 1976 local elections (A. Maghraoui 2002: 29). The Western Sahara issue had greatly increased the king's legitimacy as defender of the country's territorial integrity and symbol of its national sovereignty, and it had tilted the balance of power vis-à-vis the opposition parties in his favor. Having achieved such political unanimity, the king seized the opportunity to "normalize" political life and bring parties into the system (29). The 1976 charter was also an attempt to ensure the completion of the goals of the Green March—the undermining of support for the Polisario Front and the integration of the Western Sahara—by offering the Western Sahara some degree of local autonomy (Bergh 2007: 94). Finally, the charter offered the regime a means of addressing the economic crisis as a result of the drop in international prices for phosphate (and the regime's unwillingness to remove subsidies). Confronting a growing public debt and (despite some reforms) a growing gap between haves and have-nots in the country, decentralization was viewed as a way to address the debt by downloading responsibility for rural infrastructure and social services to municipalities (Harrigan and El-Said 2009b: 113). Hence, as Bergh (2007: 94) states, "in the governments' view, economic expansion and attempts to deal with regional disequilibria went hand in hand with the increase in participation and democratization through decentralization."

For their part, political parties were attracted to municipal politics by the expansion of municipal budgets, the enlargement of local council powers and independence, and the revision of the local election procedures to allow for greater transparency (A. Maghraoui 2002: 29). The 1976 Municipal Charter extended the powers of the municipalities by granting councils greater responsibility for the management of local affairs and transferring the power to execute council decisions from the representatives of the central authority (the *qaid*) to the elected president. Although operating with highly limited financial and human resources, municipal presidents were given responsibility for managing the budget and local administration and for overseeing the civil registry and the local police (Khattabi 1996). The president also was made the hierarchical head of the municipal staff (Bergh 2007: 94). Just as importantly, the communes were considered, for the first time, to be a framework for economic and social development (95).

That the parties saw decentralization as an opportunity (and not as a threat, as in the case of Jordan's parties and independents) had much to do with their institutional strength. As discussed in chapter 1, the main political parties in Morocco, particularly the Istiqlal, have long histories, unlike in Jordan where party organization was interrupted by approximately thirty years of martial law. In Jordan, the intellectual and ideological decline of the left both in the region and globally made it particularly hard for the country's leftist and socialist parties to reconstitute themselves after martial law was over. When they failed to gain popular support, most of them withered away; others remain so tiny they rarely won a seat in national elections (Hamid 2014: 132). Political party life in Jordan was then given another blow when the state resorted to repression in the 1990s (133), in particular with the imposition of the 1993 electoral law. The 1993 law and those electoral laws following it, as discussed in chapter 2, privileged tribal independents over ideologically based political parties. This was not the case in Morocco, where the older established parties had an uninterrupted history and large networks of associated organizations and trade unions.

The Istiqlal, for example, is associated with La Jeunesse Istiqlalienne (The Istiqlal Youth) and Femmes Istiqlalienne (Istiqlal Women). They also have organizations that tackle illiteracy, education, and human development. The Moroccan Union for Workers and the Moroccan League of Basic Education and Struggle Against Illiteracy are controlled by the Istiqlal Party (El-Maarouf, el Fahil, and Kuchejda 2009: 265). For all their weaknesses, the main parties had institutional structures—albeit top-heavy ones—with national headquarters, regional leadership, and local branches, even if the latter were passive between election periods (265). Thus, with the 1976 decentralization, the parties could effectively establish branches most anywhere in the country and bring local elites and their votes (clients) into the party. In rural municipalities, where ideologies are less important than personalities, the parties relied heavily on local elites. In the urban municipalities, where the ideological identification of the voter plays a greater role, they were less required to do so (263; M. Zaki 2010: 88). In this manner, the parties were able to establish branches and solicit elites throughout the country in 1976.[6]

Part of the reason that parties are relatively institutionalized in Morocco is due to the makhzen itself. On more than one occasion, after having weakened them, the monarchy sought to reinforce the parties institutionally in order that they remain viable and can (be co-opted to) legitimate the political system. For example, the king required all candidates for the 1984 parliamentary elections to be members of a party. If the parties were to be enlisted in the government's job of control, they had to have some institutional organization and strength (Zartman in Lust-Okar 2005: 133). More recently, the 2007 electoral law required all parties to have a statute and a program. In an effort to inject new blood into parties, the regime also stipulated that all parties include as part of their statutes the proportion of women and youth to be involved in the governing body of their party. It also has attempted to prevent the phenomenon of *transhumance* or "grazing" (as in the grazing of sheep), a term used in Morocco to describe how politicians switch from one party to another to "graze" for opportunities to access patronage (see below) (Buehler 2013a: 144).

Decentralization thus provided the institutional means to integrate new urban and rural notables into the makhzenian system (Abouhani 2006b: 64). With the 1976 charter, local elites gained access to decision-making bodies that could directly affect their interests. (Until this point, the appointed representative of the central authority of the qaid held all executive powers while the elected committee merely had a consultative role.) Those elites consequently flocked to the various parties (see chapter 5). Through patron-clientelism, the parties co-opted notables and leaders from the local area into their respective parties "in the expectation that these figures [would] be able to 'deliver' the support and votes of their local area or community" (Willis 2002: 14). When the Istiqlal and USFP entered municipal politics in 1976 and established local branches for the first time in many municipalities, both parties had to enlist local candidates—often landowning notables (see chapter 5)—who had no commitment to either party. As a consequence, many of these notables were willing to change affiliations either as a result of administrative pressure or because it suited their interests. Thus while the (former) opposition parties won the majority of seats in several municipalities in 1976, they soon were paralyzed by transhumance and by the corruption scandals that plagued many municipalities as a result of the immense wealth now at stake in municipal politics (A. Maghraoui 2002: 29).

In fact, it can be argued that this was part of the makhzen's strategy in granting municipalities greater powers in 1976—knowing the effects of transhumance—to weaken the political opposition (A. Maghraoui 2002: 29). Since independence, the monarchy had used arbitrary political appointments, the use of gift exchange, personal favors, family ties, and other forms of patronage to integrate the political parties into the neo-patrimonial makhzen system.[7] It was a system, as Liddell (2010: 317) explains, that saw political elites constantly at the mercy of the palace's whims, rewarded with government spoils when in power and cultivating future alliances to seek a return to favor when forcibly or arbitrarily distanced from the palace. Patron-client relations thus became ingrained as a modus operandi for political elites with patron-client networks permeating the political parties. This soon came to be reflected in increasing transhumance, which continues today: politicians leave one party for another perceived to be closer to the makhzen, and political parties seek to co-opt influential persons who can attract votes to the party list (via name recognition, tribal affiliation, or vote buying) (Buehler 2013a: 144). Within this context, it was not surprising that, in 1976, local notables would use the opportunities and resources granted by the charter to the municipalities in order to enhance and enlarge their patron-client networks. Following the 1976 elections, these notables took over the local branches of the opposition parties and rose through the party ranks. They soon dominated the national congresses of the so-called opposition parties where they played an important role in curbing the parties' former criticisms of the palace—the ultimate patron (Monjib 2014: 2–3).[8]

By the end of the 1990s, most political parties, including opposition parties, were "little more than large-scale interlinking patron-client networks" (Willis 2002: 14) that privileged self-interest over platforms or programs. Despite the threat privatization had posed to the monarchy's ability to employ economic resources in order to maintain its clientelistic networks, its facility to draw on rents and use patronage to cement its rule had remained largely unaffected (Denoeux and Maghraoui 1998: 77; A. Maghraoui 2012: 60–62). While there had been a redeployment of the state with privatization (Guazzone and Pioppi 2009b: 6), the state had not been undermined as the ultimate source of rent. Indeed, by acquiring the newly privatized state-owned companies, the king had become the premier private entrepreneur in Morocco, gaining access to "a new flow of resources that allowed [the monarchy] to maintain its large network of patronage" (Willis 2012: 245). In 1980, the royal palace bought a substantial interest in Omnium Nord-African (ONA), a major conglomeration. ONA then acquired newly privatized state-owned companies and assets to become the largest "private" company in the country (245). Via ONA, the regime was able to successfully penetrate and control the expanding private sector. Thus, as the state withdrew, the makhzen moved in.

Regime domination of the economy was further reinforced by the simple fact that the bidding and awarding of contracts for the partial privatization (public-private partnerships, PPPs) of public companies lacked transparency. The *walis* (regional governors) determined who received contracts (Bogaert 2011: 78). Yet the walis were appointed by the Ministry of the Interior (MoI) and were directly accountable to the minister, who was himself directly appointed by the king. In this way, even the new generation of entrepreneur elites that formed in response to the call to reorient the economy developed strong roots in the existing system and consequently little interest in politically challenging it (Catusse in Willis 2012: 248). As Willis notes, "whilst there has been a significant increase in the numbers of businessmen and entrepreneurs entering the Moroccan parliament since the 1990s, most have done so as members of political parties allied to the Makhzen or as independents" (248).

At the time of Hassan's death, in 1999, the monarchy thus remained fully in charge politically; meanwhile, the political parties, including the opposition parties, were increasingly perceived by the public as corrupt and incapable of bringing about a process of political liberalization. Already weakened by the preeminence of individual leaders within the parties and of patron-clientelism, alternance further weakened any ideological leanings the so-called opposition parties may have had (Willis 2002: 16). The main political parties, if not the political system itself, had lost much of their credibility with the population (D. Maghraoui 2008: 197). The new king would need a new elite to legitimate the monarchy. Toward this end, the 2002 and 2009 charters would attempt to valorize a new civil society elite and, in so doing, co-opt and depoliticize it by bringing it into the king's new expanded coalition.

The Parti de la Justice et du Développement

If Hassan's coalition strategy was to bring the included opposition closer to the monarchy, it also put pressure on the "excluded opposition" to accept the regime's rules of the game or be repressed "on the outside." Using this strategy, the regime sought to divide Islamic Youth (IY, al-Shabiba al-Islamiyya), the radical Islamist group responsible for the 1984 riots, to crush those elements that remained defiant of the monarchy, and to bring other elements into the fold. It was out of this strategy that the Parti de la Justice et du Développement (PJD, Justice and Development Party) eventually emerged. The group of Islamists who splintered from the IY and would later create the PJD renounced all violence, accepted the legitimacy of the monarchy, and began to work according to the rules of the game. Eventually, the monarchy allowed the group to run in the 1997 parliamentary elections as part of an already existing party, the Mouvement Populaire Democratique et Constitutionnel (MPDC, Popular Democratic and Constitutional Movement). Following its electoral success, Youssoufi offered the MPDC a position in the government of alternance; it declined. By refusing to become part of the government, the MPDC was able to credibly retain its title as an opposition party. It furthermore remained outside of the vast patronage networks through which the monarchy manipulated and undermined the (former) opposition parties. One year later, it renamed itself the PJD and established itself as the country's only real opposition party. As chapters 5 and 6 demonstrate, the 2002 and 2009 charters would offer a very different set of incentives to the PJD than to the other "opposition" parties. While the latter would be attracted by the opportunities to maintain and even expand their patron-client ties, the PJD would adapt its rationale for public actions and its program to the regime's good governance and decentralization efforts in order to mount successful challenges to those parties propped up by patron-clientelism.

Although officially established in 1998, the roots of the PJD go back to the 1970s. Its origins can be found in the IY, a radical clandestine group founded in 1969 by Abdelkrim Mouti, an inspector of primary education.[9] Mouti was influenced by the writing of the Egyptian radical Islamist thinker Sayyid Qutb, and he called for the liberation of Moroccan society from its state of *jahaliyya*, the ignorance of divine guidance that existed in pre-Islamic times. Mouti and his followers deemed the use of violence as legitimate in order to overturn the jahaliyya and achieve an Islamic state. Yet while the group conducted clandestine activities, it also had a legal public face—a religious and educational association that offered Islamic education and organized summer camps and public health campaigns—which allowed it to educate and recruit members (Wegner 2011: 21). However, the regime's tolerance of the group came to an end when IY members assassinated a leftist labor leader in 1975, and when the group called for a Moroccan revolution along the lines of the 1979 Iranian Revolution, and mobilized the poor in the Casablanca food riots in 1984, to name just a few examples. In accordance with the regime's divided structure of contestation, the regime officially banned the IY in 1976; Mouti was condemned in absentia to a life sentence, and the militants of the organization were persecuted (Wegner 2011: 22; Wegner and Pellicer 2009a: 160).

The banning of the IY did not bring its end, and the organization continued to operate clandestinely. Nevertheless, the strategy did seriously weaken the IY, and its members split into four factions. The largest of these, and the one to which the majority of members eventually belonged, was the Islamic Group (IG, al-Jama'a al-Islamiyya) (Wegner 2011: 23). While this faction remained originally loyal to Mouti (who maintained his control over the group and its organizational structure from exile), it formally broke away from him in 1982 when Mouti became increasingly authoritarian and radical. In the context of the violent strikes of the early 1980s, the IG was born; among its members was Abdelilah Benkirane, the current leader of the PJD. The IG differed from the IY in several regards, the most important being that it explicitly accepted the legitimacy of the monarchy—both politically and as the tutelary head of the state religion—and renounced the use of violence. Instead, the IG promoted Islamic values though gradualist and peaceful means (Willis 1999: 46). In other words, it sought to be "included," at least in political competition. In 1983, the IG formally applied for legal recognition as an association. The regime rejected the application; however, it tolerated—to a certain extent—the group's activities (Wegner 2011: 23). Aware of the authorities' nervousness regarding any organization laying claim to Islam (Willis 1999: 47), in 1992, under Benkirane's leadership, the IG changed its name to As-Islah was At-Tajdid (Reform and Renewal, RR) in order to eliminate any misperception about a potential claim to exclusive representation of Islam (Wegner 2011: 23). This time, the application was successful, and the RR was legally recognized.

IG leaders had decided to enter politics as early as 1988. Thus, within weeks of its name change, the RR announced the creation of a political party, the National Renewal Party (NRP, Hizb At-Tajdid) (Willis 1999: 47). The party's application for official recognition was rejected in 1989 and again in 1992. However, the regime, in the hopes of co-opting the Islamists, did allow it to field candidates in the 1997 elections under the banner of an already existing party (Wegner 2011: 26): the MPDC, an "empty shell" of a party led by Dr. Abdelkrim al-Khatib, a prominent figure of the nationalist movement (Buehler 2013a: 142; Willis 1999: 48). The RR began discussions with the MPDC in 1992–1993, and, by 1996, the RR had formally entered the MPDC's highest executive council, the General Secretariat.[10] While, as Willis (1999: 48) states, some viewed the Islamists' entry into the party as a coup (the Islamists preferred to view the relationship as a coalition), al-Khatib remained president and leader. The RR, which changed its name to the Movement for Unity and Reform (MUR, Harakat al-Tawhid wal-Islah) after merging with other groups in 1996, also continued as a separate association with social and educational activities (Willis 1999: 48).[11] It was to provide the social and religious backbone of the future PJD (see chapter 6) (A. Maghraoui 2015).

Running on a moralist platform calling for the reinforcement of religion in Morocco, the Islamists ran for elections for the first time in 1997, the parliamentary elections that would eventually see Youssoufi as prime minister. They won a small yet significant number of contests (nine seats, plus an additional five seats via bi-elections, out of a total of 325 seats) given the limited number of districts in which they ran and the discrimination they experienced at the hands of the authorities (Willis 1999: 51–53).[12] Shortly thereafter, as the number of Islamists in the MPDC increased to the point that they made up the party's governing council, the empty shell of the MPDC was abandoned. The PJD was created under the watchful eye of the state in 1998 when over 200 smaller Islamist organizations merged into the renamed MPDC (Buehler 2013a: 142; D. Maghraoui 2015).

Following its victory, Youssoufi offered the MPDC/PJD a post in the government. After significant internal debate, however, the party decided against participating, out of concern that it would be seen as aligning with parties associated with elitism and corruption and that it consequently would lose its electoral base (Willis 1999: 56–58). It opted to remain in the opposition and staked a position according to which it was supportive of the government of alternance but reserved the right to be critical (and in fact, it regularly challenged the government, particularly over issues with religious aspects; see chapter 6) (58).

Having established itself as a viable party at the national level, the PJD would run again in the 2002 parliamentary elections and turn to municipal elections for the first time in 2003. The 2003 Casablanca bombing (see below), however, would force the PJD to rethink not only its strategy but the entire rationale—heretofore based on moralistic grounds—for its platforms, policies, and political actions. The 2002 and 2009 charters would play a pivotal role in this transformation (see chapter 6).

Political Liberalization Under King Mohammed VI:
New Bottle, Old Wine

The 1976 Municipal Charter remained in place until 2002, by which point it was sorely outdated. More importantly, it was no longer useful to the regime. With few improvements to the economic situation and most political parties, if the not the political system, discredited, the regime had to seek new ways of legitimizing itself. Thus when King Mohammed VI came to power in 1999, he announced a "new concept of authority"—one requiring the involvement of citizens in the search for solutions and the execution of responsibilities (Bergh 2007: 99). He also placed fresh emphasis on economic reform and political liberalization, openly stressing the importance of human rights and freedom of speech and embracing the international development discourse of "participation," "decentralization," "good governance," and "gender equity" in his public rhetoric (Bergh 2007: 99,

2012b: 411; Berriane 2010: 89). Greater freedoms of association were introduced, and the procedures for the creation of NGOs were relaxed (Dimitrovova 2010: 525); as a result, an impressive number of NGOs were soon established (Cavatorta 2006: 216; Khrouz 2008: 43). This new direction, and particularly its embrace of the good governance agenda, intensified after the 2003 Casablanca bombings (see below). Partnering with civil society actors and including them in decision-making at all levels of government became, and remains, part of the language and official discourse of the king and highest level of state officials (A. Maghraoui 2008: 214). Yet within a relatively short period of time, it became clear that while the monarchy sought to empower civil society, it also sought to depoliticize it and harness it to its own agenda.

In 1999, Morocco entered a new "political dispensation" (Tozy 2008: 41), one that stressed new modes of governance and encouraged the rise of civil society and the left as new sources of political leadership. Mohammed VI built his political liberalization efforts on the overtures toward civil society that his father had initiated in the 1990s. CSOs had increased both in number and in diversity throughout the 1990s as the rejection of applications to register new associations grew less common. World Bank and IMF structural adjustment policies also played a role in the increase in CSOs. Morocco's SAP, as discussed in chapter 1, had weakened the ability of the Moroccan state to provide jobs and services to its population, particularly the poor. As a consequence, a growing number of CSOs—many of which were supported by international NGOs—had materialized to provide the services the state would not or could not (Dimitrovova 2010: 531; A. Maghraoui 2008: 197;).

The associations that had emerged in the 1990s were very different from their predecessors. Historically, civil society actors in Morocco have been closely associated with political parties. The nationalist movement against the French protectorate had reached deep into civil society sectors for support (Sater 2010: 22). In the decades following independence, CSOs had continued to be closely tied to the political struggle between the movement and the monarchy. In the lead-up to the popular referendum on the country's first constitution in 1962, for example, political parties had mobilized CSOs to their respective sides (Sater 2002b: 102, 104). However, CSOs' lack of autonomy from political parties and their consequent inability to articulate any independent goals or purpose had weakened their activities (106).

Frustrated by this state of affairs, CSOs, particularly women's associations, began struggling to become institutionally and financially independent from political parties (Dalmasso and Cavatorta 2010: 221).

In addition to those associations that had been affiliated with political parties, there were also associations that had been established more or less by the makhzen. These "regional associations"—purportedly set up to focus on regional economic, social, and cultural development—had been created by the intellectual bourgeoisie (often by former ministers or other members of the makhzen) at the initiative of the palace (Sater 2002b: 112). As Bergh (2007: 105) notes, their aims had been to co-opt urban elites to counterbalance the influence of political parties and to control the population due to security concerns. By the mid-1990s, the regional associations had been largely discredited and had begun to be replaced by new NGOs, formed by educated younger members of the urban middle classes disappointed with the policies of the traditional parties (Zemni and Bogaert 2006: 119).

Under Mohammed VI, there has been a proliferation of a new type of CSO—with the most prominent being women's, human rights, and Berber NGOs, as well as development NGOs (Khrouz 2008: 43). These types in particular benefited from the growing transnational discourse about democracy, human rights, and the environment (A. Maghraoui 2008: 198). The new CSOs under Mohammed VI tend to have autonomous origins, rooted in neither the political parties nor the regime, and, on the whole, they are in keeping with international rights-based discourses. The new CSOs also are politicized in the sense that civil society activists have increasingly spilled over into the political sphere (Eibl 2012: 51, 52).[13] In 2002, civil society activists intensely and successfully lobbied for a new and less restrictive law of associations. CSOs similarly entered the political sphere in the lead-up to the 2007 parliamentary elections, when the Daba Association, largely composed of leftist activists, entrepreneurs, and technocrats, began a campaign to increase voter turnout and to encourage members of the "new elite" to join political parties (52; L. Zaki 2009b: 244).

However, after only two years in power (and strikingly similar to King Abdullah II of Jordan), it was clear that King Mohammed VI "was more or less replicating his father's techniques of power brokerage" (Zemni and Bogaert 2006: 107). The foundations of formal political authority remained "fluid, ambiguous and relative" (107), and there was little accountability. Just as importantly, the regime only allowed dissent as long as it did not challenge the monarchy's legitimacy or go beyond "red lines": the king and monarchy in general, the country and territorial integrity (in other words, the country's claim to the Western Sahara), and Islam (Dimitrovova 2010: 524; A. Maghraoui 2008: 195). As Cavatorta and Dalmasso (2009: 492) state, organizations that refuse to play within the given constraints or are too politically controversial, face harassment from the authorities and are ignored or deprived of funds. Genuine opposition associations, for example, are not granted the declaration or license of *utilité publique* (public utility), this status (which the palace-"inspired" regional associations enjoy) ensures associations a degree of financial autonomy by allowing them, for example, to receive tax-deductible private donations (494; Bergh 2007: 105).

Most importantly, the monarchy began to take up and transform certain civil society ideas and proposals into concrete measures, but without giving credit to the original proponents (Bergh 2007: 110–11). Indeed, the state's capacity to participate in the construction of civil society's discourses is one of the most striking features of Morocco's civil society even today. The mushrooming of civil society activism since the ascent of Mohammed VI to the throne has included the creation of a significant number of royal committees and quasi-NGOs, all of which are based on issues initially raised by civil society; civil society is then invited to take part in these committees and organizations (A. Maghraoui 2008: 194). After adopting a dominant theme, institutions such as the Equity and Reconciliation Commission, the Royal Institute for Amazigh Culture, the Royal Commission for the Reform of the *Moudawana* (family code), the Royal Consultative Council for Saharan Affairs, the High Authority for Audiovisual Communication, and the Initiative Nationale du Développement Humain (INDH) (see below) direct resources into the dissemination of a politically neutral interpretation of that theme (Sater 2002b: 113). While appearing responsive and inclusive of civil society, the monarchy redirects civil society efforts in a less politicized and thereby more acceptable direction. The monarchy thus has become significantly more influential in defining discourses that are initiated by civil society and in determining how they are activated and implemented (102). By penetrating the discourses initiated by civil society and participating in the construction of these discourses, the regime is able to shape the extent of civil society criticism (113).

In this context, the INDH was to have the most profound impact on municipalities throughout the country. The INDH encouraged, if not inspired, the proliferation of CSOs, particularly those focused on local development. Yet successful CSOs, those that the INDH funded, were ones that offered apolitical—technocratic—solutions to the socioeconomic problems facing Morocco's municipalities. They were, in other words, focused on enhancing the effectiveness and outreach of development projects ranging from literacy to income generation to sports, not on political reform. The 2009 charter essentially aimed at luring these technocratic civil society activists into municipal politics.

Good Governance and the Initiative Nationale
du Développement Humain

The regime's efforts to harness civil society to its agenda and to depoliticize it in terms of its analysis of the nature of the causes of the country's socioeconomic problems—and, as a consequence, its discourse and activities— can be clearly seen with the INDH (launched in 2005), the king's *chantier de regne* (a reign-long effort that will define his legacy in the long term). Promoted by the king, led by the prime minister, and implemented by the MoI, and with US$1.2 billion in funding (60 percent from the Moroccan central government, 20 percent from local governments, and 20 percent from international donors, in particular the World Bank), the INDH became the government's primary program for poverty reduction following the 2003 Casablanca bombing (Harrigan and El-Said 2009b: 130).[14] The importance of the INDH and the partnership between the state and civil society that it represents cannot be understated. The INDH is the only public policy in Morocco that has its own slogan, logo, and even its own anniversary. Based on citizen participation and joint partnerships between the state, private companies, and CSOs, the INDH focuses on social services, employment creation, and programs to combat the poverty of the most vulnerable groups within society (Bergh 2012b: 411). It thus reflects the logics of two of the most dominant approaches to economic reform undertaken by Morocco. On the one hand, it follows a long historical trajectory of the monarchy providing social welfare in place of and at the expense of any potential policies or initiatives by elected party representatives. On the other hand, it follows the logic of privatization, with social welfare now privatized and depoliticized into the hands of civil society.

The 2003 Casablanca bombing had a profound effect on the monarchy, political parties, and civil society alike. (It would ultimately lead to a new charter in 2009.) With many of the twelve bombers coming from the Casablanca shantytown of Sidi Moumen—a part of the city with makeshift homes built atop a garbage dump—the bombing cemented the belief that Islamist terrorism was fueled by social injustice and poverty (El Amrani 2009: 315). The king responded by establishing the INDH. While the promotion of the local level has been a central component of reforms since the end of the 1990s, the INDH is fundamentally different from the king's earlier initiatives (see below) in terms of its structure and mandate. The INDH complements other programs dealing with poverty and social exclusion; however, it reflects international norms concerning good governance and (theoretically) supports the government's efforts at decentralization and local governance with a greater role for civil society in identifying, planning, and executing local development projects (Harrigan and El-Said 2009b: 130). The INDH thus places particular emphasis on including the public—via NGOs in conjunction with municipal representatives—in the process of decision-making (Bergh 2012b: 411; Berriane 2010: 93).

That being said, Mohammed VI's announcement of the INDH, among other programs such as Villes sans Bidonvilles (Towns Without Shantytowns), which the INDH was then to absorb as part of its mandate, must be understood as part of a historical trajectory by which the monarchy, rather than elected party representatives, grants social welfare. As a consequence, party representatives appear unwilling or unable to do so. It is part of a larger history of efforts by the monarchy to use social welfare programs to gain support at their expense. Since Morocco's independence, in 1956, social policy and social protection have been seen as the domain of the monarchy (Harrigan and El-Said 2009b: 111) with the king considered the "guarantor of social welfare and provider of services to the poor" (112). Mohammed V introduced free education and medical care as well as guaranteed employment for secondary and post-secondary graduates. Whenever social tension arose over economic decisions, such as subsidy reductions in 1981, 1984, and 1990, Hassan II would announce the reversal of government policies in order to appease the population (112). Following the unrest in 1984, for example, he announced the end of price increases for basic food, the initiation of a slum-clearance program, the building of new low-income housing units in Casablanca, and the financing of 10 million new working days (113). The social issues that arose in the 1980s and 1990s thus were the result less of a "brutal disengagement on the part of the state" than of the accentuation of the weaknesses of an already modest state social security system (Catusse 2009: 201). That Morocco's lower and middle classes were so vulnerable to the dislocations associated with the SAP was the result of a state that had been (and continues to be) particularly modest and ad hoc in terms of providing social security for its citizens (201; Harrigan and El-Said 2009b: 112–18).

The INDH continues this strategy of offering social services in the stead of, and at the expense of, elected party representatives. The state's partnership with civil society sends the message that nongovernmental actors are important and that the new structure of state power relies on a broad coalition with civil society (Sater 2002b: 115). As a consequence of the king's elevation of the status of civil society and its inclusion in institutions such as the INDH, Morocco witnessed an explosion of new CSOs. In the province of El Hajeb alone, the number of associations jumped from 450 to over 830 between 2004 and 2010 as a result of the INDH (Bono in Bergh 2012b: 414).

The INDH's focus on individual responsibility for employment and social mobility (Zemni and Bogaert 2006: 119)—as opposed to presumably relying on the state—furthermore serves to strengthen the monarchy and regime not just at the expense of other institutions but at the expense of the political. As D. Maghraoui (2008: 207) explains, "The idea of development through local civil society actors becomes consistent not only with the privatization process of solving social and economic problems, but also with the 'depoliticization' of the Moroccan political scene . . . when the monarchy stresses the discourse of privatization and good governance, it is simultaneously evoking a technical language that sees efficiency and procedural questions, not structural political issues, as the main problems that face Moroccan society."

The INDH not only renders public activities private, but it institutionalizes these private activities and regularizes them in a "mechanism of action which is alternative to that of the representative political institutions" (Catusse 2009: 207). It thus serves to marginalize political institutions and to "de-ideologize" essentially political issues (212).

The INDH demonstrates how politicization and technocratization have gone hand in hand in Morocco. Civil society activists, particularly those working in the field of socioeconomic development, have increasingly entered municipal politics, yet they largely have done so as technocrats operating within the bounds of the monarchy's depoliticized discourse and largely addressing political problems with technical solutions. As the beneficiaries of the monarch's good governance agenda, and the INDH in particular, they view the solution to the ailments affecting Morocco's municipalities as a technocratic exercise in implementing socioeconomic development projects.

The 2002 and 2009 Municipal Charters

The INDH and, to a lesser extent, the 2002 charter were two of the reasons Mohammed VI was nicknamed the "King of the Poor." The new 2002 municipal charter was to encapsulate the values of his rule: the protection of public services, local affairs, and individual and collective liberties, as well as "direct contact with the citizens," "treating their problems on the ground by associating them in the search for appropriate solution" (Bergh 2007: 99–100). The driving motivation for the 2002 charter's promulgation lay in the crisis of state legitimacy as a result of the economic dislocation and democratic deficit and in the increased international attention on Morocco (largely, but not solely, due to the "boats of death" discussed in chapter 1). In 1995, a World Bank (WB) publication highlighted the weaknesses of Morocco's administrative system (among other issues) and triggered a national debate that put decentralized administrative reform front and center on the Moroccan public agenda (Catusse with Cattedra and Idrissi-Janati 2007: 113). The WB identified poverty reduction as needing immediate attention. Morocco also needed to be—or at least perceived to be—seriously embarking on the transition toward democracy (Bergh 2007: 100). Beginning with the king's declaration to address the issues raised in the WB publication, a series of administrative reforms were put into place. Within this pressing context, reformers identified the 1976 charter as impeding councillors, particularly in the larger cities where the riots of the last two decades had occurred, from providing adequate services. International donors, including the UN Development Programme, the U.S. Agency for International Development, and the French government, were increasingly promoting good governance and decentralization, and both issues soon came to be explicitly inscribed in the country's democratization path (Bergh 2007: 114). The monarchy promoted the 2002 Municipal Charter as a first step in the devolution of powers to the municipalities; municipalities were framed as the central actor in local development. After the 2003 Casablanca bombing, the 2002 charter was revised to better address the economic problems presumed to underlie Islamist extremism and married to the king's regionalization plan. Civil society was introduced into municipal decision-making, paving the way for the country's new technocratic civil society activists to have input into municipal decisions. With the 2009 charter, the king further cemented his image as a political reformer, tying decentralization and regionalization together with development. As was the case in 1976, the 2002 and 2009 charters provided the bait for civil society to enter the political system and ultimately to depoliticize local politics.

Prior to Mohammed VI's ascension to the throne, the Moroccan government had already undertaken a major reorientation of its policies to coincide with the WB's increased emphasis on poverty and social exclusion (Catusse with Cattedra and Janati 2007: 114). Beginning in the 1990s, the WB had begun to pay increasing attention to Morocco's social welfare policies—a shift that followed its "own acknowledgement that its policies in the past had failed in respect to a reduction in income inequality and the provision of services to the poor" (Harrigan and El-Said 2009b: 125). In 1997, the government introduced the Social Priority Programme, which includes programs for electricity (PERG), water (PAGER), and rural roads (PNCRR), as well as a poor area development program (BAJI) (127). Upon coming to power, Mohammed VI established several new social-welfare bodies, such as the well-funded Mohammed V Foundation for Solidarity (1999) and the Hassan II Fund for Social and Economic Development (2000) (128).

By 2002, it had become apparent that Morocco's cities simply were not functioning and that this dysfunction was contributing to social unrest. The administrative measures the regime had undertaken in the name of security proved to be one reason services were inadequate or unavailable. In order to break up potentially explosive congregations of people (particularly in the cities), the regime had progressively divided the country into increasing numbers of municipalities. From 1976 to 2002, the number of territories, institutions, and actors progressively multiplied. This included the major cities with Casablanca, for example, being divided into twenty-nine urban municipalities (with 1,147 city councillors) by 2002 (Catusse with Cattedra and Idrissi-Janati 2007: 119). Beginning after the 1981 riots, Casablanca's administrative territories and jurisdictions were reconfigured with each subsequent crisis; Catusse counts seven different territorial configurations in Casablanca between 1977 and 2002 alone (118–19). It goes without saying that none of these reconfigurations meant a dispersal of power—power remained in the hands of the central authorities or, beginning in the 1990s, in those of the representatives of the central authorities (see below).

Dividing cities into more and more municipalities, however, soon presented serious obstacles to city management and the provision of services. Quite simply, there were too many municipalities all working in a noncollaborative fashion without an overall vision or direction (Serraj 2003). The result was that it was difficult to undertake citywide projects such as infrastructure or public transportation. These challenges were exacerbated by the privatization of services and state-run corporations and the consequent multiplication of actors in "local" service delivery (Rifi 2003). Entire jurisdictions had been transferred to international private groups (such as Lyonnaise de Eaux) that provide services (in this case, water). Elected officials at the municipal level had little to no input into the array of external services being brought to their municipalities (Saadi 2012).

Even without these important changes over time, the 1976 charter had done little to foster democracy or to improve the running of local administrations (D. Maghraoui 2002: 29). The charter was extremely contradictory, using a language that emphasized decentralization yet imposing control over many decisions and activities of the municipalities (Darif 2003). As Bergh (2007: 96) states, the municipal councils in reality "were only carefully-controlled providers of mundane services: sewers, street cleaning, garbage collection, bus stations, markets, and slaughter houses." The MoI still had substantial control over all decisions; the councillors themselves and municipal councils had little autonomy. The representatives of the central authorities had the right to annul the election of a president, to "declare resigned" council members or suspend the council, to convene an extraordinary session without consulting the president (and to set the agenda for the sessions), or to sit in on any council meeting. A president could be replaced if he refused to carry out decisions the central authorities desired. The central authority representatives also could declare any council decision null and void if it was deemed outside of the sphere of interest of a local authority (with the MoI authorities in charge of determining what was considered to be inappropriate) (95; Darif 2003).

If the 1976 charter was intended to lure opposition parties into the political system, the 2002 charter was an attempt to do the same vis-à-vis the civil society activists that had come to the fore as a result of the king's good governance agenda. The 2002 Municipal Charter was promoted as a step toward proximity, sharing authority and giving responsibility to local elected people.[15] In keeping with Mohammed's proclaimed new concept of authority, municipalities were put at the center of a vast plan for Morocco's territorial administration (Catusse with Cattedra and Idrissi-Janati 2007: 115) and were given a role in reducing poverty and exclusion. Municipal councils were offered a consultative capacity with respect to projects undertaken within the communes. More importantly, the council was to undertake community work or "local actions" (*actions de proximité*) that would mobilize the citizenry, develop a public conscience, and improve the environment, all of which was to promote the creation of local associations (Bergh 2007: 101). According to the charter, the council was also responsible for undertaking activities for awareness raising, communication, and information (101–2). Communal councils were expected in addition to enter into partnership agreements with local associations.

To increase efficiency, the 2002 charter significantly increased the walis' (regional governors') authorities. Municipal council decisions would no longer have to be approved in Rabat; rather, the wali, the representative of the MoI at the regional level, would perform that duty.[16] The charter also reinforced the power of all presidents as the executive heads of their municipalities (Catusse with Cattedra and Idrissi-Janati 2007: 123–24). Cities of more than 500,000 inhabitants (fourteen in total) were unified under the authority of one central municipal council. At the head of each of the newly fused cities, the charter established a new supra-council comprising the presidents and vice-presidents of the urban *arrondissements* (boroughs, or *da'erah* in Arabic) that made up each city. Consequently, Casablanca went from being a city with twenty-nine urban municipalities to a city of one municipality with sixteen arrondissements (each with its own council of limited jurisdiction) and a total of 131 councillors (118–19).[17] The head of the supra-council, the president of the city, was invested with more powers.

In direct response to the criticisms that councillors were incompetent or poor administrators at best and corrupt ones at the worst, the charter specified the required education level for presidents and secretaries-general (primary school education and literacy, respectively) and specified the processes for recording the minutes of all council sessions (Catusse with Cattedra and Idrissi-Janati 2007: 124). It furthermore defined the responsibilities of the elected mayors and councils, streamlined administrative and financial procedures, broadened the municipal revenue base, and introduced new cooperation mechanisms. It expanded the president's sphere of control to cover most local issues except for those dealing with public security and issues related to public liberties (which were the responsibility of the regional governor) (Bergh 2010a: 114). Finance, taxation, and municipal property; planning and land management; local public services and utilities; hygiene, sanitation, and the environment; and equipment and sociocultural activities now all fell under the purview of the municipal councils (Nachatti 2003).

The 2002 charter was not to stay in place for long. The 2003 Casablanca bombings were followed by two more attacks, in March and April 2007, when another seven suicide bombers—also predominantly from Sidi Moumen—blew themselves up in Casablanca. As a direct response to these bombings, the regime issued the 2009 charter as an attempt to quell the general discontent over the lack of improvement in governance and services and the more specific problems confronting cities with growing shanty-towns (Serrar 2008). Yet if the 2009 charter was to address the economic problems that triggered the 2003 and 2007 bombings, it also aimed at resolving the issue of the Western Sahara (El Amrani 2009: 315). As with 1976 charter, regionalization, and specifically the integration of the Western Sahara, was to go hand in hand with the increase in participation and so-called democratization through decentralization (Bergh 2007: 94).

In a 2008 speech marking the anniversary of the Green March, the king announced his regionalization plan—"a one-size-fits-all system in which all Moroccan regions would enjoy more self-government, with the Western Sahara treated like any other region" (M. Ottaway 2013: 1). As Ben-Meir (2011: 77) summarizes, the king's regionalization road map called for decentralizing authority to the people and institutions of the Western Sahara so that they could manage their own affairs while remaining under Moroccan sovereignty. Morocco's position toward resolving the territorial dispute over the Western Sahara thus was embedded within the kingdom's decentralization plan and promoted as a national regionalization plan, with the Saharan provinces among the first regions to experience the benefits of "advanced decentralization" (M. Ottaway 2013: 1).

Discussions concerning regionalization date back to 1997. Administratively, as discussed in greater detail in chapter 5, local collectivities are under the jurisdiction of the MoI and essentially consist of four types: regions (12), prefectures (13), provinces (62), and municipalities (1,503).[18] Regions are the largest administrative unit and are subdivided into prefectures and provinces (urban and rural, respectively), which are further subdivided in districts (*cercles*) and urban municipalities (221). Districts are subdivided into rural municipalities (1,282). In larger cities, as noted above, the municipalities are comprised of arrondissements. Regions were created in 1971 but were not given legal recognition as a territorial collectivities at that time; constitutional amendments in 1992 and 1996 gave them legal status (Bergh 2007: 80). In 1977, a decree assigned walis representing the central government at the regional, provincial, and prefectural levels responsibilities for coordinating and monitoring the performances of the deconcentrated services of the line ministries in order that they would ensure the coherence of different sectoral policies within the territories they oversaw (World Bank 2009: 10). Walis furthermore were given responsibility for implementing central government laws, ensuring public order and safety, and monitoring the elected municipal councils. A 1993 decree expanded walis' authorities to include the implementation of ministerial decisions in the provinces and prefectures, as well as the responsibility for public servants, including their appointment or dismissal (10).[19]

From their very inception, walis have played a key role as representatives of the monarchy in security and economic development. Any devolution of powers to the wali consequently would have little to do with democratization. In 1997, a decentralization and regionalization law was passed, officially creating today's sixteen regions (*wilaya*) with (weakly empowered) legislatures. The 1997 law designated regions as promoters of the broad-based social-economic development of the respective regions. Their socioeconomic role was strengthened in 2002 when a royal letter concerning the "decentralized management of investment" granted walis the responsibility to create regional investment centers (RICs) that centralize the services for investors, Moroccan or foreign (Catusse with Cattedra and Idrissi-Janati 2007: 126; Filali-Ansary 2009; World Bank 2009: 10–11). The history of the creation of regions parallels that of other territorial administrative units in that their growth and development was driven by political crises. Catusse notes that the king only referred to walis (regional governors) as an institution for the first time in 1981—following the urban riots, he named the wali as the governor to the prefecture of the region of Casablanca. Between 1983 and 1997, the wilaya was extended to all regions—each time triggered by political unrest. After the riots in 1990, the cities of Fès, Marrakech, and Meknès were divided into several prefectures and the wilaya charged with coordination and security.

While regions were ostensibly given legal status as local entities in 1997 in order to diminish regional economic inequalities, the true goal was political stabilization (Chahir 2003). The central authorities had no intention of ceding to demands for autonomy by ethnic and other minorities in the Sahara and elsewhere; instead, they sought to integrate these leaders and their demands. As a strategy, the decentralization and regionalization law had two components. The first was to reduce the popular frustration with the socioeconomic crisis facing the country at that time. The second was to increase the legitimacy of the monarchy by seeking new alliances and support.

The king brought regionalization, the issue of the Western Sahara, decentralization, and development all together for the first time when, in a 2006 speech, he announced the strategic need to evaluate Morocco's experience in local democracy and to give new impulse to decentralization and regionalization (Serrar 2008: 17–18). Regional reform was once again on the agenda as the king created the 2006 Advisory Committee for Saharan Affairs (M. Ottaway 2013). Although a cease-fire was negotiated in 1991, there still remains no final status agreement on the Western Sahara between the Polisario Front and the Moroccan state—despite numerous rounds of negotiations. In an effort to break the impasse, in April 2007, Morocco unilaterally submitted a proposal to the United Nations Security Council that granted a degree of autonomy to the Western Sahara. The proposal, the Initiative for Negotiating an Autonomy Statute for the Saharan Region, called for the Western Sahara to exercise control over local affairs through an elected legislature and executive authority, while the central government in Rabat retains control over foreign affairs, defense, currency, postal service, and religion (2). By 2008, the autonomy initiative, as it was known, had transformed into the one-size-fits-all plan in which the Western Sahara was treated like any other region.

Within this context, the MoI launched, for the first time, a series of workshops throughout the country's regions, headed by legal experts and involving council members and civil society representatives, on how to improve the 2002 charter. With crumbling infrastructure, collapsing buildings, and terrible roads throughout Morocco, the 2009 charter was to address the inability of municipalities, particularly in growing urban areas, to fulfill the service-provision roles granted to them under the 2002 charter by way of greater inclusion. While the workshops were aimed more as a legitimizing ritual ("Décentralisation" 2007), they contributed toward diagnosing the main problems facing the local management under the 2002 charter, namely: the overlapping and ambiguous functions and jurisdictions between levels of government; the political infighting within local governments; fiscal constraints and the lack of strategic planning; and, above all, the suffocating weight of the supervisory powers of the MoI ("Ce que l'intérieur" 2008; Chmirou 2006; Laabid 2008; see also "Bilan positif" 2005 and "Décentralisation" 2007).

Indeed, within six months of its adoption, the 2002 charter had already attracted a barrage of criticisms, with political parties and municipal presidents and councillors arguing that its shortcomings were having a negative impact on service provision (Laabi 2004). The 2002 charter had not altered the weight of the control of the central powers approvals, for an inordinate number of decisions were still required from the central authorities. Local officials consequently complained of being treated as "legal minors," and all the major political parties, including the Istiqlal and the PJD, called for a weakening in state *tutelle* (tutelage) ("Ce que l'intérieur" 2008; Filali-Ansary 2009; Sedjari 2004; see also "Consacrer" 2004). Just as importantly, much of the 2002 charter had been ambiguous in its language, leaving presidents and councils unclear of their exact prerogatives, creating confusion and granting the representatives of the central authorities extremely wide leeway to step in and exert their authority (see chapter 5) (Douichi 2005; Filali-Ansary 2009; C. Laâbi 2004).[20] Councillors argued that the prerogatives and interventions of the regional governors and the municipal presidents needed to be more clearly defined and specified; the lack of clarity was leading to the neglect of issues as they "fell between the cracks." The political parties also overwhelmingly criticized the lack of collegiality in councils. Parties and observers blamed the infighting in councils on the lack of majorities in the communal councils as a result of the electoral system (see chapter 5), leading councillors to be more concerned with political calculations regarding coalition formation and maintenance than with the quality of council management (see "Gestion communale" 2010). The PJD consequently demanded a revision in the manner in which presidents were elected. The USFP demanded the requirement of a university education for all presidents and training for all councillors on the provisions of the communal charter ("Ce que l'intérieur" 2008). Political parties argued that these would increase the professionalism of the councils and reduce corruption (Filali-Ansary 2009; Hamrouch 2008; Jaidi 2003; Khamliche 2002; Lahlou 2008a, 2008b; Nachatti 2002). Local officials also complained that the unbalanced distribution of power between the presidents and the rest of the councillors was contributing to the ongoing inability of municipal councils to accomplish anything. In many cases, presidents had refused to delegate any of the powers entrusted to them by law, essentially monopolizing all decision-making. This imbalance had further divided and weakened councils.

Prepared and presented with much fanfare, the 2009 charter delegates more decision-making responsibilities to municipalities.[21] It grants greater responsibility for slaughterhouses, bus stations, lights, roads, landfill, green space, sewage and garbage, and, most importantly, urban management to municipalities. It designates some responsibilities as requiring a posteriori approval from the representatives of the central government as opposed to a priori approval. The charter furthermore provides inter alia formal legal status to groupings of municipalities and enables them to act as special-purpose vehicles (World Bank 2009: 10).

Most importantly, the 2009 charter formally brought CSOs into municipalities' decision-making structure and recast local politics as issues of development. The 2009 charter builds on the 2002 charter by requiring all municipalities to play a role in reducing poverty and exclusion. In this regard, municipal councils are to undertake community work or "local actions" (actions de proximité) that will mobilize the citizenry, develop a public conscience, and improve the environment, all of which should promote the creation of local associations (Bergh 2007: 101). Municipalities thus are expected to financially aid local associations and to enter into partnership agreements with them—for these partnerships they commonly receive INDH grants (see chapter 5). For the first time, municipalities were furthermore charged with establishing consultative committees for "equity and equal opportunities" consisting of members of local associations and civil society. Finally, based on feedback received from the committees, municipal councils are to create local development plans (plans communal de développement, PCDs).[22]

With the 2009 charter, the monarchy thus further enlarged its position "as a central point of reference" (Sater 2002: 116). Having played a key role in the construction of civil society's discourse of political reform, the king further positioned himself as the political reformer by granting the country's new technocratic civil society activists—in keeping with the international good governance and decentralization agenda—a legislated role in municipal decision-making. At the same time, the 2009 charter did not address, or only partially addressed, the main criticisms of the 2002 charter. This was not unintentional.

Conclusion

The "varying situations," to use Nellis's phrase, that explain why Morocco has taken steps to decentralize while Jordan did not can be explained, to a large extent, by the Moroccan regime's change in coalition strategy following 1972—its decision to reduce its dependence with the Berber elite and widen its coalition—and by the ability and willingness of key players to take advantage of decentralization. Since 1972, the monarchy in Morocco has repeatedly broadened its coalition strategy by co-opting a widening circle of opposition figures and civil society actors. Decentralization reforms are a tactic or tool in these efforts, serving to present the monarch as a political reformer, forge stronger ties with important segments of society, and legitimate the regime. Central to the monarchy's success in 1976 was the fact that Morocco's opposition political parties saw decentralization as beneficial since they were able to take advantage of it by opening local branches and absorbing new elites, resources, and votes (clients). This worked to the regime's advantage in several ways. As local elites were drawn into the opposition parties by opportunities for patronage and climbed up the party ranks, they curbed their parties' criticisms of the regime. Most importantly, as discussed in depth in chapter 5, the charters maintained, if not enhanced, opportunities for patron-clientelism, thereby sustaining the makhzen's system of neopatrimonialism.

In 2002 and 2009, Morocco's new technocratic civil society activists were similarly lured to enter the political system by the prospect of better realizing their development projects offered in municipal charters. Empowered by the regime's good governance agenda and its discourse of partnering with civil society—as well as the establishment of the INDH—the 2009 charter appeared to be the embodiment of the good governance agenda and offered civil society activists the positions they had been expecting.

Yet while the 2009 charter positioned the king as a political reformer, it was less clear if political reform was the intention or the outcome of the charter. Indeed, few of the issues raised by local officials and the political parties vis-à-vis the 2002 charter were addressed in the 2009 charter. The charter remained ambiguous in its delineation of functions and jurisdictions, doing little to clarify who does what. As discussed in chapter 5, the new charter did not specify any clear or explicit mechanisms for the participation of CSOs or partnerships with the municipalities, the private sector, outside agencies, or other development actors (Tarik 2008). The inability of parties to form majorities remained a problem (Aswab 2010). Furthermore, while strengthening the role of the president, the charter did not enshrine mechanisms by which the president must delegate powers.

Municipalities thus would continue to be marked by confusion over ambiguous areas of jurisdiction and by infighting—both of which would continue to hinder their ability to provide adequate services. Yet, as I argue in chapter 5, this obstruction, too, serves to benefit the regime by justifying the need for tutelle in order to guide councillors, coordinate different entities and activities, and impose better fiscal management (Rousset 2003). Stated differently, the end result is that the authorities of the central state are required to come rescue municipalities—and thereby citizens—from their own elected officials.

CHAPTER IV

The Destabilizing Effects of Centralization

I f, as the previous chapters argue, authoritarian rulers employ both centralization and decentralization as tactics of larger coalition strategies aimed at maintaining their rule, are the tactics equally effective? Looking specifically at the issue of elite capture, this and the following chapters examine municipal politics in Jordan and Morocco, how they differ as a result of the respective two monarchy's different strategies and what these differences mean for regime stability. This chapter demonstrates that the inequality between municipalities in Jordan in terms of funding and resources discussed in chapter 2 is reproduced within its municipalities. Indeed, a closer look at Jordan's municipalities indicates that the inequality within municipalities occurs between tribes and between clans within tribes. I argue that the competition between tribes and clans for limited resources and services, many of which can only be accessed via *wasta*, is having long-term repercussions. Jordan's ongoing centralization of powers and resources is dividing and fracturing tribes, the very bedrock on which monarchical support is based.

The centralization of municipal decision-making, the inadequate funding, and the networks of wasta within which Jordan's municipal councils must operate have created a local political dynamic of intense competition for resources and services between tribes/clans and have engendered tribally based elite capture whereby mayors and councillors engage in a system of mutual exchange seeking to ensure that their tribes/clans—and only their tribes/clans—receive these resources and services. Those tribes/clans with no representation on council, particularly in rural areas, receive few to no services. At best, they receive them at a later date. Operating within a tribally based patronage system at the national level, municipal politics is similarly tribally based, to the advantage of some and the disadvantage of others.

These dynamics came to the fore with Jordan's amalgamation (see chapter 2). Amalgamation reduced the number of mayoral positions and the number of seats individual tribes/clans could realistically win on a council; it thus reduced the number of access points to wasta and thereby the number tribes/clans that could benefit from "exchanges" between councillors. As a consequence, amalgamation exacerbated not only the discrepancy between towns at the center of municipalities, which benefited from the majority of resources, and those geographically distant from the center but also the discrepancy between tribes/clans—that is, between the ever smaller number of tribes/clans that had seats on council and those that did not.

Centralization has engendered frustrations and resentment among municipal actors—including and perhaps especially pro-regime actors—not only with the shrinking access to wasta but with their dependence on wasta, donors, and royal patronage; even the most successful of municipalities are unable to accomplish the most basic of tasks without essentially asking for help. Tribes and clans see the difference within municipalities and between municipalities, with some municipalities receiving more and others less as a result of patronage and patron-clientelism. In the context of shrinking resources and few avenues for municipalities to generate their own wealth, the wasta that lies at the heart of municipal politics creates an inherently unstable situation; it fractures tribes and pits pro-regime elites against each other in an effort to access wasta at the top.

Wasta, Municipalities, and Tribalism

As discussed in chapters 1 and 2, tribal ties remain an important aspect of political life in Jordan. This is a result of monarchical strategies of legitimation and the "institutional clientelism" that has developed over time as a result of Jordanians trying to protect themselves from the hardships of life (Harrigan and El-Said 2009b: 51). Patron-clientelism, largely but not solely based on tribal ties, shapes all elections in Jordan, national and municipal. As noted, Jordanians refer to these ties as *wasta* (mediation). While historically a form of mediation according to which the mediator or wasta performer was rewarded with social prestige, today wasta is a "contract-based *wasta*" according to which votes are exchanged for favors (Cunningham and Sarayrah quoted in Harrigan and El-Said 2009b: 51). Mayors, municipal councils, and municipal employees are central to the clientelistic networks that make up national-level politics. Indeed, municipal politics is an extension of these clientelistic networks within which both MPs and mayors must be considered as points of access through which services, employment, and resources are accessed and flow. Wasta determines who—which tribe, clan, or family—does or does not receive services at the municipal level. The end result is that municipal politics is an informal system of exchange whereby votes or jobs or other favors are exchanged for services and tribalism is reinforced. The details of this exchange are commonly determined prior to elections, with electoral outcomes consequently decided before election day. Tribally accessed services, not ideology or policies, define municipal politics, as does the increasing competitiveness between tribes/clans as resources become increasingly scarce and the gap between haves and have-nots increases.

As I discuss in chapters 1 and 2, stability in the Hashemite monarchy depends on the distribution of strategic rents to Jordan's Transjordanian population in general and its tribal elite in particular in return for political support. Importantly, as Lust-Okar (2009: 8) states, because the regime relies on mediating competition over state resources for stability, it restricts access to resources and thereby reinforces the roles of societal elites who can provide points of access. As a consequence, wasta and informal institutions are vital to maneuvering in the public sphere—for finding jobs, doing business, getting permits.

Elections are the dominant mode by which patronage is distributed. Constitutionally, Jordan's parliament is endowed with the powers to create, amend, and pass legislation (a group of ten parliamentarians may propose legislation, which is then assigned to a committee for review), but there is no rule as to how long it may sit with the committee. Thus, few, if any, proposals come to the floor for discussion. With parliamentarians handicapped in their ability to legislate—the role of MPs in Jordan is largely restricted to responding to legislation presented by the government.[1] Elections do not serve as battlegrounds for policy making but for access to state resources (Lust-Okar 2009: 10). Lust thus describes Jordan's electoral system as one of "competitive clientelism" whereby parliamentary representation revolves around patronage and voters determine their choices based on their perception of who can deliver the goods (10; Lust-Okar 2001). Voters look to MPs, for example, to hire their sons and daughters in government ministries in Amman—candidates who are perceived as having the connections, the wasta, to provide this and other types of services, get elected.[2] Those who can appeal to their MP as a member of the same family, tribe, neighborhood, or village are more likely to gain help (and indeed, with shrinking access to resources, they are the only ones likely to do so) (Lust cited in Clark 2012: 361). Voting thus acts to strengthen clientelism, specifically tribally based clientelistic networks.

The services MPs can provide can be quite extensive, creating a web of clientelistic ties that extend throughout the public and private sectors (Clark 2012: 360). MPs utilize both personal connections and their office to create these networks. While MPs use their personal discretionary budget to hire their supporters, much of their time is spent going from ministry to ministry, to the University of Jordan, and so on, developing networks to provide the jobs and other favors their constituents demand and to resolve various issues. It is through this time-consuming process that MPs find jobs in government, positions in the university, and licenses for the pilgrimage for their constituents. MPs can be deeply involved in big business, too. They may use their ministerial networks to ensure the transfer of money from one ministry to, for example, a contractor, who is still awaiting payment after completing a government building project. Or they may use their networks to secure a permit from the Ministry of Education for a private school, even if it does not fully meet all the requirements. MPs are thus constantly developing networks within their locality, where they were elected, and in Amman, where their seat in government lies.[3]

Consequently, MPs are deeply invested in the municipal politics in their districts. MPs enlist the help of municipal mayors to address the demands of their constituents, and they reward them for their support. At a basic level, MPs seek to assure their respective reelections by creating employment in their electoral districts. In doing so, mayors are pressured to create job positions in the municipality and put them in their budget (see below).[4] Paraphrasing the former head of one municipality's local development unit (LDU, see below): "The prime minister, Council of Ministers, ministers, and MPs all interfere in municipal affairs. All kind of interventions exist. . . . MPs call the mayor to appoint people and to promote and reward employees. They also call the mayor to direct services, especially those related to infrastructure . . . to the areas that elected them."[5] Others agree, arguing that MPs most commonly interfere in the details of municipal council work for employment-related reasons.[6] As one former councillor confirmed, in return for their votes, "people expect both personal and public services. But mostly they expect personal favors in return . . . most likely employment."[7]

It also is not unheard of for MPs to use their positions against those who did not vote for them by ensuring that areas that supported an opponent do not receive a service—for example, a minister may be requested to put a municipality last on a list of recipients.[8] MPs, ministers, or perhaps even someone in the royal *diwan* may also pressure mayors on behalf of others—influential families, unsuccessful at directly pressuring their respective mayors to hire their sons or daughters or to issue an illegal permit, use their contacts in Amman to pressure the mayor on their behalf. They may also use their contacts in Amman simply to stifle a municipal proposal.[9] As one municipal employee stated, "Wasta has many avenues—through the mayor and members of the municipal council or through people who own them, and through members of parliament."[10]

However, if MPs can be considered points of access, so too can mayors within their municipalities. In the context of shrinking resources, responsibilities, and power, tribal actors at the municipal level compete against one another for access to the mayoralty and to municipal councils and the consequent opportunity to develop and expand patronage networks to meet the local demands of their families, clans, or tribes (Clark 2012: 361). The fact that municipalities cannot provide all their services adequately with their available budgets has meant that municipal councils have become sites of contestation between individuals and groups seeking to ensure that they and their extended family/clan/tribe receive services (or receive the service first). As one former mayor simply stated, "The budget of municipalities is very small, and it does not help to implement big projects for all people, so members of the council compete on small projects and give preferences to their own clans."[11] Municipal politics, under these conditions, is a system of mutual exchange whereby decisions in council are made on a tit-for-tat basis—often decided prior to the official elections.

Within the municipality, the most important post by far is that of the mayor.[12] Mayors provide an important "point of access" not only to local resources but also to MPs and the resources and/or wasta they have accrued. Indeed, the degree to which a minister or MP is successful in influencing a mayor depends both on the status of the MP/minister—his tribe in particular—and on the strength of the mayor. As one political observer stated, being an MP is not enough, status and wealth are what count: "In al-Karak, only a Majali [family member] can pressure a mayor."[13] Conversely, the degree to which a mayor can resist pressures from other power centers depends on his/her status and, of course, personality.[14]

In terms of municipal councils and the running of municipalities, decision-making power lies overwhelmingly in the hands of the mayor. As one frank former mayor stated, "The law gives the mayor authorities and he uses them . . . to help those who elected him."[15] Quite simply: "The services are historically distributed according to who elects the mayor and who does not. The ones who elected him get street lights and their streets are paved. The others do not get these services."[16] While the mayor cannot help everyone in a tribe, he can help "key figures in the tribe, those who influenced the other members in the tribe to elect and support him."[17] The routinization of internal procedures and the delegation of authority to units and committees all lie in the mayor's hands. Indeed, during the period under study, mayors had fourteen powers that required no approval from their respective municipal councils. A mayor could sign contracts, tenders, mortgages, rents, and loans; begin legal actions on behalf of a municipality; put the boards' decisions into effect; and follow up on and collect the municipality's debt. He furthermore prepared the year-end final accounts (Ahmaro 2014: 74–75).

Mayors also play an important role in determining who receives university admission or a scholarship from the royal diwan, as it is the mayor who nominates candidates from his/her municipality and forwards them to the royal diwan.[18] They can raise the price of lands simply by extending streets to them.[19] As one former councillor admitted, councillors

can pave roads, as I did. They can propose opening new roads to raise the prices of their land. They can invite whomever they want to attend meetings with officials. They can distribute the national aid. They can distribute the royal grants, employment, lighting streets for some people [the municipality can erect five to ten lighting poles on its own expense]. The elected council appointed employees for each of the council members. The mayor is the most important one in terms of providing services after the prime minister. We are not a state of law; we are a state of tribes.[20]

Mayors and other council members follow through on their promises in a variety of ways. The dynamics usually are simple; indeed, most abuses are conducted under a legal cover. As one civil society activist stated: "Most mayors do not read the laws; they pay attention to the lands within the municipal boundaries. The municipal [administration] finds the legal means for the mayor to violate the laws." Other times it is simply a matter of blatantly ignoring the law: "The system of tribal privileging works according to the tasks of the municipality. For example, the municipality makes tax exemptions; it can punish or turn a blind eye to construction violations of regulations, it employs, and it can turn places into commercial zones, or even public lands into commercial lands. In all tasks the mayor benefits his family and his tribe first. There are people from the mayor's tribe who used the public roads to expand their building or to construct new buildings, and the municipality turned a blind eye to them."[21]

In other instances, the make-up of the council itself ensures that certain tribes or clans benefit while others do not. Referring to his own council, one municipal employee stated:

A member from one family at the Mazar municipal council will be biased to his tribe in giving services. The municipal members can give priorities to their own families and their tribes in employment, opening roads, lighting streets, giving permits for construction and employment. For the Mazar municipality, one-third of the council members are from [the village of] Mazar, and they are biased in term of services to Shirman and Jarah tribes. Seventy percent of the employees in the municipality of Mazar are from [the village of] Mazar . . . the members can find ways to get around the laws. They are doing this in a legal way. . . . They vote on opening a road, for example, even if it is not necessary; in return they pass something else like lighting the road for other members.[22]

The informality and personalization of the system means that tribes and/ or clans compete against each other for resources and services. It becomes crucial that each clan has some sort of representation in the municipal council. As candidly described by one former mayor:

The mayor and the council members help their clans by appointing employees, services, and preferences. Sometimes they approve projects because they help all the people within the municipal boundaries, but most of the time the projects they approve, like paving roads or lighting streets, are only to please those who elected them. . . . [Consequently] some people ask for roads and they get them while they do not need them; others need roads and they do not get them. It is based on the relation with the mayor and municipal council members. The areas that do not have members in the council, they do not receive services, even though they deserve to get them.[23]

One of the greatest powers a mayor has is his ability to hire temporary workers without the approval of the Ministry of Municipal Affairs (MoMA). These hires are intended for small jobs requiring manual labor, largely "for those who cannot read or write, for work such as digging and cleaning."[24] As discussed in chapter 2, a mayor cannot hire anyone for a permanent position as an employee of the municipality without the MoMA's approval. In seeking to serve his constituents—specifically those who voted for him—mayors often hire those who hold academic degrees—engineers, accountants, administrators—as daily laborers. While on paper they are employed, for example, as a cleaner, in practice they are working in the field for which they were trained, such as an engineer.[25] Or they may be hired as supervisors, but they are given no workers to supervise.[26] Eventually, the mayor makes an argument for an additional employee, enters it into the budget, and seeks approval from the MoMA. Daily laborers thus turn into permanent employees.[27] The end result is overbloated staff. You often find "the daughter of the mayor, her husband, and their son working in the municipality."[28] One municipal employee readily admitted that in the municipal government in which he is employed, "there are thirty-two managers, twelve of them without assistants or employees. They do not even have departments. They cost the municipality 35,000 JD extra every year."[29]

These hirings may be part of the "bargain" with an MP or minister in order to gain votes. But they also may be a means of ensuring the smooth flow of decision-making in the municipality; in other words, they are intended to appease councillors. As a United Nations Development Programme consultant perceptively observed: "According to law, the council must approve a mayor's decisions. But in practice, a mayor will have two people on council with him who are from the same clan as the mayor and vote as he votes. In addition, he makes sure everyone else is in his back pocket by hiring someone from each of their tribes or clans; in this way the council is fully with him and he can do as he pleases."[30] A civil society activist, when referring to the electoral struggle between candidates representing two leading families in his municipality, concurred, stating that one of the causes of the inflation of employees is that the mayor "makes sure to hire employees from the other family in order to avoid problems."[31] As one former mayor explained, he hired equally from the different clans in his municipality—rotating the positions through the various clans. While he acknowledged that this system was not merit-based, he argued that it both kept the peace and created employment, which is, as he stated, part of the municipality's job.[32] As this same former mayor elaborated: "We had . . . a vacancy for an accountant, and a deputy called me to employ someone from one of the towns. But I did not agree. . . . I told him if I want to employ that person I would have to employ other people from other villages. So I asked the deputy to give me three more vacancies in order to employ this man. He could not do that, so I did not employ that person, and the vacancy remained unoccupied."[33] When mayors make no attempt to keep the peace, they pay the price. There have been several incidents when entire councils resigned as the result of a mayor refusing to hire for nonmerit reasons.

What we find therefore is that municipal councils are dominated by an informal system of exchange: "The members, for example, agree to pass some decisions for the mayor, including opening some streets for his land or to the land of members of his family to raise its price; in exchange, the mayor provides services to other places that might be of importance to the members of the council. If you do not have a member in a council, the chances to get services are very limited, for you need to exchange something in order to get services. The members in municipal council exchange their votes for services to them and their tribes."[34]

As one former councillor stated, the mayor is not "getting away" with anything. Rather, all his actions have received approval from the other council members. In other words: "All of them benefit so no one protests the corruption. The members cover each other."[35] In a different interview, he stated it even more bluntly: "You came to my house through a paved road. If I were not a member on the municipal council, the road would not have been paved. . . . I am very frank, I will tell you how the municipality works. They pass things for me, and I pass things for them."[36]

The former councillor describes the system as such: "Let us assume that I am the council member of Hufa village in the municipality of Mazar. It is in my interest to employ people from Hufa or to open new roads in Hufa, so I cooperate with the mayor. In return for his support, he passes for me what I want."[37] He continued that it is not unheard of, however, for alliances to form for or against the mayor's wishes.[38] The same interviewee recalled an incident when eight of the fourteen councillors wanted to dismiss an engineer due to the large number of complaints lodged against the engineer (all of which were from the engineer's own tribe). When the time of the vote came, the mayor entered an agreement, "a promise," with one of the eight; with their numbers down to seven, the councillors were unable get the decision passed.[39]

In urban municipalities, where tribal ties may have broken down or tribal diversity may be greater, wasta often determines the prioritization of who will receive a service first.[40] In other words, the coverage of services usually is universal (eventually), but wasta determines when the service is offered and its quality. In rural municipalities, however, as one municipal employee stated, "The impact is clear. Some people get services, and others do not."[41]

Of course, both the MoMA and the Cities and Villages Development Bank (CVBD, a bank under the authority of the MoMA designed to lend municipalities necessary loans, primarily for development projects) play integral roles in these networks. A former consultant to the CVDB succinctly summarizes the role the MoMA and CVDB play in the web of wasta in which the municipalities are enmeshed:

The MoMA must approve all hiring. The MoMA however can only approve a hire if the hiring is built into the budget, if the mayor builds the hiring into the budget and creates a new space for the person. . . . The MoMA cannot reject a hire if it is in the budget, if there is space. Therefore, the mayor is the main factor in hiring. And if the MoMA objects, saying there is no money in the budget for a new hire, then the mayor goes to the MP—there is like a contract between him and the MP—they hire someone for three months and then make a case for his permanent hire, and the MP puts pressure on the CVDB to lend money for the hire. So if the MoMA says you have no money, you get money through the MP. The minister of the MoMA is also the head of the CVDB. Any MP who wants money for a municipality goes to the CVDB.[42]

As the consultant exclaimed: "Any MP who needs money has a bank to go to!"[43]

Just as importantly, the working relationship between the MoMA and municipalities—including municipal audits—depends on the personal relationship between MoMA officials and the mayors. Paraphrasing this same CVDB consultant: municipal governments do an estimated budget each November, which is then sent to the MoMA for approval. But in general, the municipalities do not have the expertise to do the budget properly, so a MoMA representative meets with the mayor and the head of the financial department in the municipality. If the mayor and the MoMA representative have good relations, the budget is approved, including any spaces created for the hiring of new employees. While there are audits of tenders, the MoMA's audits strictly examine the finances, not the cycle of budget making. Again, personal relations dictate: if the auditor does not like the mayor, he writes a bad report, but if he likes the mayor, he writes a good report.[44]

The same CVDB consultant goes on to explain that this dynamic is replicated in the CVDB: weak mayors do not get money transferred to them if they have a debt, but strong mayors do.[45] As he complains, when a municipality declares bankruptcy and its equipment is removed, the CVDB goes right back in and gives it back to them.[46] As one former employee of the MoMA complained: "The CVDB is not a bank, it's a fund!"[47]

Wasta also means, however, that should a mayor seek to fire someone, he is rarely if ever able to solicit approval from the MoMA. Upon coming to power, the former mayor of Ajloun found a vastly bloated staff of over 400 employees in the municipality, only a fraction of which, he estimated, were needed. Yet when asked if he could fire any of them, the response was simple: "No, no one will support you—here in the municipality or in the MoMA."[48] This was echoed by the former mayor of al-Zarqa'. When he reported to the ministry that he did not need 35 percent of his employees, he was not given approval to fire a single worker.[49] Similarly, the former mayor of Shoaleh, elected in 2007, readily admitted that despite a lack of qualified personnel, the municipality is overstaffed with, according to the mayor's calculations, 50 percent of the staff being redundant. Fifty-two percent of the municipality's budget was going toward salaries. Yet while the MoMA had approved all of the mayor's requests for hirings (three engineers), it did not approve any of the mayor's requests to fire employees.[50] Reflecting on the municipality of Jerash's bloated number of employees, the general manager of the municipality concurred: "We are 80 million JD in debt to the CVDB; 60–70 percent of the municipality's budget goes toward salaries! And the rest goes to costs such as electricity. As a result, there is no budget available for any projects. The number of employees and workers is 700! . . . We can't bring the number down. The best we can do is increase their competence. Every council hired [their own] people . . . as [temporary] workers and got MoMA approval; then they would shift them into employees."[51]

Informal institutions thus determine the running of a municipality: tribes over parties and clientelism over the rule of law. While this system of exchange ensures services and personal favors for those who dominate the council, it does not do so for those who are not represented on the council. All the tribes in one municipality may not get representation on the council. And in cases where one tribe dominates a municipality, all the clans of that tribe may not have representation. Municipalities are thus divided along tribal or clan lines. Tribal or clan relations have become increasingly competitive as the gap between tribe and clan "haves and have nots" has increased (Clark 2012: 364).

The citizen also is, more often than not, a "have not." Mayors are inundated with requests and complaints. The former mayor of Wasatiyya for example, stated that he directly receives a minimum of five requests per day from people seeking employment (Farawati 2010: 43). Meetings with mayors are often interrupted as citizens enter the room (in some cases, barge into the room) making demands. When Rana Hejaya was mayor, she eventually removed the door to her office to ensure that everyone felt equally welcome and no one was offended. At the same time, once elections are over, mayors must turn their attention away from the citizens and toward internal council politics. As several interviewees stated, once in office, the mayor "turns his back to the demands of the people" for the simple fact that he needs the support of the other council members—not the population's—in the ongoing system of exchange that makes up municipal politics (Clark 2012: 372).

The consequences of this system of exchange are evident and multifold. At a very basic level, the restricted nature of municipal resources and responsibilities reinforces tribal units as the most important political bodies in municipal politics. As one political researcher stated: "The nature of municipalities as a service provider controls the relationship between the people and the municipalities, and this reinforces tribalism."[52] Predictably, municipal elections revolve around tribes and tribal alliances, not parties, platforms, or ideology. Indeed, electoral outcomes for mayor and council members commonly are decided prior to the official elections; in other words, the details of the exchange are decided within and between the clans or tribes before the elections, determining who runs and who gets elected.

As discussed in chapter 2, the electoral system at the municipal level has been modified numerous times.[53] Just as at the parliamentary level, the one-person-one-vote system first instituted in 1993 (and only fully eliminated in 2015; see chapter 2) had a significant effect on municipal electoral outcomes.[54] Namely, it exacerbated the competition between clans within tribes for seats on the councils. The one-person-one-vote system favored tribes over ideologically based parties, but it also fractured tribes, pitting one against another and even clans within a tribe against each other as they competed for council seats (Clark 2012: 365). The one-person-one-vote system heightened competition between and within tribes by enabling smaller tribes and weaker clans to compete and be elected to municipal councils and by making it difficult to establish pacts, by which mayoralties were traditionally rotated among tribes or clans.[55] It remains to be seen what result the new decentralization and municipalities law will have on the scheduled 2017 local elections.

The impact is evident in how elections are conducted. Political parties, policies, and even platforms are absent from municipal elections. As one activist from Jerash concisely summarized: "First of all, municipal elections are not political. Whoever runs for elections says that he is running to provide services and discards politics from his speeches and platform. Second, the parties do not nominate candidates; it's the tribes that do so. In the last election, every tribe held meetings to nominate a candidate. If there is more than one candidate, they make an election inside the tribe. Inside the tribes, there are candidates who pay money to get nominated."[56]

As a civil servant from Jerash elaborated: "Elections in municipalities are tribal-based. In a rare case the candidate of a tribe might be affiliated with a political party. This might give the impression that the election in his area is ideologically based. But it is not true, it is just a coincidence. The candidate . . . in such a case uses the tribe and his party support to compete. But without the support of his tribe he would not run from the very beginning."[57] Indeed, paraphrasing a former councillor, voters, seeking someone with wasta, "refuse to vote for someone based on ideology."[58] This former councillor argued that a candidate had lost the last election because he had run under a party label; the previous elections he had run as a tribal candidate and had won. While many interviewees argued that parties may have a foothold in cities where diverse peoples live and, consequently, candidates need party organization and support to win, this is not the case for the vast majority of Jordan's municipalities.

The tribal system is so entrenched in municipal politics that Palestinians, even in municipalities with large concentrations of Palestinians, often vote as blocs, making alliances with different tribal candidates in exchange for positions on the municipal council or for specific services (Clark 2012: 365). In municipalities like Jerash, Palestinians in camps are approached by candidates—usually Transjordanian—through friends or mediators who are supporters of the candidate. The Palestinians hold meetings for the candidates in the camps with candidates making promises and, based on these, alliances with different blocs of Palestinians.[59] In this manner, Palestinians also engage in Transjordanian tribal politics.

Similarly, Islamists choose candidates who are supported by their tribes. According to numerous interviewees, members of the Muslim Brotherhood (MB), prior to its disbandment in 2016 (see chapter 2), chose candidates who were supported by their tribe; if they only chose candidates based on their affiliation to the MB, those candidates would stand no chance of winning. There is no reason to believe that any of the three Islamist parties that have emerged from the original MB, including the Muslim Brotherhood Society and the Islamic Action Front (IAF), which headed a list called the National Alliance for Reform (see chapter 2) in the 2016 parliamentary elections (particularly as the elections continued to produce a tribally dominated parliament), will act any differently. As one interviewee stated, tribes will often vote for MB candidates since the "Muslim Brotherhood chooses tribal candidates so that the candidate can get both tribal and party votes."[60] A former mayor elaborated: people do not vote for the MB because of political affiliation; they do so because the candidate is "liked as a person."[61] Others pointed out that despite the party label, MB candidates not only work with the tribes and get elected through the tribes, but they take no political positions—not even regarding municipal amalgamation (see below). Just as all other candidates, "they do not have a program or a vision regarding municipalities."[62] A civil society activist confirmed this: IAF candidates "run on a platform to provide services; they do not talk politics."[63]

Clans or tribes hold their own internal (pre-) elections. The aim of these elections is to best secure the limited available resources and, as a result, services. Within the tribal elections, tribe and/or clan leaders try to build a consensus around candidates to ensure their electoral success in the official elections. The elections proceed in relatively similar ways. As one interviewee in Jerash, a municipality with a large Palestinian population, explained: "All municipal elections . . . are tribally based. We do not have elections based on ideology or a party system. . . . Each tribe wants to lead the municipality for its own benefit. Normally, the tribe members meet and elect one from within. Sometimes one of them seeks nomination by his tribe, and sometimes the tribe chooses one. If one of them decides to run for election against the will of his tribe, the tribe simply does not give him any votes."[64]

A businessman from a municipality dominated by Bani Hassan, Jordan's largest tribe (albeit one not highly represented in positions of power), concurred. When asked how the process of nomination for elections occurs, he stated: "First inside the small family, then to the bigger, the clan, and finally to the tribe. . . . I tell my family that I want to run for election, or one of them asks me to do that. If we agree on that in the family, we ask the support of our clan, which meets to discuss the issue. If it agrees, we then hold a bigger meeting among the tribe." If there is someone else who wants to run, "we discuss this issue in the tribe. If we can't agree on one, we just hold an internal election."[65] Competitive elections are often the last resort, with tribes preferring a consensus over a candidate. However, when tribal leaders cannot succeed in convincing one or more of the candidates to voluntarily withdraw, internal elections are held. Paraphrasing an interviewee from a municipality dominated by an influential tribe, the Naimat: "Whoever wants to run first speaks to his family. If the family is in agreement, then he seeks approval from all the clans within the village. If they grant him approval to run as a candidate, he then approaches the Naimat tribe within the Ail municipal boundaries in order to get their approval. If more than one nominates himself, the tribal leaders start to convince some of them to quit until one remains as the candidate for Naimat. Normally, the tribal leaders are successful and the tribe only has one candidate. If not, we run internal elections."[66]

In a group interview at a "mixed municipality," several local citizens, including a municipal employee, agreed: "It is very simple. If I want to run for election, I will go first to the family to inform them and to get their opinion. If they welcome the idea, we hold a meeting for the bigger branch of the family. If the branch of the tribe approves me, we hold a meeting for the tribe [the Amawi tribe]. There might be other candidates from the other branches of the tribe; if so, we run election inside the tribe. Who wins will be nominated as the tribe's candidate. . . . It is very possible [that someone from my tribe nominates me] but in the end the tribe must meet to decide who the candidate is."[67] Sometimes the names of the competing candidates are simply written on pieces of paper and one is drawn.[68]

In diverse municipalities, the need for and occurrence of alliances and agreements between clans is more prevalent, with, for example, one clan being promised services in exchange for another clan's candidate being granted the position of mayor. Similarly, as discussed in greater depth below, when different clans of the same tribe perceive that their needs will not be represented on the council, they may run different candidates.[69] It is also not uncommon for smaller tribes/clans to make alliances to compete against a more dominant tribe/clan. As one civil society activist from Jerash stated, not all clans are satisfied with the choice of candidates, as happened in recent elections in Jerash, when a coalition of small tribes ran against the largest tribe.[70]

Alliances form and shift. In al-Mazar al-Shamaliyya, for example, a municipality dominated by two large families or clans and several smaller ones, the dynamics change with, in general, the two larger families competing for the votes of the smaller ones. As a former councillor stated, there are two big families in the village, Shirman and Jarah, both from the Bani Hassan tribe. Candidates from these two tribes make alliances with the smaller families/clans in the town in order to secure votes. Thus, "for example, the Shirman family goes to Abdulmuhsen family and make agreement with them. Abdulmuhsen would give us the mayor, and we would give them a member in the council."[71] In a different interview, the same former municipal councillor stated that when he became a candidate of the Shirman clan, he knew "that some of the Shirman members would vote for the candidate of Jarah clan. Maybe they did not like me. Because of that, I did not depend only on the votes from Shirman. If I was sure all the Shirman clan members would vote for me, I would have relaxed because the number of Shirman members is more than the number of Jarah, so

I also made a secret agreement with some members of Jarah clan and other small clans. . . . As a Shirman clan, we offered to elect their candidates, and for others I offered to represent their interests at the council."[72] If, however, it looks as if candidates from other towns in the municipality are placed to win the mayorship, then "the Shirman and Jarah unite against the other candidates from the other towns. Jarah and Shirman are both from Bani Hassan tribe. Jarah grandfather is Bani Ali, and Shirman grandfather is Bani Yahya. They meet and agree on one candidate."[73]

The reduction of municipalities to little more than garbage collectors, the lack of sufficient resources, and the prevalence of wasta (determining who runs for elections and who gets elected) all result in new faces having difficulty entering politics; people with political ambitions and/or grievances simply do not enter political races at the municipal level. As one former mayor stated, people either become apathetic or take to the streets (Clark 2012: 363). Most educated professionals avoid local politics; meanwhile, the youth turn to the streets (where, as one former mayor stated, the Islamists get them). Another former mayor concurred, arguing that while citizens in the rural municipalities are not political, they are angry. For this mayor, properly functioning municipalities are needed to stop terrorism.[74]

Those who do enter municipal politics, as noted above, do so as tribal representatives. While in some municipalities there has been a shift toward more merit-based criteria for the election of the mayor, these mayors continue to rely on tribal backing. Consequently, even if they represent a new face, they do not represent a new way of conducting politics or a new vision.[75] As one former mayor stated, even the new faces "are like the previous ones. The municipality work is clear, and it is all about paving roads, opening new ones, lighting some streets. The division of work is decided by the council members."[76] The most important posts are the "mayor, his deputy, and the head of the land development committee because of its role in raising land prices."[77] Municipal politics is not a springboard to national politics; rather, it is a platform for prestige and personal and family interests. Councillors are elected based primarily on tribal considerations and secondly because they "have a strong personality and a strong relationship with the state."[78] If ideological considerations are involved, they come as a third consideration, well below the other two. Citizens overwhelmingly vote for some in their family as opposed to the most qualified person. Until 2012, mayors only needed to be able to read and write—MPs had voted against raising the level of education as a requirement for the mayoralty.[79]

Municipal politics in Jordan thus runs along tribal lines—not ideology and experience—with services being dictated by tribally based wasta. With highly limited resources and decision-making powers, Jordan's municipalities revolve around a system of exchange that encompasses not only multiple lines of wasta to Amman but "deals" among candidates and councillors. Candidates are chosen by their tribes, and alliances are made— based on tit-for-tat exchange—prior to the elections to secure votes and essentially determine electoral outcomes. It is a system, as I elaborate on below, that fragments and pits tribes against tribes and clans against clans for limited positions and shrinking resources. It is also a system in which the mayor's tribe/clan and his/her alliance partners capture all resources and services and distribute them, most commonly, to their own tribes/ clans and not others.

Municipal Amalgamation and Elite Capture

In the increasingly competitive environment for resources as a result of the SAP and, most recently, the influx of Syrian refugees (see chapter 2), Jordan's wasta-based system has led to the fracturing or splintering of tribal units along clan lines.[80] These dynamics were clearly revealed when Jordan amalgamated its municipalities. Amalgamation deepened elite capture; by reducing the number of municipalities and thereby the number of mayoral and councillor positions, it reduced access to, and consequently increased the competition for, wasta, also diminishing the number who benefited from wasta. Certainly, the 2011 municipal protests noted in chapter 2, in which protesters demanded the redrawing of municipal boundaries, exposed the fragility of the system. They revealed growing fragmentation and alienation among the social groups that support the monarchy the most.

As also discussed in the chapter 2, in 1990, Minister of Municipal Affairs Abdel Razzaq Tubaishat introduced amalgamation as a solution to the municipalities' economic problems and inefficiencies.[81] Presented to parliament in 1993 and ratified in 1994, amalgamation took place in 2001. The MoMA defends amalgamation, arguing that in most cases it worked. Municipalities were able to save on equipment, such as garbage trucks, by reducing unnecessary duplication. This was not the case in all newly amalgamated municipalities, however; in other cases, such savings either did not happen or were perceived to be not as important or not enough to outweigh other perceived negative effects of amalgamation. In numerous municipalities, mayors complained that amalgamation had resulted in a disproportionate increase in their expenses, as the municipality now had to provide services to a larger area. Due to small and dispersed populations, the additional tax revenue that came with amalgamation did not cover the additional service-delivery expenses. In other cases, a municipality relied heavily on the resources generated from one particular area or village; when this area was amalgamated with a different municipality, the original municipality lost an important source of income and was financially weakened.[82]

In some cases, services became even more uneven because they simply were not located in or did not extend to villages that were, at times, as much as 60 kilometers from their new municipal administrative centers.[83] In other words, amalgamation exacerbated elite capture. As a municipal employee summarized: "Amalgamation affected negatively municipal work as the services were directed to the areas represented by powerful people on the municipal council, like the mayor, at the expense of the less represented areas. Also the cost of the service became higher because the amalgamation happened without any proper research. Some areas are remote, and including them in the municipal boundaries cost the municipality a lot of money. In addition, the hiring policy was not fair. More employees from the influential areas of the municipality were hired than from other areas. This led to the protests."[84]

A former municipal councillor provides another example from the municipality of al-Mazar al-Jadida:

Amalgamation concentrated all the projects in the village of Mazar. The other villages do not have these projects. In Mazar we have the center for information technology, the municipal hall (Dar al-Baladiyya), which cost 35,000 JD, a complex for rent that cost 500,000 JD, and the gas station. If Mazar were not the [administrative] center, it would not get these projects. The main visitors come to the center. The government institutions are located in the center. So the other villages believe if they have their own municipalities, they would get the same privileges. . . . All these projects are in the village of Mazar because one-third of the people from the district of Mazar live in the village of Mazar, and four members of the municipal council and the mayor come from the village of Mazar, so they have a big say in a council of fifteen members. . . . Since the services are concentrated in the center . . . , towns like Rihaba and Der Yousef asked for a separate municipality. Voting inside the municipal council is very important; it imposes how services are distributed. Some projects can be made in other towns, like the school that is being built in Rihaba by USAID, but not all projects. The donors come to the center, and the center decides where the projects will be established. Some projects are not good for the other towns because there is no public transportation between some of the towns and Mazar; for example, there is no public transportation between Rihaba and Mazar. . . . Mazar did not protest because it is in its interest to remain the center of all towns. Hufa did not protest because the people there are from Mazar. Habsha and Der Yousef and Rihaba applied for separation.[85]

The councillor elaborated: "The main projects are in the village of Mazar. The complex and the gas station are in Mazar. Also, when the municipal council built the complex, the gas station, and the municipality building, it needed more money to complete the projects. So what the municipality did was redirect the allocated money for Rihaba, money allocated for paving roads in Rihaba, to complete the projects in Mazar. The members of the municipality's other villages found out, and that was one of the reasons for the protests."[86]

Elite capture was further deepened by the fact that amalgamation also decreased the number of elected representatives by amalgamating several municipal councils into one new one. Municipal councillors complained that their villages now had less chance of being represented on the council or that their voice in the council was much weaker since the councils now represented a larger number of people.[87] A municipality such as Husn, for example, was now amalgamated into a much larger municipality—in this case, Irbid—where it proportionally had fewer representatives on a much larger council.[88] With larger electoral districts, and therefore larger voting populations, even large tribes were now not able to secure enough votes for a seat on the council without reaching outside the tribe (Clark 2012). Amalgamation thus created a situation of increased competition and alliances—with service delivery increasingly concentrated and centralized in the municipal center as a result of tribal or clan biases (those who dominate the council) or as a result of geography (or both).[89]

As discussed in chapter 2, in October 2011, the municipalities erupted into protests demanding the undoing of amalgamation. By separating, more municipalities would have their own mayor and hence the wasta, jobs, and services that come with him.[90] Consequently, those who protested were, by and large, the smaller and less influential tribes and/or clans demanding their own municipalities in the hope that they could establish tribally based clientelistic networks that would work to their favor. As one interviewee stated, "Amalgamation reinforced tribalism. Those areas that did not vote for the mayor were discriminated against, and this encouraged them to demand their own municipality. The main reason the tribes demanded separation is to have their own mayor in order to serve their relatives."[91]

One interviewee in Birayn explained what transpired in his municipality:

When the authority did the amalgamation, it put five towns of different clans together without allocating enough resources to the new established municipality. Birayn is very big; it covers 250 square kilometers. Because the services are all located at the [administrative] center of the municipality [the town of Birayn], the people near the boundaries of the municipality need to travel 15 kilometers to get their services. Some of them have to travel to al-Zarqa' first, then to Birayn, because there are no roads between Birayn and their villages. Of course this situation increases tribalism. With the lack of resources, the Ghewri clan at Birayn municipality will give the services first to the people in village of Birayn and the other clans will protest. Whether the government did that intentionally to increase tribalism or not, I cannot say, but this is the result. When each town has its own municipality, the relationship between clans will be better. . . . The mayor of Birayn employed his son and the sons of his sisters in the municipality. Some other members employed their sisters. Of course this infuriates the clans that could not employ their relatives in the municipality . . .

At first we sent a petition to the minister of municipal affairs demanding that Birayn be divided into two municipalities, with the villages of Birayn, Sarout, and Alouk constituting one and Um Ruman and Kamshah the other. When the minister did not respond, we met the al-Zarqa' governor and the interior minister. Both of them promised to speak with the prime minister. But nothing happened. So we decided to escalate our demands by boycotting the registration for municipal elections, and we threatened not to send our children to school, and we organized a sit-in at the Ministry of Municipal Affairs. In the end, the minister of municipal affairs agreed to discuss our demands in the presence of some deputies and the mayor of Birayn. The minister agreed to reexamine his initial decision of keeping all five towns amalgamated into one municipality. Then we were informed that his final decision remained the same, so we gathered again and decided to stage a sit-in at the Prime Ministry Council until our demands were accepted. . . . The minister of municipal affairs met us in the presence of . . . the speaker of the parliament, and he agreed to separation. . . . We met with the minister of municipal affairs in early October 2011 and the sit-in at the Prime Ministry was approximately ten days after that. Around 100 people came to the sit-in . . .

Frankly, there is one clan that creates trouble in Birayn, the Khalaileh clan. They are in Um Ruman and Kamsha. So it is better for them and for the rest of the clans that they have their own municipality. . . . We are all Bani Hassan, but Bani Hassan are almost half a million people in Jordan. In the boundaries of new Birayn municipality there are Ghweri, Khalaileh, Zawahreh, Omoush, Shdefat, and Zioud.[92]

While the protests occurred at the same time as the Arab Spring, and the Arab Spring protests were no doubt an inspiration for the municipal protestors, the immediate cause of the protests (almost ten years after amalgamation was implemented) was the proposed electoral districts for the 2011 municipal council elections. When it was announced that each municipality would only have one electoral district (rather than several, as had been the case prior), protests broke out against further concentrating wasta and services into the hands of a few.[93] In response to the protests, the MoMA announced that any village with a population of over 5,000 could apply to be its own municipality.[94] Approximately 180 towns and villages applied for separation, an indication of the widespread dissatisfaction.[95] In the end, seven new municipalities were created, bringing the total number of municipalities to 100.

Jordan's tribally based hyper-centralized system thus has had a destabilizing effect at the municipal level. The municipal protests were disruptive in of themselves; however, when who was protesting—the tribes—and why—the lack of access to patronage—are taken into account, their destabilizing nature becomes evident. The protests revealed not only the frustration of the tribes but also the splintering occurring within and between the regime's coalition partner. Indeed, while the dynamics of Jordan's elections and municipal politics repeatedly revitalize tribalism, this is not occurring without the simultaneous frustration with a system that privileges certain tribes/clans. The municipal protesters were not demanding greater democracy; they were demanding equal Transjordanian access to the pie—in this case, wasta.

If Only the King Would Help

A look at municipalities' LDUs (see chapter 2) provides an example of the destabilizing nature of the frustrations experienced at the municipal level. In many cases, if the LDUs were active at all, their projects failed as mayors succumbed to the system of exchange that defines municipal politics in Jordan—with decisions, such as the location of a project, being determined by wasta, not by relevant criteria. But it is important to note that successful LDU projects also need wasta in order to be successful. With few means to help themselves, municipalities are repeatedly reliant on wasta and external assistance—even when the goal of the LDUs is for municipalities to develop themselves—if their LDU projects are to be successful. In Jordan's hyper-centralized system, success stories are rarely replicable; each project involves the same degree of red tape, wasta, donor aid, and, often, direct royal patronage. This is, for mayors and especially the most civic-minded and committed mayors, disheartening at the best.

In 1993, in one of the first attempts to reckon with the economic crisis and the lack of the most basic service delivery in many of the country's municipalities, the MoMA began encouraging municipalities to establish LDUs to assess and develop economic opportunities in their areas and to create long-term development plans (see chapter 2). In the majority of municipalities little came of this initiative. Municipalities either failed to establish LDUs or failed to be effective at generating projects. If they existed at all, the LDUs generally suffered from one or both of the following problems: either the mayor, to which LDUs report, failed to see the potential or take advantage of them or he was unwilling to grant them the type of authority they required to be effective and/or they were inappropriately staffed with underqualified or misqualified personnel.[96] Some mayors simply closed their LDUs. In 1995, however, the German Development Cooperation (GIZ, formerly the GTZ) began working with three municipalities to help them establish LDUs with qualified personnel (largely planners and engineers, some of whom were already working in the municipalities and some of whom had to be hired) and to provide training (lasting 1.5 years) to the LDUs and the municipalities as whole. The end goal of the project was to help LDUs create development plans and strategies for three years, based both on public consultation and in-depth research into resources, capabilities, and long-term feasibility. The GTZ project was the groundbreaker in terms of LDUs.[97] Approximately ten years later, the European Union and several other international donors, including the U.S. Agency for International Development (USAID), the Millennium Challenge Corporation (MCC), and the World Bank emulated and/or built on the GTZ's initial work in the three municipalities.[98]

Several—albeit few—success stories can be found from among the donor programs (see below). More commonly, however, the LDUs did nothing, or their projects were ill conceived and the municipalities had difficulties attracting investors, as they were aware of local corruption, the distance from the market in Amman, or the lack of chambers of commerce. Within a relatively short period of time, several were either not in operation or not profitable. An aluminum factory in Birayn, for example, that was part of the MCC program—and an early success story—ran into difficulties from steep competition and was forced to close for a lengthy period to make adjustments.[99] In many cases, public consultation was either minimal or nonexistent. As one association head complained: "There are no meetings with civil society. I am the head of the [local] cultural forum, and I never got an invitation to meet the LDU members. The LDU was created to get the money from the European Commission; it ceased to work after that. Besides, who are the members of this unit? One of them is holding a bachelor degree in shari'a, the other in Arabic languages, and a third in children's education. One of them was appointed to the unit because a deputy spoke with minister of municipalities to appoint him."[100]

The LDU projects commonly became subsumed under the logic of the informal system of exchange that is municipal politics. In one case, a municipality successfully completed the EU program and built a multiuse complex with EU funds. While the decision to build the complex was part of an open process, as required by the EU, the decision in terms of where to locate the complex was not. The complex was built on land bought from the former mayor's friend—despite its relatively undesirable location. In exchange for their support, the mayor granted family members of those council members who voted in favor of the land purchase employment in the municipality. The municipality has had difficulties finding someone to rent the complex, which is located below street level (Clark 2012: 371).

Even the (limited) success stories are by-and-large not replicable. The lack of authority and resources as a result of centralization means that municipalities, even the successful ones, remain dependent on wasta, donors, and royal patronage. Donors are needed for the next project; wasta is needed for the land, a RONGO (royal NGO) may have to cover some expenses, or the King Abdullah Fund may have to sweeten the pot to attract investors. Each time is the same. In the long term, it is an unreliable system of ongoing and frustrating dependency, one that is often negatively perceived by municipal mayors as begging. In the end, they see the king as their only hope.

Qreqra w Finan, located in Wadi Araba in the governorate of Aqaba, provides an example of a particularly impressive LDU success story; at one point it was quite literally the poster child of the EU. The population of Qreqra w Finan is almost entirely employed in agriculture and suffers from low education levels, high unemployment among the youth, and 55 percent poverty rates.[101] It is one of the poorest municipalities in the country. In 2006, the municipality established its LDU and, after extensive consultation with the local population, decided to start a rose farm. The EU provided the funds (approximately 350,000 JD / US$492,610 / 364,657 euros) for the farm's establishment. The farm was completed in 2009; for the first four months—until the roses were ready for sale—it received financial support from the Jordan River Foundation and the Aqaba Special Economic Zone Authority. A rose farm was chosen for several reasons, the most important of which being that roses require significantly less water than traditional agriculture (particularly tomatoes, the dominant crop in the area). According to the previous mayor, the cost of water for growing roses is only 10 percent of growing the fruits and vegetables normally produced in the region because the water can be recycled (an important factor in a region where water resources are lacking). In addition, every 30 *dunums* (a dunum is approximately one acre) of a rose farm employs one to two people. Whereas with traditional agriculture, in a good year, a local farmer would only earn 1,000–1,500 JD (US$1,407–2,111 or 1,041–1,562 euros), the eight greenhouses that were established via the EU project employ six people, all of whom receive steady incomes (as opposed to seasonal incomes) of not less than 200 JD per month (US$281 / 208 euros). In 2010, after only approximately one year in production, the profits from the farm (the roses are driven to and sold daily in Amman) were estimated at 40,000–50,000 JD (US$56,298–70,372 or 41,677–52,096 euros).

Shoaleh, situated in northern Jordan (Irbid governorate) on the border close to the Golan Heights was also a participant in the EU project. Its 14,000 inhabitants also work primarily in agriculture and/or the public sector (predominantly the army). In consultation with the public, the municipality established an olive press factory, which first began operating in 2009. With the EU grant money, the municipality contributed 40 percent (approximately half a million JD [US$704,000 / 521,000 euros]) of the costs while the private partner contributed 60 percent (approximately 1 million JD [US$1.4 million / 1 million euros]).[102] Based on a call for tenders, a Turkish company provided the oil presses. Within the first year of operation, the press was making a profit and employed twenty-five local people, three of whom work year round.

RONGOs also have helped municipalities in their efforts to undertake revenue- and employment-generating development projects. In cooperation with the King Abdullah Fund, the municipality of Shobak in the southern governorate of Ma'an established a clothing factory employing sixty to seventy young women.[103] The council approached the fund after it had no success in finding investors. The municipality provided the land, and the fund built the necessary infrastructure to lure investors previously unwilling to seed a project in a municipality far from the main market of Amman and often plagued with transportation difficulties in the winter.[104]

Similarly, the King Abdullah Fund was able to attract businessmen to invest in Julfar, a factory producing interlocking paving tiles located in the northern Jordanian municipality of Wasatiyya. The factory was the brainchild of Mayor Imad al Azzam, elected in 2007. After consulting with local businessmen regarding which types of employment investments would best benefit the population, the mayor, on behalf of the municipality, made them an offer they could not refuse—a plot of land with four buildings for the factory and administration for free, with no fees for five years. The land, 10 dunums in total, was bought and paid for by the municipality at a cost of 200,000 JD while the construction of the buildings was paid for by the King Abdullah Fund. The total investment costs for the factory owners was 1 million JD. Three Jordanian investors agreed to contribute a combined total of 50 percent; then they convinced their partner in the United Arab Emirates to contribute the remaining 50 percent. The only conditions on the four investors was that they hire and train 300 local Jordanians over the course of the five years and that the employees earn twice the salary other workers earn in industrial areas in Jordan.[105]

Yet it is questionable whether these success stories can be replicated while municipalities labor under the paralyzing effects of overcentralization. Despite having been charged with the creation of LDUs, the vast majority of municipalities lack the authority, resources, and land to implement any development plans. They must go through the same wasta-dependent process for each and every project. Frustrated with or stymied by red tape, running out of or having no luck with wasta, having lost faith in the state institutions, mayors are forced to appeal to the king for help as their last resort.

Ministerial approvals for municipal decisions are often arduously long. While the MoMA is directly responsible for all municipalities, the governor (appointed by the MoI) is responsible for all public order, security, and law in his governorate.[106] As part of this role, he supervises the functioning of all ministries in the governorate. In addition, governors are to coordinate economic development, including creating a favorable climate for investment (Ababsa 2015). As such, numerous decisions must also go by his desk. Municipalities must obtain MoMA approval for virtually every decision, and both MoMA and the governor's approval for most decisions. Indeed, the MoI has exerted increasing control over municipalities with time. It has a department at the governorate level responsible for security and, particularly in the larger municipalities with a Palestinian and/or Islamist presence, keeps a close eye on councils, whom they hire, their policies, and their comings and goings. The *mukhabarat* (General Intelligence

Agency) has been known to put pressure on mayors when displeased with a council decision. Its interference in election results is also well known, with one former mayor stating that he was directly told not to run for office again because the winner had already been predetermined. In Jerash, interviewees are open about the fact that the state would never have allowed the MB to win for the simple fact that the mayor is on the Jerash festival committee and the (old) MB was against the festival.[107]

The frustrating and slow approval process is made clear by one former mayor's experience. After receiving approval of his municipal budget—which included expenses for the construction of a new building—the mayor filed the papers at the MoMA to be granted permission to build a new building. The paperwork sat at the MoMA for some time before it was sent to al-Karak, the governorate, where it remained for five or six more months. In the former mayor's words, the papers just sat there until the financial year came to an end and the municipality was unable to send out a call for tenders. The former mayor thus had to begin the entire process again from scratch, with the insertion of and approval of the building in the next budget. This was after, the frustrated former mayor literally shouted, the MoMA had informed the governorate of its approval.[108]

The fact that multiple agencies—agriculture, tourism, and the like—have jurisdiction over various "municipal services" also at times means that municipalities simply cannot get things done—either due to the agonizingly slow decision-making process that results from hyper-centralization or due to simple "turf" issues. The municipality of al-Mazar al-Jadida provides a telling example. Its EU-assisted development strategy identified the municipality's most valuable long-term asset as wind power.[109] The plan envisioned the eventual erection of a wind farm generating 5 megawatts of electricity—with the goal of selling electricity to other parts of the country thus bringing sustainable jobs and money to al-Mazar al-Jadida.[110] Toward this end, in early 2009, the municipality entered an agreement with a German company to build a wind station. Progress on the project could not proceed, however, without approval from the Ministry of Energy. After a yearlong delay caused by a string of demands by the ministry for a variety of permits—and with no indication of a final approval in sight—the mayor went public and complained to the media about what he saw as the stalling of the project. Shortly thereafter, the minister personally came to the municipality and gave his oral consent to the project. By this time, however, the German company had pulled out; the delay (and with no written contract in sight) was simply too long.

The tight financial leashes under which municipalities operate also frustrate mayors and slow all procedures. Generally, expenses can only be made if they are in the budget. Even the majority of emergency expenses cannot be dealt with without the MoMA's approval. Thus, when, in the municipality located in the governorate of al-Karak—where the frustrated mayor loudly complained of the slow approval process—a machine broke down and required a 17,000 JD repair, the municipality was not able to address the issue until the MoMA gave its permission.[111] The same applies to garbage trucks and other equipment needed on a regular basis. It is not uncommon for a municipality to have a fleet of unusable trucks. Even after an expenditure has been approved in the budget, additional approvals are required at the time of purchase or the hiring of an employee. Budgetary approval is not sufficient. The sheer volume of approvals and the slowness of the bureaucracy require mayors to make their cases in person. Consequently, the vast majority of mayors drive at least once a week to the MoMA in Amman to have various forms signed and requests approved—even when the drive is three to four hours each way. As one former mayor stated, everything has to be done in person, not by computer or by phone, and sometimes, when you arrive at MoMA headquarters in Amman, the person you need to meet is not even there.[112]

Birqish, a municipality in the northwest of the governorate of Ajloun and a participant in the USAID/MCC municipal-strengthening project, provides another example of the frustrating effects of centralization. With a view of Jebel Sheikh (Mount Hermon) before you head down into the forested valley in which the village is situated, Birqish is located in a breathtaking corner of Jordan. It is little wonder the former mayor describes the municipality as a tourism area. Yet (until very recently, see below), the municipality received few tourists, had a negligible number of people employed in tourism, and received no profits from its sites, which are under the control of the Ministry of Tourism and Antiquities.[113] Tourism plays almost no role in Birqish's economy. The area boasts hiking trails; the "Jesus Cave," where Jesus and his followers are believed to have rested on a return journey to Jerusalem after fleeing Herod's soldiers; a series of underground caves boasting an impressive array of stalactites and stalagmites; and three stone wheat grinders of historical interest. Yet until recently, the sites were poorly advertised by the

Ministry of Tourism and Antiquities and remained relatively unknown to tourists, including Jordanian tourists. There were no tourist facilities at any of the sites or in the town. The municipal council was even stymied in its attempts to develop tourism. Available land in the municipality is under the control of the Ministry of Agriculture. The municipality possesses a few unused dunums; however, these lands are too small and fragmented to be of value for any substantial building project. When the municipality requested 56 dunums of land from the Ministry of Agriculture to develop a tourist center, the minister simply refused.

As part of its MCC training, Birqish was able to build a multipurpose hall that serves the local community by providing rooms for rental for weddings, for example (a tourist hotel was raised as an option but was deemed unfeasible). MCC provided the necessary funds to build the hall (approximately 350,000 JD) and also donated two garbage trucks, a pick-up truck, a water tank, a sewage tank, 100 garbage containers, and 200 units for lighting. The municipality was required to provide the land for the hall. As noted, Birqish's limited municipal-owned lands are already being used for other purposes or are unsuitable for development. The municipality did get its land, but only by sheer luck—the Ministry of Roads and Transportation had recently built a road in the village of Birqish, directly in front of the municipal hall, and had not used all the land under its jurisdiction. The mayor contacted the minister and requested this land be donated, as it was essentially useless to the ministry; the minister agreed. The hall was built but only as a result of events that can most likely not be replicated. Indeed, the municipality has attempted several new projects, but each time it has been stymied due to the lack of land. As the previous mayor stated, "the only solution is through the king himself."[114] If the king comes to Birqish, the municipality will ask him for lands.[115]

Qreqra w Finan, home to the successful rose farm, is also paralyzed in its ability to develop further. The desired expansion of the factory will be difficult as the municipality also owns no lands. Qreqra w Finan is unique in that all lands are owned by two associations. In the early 1970s, in response to tensions over land between the two tribes that live in the area, King Hussein personally visited the area; as part of the solution he reached with the tribes, each tribe created an association (the Wadi Arab Association and the Amareen Association). The lands were divided into two and the associations given ownership of the lands. Each citizen was given the same amount of land (1.5 dunums) for housing. All land is essentially communally owned by one association or the other (since the 1970s, some people have moved away and sold their land to other people, so plots for housing now vary considerably). In order to build the rose farm, each association agreed to donate land toward the project. Consequently, in the case of Qreqra w Finan, the private investors are the two associations, which also now receive part of the profits.

The municipal council's goal is to expand into the European market. It has several other projects it wishes to develop, such as a dormitory for girls attending university in Aqaba. Moving forward, however, will difficult. Municipal land ownership is a condition of most donor projects—World Bank and USAID/MCC projects both require it, for example. Consequently, the municipality must convince either both associations to give up land (which entails convincing farmers to abandon their traditional source of income, farming) or one or more (national) ministries to do so. The Jordan Valley Authority, under whose jurisdiction the municipality falls, refused to grant the municipality the five dunums it requested for the dormitory. Similarly the prime minister's office refused, citing the anticipated Red Sea–Dead Sea project. As the former mayor, clearly distressed, stated: "The Bedouin man is ready to sell his possessions to educate his daughter, his daughter! There are huge changes going on. But where will the university graduate work later?"[116] How, he asked, is the municipality to develop any plans that can make it self-sufficient? That can reduce unemployment? As was heard in many other municipalities, the only solution was the king. The former mayor planned on approaching the king when he came to the municipality to inaugurate a housing project for the poor and presenting him with a list of demands. This, he said, was the only hope. Unsurprisingly, the mayor—a young and educated man with good career prospects elsewhere—decided not to run for reelection; like everyone else, he stated, he likes success. While the municipality achieved some success, he only sees a "dark future."[117]

While the details of Qreqra w Finan are unique, the struggles for approvals, resources, and land are not. When central municipalities took over municipal functions, they also acquired municipal lands and resources. Thus, as noted in chapter 2, Jerash receives none of the revenues from its Roman ruins, neither do Shobak or al-Karak from their castles, nor did Qreqra w Finan from the eco-lodge in Finan when it was still publicly owned. Major operations owned by the central ministries located in the municipalities furthermore do not pay taxes. While the municipality of al-Hashemiyya al-Jadida suffers the environmental consequences of the oil refinery located on its borders, the oil refinery does not pay any municipal taxes.[118] The municipality is in effect a dumping ground for Amman's uglier industries. Mayors often look out over large amounts of undeveloped land that they are not allowed to use because that land belongs to a ministry. In Shoaleh, the previous mayor managed to convince the Ministry of Tourism to transfer a small amount of land to the municipality so that it, together with the Royal Society of the Protection of Nature, could develop a tourist site overlooking the Golan.[119] Other municipalities appear not to have the same personal relations and have not been as lucky. Al-Khaldiyya was similarly lucky, as the Ministry of Agriculture transferred 20 dunums in order that it could develop a park. However, the fundamental problem remains the same even for these two municipalities. They remain without the resources or the land to develop any new projects, even income-generating projects. They remain dependent on the patronage of others.

Some municipalities have purchased land in order to undertake projects. However, those selling the land often raise the prices when a public agency is involved; this is one of the reasons why donors make land possession a criteria. The municipality of Ail, in the southern governorate of Ma'an, provides a good example. Ail was a participant in both the GTZ project and the EU project and is considered a success story. With the GTZ, the LDU worked with local associations and, based on their input, decided to enter a public-private partnership and build a gas station. The GTZ provided the municipality's portion of the investment. The municipality purchased the land. However, the price of the land pushed the cost of the entire project up to 650,000 JD (Clark 2012: 371).[120] While the gas station was needed in the area, and provides both a monthly income of 3,000 JD from the private investor who pays annual fee to rent and run it and some limited employment, it will require decades for the municipality to recoup its investment. In this case the funds were provided by the EU. If the municipality wants to move forward with any new development plans, it will again require a donor or the king to pay for it.

It is little wonder that in municipality after municipality phrases such as "If only the king would visit . . ." are regularly heard. At issue is the fact that municipalities must rely on wasta and handouts to get things done, particularly the development projects they are charged with doing. This is not lost on mayors who recognize that one success does not mean another when the main obstacles are institutional. It is not uncommon for mayors, councillors, and citizens to speak of state failure. As one civil servant observed: "The failure of the municipalities is an indication of state failure. We do not have institutions in this country; the only institution is the tribe."[121] Donor support is required for large and small projects. In one municipality, for example, the mayor even had to solicit the support of a donor to build a fence around a school after waiting years for the Ministry of Education to do so. Yet donor aid is not always forthcoming. Some mayors see asking for donor money as simply shameful—putting them in the position of a beggar.[122] It is a frustrating and depressing trap by which municipalities cannot help themselves. In the end, they turn to the pinnacle of the wasta system, the king himself. As a University of Jordan researcher stated: "People have lost faith in institutions so they look to the king."[123]

Royal Patronage: Those Who Get the Most May Be the First to Complain

It is to be expected that municipal mayors and councillors see turning to the king as their only option. While municipalities in the north are less dependent on royal patronage than those in southern Jordan, since they have greater economic possibilities in terms of agriculture and ease of access to Amman, royal patronage is prevalent throughout the country. For many, royal patronage is essential to running the municipality, providing services, and sustaining LDU projects. Yet councillors and citizens are frustrated, if not increasingly angry, with this dependent status both because, in the absence of other alternatives, they require patronage and because they perceive an unequal distribution of royal patronage. The degree to which some municipalities have, or rather are bestowed with, wasta and royal patronage and others are not is a source of contention. To be sure, royal patronage is appreciated; however, municipal mayors and councillors point to the inequality and irregularity of royal patronage. As I demonstrate below, even highly privileged tribes can feel a sense of injustice.

The king regularly tours the country for royal visits or to inaugurate schools and other institutions founded or funded by the king. The king's visits provide opportunities for him to bestow his generosity and for citizens, including municipal representatives, to demand it. The king's—or royal diwan's—presence, however, is felt far more than just at royal visits. The mayor nominates students to receive university scholarships from the royal diwan.[124] The municipality, in coordination with the *mutasaref* (the head of the *liwa'*, or administrative district) and the Ministry of Social Development, also puts forward names of the poor in need of financial aid. In municipalities throughout the country, truckloads of food are delivered to designated families by a RONGO on a monthly basis.[125] Citizens further can apply directly to the king, via the royal diwan, for financial grants, educational scholarships, and even treatment in hospitals. Here, too, wasta is employed to ensure that their demands "move on" at the royal diwan and are addressed from among the large numbers of people making the same requests. People contact MPs and ministers to help them at the royal diwan.[126] As the University of Jordan researcher stated: "People try to get in touch with the king—it is the shortest route to access services and jobs. Royalty is very open. It is very easy. The royalty moves around a lot, and people have petitions ready. And royalty want to be open, especially after Tunisia and Egypt. And you can email a request to the royal diwan, and the emails are acknowledged. The emails are collected and given to the king, who then directs the requests to the PM or whomever for the appropriate decision or action."[127]

During royal visits, the informal patronage system is quite formalized by the state. In preparation for these visits, the formal state structure is enlisted not only to greet and honor the king but to help facilitate royal patronage. Representatives come prepared with a list of items they would like the king to provide—many of which are basic services. As a former councillor recounted of the king's visit to his municipality, in preparation for the visit, the consultative council for the district—appointed by the governor, the mutasaref, and the MoI—determined who would be invited to meet the king at the reception and what would be on the list of demands presented to the king. He was chosen to be among those receiving the king. The committee requested a new school, a health center, a building for a youth center, buses for the youth clubs, and financial support for a local chartable society. Following the visit, all the committee's requests were met (with the charitable society receiving 40,000 JD). In addition, the numerous citizens who passed envelopes with personal requests for financial support to the king's assistants each received 200 JD. The king also gave 500 JD to each female student and teacher at the school where the reception took place.[128]

Two occurrences during this event are particularly noteworthy. The first is how the committee justified the requests to the king: "When the king visited . . . we told him that from [our municipality] we do not have any minister or deputy minister, and we do not have any general director in any ministry."[129] What is interesting is not just that the municipality made its case based on the logic of wasta but that it made it clear that it felt it was not getting its fair share of royal patronage and deserved more. Furthermore, the former councillor, while pleased, remained disappointed with what the municipality achieved as a result of the visit. As this was the first visit to the municipality by a king "since Jordan became a state," he felt the committee should have demanded more—the employment of 1,000 young men in the military and the establishment of a university college.[130] Having been relatively neglected, the municipality (or more accurately, the tribe) was owed more. It should have demanded what other municipalities had received.

This sentiment is not unusual. The former mayor of Qreqra w Finan who established the rose farm, for example, when lamenting the seemingly futile state of affairs as he tried to develop his municipality, stated that when he listens to other mayors, he sees the difference—that his municipality does not have as much as others. Quite simply, he added, "we are not supported. We had all our own ideas and did all our work on our own. And we see the difference."[131] In another municipality, I heard the same:

> The deputies and the ministers do not inform the king of the people's urgent demands. That is why we demand his Excellency, the King, to visit Ail. He will listen from us directly and solve the problems. We are still living in the age of wasta, and the deputies do not inform the king of everything. The wasta helps only the more influential people, the deputies and ministers. The Naimat tribe comprises more than 70,000 people, but you would not find a minister, an ambassador, or cultural attaché from Naimat. . . . The king will order the creation of a health center. . . . The king does not know we need one. The deputies and ministers hide the demands of people because their priorities are their own interests. . . . The last time a senior official visited Ail was eight years ago. . . . Since then, no officials have visited. We have what I call the system of fetishization. There are some appointed officials. Those who are around them and follow them benefit from the system: they become ambassadors, get scholarships and training outside the country. But the others get nothing. This is completely unjust. . . . The sons of Majali, Sharaiedeh, and Tel

families are benefiting a lot from the system, but other families are alienated.[132]

Keep in mind that this was spoken by someone from a tribe that most others consider quite powerful.

What we find is that municipalities are essentially reliant on and embedded in a system of wasta and handouts. As Lust-Okar (2009: 9) reminds us, in times of restricted state resources, those who are the most dependent on wasta may be the first to challenge the regime. Indeed, while the protests in opposition to amalgamation were fundamentally different from the (simultaneous) 2011 Arab Spring protests for greater political opening, the two are not unrelated in the sources of their mutual frustration. As one interviewee stated: "There is a link between the lack of services and corruption . . . and the protests in Jordan. As I said before, when the people in Birayn know that the mayor has employed his son and the sons of his sister in the municipality, they of course become angry. Similarly in al-Zarqa', the mayor employed his sons and their wives in the municipality. Of course the people see that as corruption and they protest against it."[133]

A state employee in Jerash echoed this opinion. When speaking of the protests against amalgamation, he asserted: "The big picture is the people's frustration. . . . I want to say, tribalism is changing. Today inside each tribe, there are rifts. . . . I am not saying the tribal system is disappearing; I am just saying Jordan is changing. Tribalism can no longer sustain the regime. The number of educated people has increased, and the regime cannot satisfy all of them. The regime still believes that if it satisfies the tribal head, the tribe will support it. This does not work anymore. We need a system where all the people are treated the same way."[134] These words have the same ring as the demands made by some of the Arab Spring protestors— that the regime treats Jordanians as subjects, not citizens. Transjordanian youth thus demanded "rights and not grants" (*huquq la makarem*) (Yaghi and Clark 2014: 248).

The Vicious Circle of Centralized Control, Wasta, and Poor Services

The frustration, sense of injustice, and instability caused by Jordan's hyper-centralized tribal system is exemplified by the fact that while encouraging municipalities to develop themselves, the regime not only is unwilling to grant municipalities the authority or resources to do so but appears to have little confidence that they can do so. Indeed, municipal mayors and councillors—the majority of whom are Transjordanians—are accorded little respect. This also does not go unnoticed by municipal actors—the same actors the regime seeks to privilege.

The high degree of Jordan's centralization, and the fact that the center clearly feels it can do development projects far better than the municipalities and their LDUs, is perhaps best demonstrated by the fact that the region in which al-Mazar al-Jadida is located will now have a wind farm and that a "special economic development zone" (promoting environmental sustainability and the development of its historic landscape) is being developed in Birqish. While municipal efforts to develop these two projects were thwarted, they are now being developed and bestowed "from above." The special zone is a royal initiative. The wind farm is to be an upcoming phase in the kingdom's larger plans to develop wind energy (with the first project being built in the south).[135] Much like the castle in Shobak or the ruins in Jerash, neither municipal council will play a role in the development of these projects or receive any of the direct profits.

More telling is the treatment of mayors themselves. In 2011, in the midst of the confusion over the creation of new municipalities and the government's flip-flop as to whether the 2011 municipal elections should go ahead or be postponed, the government dismissed all municipal councils and appointed new councils in their stead. Elections were not held again until 2013, six years after the previous elections.[136] Mayors and councillors at the time were not informed of the dissolution of their councils. Asked about it, one Transjordanian mayor stated: "I heard that the municipal councils were dissolved on the TV. No one called me to inform me or to explain to me the decision. I sat after the news three days at home. I did not leave. Then I found it proper to go to the municipality to give the appointed mayor information about the municipality. . . . No one called me. The state treated us as if we did not exist."[137]

Mayors in Jordan are caught in a predicament—a vicious circle in which their lack of authority and resources fosters a culture of wasta and corruption; this same corruption then prevents them from being able to develop their municipality (or to be perceived as capable of development projects). It is difficult for even the most well-intentioned mayor to escape. The story of one former mayor in a municipality in the north says it all.

When the mayor came to power in 2007, he found a staff of 250 employees and 65 percent of the budget devoted to wages. In under three years he brought this percentage down to 55 percent—an impressive feat given that he hired thirty-five new employees.[138] He was able to do this by increasing the size of his general budget. According to the mayor, he saved the municipality 120,000 JD (US$168,895) annually on fuel by eliminating private use of municipal vehicles alone. He did so by installing a hazard analysis and critical control point (HACCP) system. While HACCP was originally designed to ensure food safety, it is essentially a quality control system that can be applied to any field. It helps the municipality identify where bribery may take place and puts systems in place to prevent it from happening. One part of the HACCP system is simply to require all steps in each procedure within the municipal offices to be acknowledged with a signature. There is now, put simply, a paper trail, and missing signatures can easily be identified. In addition, the former mayor installed surveillance cameras in the municipality building and a finger scan system. According to him, these measures brought the municipality an additional 350,000 JD (US$492,610) by the end of 2009. Yet this same mayor is the one who had the municipality's multiuse complex built on his friend's property despite its poor location (see above).

In 2010, the mayor stated that he was certain that he would not run again—the responsibilities and the pressures to succumb to bribes were too great; he readily admitted that there continue to be regular and numerous attempts to bribe him and municipal council members (usually to hire someone). Mayors throughout the country expressed the same words, that the pressures to be corrupt were simply too great. Even the most well-intentioned mayor is not immune to pressures of powerful families and their wasta in Amman or the local system of exchange.

In the end, municipalities continue to have crippling debts and provide dismal services. Based on an investigation conducted by Jordan's accounting bureau, Ahmaro (2014: 73) documents that municipalities suffer from permanent financial deficiency and budgetary insufficiency and continue to take loans in order to pay wages and salaries instead of financing development projects. Moreover, loans regularly go unrecorded in their financial books. Municipalities suffer from delays in the performance of their duties, the payment of liabilities, the recording of financial transactions, the reconciliation of banking and other accounts, and in the preparation of year-end financial statements. Budget and accounting records are either delayed or not maintained at all. There are chronic delays in the depositing of funds into bank accounts. Municipal governments continue to suffer from a lack of qualified staff and exercise little control over their employees. There is an absence of internal control units, or unqualified staff are conducting its tasks. Unauthorized staff commonly collect cash, make entries into the accounting system, and conduct audits. There is a lack of control over municipal warehouses and fleets (garbage trucks, for example). There is also strong evidence of the incorrect calculation of taxes and fees on occupational and building licenses (or issuance of illegal occupational and building licenses).

Furthermore, studies find that as a consequence of hyper-centralization and associated wasta, citizens are marginalized and alienated from municipal politics. Because central ministries provide most services of significance, such as education, directly to citizens, citizens increasingly view their municipalities as irrelevant or ineffective, and they look elsewhere for solutions to the problems confronting them. Quoting a Friedrich-Ebert-Stiftung report: "If Parliamentarians provide services, this leads to the conviction among people that a deputy is more capable of this than the local council. This causes people to underestimate the work of local councils and to not deal seriously with them. In some cases they may even pass by the local councils and their procedures" (Hussainy 2014: 7). No critical voice—by any party, including the IAF, or any NGO—was raised when the democratically elected mayors were replaced for two years in 2011–2013 (see above). In very concrete terms, this alienation also has meant, for example, that municipalities have difficulty collecting local taxes and fees—thus exacerbating the poor service delivery (Center for Strategic Studies 2004: 6).[139]

Conclusion

A view from Jordan's municipalities demonstrates that while the regime maintains and revitalizes tribalism through elections (despite the monarch's proclaimed desire for a "parliamentary government based upon political parties" (Sowell 2016) and the creation of territorial units, their funding, and royal patronage, centralization in Jordan is dividing and fracturing tribes and clans as they compete for wasta. Certainly, amalgamation brought to light the competition between tribes and clans for mayoral positions and access to wasta. Jordan's municipalities, which are overwhelmingly Transjordanian-dominated, are embedded in the ethnic- or tribal-based wasta that emanates from Amman, where MPs are elected based on the services they can provide and where municipal-level service delivery decisions are by and large made. When proposed changes to the municipal electoral districts in 2011 threatened to further increase the competition between tribes/clans by reducing the number of avenues to wasta, they sparked demonstrations demanding the redrawing of municipal boundaries—the undoing of amalgamation.

Yet this chapter also indicates that the frustration that erupted among Jordan's tribes and clans in the municipal protests cannot be understood as an isolated event. Municipal LDU success stories reveal a sense of discouragement and, importantly, a sense of injustice as mayors are forced to rely on donors, the whims of ministers, and royal patronage to accomplish their goals. Even mayors in municipalities dominated by what are considered the most powerful tribes look to other municipalities and see the unequal and essentially ad hoc nature of what municipalities receive, and therefore are able to do and provide. While municipal demands remain limited to better funding and access to resources, they certainly have a familiar ring to those of Jordan's Arab Spring activists' protests—rights, not grants.

That citizens quite simply are receiving inadequate services, and most definitely unequal and unfair services, as a result of elite capture cannot be removed from this picture of political instability. Indeed, in the vicious circle of Jordanian municipal politics, wasta—which simultaneously privileges (some) Transjordanians while contributing to the poor service delivery—also ensures that merit and qualifications are not the criteria on which tribes/clans select their mayors in the majority of municipalities. Mayors furthermore do not take any experience they may gain to the national level, for few mayors seek office as MPs. MPs similarly run for office based on their ability to access wasta. Jordan's "municipal mess" also has long-term consequences for national politics ("Jordan's Municipal Mess" 2011).

As I demonstrate in chapter 5, municipalities in Jordan and Morocco have much in common beyond poor service delivery. In both cases we see how elites pursue their own goals and agendas. In Jordan, the elite capture of LDU resources and services did not occur as a result of the "wrong people" being in mayoral positions. Elites seize the opportunities available to them to advance their political agendas; in a system dominated from the top by tribal-based wasta, the LDUs were subordinated to the established patterns of political contestation (Clark 2012). The same can be said of Morocco, where councillors have taken advantage of the opportunities that decentralization offers them to further their political agendas. Yet while decentralization in Morocco offers pro-regime elites increased access to resources, centralization in Jordan has consistently reduced access by the very elites considered the bedrock of regime support. While reducing access to wasta, the regime in Jordan has simultaneously offered few new institutional avenues by which mayors and councillors can improve service delivery in their municipalities. In the long run, this will have political consequences.

CHAPTER V

Elite Capture and Regime Stabilization in Morocco

A s discussed in the introduction, economic reform does not take place on a blank slate. Rather, it takes place in politico-institutional contexts that play important roles in adapting or molding the reforms themselves. This chapter and chapter 6 examine how local actors adapt to and thereby adapt Morocco's good governance and decentralization reforms. They investigate how local political elites and parties strategically use decentralization reforms to maintain or gain political power. The two chapters also examine the extent to which, and how, these "adaptations" play a role in stabilizing Morocco's authoritarian regime. The answers to these questions, I argue, depend largely on the local actors themselves, their context and institutional practices, and specifically whether they lie inside or out of the web of royal patronage and the networks of patron-clientelism. In this chapter, I focus on the "palace," "royal," or "administrative" political parties and the "traditional" or "loyal" opposition, such as the Istiqlal, which, as discussed in chapter 1, are marked by their co-optation and reliance on patron-clientelism; in chapter 6, I examine the Parti de la Justice et du Développement (PJD, Justice and Development Party), which, at least until 2011, lay outside of these networks of patronage as a result of its oppositional stance.[1] Until that time, the PJD rejected any associations that could draw it into the regime's networks of patronage; at the same time, it was simply not privy to them. I argue that in both cases, local elites strategically exploit decentralization to their political advantage, namely to gain or maintain political power. All local actors seize the opportunities the reforms have to offer to advance their political agendas. What differs is which opportunities best advance those agendas.

Decentralization reforms offer new opportunities by which the administrative parties and those of the former opposition can capture additional power and resources and thereby maintain or even expand their networks of patron-clientelism. At the heart of these opportunities for elite capture lie the multiple mandates that elected officials may simultaneously hold as a result of the good governance and decentralization reforms: municipal councillors may establish multiple nongovernmental organizations and, since heads of these organizations apply to municipal councils for funding, sit on the committees that judge which organizations receive funding and are granted funding. All of these capacities serve the needs of councillors, their families, and/or their clients. To be sure, it is relatively common globally for elected officials to gain votes via the distribution of benefits and services under the cover of a nongovernment organization. Yet with Morocco's decentralization reforms, elected officials establish associations with the express purpose of capturing resources and decision-making powers designated to civil society organizations (CSOs), and they do so legally; indeed, this appears to be the intent of the reforms. Local elites thus are able to maintain the patron-client ties that sustain them. In doing so, elected officials maintain, and even reinvigorate, the neo-patrimonial system of the *makhzen*.

In this chapter, I also make the argument that if local elites are engaging in elite capture, they are doing so in a context in which decentralization reforms keep political parties at the municipal level relatively powerless and divided among themselves. This is by no means accidental; again, to a large extent this was the intended outcome of the charters. Despite ample criticisms of the 2002 charter, the regime maintained the very shortcomings that critics pointed to as responsible for the inadequate state of services in Morocco's municipalities. The 2009 charter maintains not only the suffocating weight of *tutelle*, as noted in chapter 3, but also the vague and ambiguous delineation of powers and jurisdictions of the 2002 charter, enabling representatives of the central authorities to use their vast discretionary powers to intervene in and often impede the effective functioning of the councils. The electoral system at the municipal level continues to be one that produces minority governments and fragile coalitions that commonly result in a paralysis of effective decision-making. The 2009 charter also continues to allow for the concentration of powers in the hands of the municipal president (the Moroccan equivalent of the mayor) without any provisions for the distribution of these powers to councillors. Presidents' discretionary powers, in combination with their personal wealth and status, enable municipal presidents to engage in politics dictated by their personal gains. This power imbalance—with the president's authority far outweighing that of other councillors, or even that of the secretary-general and the employees of the Ministry of the Interior (MoI) working in the municipality—commonly means that members of the municipal staff are complicit in the corruption. As citizen participation and service delivery suffer, both the elected officials and the electoral system are discredited, leaving the king, by way of the representatives of the central state or the programs he has initiated, to come to the rescue of the frustrated and angry citizen by directly providing the necessary infrastructure and services that elected officials appear unable, unwilling, or simply too corrupt to provide.

Indeed, the ineptitude and/or corruption of locally elected officials (which, at best, the 2009 charter did nothing to prevent) serve to underscore the notion of the king as reformer. The monarchy, having devolved power to elected officials, is still, in the end, the body that best takes care of its citizens, much as it supposedly has done historically via various social welfare programs, including the Initiative Nationale du Développement Humain (INDH, see chapter 3). The failures of municipal councils enable the king to "rescue" municipalities with a project imposed from above, whether an equalization project or an INDH one.

In the end, Morocco's decentralization reforms are contributing to the stabilization of the authoritarian regime. By facilitating the weakness of political parties and facilitating elite capture, neo-patrimonialism is maintained and the role of the king as a political reformer is strengthened. As I discuss in the chapter 6, Morocco's opposition party, the PJD, operates within the same politico-institutional context, yet it has grasped onto a very different set of opportunities that the reforms offer and effectively challenged the hegemony of the state. Yet here, too, we see how its responses to the charter serve to stabilize the authoritarian regime, for its own discourse—a technocratic discourse of "getting things done"—reinforces the king's.

Deconcentrated and Decentralized Structures
of Authority in Morocco

As noted in chapter 3, Moroccan municipalities operate within the context of two parallel structures—what are known as the "de-concentrated" structure of administrative authority derived from the central powers and the "decentralized" structure of elected authority derived from direct and indirect elections. Taking its orders from above, the deconcentrated administrative structure is not intended to respond to demands from below. It is far more powerful than the decentralized elected bodies in terms of its supervisory authorities, its decision-making powers, and its financial resources. The good governance and decentralization reforms discussed in chapter 3 were introduced within this context and were presumably meant, to some degree, to alter these relations of power. On paper, the reforms are based on a "bottom-up" process according to which citizens' and civil society's input is meant to initiate and shape the process; such input was intended to bring the municipal services more in line with what citizens need and want, and to encourage citizens to act in a "watchdog" type of role, ensuring that their demands are in fact met. The reforms were, in other words, ostensibly intended to strengthen the decentralized structures of elected authority. In practice, however, the 2002 and 2009 reforms have served to strengthen the deconcentrated structures of administrative authority. While executive powers have been devolved to the municipalities, they remain under the same structures of control, albeit now in the hands of the representatives of the central states as opposed to Rabat. Moreover, the 2009 reforms continue to grant *walis* and governors vast formal and discretionary powers over municipal decisions and finances, and both of these representatives of the central authorities use these powers to "call the shots" and subvert the bottom-up process. Good governance and decentralization reforms have strengthened the state vis-à-vis elected officials; the latter are simply bypassed or choose to toe to the line. These dynamics are clearly seen both with the making of the *plans communals de développement* (PCDs, local development plans) and with the INDH.

Morocco's administrative and territorial units (the local collectivities)—regions, prefectures, provinces, and municipalities—fall under the deconcentrated structure of authority. As noted in chapter 3, beginning at the top, Morocco is divided into regions, which are headed by appointed walis (regional governors); these are further subdivided into prefectures (centered on large cities) and provinces (rural and centered on smaller cities), which are headed by governors. A wali is also the governor in the province or prefecture in which he resides. Consequently, walis and governors may be one in the same, and the term *wali* commonly is used for both positions. The provinces/prefectures are divided into municipalities: urban municipalities are headed by *pasha*s while rural municipalities (those with populations of under 35,000) are headed by *caid*s. Below the pashas and caids are lesser administrators, such as the secretaries-general appointed to every municipal hall or center. All of these administrators are appointed and receive their authority from the top. There is no hierarchical relationship between the three administrative/territorial levels; no local collectivity exercises authority over another.[2] Rather, they each report independently to the MoI in Rabat, which is the *organe de tutelle* (administering authority) for all local collectivities (or, as one former municipal president put it, the *ministre de la tutelle*—minister of guardianship). Within the MoI, municipalities fall under the jurisdiction of the Direction Générale des Collectivités Locales (DGCL, General Department for Local Communities). It is responsible for the budgetary, technical, and judicial supervision of all councils (Catusse with Cattedra and Idrissi-Janati 2007: 120).

Parallel to this "top-down" structure is the "bottom-up" decentralized structure of the elected bodies. Although they have statutory powers and state-provided financial resources to perform their duties, none of the elected bodies have legislative powers (Madani, Maghraoui, and Zerhouni 2012: 34–35). Beginning at the bottom, each municipality is headed by an elected council with a president (mayor) who has a six-year mandate. Provinces/prefectures and regions also have elected councils. The provincial/prefectural councils are indirectly elected via a variety of intermediary bodies; elected municipal council members are one such body and vote for a portion of the council seats. As of the 2011 constitution, regional councils are now elected by direct universal suffrage (the first elections were held in 2015). At the top of the decentralized structure lies the indirectly elected Chamber of Councillors, which forms one house of the two-house parliament (see chapter 3).[3]

The representatives of the central authority represent the executive power of the territorial collectivities, and they have powers delegated to them by various ministries, including the MoI (Madani, Maghraoui, and Zerhouni 2012: 34). All elected bodies—the municipal councils, the provincial/prefectural councils and the regional councils—are subject to the supervision of the pasha/caid, governor, and wali respectively. The high degree of tutelle these representatives of the central authority exert over elected councils is justified by the presumed apolitical and technical know-how of the representatives of the central authorities.

The 2002 and 2009 reforms did not, and were not intended to, alter these basic structures of authority. As discussed in chapter 3, the reforms did devolve additional authorities and responsibilities to the municipal councils; they increased the executive powers and the scope of responsibilities under the jurisdiction of municipal councils. Most importantly, they changed the decision-making process so that municipalities are now expected to address municipal problems by way of a civil society solution. As of 2009, all municipalities must prepare a PCD (see chapter 3) and establish consultative committees for "equity and equal opportunities." In keeping with kingdom's increased focus on good governance and participatory development, the "equity and equal opportunities" committees are to comprise local associations; economic actors, such as shop-keepers or farmers marginalized groups, such as unemployed university graduates and the physically challenged; women; and ordinary citizens and to build civil society's demands and feedback into the municipality's PCD.[4] The council is to undertake community work by promoting the creation and activities of local associations. In this regard, municipalities are expected to financially aid and enter into partnership agreements with local associations.

However, as noted above, the reforms also increased walis' authority by devolving to them the power to approve municipal council decisions. Rather than the central ministry in Rabat, the wali, the representative of the MoI at the regional level, now performs that duty. The 2009 charter thus did not reduce the degree of tutelle over municipalities. Walis' and/or governors' approvals are required for all decisions municipalities make, even if some of them are now, according to the 2009 charter, a posteriori rather than a priori. Walis' and governors' formal powers of approval continue to be augmented by their vast discretionary powers, many of which are, as discussed in chapter 3, the result of ambiguous areas of jurisdiction whereby their responsibilities and municipal responsibilities overlap or whereby the jurisdictional boundaries are unclear. This can be clearly seen both with the making of the PCD, which lies at the heart of the reforms made to the 2009 charter, and the INDH. While both are, theoretically, premised on bottom-up processes, in practice they are decidedly top-down processes that serve to strengthen the authoritarian state at the expense of elected officials.

The making of the PCD is not only a required but a necessary tool by which municipalities lay out their development objectives and secure ministerial funding for their desired projects, should they be approved. Municipal expenditures on the basic administration and running of the municipality (particularly wages) consume most of their budgets, leaving little with which councils can invest in development projects.[5] Consequently, the creation of a PCD is central to a municipality's ability to address economic and social issues. The making of the PCD should be a bottom-up process. Yet civil society associations are commonly excluded from the process. At best, the process is dominated by the municipal council, which claims to speak on behalf of civil society. More commonly, it is determined from above by the representatives of the central authorities either by contracting the PCD out to a private firm or by imposing a plan. Municipalities require not only the governor's approval for the PCD but his support as an intermediary vis-à-vis the ministers who also must approve the plan. Municipalities' dependency on the governors is compounded by the lack of budgetary autonomy from the central state. In the end, the majority of municipalities simply accept what is given to them.

Theoretically, making the PCD begins at the municipal level: the municipal council, in consultation with civil society, prepares a list of projects it would like to undertake. It then sends the proposed PCD to the relevant ministers and the MoI for authorization. Once approved, a *bureau d'études* (consultancy firm), responding to a call for tenders (commonly launched by the governor and on behalf of all the municipalities in the province), does a diagnostic study of the proposed projects and the final PCD is completed.

In practice, the making of a PCD can vary significantly. Indeed, the integration of civil society varies dramatically from municipality to municipality.[6] Despite civil society's theoretically pivotal role, the 2009 charter does not lay out any guidelines on how to establish the committees for equity and equal opportunities.[7] How and the degree to which civil society must be integrated into decision-making also is not specified. While there are examples of municipalities that have monthly meetings with civil society via their committees for equity and equal opportunities, most municipalities have not established a committee or, if they have, only meet with it perhaps once per year. Given that many councillors also are heads of associations, municipalities appear to regard these councillors' opinions as sufficient to represent the voice of civil society.

Moreover, particularly in the rural municipalities, neither civil society nor the council may be involved in the making of the PCD. Most municipalities do not have the resources or knowledge to undertake a PCD (training continues not to be provided to councillors), so in some provinces, much to the frustration of municipal councils, governors have asked a university, such as al-Akhawayn University in the province of Ifrane, to develop PCDs for all of the municipalities. Al-Akhawayn therefore technically would consult with civil society and procure all necessary logistical and diagnostic data to complete the PCD. In other cases, however, "the general picture . . . is one of a 'souk' (market) of PCDs where the main winners are . . . consultants, contracted either by the Ministry of the Interior on behalf of the poorer communes, or by the (wealthier) communes themselves . . . many consultants . . . simply deliver the final product to the communes" (Bergh 2012b: 421). In many cases, the consultants do not involve civil society at all.

Regardless of the process, the governor plays a crucial role. When a council prepares its initial list of proposed projects, the province must vet the proposals. Before the proposals are sent any further, the governor visits the municipality to determine its level of need vis-à-vis a specific project. Only after this stage do the proposed projects receive ministerial consideration. Here, too, the governor plays a pivotal role as an intermediary in pressuring for greater investment. His approval and support are crucial; a municipality has a far more difficult time in getting large-scale projects promoted and approved if there are personal or political clashes with the governor or if the mayor does not have a form of leverage, as discussed below.[8]

Financially, municipalities are highly dependent on the central state; the 2009 reforms did little to change this, despite complaints from local officials (see chapter 3).[9] Much like Jordan, municipalities rely on (inadequate) state transfers and have little to no margin of autonomy (Catusse with Cattedra and Idrissi-Janati 2007: 120).[10] Moroccan municipalities depend on the central state for 75 percent of their operating revenues. Municipal public expenditures are overwhelmingly financed by value-added tax (VAT) transfers—approximately 43 percent of municipal operating revenues come from the portion of the VAT that is transferred to municipalities (Ministère de l'Intérieur 2009a: 170). Other taxes, such as the urban tax, business tax, and supplementary urban tax—all assessed and collected by the central government and transferred to the municipalities—make up approximately 32 percent of the operating revenues (170). The various local taxes and fees municipalities may collect (on slaughterhouses or construction, for example), amount to approximately 25 percent (170).

The end result is that municipalities continue to be on a tight leash, unable to do much that does not toe the MoI line.[11] Due to the lack of budgetary autonomy, one study notes, most councils do not try any show of force but prefer to plead the case for their proposals to the minister or his local representatives. This is only possible, however, "whenever the council had the jurisdiction, political will and logistical ability to do so" (Catusse with Cattedra and Idrissi-Janati 2007: 120). In most cases, paraphrasing one international democracy-building organization, successful presidents "play the game of being partners to the Ministry of Interior; they cede authority to the Ministry of Interior; most mayors try to implement the system as it is."[12] As the study continues, geographic proximity to Rabat and political support are often an advantage, but this task is clearly more arduous for the more modest and remote councils. Most presidents, according to one former president, are "like servants" to the governor. The ones who have a vision, he continued, have confrontations with the governor.[13]

The abovementioned dynamics also can be seen in the INDH process. The 2009 charter requires municipalities to create INDH committees to review INDH applications. They also are encouraged to undertake development projects with civil society; if they do so, they qualify for INDH funds. Yet, again, while theoretically a bottom-up process, in practice, the INDH decision-making process is top-down and largely in the hands of the representatives of the central government, namely the Division de l'Action Sociale (DAS, Social Action Division) in the MoI and the governor (Berriane 2010: 104–7). The local INDH committees are largely irrelevant to the INDH decision-making process; association leaders commonly go directly to the governors with their funding demands.

The INDH comprises four programs: (1) combatting social exclusion in urban areas; (2) combatting poverty in rural areas; (3) combatting vulnerability by aiding those who are disadvantaged (such as the homeless and the physically challenged); and (4) a cross-cutting program intended to focus on human development in all nontargeted rural and urban areas.[14] Approximately half of all projects are carried out under the cross-cutting (*transversal*) program, which, unlike the other three programs, is based on a call for proposals from civil society at the provincial level and is funded by a provincial competitive fund.[15] Technically, once again in keeping with the spirit of good governance, this process begins at the bottom with local-level NGO leaders representing the interests of the population (Bergh 2012b: 416–20; Berriane 2010: 93–94). Local NGOs design projects—usually with the help of the municipality or province—and propose them to the Local Committee for Human Development (CLDH) for their municipality. CLDHs are headed by the municipality president and include councillors, civil society representatives, and ministerial representatives or civil servants employed by the MoI at the provincial level.[16] The CLDH forwards the local initiatives for human development (LIHDs, the development plans and projects designed by the LHDCs based on the proposals) to the provincial level where the Provincial Committee for Human Development (CPDH), the head of which is chosen by the governor and which also includes civil society representatives, grants final approval for the LIHDs.[17] At the provincial level, the DAS oversees all the LHCDs beneath it and reports directly to the governor (Bergh 2012b: 417). The National Coordination Unit, located within the MoI, is responsible for the daily management of all the programs (416). A strategic committee, headed by the prime minister, is situated at the top of the pyramid. It is in charge of budget allocations, training, communication, convergence strategies, and the monitoring of evaluations (416).

Yet, as Berriane (2010: 104) states, it is unclear how the local and prefectural committees actually function and the degree to which NGO leaders who are taking part in them are encouraged to actively participate. Furthermore, as she argues, it appears that the councils are largely "spaces in which participation is merely staged and where decisions are effectively taken by the Prefecture under the supervision of the governor" (104). Zemni and Bogaert (2011: 412) concur, pointing out that the governors are not elected but directly appointed by the king, which proves a direct bypassing of local elected bodies in favor of a top-down approach in which the king and his "agents of authority" call the shots. Moreover, governors have a significant degree of discretionary power in determining funding. Commenting on the cross-cutting program, Bergh (2012b: 422) reveals that the selection criteria for the call for proposals leave considerable room for the CHDH to maneuver; in addition, the CHDH can amend ineligibility criteria "according to local specificities" —provided that the proposal even makes it this far. DAS staff can reject a project proposal on grounds of nonadherence with the vaguely defined program objectives. That the governor also is designated as the *ordonnateur du budget* (official with power to authorize expenditures)—as opposed to the Ministry of Finance—grants him even greater powers (419).

Indeed, Cavatorta and Dalmasso (2009: 494) argue that the distribution of INDH grants is based on political quietism as opposed to merit, with the end result being the "domestication of associational life." With nontransparent criteria and decision-making processes, certain actors are systematically excluded from participating in the selection process and/or from receiving funding. Actors who "are already known to local authorities and who fit into the promoted profile of civil society actors are favored" and projects that present themselves as having no political agenda are those that are successful (Bergh 2012b: 415–16, 417; Bergh and Rossi-Doria 2015: 203; Berriane 2010: 101).[18] Thus, while creating links to civil society, the INDH also strengthens those associations that fit with the view of the state and present no threat to it. INDH furthermore offers the state the opportunity to infiltrate NGOs and co-opt them.[19]

The INDH thus undermines the elected councils, strengthens the representatives of the central state, and legitimizes the king by providing a new role for the monarchy as an agency that delivers social services.[20] It creates a direct link from the representative of the king to civil society; NGO representatives who bypass the elected president and go directly to the governor have a far greater chance of getting funded.[21] In fact, the majority of NGOs take their proposals directly to the CPDH, not to the CLDH.[22] The INDH program overlaps and competes against the PCDs of the charter, with the state triumphing over elected officials and the INDH over the charter. In the words of one political analyst, the 2009 Communal Charter has no real impact—it is the INDH that has a real impact on the population. This is because, as he stated, the charter is only an opening while the INDH is under the control of the central authorities, the governors, and has far more power than any municipal council.[23]

The Discretionary Powers of the Representatives of the Central Authorities

At the heart of the decision-making processes of the PCDs and the INDH are the vague and opaque decision-making processes that grant governors significant discretionary power over municipalities and enable them essentially to usurp municipal roles and responsibilities. This is reflective of the system of control that dominates the entire deconcentrated structure of authority. Under the 2009 charter, jurisdictional overlap and confusion continue to grant representatives of the central state a broad range of informal powers above and beyond the formal powers they possess. As with the PCDs and the INDH, the approval (and the speed at which the approval is granted) of day-to-day municipal decisions often hangs on political or personal criteria. It is a highly arbitrary system, and the ease by which municipalities are able to successfully conduct their work is often determined by the personality or the political persuasion of the governor. This serves to undermine the elected councils but not the authoritarian regime, for it enables the state to come in and directly provide the services that the elected councillors are apparently unable or unwilling to do. As indicated above and in chapter 3, this may be the intention of the jurisdictional overlap and confusion.

As discussed above, walis and governors act as crucial kingpins between players—ministerial representatives, representatives of the deconcentrated services of the states, and private actors.[24] The walis of the regions and the governors of prefectures and provinces not only enforce laws, implement regulations and government decisions, and exercise administrative control on behalf of the state, but they also coordinate the activities of the dispersed offices of the central government and ensure their proper functioning, and they assist municipal presidents in implementing plans and development programs (Madani, Maghraoui, and Zerhouni 2012: 36). In addition, they are empowered to take "all necessary measures" with respect to economic and social matters, such as professional development, the promotion and coordination of private (foreign and domestic) investment via the regional investment councils (RICs), and the establishment of industrial zones and business parks (Filali-Ansary 2009).[25] Prefectural and provincial councils similarly are required to promote investment by participating in planning and promoting business parks and the like. They may sign agreements among themselves or with other local entities for the development of projects of common interest. They may also, on their own or in partnership with the state, region, or one or more rural communes, take all actions likely to promote development and support development programs in rural areas (ibid.).

Walis' prerogatives are thus quite extensive. They and other representatives of the central authorities continue to have a large supervisory role over municipal councils. State tutelage manifests itself in the daily workings of the municipal council in different ways, the most obvious being that, despite the devolution of greater responsibilities to municipal councils, councils continue to require approvals from the representatives of the central authority on an inordinate number of decisions, particularly in regard to financial matters. The 2009 charter grants walis the power to approve municipal budgets, in place of the MoI in Rabat; budgets, loans, guarantees, new accounts, franchises, or any act involving money passed by communal councils all require the approval of the governor or wali (Filali-Ansary 2009). As one former president stated, to be successful, a project must have the same aims as the state.[26]

Municipal governments have little sole (as opposed to shared) jurisdiction, even over affairs that constitute local services (*services de proximité*). The jurisdictions of the various territorial collectivities are "rarely defined with any precision, but as representatives of the King (and officials from the Minister of Interior) they concentrate more powers and resources than the elected authorities. Extreme confusion exists among the multiple jurisdictions that plot, share and trace the contours of the urban political and administrative landscape" (Catusse with Cattedra and Idrissi-Janati 2007: 117). Thus, while the region is responsible for economic planning, the provinces/prefectures are charged with matters that relate to rural development, coordination between municipalities, and provincial or prefectural property. Little has changed from the 2002 charter; approximately 70 percent of their roles and prerogatives continue to be similar (Filali-Ansary 2009).[27]

This jurisdictional confusion—which, as Catusse with Cattedra and Idrissi-Janati (2007: 117) concur, is not by accident—is further exacerbated when one takes other ministries into account. At the regional and provincial levels, there are the various line ministers representing their respective ministers, such as the minister of health, in Rabat. The ministerial structures are similarly top-down, with neither ministers nor line ministers accountable to any elected bodies. Municipal presidents have no direct relationship to line ministers and must take any issue or complaint directly to Rabat; these complaints are then transmitted back down the chain of command. This creates an even greater degree of confusion regarding jurisdictional authority. While municipalities are responsible for basic services involving public health and safety, for example, local clinics are under the Ministry of Health and not under the jurisdiction of municipal governments. Municipal councils consequently complain that the legislation is contradictory and consequently unclear—they often do not know when they must seek approval of a ministry and when they may act alone.[28]

The conflicting jurisdictions also mean that walis and governors of the prefectures/provinces have the maneuverability to essentially usurp prerogatives from council presidents (Filali-Ansary 2009). In the case of one municipality where the DGCL, the province, the Ministry of Youth and Sport, and the municipality all contributed money toward the building of a sports complex, there were ongoing disputes concerning who would run the complex after it was built. While the charter states that municipalities are qualified to run them, the governor also has the right to withhold approval, which in this case he did.[29]

Thus, much like Jordan, municipalities often have little control over services theoretically under their jurisdiction.[30] Councillors regularly complain that they have to rely on the province/prefecture to execute many of their decisions—even those involving mundane matters. As a consequence, as one frustrated former councillor complained, council decisions often have little impact, which ultimately has a negative effect on the credibility of the municipal council.[31]

Even in those issues areas where council decisions are approved, the process is frustratingly slow. One former president of a small rural municipality expressed a common complaint when noting that her municipality had been waiting for two months for the wali's approval for the purchase of one roller for the paving of local roads—a purchase that had already been approved in the budget by the MoI.[32] At that point, it had been five months since the municipal council voted to purchase the roller. Similarly, the approval process for basic maintenance of a municipality—small- and medium-sized projects such as painting a municipal hall—can take an inordinately long period of time. As the same president explained, the municipality must first issue a tender, which must be validated by the province. The province regularly takes one to one and a half months to do so. Once the tender is posted and the municipality decides to award a contract, the decision must be approved by the governor; this can take a minimum of twenty days. Once approved, the municipality may then go through all the bureaucratic steps in order for a company to actually conduct the work. This can also take another twenty days. In the end, a small painting job can take three months or more before work can even begin.[33]

In other cases, delays are due to the lack of coordination between ministries, specifically the lack of horizontal ties and what often amount to overlapping functions, conflicting interests, and the right hand not knowing what the left hand is doing. A telling example is provided by the rural municipality of Oulad Ghanem, a seaside municipality located south of the city of al-Jadida. Oulad Ghanem has 20 kilometers of beach coast protected under the Convention on Wetlands (known as the Ramsar Convention, for the city in Iran in which it was signed), an intergovernmental treaty providing "the framework for national action and international cooperation for the conservation and wise use of wetlands and their resources."[34] Of central importance to the treaty is the protection of waterfowl habitats. Oulad Ghanem's coastline is an important site for migratory birds, and two endangered species of birds winter in the area. Importantly, signatories of Ramsar commit themselves to the "wise" or sustainable use of wetlands. However, while development is not prohibited in Ramsar-protected areas, Oulad Ghanem has been unable to obtain ministerial permission to develop its coastal area or to attract (much-needed) investment.[35] A former president first approached the minister of water and forestry, who acknowledged that Ramsar merely regulated protected areas and placed the blame on both the provincial and regional levels for blocking all development along Oulad Ghanem's coastline. He subsequently approached officials at both the provincial and the regional levels and pleaded his case with documented evidence in hand that Ramsar is not intended to prevent development. When these efforts had no effect, he arranged for the minister of the environment to meet with provincial (MoI) authorities. With a continued lack of positive results, he then turned to a strategy of bringing representatives of the central authorities to both the regional and provincial levels. At the heart of the problem, the former president complains, is the lack of communication between different administrative bodies: "The true obstacle is the administration!"[36] In essence, he was trying to establish the types of horizontal ties that the system does not allow for. What is remarkable about these events is that the majority of these actions took place while he was no longer president; he was both a member of the provincial council and a member of parliament![37] His clout enabled him to make these linkages;

it was unable, however, to overcome the jurisdictional confusion and duplication that serves to ensure that all political change occurs from the top-down.

Jurisdictional confusion and duplication moreover mean that walis and governors have a preponderance of discretionary decision-making authority. Presidents universally complain of the personalization and politicization of the approval processes.[38] Consequently, a president's ability to carry out council decisions can vary quite dramatically from municipality to municipality. As one development worker stated, things can change a lot from wali to wali and municipality to municipality depending on who the president and wali are and their abilities to negotiate.[39] A municipal councillor echoed his sentiment, stating quite simply that it depends on "who you get." Presidents who have good personal relations with or similar political views to the pasha, governor, or wali have a far easier time obtaining approvals (or being granted the right to run their own sports complex), or to benefit from the central authorities turning a blind eye. Paraphrasing a leading member of the PJD, "it is very important that there is a good relationship between the wali and the president; the wali looks to see which political parties are in power and who is in the opposition and, based on this, can obstruct a party. When the president of the commune has good relations with the wali, the municipality works; otherwise it doesn't. Personal relations and political affiliations are fundamental."[40]

Based on technical or political reasons or simply his personal opinion, a governor may frustrate the work of a council by rejecting a proposal without any explanation, even on the last day of the three-month period during which the governor must issue his decision.[41] Other representatives may act similarly. Thus, in Kenitra, councillors were originally thwarted in their attempts to contract a new private bus company to provide transportation services when the pasha—despite significant public demand for improved transportation services—sent a report to the wali denying the municipality's need for a second company. Moreover, rather than the usual week, the municipality's request to introduce a second company sat on the pasha's desk for three months before he sent the report to the wali. Councillors attribute the delay and the rejection to political bias against the party of the president, the PJD (Clark and Dalmasso 2015: 17–20).

Conversely, however, if the governor is a friend of the president, "obstacles melt away from the commune."[42] Thus, when the former president of a municipality that has had tremendous success in obtaining various *mise à niveau* infrastructure projects ("up-grading" or equalization projects) from the king was asked about his relationship with the governor, he answered that they are both "sons of the province," adding, "we understand each other."[43] When further asked about the reasons for the municipality's success in terms of so many projects, he and the former vice-president stated, after crediting the king, that it was because the pasha and the president understand each other perfectly that there is an "*entente parfait*" (a perfect agreement). In the words of a former councillor in the same municipality, the governor and the president are good friends, "so this president can do all he wants."[44]

In another municipality, the municipality required credit to complete its projects. The president, however, preferred to avoid the Fonds d'Equipement Communal (FEC, Communal Equipment Fund), wishing to spare the municipality the interest fees on the loan. Based on family connections, she was able to directly approach the governor and receive an interest-free loan from the province.[45] As the president stated, it was only thanks to her cousin's close relationship with the governor that she was able to get an appointment, much less the funds.

The discretionary power of the walis and governors should not be underestimated; it extends far beyond their (significant) role in municipal councils' approval processes. Walis and governors also play a pivotal role in determining administrative boundaries—whether municipalities are designated as urban or rural and what or who lies inside or outside those boundaries. The process of *découpage administratif*, the drawing of administrative boundaries, including municipal boundaries, in Morocco is decreed by the MoI upon approval by the prime minister and typically occurs at the request of the governor. It is often motivated by political and personal considerations. The political changes découpage administratif can bring about can be quite significant, both in terms of the electoral outcome and in terms of the ability of council to be effective once elected. Découpage administratif can therefore be used to target and discredit a political party, a strategy that can be far more effective than ensuring its loss.

In preparation for the 2009 elections, in an ostensible effort to bring municipal governments closer to the people and to increase effectiveness, the MoI divided many municipalities in Morocco into smaller municipalities or amalgamated them with neighboring municipalities as part of a series of reforms to the electoral law in 2008. In just one of many examples from 2009, at the request of the governor, the MoI amalgamated a

rural municipality in central Morocco into its neighboring urban municipality. Overnight the number of eligible voters increased by one-third in
the 2009 elections.[46] Yet, unsurprisingly, the criteria on which découpage
was (and is) based is not transparent and certainly not publicly available.
As Catusse with Cattedra and Idrissi-Janati (2007: 117) note: "It is difficult
to obtain precise and up-to-date maps reflecting recent changes, and maps
of the various administrative perimeters are often lacking. . . . This reflects
a tradition of censorship and the withholding of information, especially
when it's a matter of seeing, in images, the relationship between territory
and politics—and even more so on an urban scale."

Eighty-five percent of municipalities were redesignated as rural municipalities in 2009. As a consequence, the 2009 reforms served to buttress
"the local pro-monarchy notables that often lead parties within these
regions" (Buehler 2013a: 144). In preparation for the 2009 municipal elections, the electoral law was reformed in 2008. The reforms introduced a
proportional representation system (replacing the previous first-past-the-
post system) for towns of more than 25,000 inhabitants while maintaining
the first-past-the-post system for rural municipalities (those under 25,000
inhabitants). The proportional list system makes it likely that large numbers of parties will win. One party typically does not win the majority of
seats; consequently, urban municipalities tend to be governed by (often
fragile) coalitions (see below). In contrast to urban municipalities, rural
municipalities use the first-past-the-post system—a candidate-centric system that works in the favor of individual candidates (that is to say, pro-
regime notables/incumbents).[47] It was no accident that the MoI designated
some municipalities with populations over 35,000 as rural (see chapter 6).

Via découpage administratif, governors also can determine the fate of
specific parties. In one municipality in which the PJD came to power in
2009, another town that had been part of a neighboring rural municipality was added to the municipality. The town, however, was originally built
illegally by its inhabitants and, as a result of its illegal status, has no public
services. The official reasons for the transfer of the town were logistical—
that the town is closer to the main city of the current municipality as
opposed to that of the previous municipal center and that the current
municipality is better equipped to provide the necessary infrastructure
and services to the (no longer illegal) town. However, councillors made
it clear that there were also political and ideological issues at stake.[48]
In order to receive electrical and water services, homeowners require

property certificates demonstrating ownership of the land. The lands on which the town is built are part of what are known in Morocco as collective lands, lands belonging to ethnic groups. In this case, the group refuses to sell its land to the landowners. The municipality's hands are thus tied; it cannot legally supply the 400 families of the town with water and electricity. Paraphrasing one councillor, the town is a bomb given to the PJD by the governor.[49] Regardless of municipal resources, the problem cannot be solved.

Municipal Presidents and the Concentration of Power

Like the representatives of the central authorities, Morocco's municipal presidents have significant discretionary powers. Both the 2002 and 2009 charters downloaded greater powers to council presidents even as the councils themselves saw their authority unchanged. As noted in chapter 3, most political parties had called for a greater delegation and delineation of responsibilities between the president and the councillors. Yet the 2009 charter did not address these concerns; presidents continue to be able to choose whether to delegate some of their decision-making powers and responsibilities to other members of the council. Furthermore, in Morocco, presidents may simultaneously be MPs, resulting in an overconcentration of representative roles in the position of the president and exclusively the president. While the practice of dual mandates is allowed in some countries, even in France, which is the most well-known for the practice of dual mandates (and the system on which Morocco's system is based), the practice is being eliminated. Add this concentration of power to presidents' potential social prestige or wealth, and the result is an imbalance of authority vis-à-vis other councillors and even the municipal administrators. Such imbalances not only divide and thereby weaken councils; they all but ensure that municipal politics revolve around the president and his family's personal interests, guaranteeing endemic corruption and the poor performance of most councils in discharging their responsibilities. The discretionary powers of presidents play a key role in discrediting elected officials, if not the entire electoral system, in voters' eyes. The paramount role of personal interests in municipal politics is particularly evident in the formation of electoral coalitions.

Broadly speaking, Morocco's municipal presidents can be divided into two categories: those who receive their legitimacy "from the top" or "from the bottom." As discussed in chapter 1, Morocco's urban bourgeois families historically fell into three broad and overlapping categories: the makhzen families, Sharifian families (descendants of the Prophet Muhammad), and commercial families.[50] The offspring of the latter, the commercial elite (dominated by Fès), were largely responsible for the founding the nationalist movement and, following 1956, dominated the political elite. Morocco's rural notability was largely created by the French (and designated the title of "notable" by the French) and comprised those who were affiliated with the makhzen as lower-level representatives of the central authorities. Much like their urban bourgeois counterparts, who solidified their status, wealth, and power by expanding into commercial ventures, for example, or via intermarriage, the rural notable also expanded his wealth and power through acquiring large landholdings. Thus, the rural (Berber) notable commonly was a large landowner whose elite status was marked by the fact that he did not do manual labor himself but employed sharecroppers. The offspring of this class benefited from French policies, were educated in the military college in Meknès or in the Collège in Azrou (see chapter 1) and became part of the Moroccan political elite concentrated largely in the Interior, Education, and Justice ministries and in the officer corps (Waterbury 1970: 116). These "agents of authority" and army officers came to form the backbone of the Mouvement Populaire (MPP) while the educated graduates of Azrou, having more in common with their urban counterparts, often were associated with the Union Nationale des Forces Populaires (UNFP, National Union of Popular Forces) (see chapter 1).

With the first municipal elections, in 1960, this small closed circle of elites entered the elections and came to dominate municipal councils. The success of these candidates was largely based on their relationship to the center, the makhzen, from which they received their prestige, wealth, and substantial support. They were also aided by an electoral system that "allowed for direct and personalized relationships between the candidates and the voters, and eliminated partisan intermediation" (Bergh 2007: 90). To be sure, by the 1970s, Morocco's elites had substantially diversified as a result of education, population growth, and urbanization. Joining the rural notable, for example, were agricultural entrepreneurs who invested commercial and industrial profits into agricultural operations. On the outskirts of cities, a new wealthy land developer also came to the fore, dividing and selling his property for residential housing and industrial development. However, much like the traditional elite, this elite, broadly speaking, benefits from central support and external resources. Simply put, similar to the tribal independents in Jordan, it is voted in based on what it can bring from the center to the municipality.

When the 1976 charter entailed the first substantial devolution of power to Morocco's municipalities, it attracted the attention of this array of elites and resulted in increased political competition at the local level (Bergh 2007: 94–96). The 1976 charter was highly limited in both the scope of the responsibilities and financial resources it devolved. Yet councils now had the executive authority to determine a variety of local decisions (with the ever-present tutelle, of course), including the issuing of building authorizations. As Abouhani (2006b: 59) outlines, it gave municipal councils the means to manage the urban space and to have direct control over land and real estate in general. At the same time, municipalities were also given authority over infrastructure (roads, water, sewers, and electricity) and other local public services (59).

The 1976 municipal reform reconfigured the landscape of local elites in urban municipalities (Abouhani 2006b: 55). Municipal councils became important arenas in which landowners and developers sought to defend or advance their interests.[51] Indeed, according to Abouhani, the accumulation by landowners of municipal council presidencies and council member mandates is one of the most noticeable phenomenon of the last decades (61). In less than a decade after the promulgation of the 1976 charter, under the pressures of urbanization, the peripheries of all major cities became highly profitable for large landowners, and councils became the arenas in which they protected and furthered these interests (61). By allowing rural migrants and others seeking landownership in the city access to their property, many landowners acquired the image of a benefactor; in return, small property owners helped ensure that the landowners were elected. Landownership thus opened the local and even national political horizon to landowners/developers, allowing them to enlarge their field of action (61). With the newly acquired political power, they were able to raise the status of "their neighborhoods" by securing services and facilities for them—thereby elevating their statuses and their abilities to acquire votes (61).

The case of Chefchaouen provides an example. As Iraki (2002a) documents, a propertied elite began dominating Chefchaouen's municipal councils beginning shortly after 1975, when the region of Chefchaouen was created and the city named its administrative center. Benefiting from land-based wealth, cultural prestige, and patronage networks, local property-holding elites were able to take advantage of rising property values as new land became urbanized in and around the city with the development of new government centers and services.[52] Their large inherited landholdings enabled them to make money through sales or investments. Property-related issues thus became critical for these families as they related to the urban administration of the city. With some brief exceptions, traditional elite families (35–80) began dominating—and, until recently, have continued to dominate—the municipal council.[53] Each profession and area of activity in which the traditional elite dominates, such as construction, has, since the 1980s, been represented on the council. Unsurprisingly, as Iraki notes, between 1985 and 1995, there was considerable growth in the number of property/construction operations and the number of building permits issued by the municipality. Approximately 70 percent of this activity was related to family-oriented construction—families with property profited from rising prices by splitting up their property and selling parts of the land—most of which was in the hands of the traditional elites (35–80).

The social prestige of presidents, the immensity of their fortunes, and their possible dual role as MP, as Abouhani (2006: 62) states, had a significant effect on the relationship between presidents and other elected officials. Abouhani's research shows that within council deliberations, the president's opinions weighed heavily on all decisions within council sessions, in many cases ending with a statement that the council approved by consensus the president's propositions. This polarization of local representation around the president becomes particularly apparent in the municipalities' dealings with the public—all information, requests, and pressures converge on the president's, and often solely the president's, desk.

This imbalance between presidential and other councillors' authority has been accentuated by the recent charters, including that of 2009. What we see over time is less a devolution of authority to municipal councils, or even council bureaus, but to municipal presidents. As the executive authority (Catusse with Cattedra and Idrissi-Janati 2007: 123–24), the president *may* delegate authority to other council members, but the charter does not require the president to do so. As a result, presidents have a significant degree of discretionary power with which they may further augment their authority vis-à-vis other councillors in the bureau. Consequently, the division of competencies differs from bureau to bureau—depending, to a large extent, on the president, whether or not there is a majority government, and the nature of the coalition. Even if they are on the council's executive bureau (see below), councillors may be completely marginalized from all real decision-making.

This imbalance in authority was particularly evident in one municipality where councillors referred to "Monsieur le Président" while the president referred to them by their first names.[54] In this same municipality, I witnessed the president (who was also an appointed member of the regional council) oblige councillors to join him for a social lunch, even refusing (upon their polite requests) to let them withdraw to their families prior to dessert. At the same time, the first vice-president (who was the only one to refer to the president on a first-name basis) simply refused to join in for lunch without any protestations from the president.[55] In fact, the president was more deferential to the vice-president than the vice-president was to him. It was unsurprising to later hear a member of the opposition state, "Il a fait le bon et le mauvais temps" (he makes the good and the bad weather) when referring to the power (both formal and informal) of the vice-president on the bureau.[56] Having delegated authority only to the vice-president, who, uncoincidentally, was the former president, the municipality essentially was being run by the president and vice-president, not the bureau. Similarly, in other municipalities, councillors consistently referred to the more powerful members of the municipal bureau—the "president and three to four members of his family"—in the third person even when they were present.[57]

With presidents commonly delegating competencies within the bureau according to political or personal criteria, it is unsurprising that "municipal work is rarely teamwork."[58] In some cases the imbalance of power vis-à-vis the *président sacré* (sacred president) means that other councillors are servile in face of the president's decisions—as witnessed in the trivial but telling example in which councillors quietly and subserviently joined in for lunch against their will. Toward this end, councillors' votes are bought, and deals are made. In one municipality, councillors complained the previous councillor could count on getting everything he wanted passed—the four or five people from his family on the council voted as he did; the rest would be bought off with a "night in a hotel." The president would furthermore, they claimed, record these evenings as fodder for potential blackmail.[59] In many municipalities, the concentration of power in a few hands results in an unstable bureau, with councillors walking out of meetings or coalitions. In these cases, councillors simply do not show up to bureau meetings; some join the opposition while others simply remove themselves from an active involvement.

The influence of landowner-developer presidents in municipal politics should not be taken lightly. This is not the only route by which today's political elites at the local level have come to power. As Iraki (2006: 79) notes, in traditional midsized cities, we can find three main types of elites: the traditional, moneyed landowner; the bureaucratic/civil servant elite; and a business/entrepreneurial elite. These replace or overlap with each other chronologically. Not all landowners—those in rural areas suffering from outmigration, for example—have subdivided their land for housing. In smaller towns, elites continue to gain their places on council based on their family's long history and lineage. However, it must be kept in mind that the urbanization rate in Morocco has more than doubled over fifty years, surpassing 55 percent in 2004 (L. Zaki 2008: 159).[60] Land and related industries are paramount in terms of bureau politicking. Landowner-developers seek power to protect and enlarge their interests by ensuring, for example, that roads are built near their property or that zones are designated for building or industry. Alternately, landowner-developer presidents may seek to prevent any public usage on or near their lands, leaving those lands intact for speculation.[61] Thus, despite the diversification of many elites' children— the sons and daughters of notables—into a variety of professions, such as law, entering municipal politics remains a priority to protect the family lands and interests. The task of managing the family interests via the position of president may rotate among the children, or even nieces and nephews, of the family, but municipal politics remains central to the family's position. The result is that municipal politics remains "all persons or personal interests."[62] As discussed above, this dynamic can most clearly be seen in the formation of electoral coalitions in urban municipalities; coalition politics often can revolve around personal and family interests.

The municipality of Tiflet is a case in point of "family politics" in coalition-building. Located near the large cities of Rabat, Salé, and Kenitra, Tiflet is one of the fastest-growing municipalities in the country, with a growth rate of approximately 3 percent per year.[63] Although designated an urban municipality, Tiflet remains predominantly rural in nature, with the majority of people working in agriculture. However, a new middle class of teachers, doctors, and dentists has relocated to the municipality. Consequently, residential development has become a source of big business and tremendous wealth. Unsurprisingly, the physical orientation of the city and its expansion has tended to reflect the property interests of the largest land-owners and decision makers. As Iraki (2002a) recounts, from the early 1980s and onward, Tiflet's real estate and land price transactions experienced the greatest leap in terms of their importance of all of the municipality's economic sectors. Land speculation is by far the greatest source of profits in the city. Similarly, rents tied to land for housing development play an important role in economic and political power and the growth of the elite.

Two well-established, wealthy families, the A'rchanes and the Berkyas, have dominated municipal politics (since the 1970s).[64] The father of the 2009–2015 president of Tiflet, M. Mahmoud A'rchane, established the Mouvement Démocratique et Social (MDS, Democratic and Social Movement), a splinter party from the Mouvement National Populaire (MNP, National Popular Movement), in 1996. The interior minister at the time, Driss Basri, favored the party. According to Iraki, A'rchane was able to attract local civil servants, teachers, and local businesspeople to his faction because they hoped to benefit from his national influence.[65]

While Tiflet's 2009–2015 municipal government was led by an A'rchane, the 2003 municipal government was led by a Berkya, which is not to state that they have not formed alliances with one another. Iraki's research reveals that in the defense of land interests, Tiflet's municipal politics are marked by short-term alliance strategies. Each family head must work to develop the necessary alliances to defend the integrity and worth of his property holdings. The more significant these holdings are, the more likely his efforts will be aimed at influencing (or avoiding) major urban planning decisions. For example, negotiations with respect to the development of an industrial zone play out between groups of landowners who either want or do not want an industrial zone on their land; the powerful landowners put forward arguments about zoning and make alliances with other groups that can best move their personal interests forward. This often involves making deals and concessions to other groups of landowners so that everyone gets something. Consequently, decisions by council tend to be based on these negotiations and not on a broader view of what may be best for the city's development.

In the early 1990s, a third family, the Khamis, entered municipal politics and dominated the councils under the banner of the Istiqlal (Iraki 2002a). The 1992 elections thus saw a rejection of some of the city's most powerful groups, including the defeat of most of candidates associated with the A'rchane family. In response, Mahmoud A'rchane worked to lure a number of Istiqlal members over to his side and forged an alliance with the Berkyas. By 1995, he had established a majority of support behind him and managed to have a vote of no confidence passed against President Khamis, deposing him and taking over the position for himself.

More recently, in 2009, the A'rchanes and part of the Berkya family formed an alliance, with the former Berkya president currently serving as a vice-president in the bureau. The alliance resulted out of an internal family dispute—a "personal issue rather than a political one" between cousins within the Berkya family. The vice-president sought to and was able to prevent his cousin from winning the elections by forming an alliance with the A'rchanes.[66] As the head of a local association quite simply stated when referring to the historical rotation of power between these two families, "C'est la réalité" (this is the reality).[67]

The fact that coalition politics revolves around personal and family interests has several repercussions—the most common being that municipal decisions are commonly not dictated by the public good. In the case of Chefchaouen, for example, the preservation of architectural heritage in the old medina, of central concern to the highly important tourist industry, has consistently taken a back seat to private interests, such as new construction on the outskirts of the city. Tourism and the old city of Chefchaouen have been neglected, even though, in the words of a representative of Chefchaouen's Association for Tourism, "All of us would have gained had tourism developed!"[68]

The Complicity of the Representatives of the Central Authorities

The prestige, wealth, and power of presidents affects their relations with other councillors and, as Abouhani (2006b: 62) states, with the civil servants in the municipal hall, local authorities, and the wali. As in Jordan, corruption would not be possible without the representatives of the central authorities, namely the secretaries-general and the civil servants working in the municipal offices. Although the MoI has a general inspection unit that regularly inspects for irregularities and an administrative court to which official complaints may be submitted for review, these avenues have little impact given the endemic nature of corruption. As with the councillors, presidents can have considerable sway over a municipality's civil servants. The granting of illegal construction permits or more egregious violations—all of which in the long run help stabilize the authoritarian regime by maintaining the system of patron-clientelism—could not occur without the complicity of local technicians and representatives of the central state.[69]

With the 1976 charter, presidents became the hierarchical heads of the municipality staffs (Bergh 2007: 95). With subsequent charters, presidents have been granted the authority to hire civil servants at higher levels, according to the MoI ranking (albeit with the approval of the MoI). While the MoI remains responsible for municipal staffing, presidents may now hire the lower ranks of civil servants within municipalities. They may also request a specific secretary-general from the MoI. These presidential powers mean that civil servants may oftentimes feel obliged to fulfill a president's (illegal) demands. The reasons range from the sheer imbalance in social prestige and wealth, particularly in a small, rural municipality, to the fact that civil servants may have favors of their own they wish to see fulfilled, such as the hiring of a relative. Indeed, councillors regularly accuse presidents of hiring staff for political reasons.[70] As in the case of Jordan, the overbloating of municipal staffs as a result of personal or political hires in many municipalities cannot be dismissed lightly. According to the president of Kenitra, when he came to power in 2009, he found 1,603 civil servants employed in the municipality when, according to his calculations, only 750 were necessary.[71] In other cases, councillors complain that presidents hire "weak" people so that they can be manipulated.[72] Civil servants may be pressed to avoid collecting local fees, such as on the rental of space in the market, in order to ensure votes for the president.[73] Tenders are awarded without any public call. Clients' palms are greased with under-the-table money as receipts for tax payment, and the entry of money collected into the books does not correspond with the amount actually paid.[74]

So important are civil servants to the ease with which elites are able to ensure their reelection that in one municipality they were part of a coalition deal. When the A'rchane and Berkya families formed a coalition in 2009, the only stipulation made by the Berkya "defector" was that the president not touch the people who were linked to the former Berkya presidency, referring to the civil servants.[75] He made no demands vis-à-vis the coalition's program, for the simple fact that "he knew that [the current president] would not touch his interests."[76]

Central to the ability of a president to bend the rules to his (and his clients') advantage is his relationship with the secretary-general of the municipality. Appointed by the MoI, secretaries-general are kingpins in the functioning of a municipality because they (since the 2009 charter) have the role of coordinating the deconcentrated and decentralized systems within the municipality, determining the organizational structure and who does what.[77] Their main job thus is to ensure that municipal council policies are implemented by the MoI's civil servants. Presidents may not hire secretaries-general, but they may put forth suggested names. It is not unusual for a president to suggest someone with whom he has a personal friendship. Thus, in the case of one municipality, the secretary-general moved from one municipality to another when the president was elected in 2009.[78]

Within this context, those who do not politically support the president, refuse to bend the rules or simply are not politically useful, are easily removed. While presidents cannot fire civil servants, with the help of the secretary-general, they can transfer them to (undesirable) positions elsewhere in the municipality.[79] One municipal employee in Chefchaouen is a case in point. Based on what he claims were purely political reasons, he was transferred to ten different jobs, including the abattoir, none of which were in accordance to his skill set.[80]

The complicity of MoI employees extends upward to the local authorities representing the central state. Should the president have good personal relations with the governor, he may quite easily aid the incumbent in being reelected. Some councillors claim that representatives of the central authorities make their preferences publicly known, thereby indirectly pressuring citizens to vote for a specific candidate. Councillors furthermore regularly complain that authorities are paid to look the other way when vote buying occurs. Accusations are made that the authorities may facilitate or aid vote buying—by not responding to reports of vote buying and other forms of electoral fraud—in order to help ensure specific electoral outcomes.[81] In fact, vote rigging is a relatively easy affair for presidents—depending on their relationships with the higher authorities, such as the pasha. Elections in Morocco are administered by the MoI, with each municipality having an electoral commission. The role of the local commission is to confirm the accuracy of the registered list of voters, ensuring, for example, that there is no duplication of names. While the "commission is the work of the *fonctionnaire* (civil servant)," the president is the head of the commission.[82] Electoral lists can be manipulated by simply leaving the names of those who are not allowed to vote on a list (with changing electoral districts, see below, they are on the incorrect list) or by allowing people to vote who are not on the list.[83] The fact that voters (during the period under study) were issued a separate identity card based on the commission's list (as opposed to using their national identity cards) further facilitated the ease of electoral fraud.[84] Keep in mind that the pasha is also on the local electoral commission.

Indeed, councillors paint a picture of central authority representatives who tolerate corruption so long as the councillor is politically acquiescent. While it could not be verified, councillors also repeatedly tell stories of councillors being asked by a representative of the central authorities (or sometimes by the president) to sign a blank check that can be used as blackmail. In Morocco, if a check bounces due to lack of sufficient funds, the penalties are harsh and include time in jail.[85] If such stories are true, the representatives of the central authorities do not just tolerate corruption but regard it as useful: if elected officials "underperform" and consequently are discredited in public's eyes, the state, in the form of the INDH or an imposed PCD or an equalization project, can step in and rescue the citizens from the incompetence and corruption of elected officials.

Transhumance

The weakness of Morocco's political parties is perhaps best illustrated by the endemic practice of *transhumance*, switching political parties to "graze" for opportunities to access patronage (see chapter 3). Transhumance has not only undermined political parties but also served to entrench local politics as family and personal politics; service delivery, as a consequence, suffers. Here, too, we see the state do little to prevent transhumance; electoral laws supposed aimed at curbing the phenomenon go unenforced as witnessed by the establishment of the Party of Authenticity and Modernity (PAM, see chapter 6). Transhumance works to the advantage of elites who receive their legitimacy "from above" because they can access a ready network of patrons to secure what they or their clients demand. Yet it is not only those elites who gain their legitimacy "from the top" who engage in transhumance; those who receive their legitimacy "from the bottom" also do so when they find themselves forced to seek the best patron for the needs of their constituents.

Transhumance is a dominant feature of elections in Morocco, national and municipal. The makhzen's creation of administrative parties and those parties' integration into the neo-patrimonial makhzenian system resulted in a network of mutual loyalties and services (Bergh 2007: 116). Indeed, most political parties are little more than interlinking patron-client networks. As in Jordan, candidates have a greater chance of being elected if they are perceived as being able to deliver material and other goods, either directly or indirectly via patron-clientelism. Within an administrative and political system based to a large extent on informality and personalities, voting is based on patron-clientelism. Consequently, voters, particularly in smaller cities and towns, are electorally loyal to a family; party ideology and platforms matter little in this system.

In the case of landowner-developer presidents, votes come, quite logically, from the constituencies who benefit the most from land development—those who live on the (sometimes illegally) developed lands; who engage in related/upstream and downstream/spin-off industries, such as construction; and those who are employees on the landowner's lands or in industries related to the landowner's properties. In all cases, a clientele with vested interests has developed around the president or council member. Take the example of one municipality where the president and his father had led the council for a cumulative total of twenty-six years (as of 2014).[86] This president stated: "Elections are done with money, and we have money. We make a lot of people work."[87]

Councillors regularly point to the lack of transparency of tenders and that contracts are given to the clients of the president.[88] Some complain about the illegal granting of construction licenses.[89] Others describe the illegal acquisition of public lands and lands designated for ethnic collectivities for private purposes.[90] Similarly, the landowner-developer furthermore provides services to clients living on his property or in his buildings in order to garner votes.[91] In the rapidly growing cities of Morocco, newly settled migrants often take up residence on illegal or underserviced lands. To maintain these clients, the landowner-president seeks to ensure that the land is not redesignated, laws regarding illegal settlement are not enforced, and that services, such as electricity or water, are brought to his "neighborhood."[92]

Only the affluent can become presidents as the pay is so small.[93] Because all presidents are wealthy, votes can and are bought in municipalities throughout Morocco. Votes commonly are bought for as little as 200 dirham (US$25).[94] Councillors complain that vote buying begins in the weeks leading up to the elections and occurs in full sight on the streets.[95] Others elaborate that vote buying occurs in two manners. The first is the organized distribution of money—by party supporters—in key neighborhoods in the days leading up to elections day (often by giving women money to distribute); the second is money distributed on voting day "by those who hide near the voting booth," for example, in a van near the polls.[96] In many cases, however, clients simply pay a visit to their patron-candidate at election time.

To be sure, there are many rural municipalities in which the rural notables have not developed their lands for housing (partially because there is no demand). Yet here, too, these notables benefit from their lineage, social prestige, and wealth and continue to have large bases of clients. They receive votes from the large networks of citizens, who, like their fathers before them, sought advice or a small loan from these notables or benefited from their patronage to the village—the donation of land for public usage, such as the building of a women and children's center. Thus, particularly in small rural municipalities, it is not uncommon for the presidency to remain in one family. In one fairly typical rural municipality, the president who heads the council is joined by her cousin, the former president, on council. Another family member was the president before that. In fact, the presidency has been in the mayor's family since independence. When asked what her electoral campaign and strategy had been during the elections, she quite honestly said that she had had no strategy. When pressed further, she was clear that she did not raise any issues during her so-called campaign. The source of her success was quite simple: she stated that she was supported by her family, and the people in the region trust her family.[97]

Unsurprisingly, when the A'rchane municipal president was asked how the A'rchanes were able to come back to power and retake the presidency in Tiflet (see above) in 2009, he replied in a fairly similar manner. He stated that they won because of the poor performance of those who governed between 2003 and 2009 (the Berkyas) and, referring to his own lineage, "since family matters, the people came back to the family."[98]

Within a context in which patrons and the number of clients they can bring to the booths determines elections, it is useful for MPs and municipal councillors alike to change party affiliation if there is a better deal—namely, better or more resources they can offer their clients—on offer elsewhere (Bergh 2007: 116). As at the national level, transhumance serves to keep parties at the municipal level weak. It also keeps "new blood" from being successful in municipal politics—without networks or resources to bring to the table, and without enough networks and resources to be ranked high on the electoral list, new faces have difficulty entering municipal politics. In the end, parties are devoid of any real ideology or platform; "like boutiques," they are only open at election time.[99] As the former president of one municipality said to me: "We vote for the person, if the head of the list is not a good one then the party does not get the votes."[100] Another councillor freely admitted that he had switched parties three times: "We change political parties following our objectives."[101] Councillors commonly "change their colors" after they are elected, with some councillors changing parties seven or eight times in six years. They abandon one "electoral horse" when there is a better horse to deliver them to their personal goals.[102] One former president appropriately referred to such councillors as electoral entrepreneurs.[103] Just as commonly, when the defecting councillor is the "head sheep," the "rest of the sheep follow" and switch parties along with him.[104] Thus, in municipalities throughout the country, five or six councillors may leave a party when their patron leaves it—they follow as clients, particularly if their patron is an MP. So pervasive and commonplace is this sort of "grazing" that in one municipality a councillor openly admitted to me that he did not know to which party he now belonged. When he turned to ask other councillors at the table, the table broke into laughter.

Yet Morocco's municipalities also are populated by a second kind of president or councillor, one located at the other end of the spectrum and who receives his or her legitimacy "from the bottom." As discussed in chapter 1, the 1980s and the 1990s witnessed a decrease in the standards of living for many segments of Moroccan society as well as a relative political opening that encouraged increased political participation among the middle classes, who had thus far been absent from politics (Iraki 2002a, 2002b). There was an increase in neighborhood associations as a result of this opening. Neighborhood associations formed to defend the neighborhood against destruction (in the case of illegal neighborhoods) or to hasten the arrival of sewers, water, electricity, and road construction, for example (Abouhani 2006b: 64–66). In the course of their work, these associations recruited people with the skills they needed to accomplish their goals; members also learned the skills of technical mobilization, organization, and recruitment in order to effectively deal with elected officials and private service providers (73). Consequently, a new type of elite who acted as a mediator between the association and the municipal council came to the fore (Abouhani 2006b: 73; Iraki 2002b). These new elites—whose legitimacy was rooted in their neighborhood identity and an ability to mobilize people and get things done—soon entered municipal politics. Yet little changed with their entry. To the contrary, neighborhood association elites who entered municipal politics in the 1990s were soon integrated into the existing system of patron-clientelism and transhumance.

Political parties could not ignore the new neighborhood association elites of the 1990s. Given their legitimacy, in terms of their local identity and their ability to mobilize, parties could not afford to. They represented too many votes that neighborhood association leaders could mobilize to the polls (for or against the incumbent councillors) (Iraki 2002b). Consequently, political parties soon sought to attract neighborhood association elites (and the votes they brought with them) and bring them onto their electoral lists. The parties' choice of candidates and their position on the list depended (and continues to depend) on the quality and magnitude of their networks, their ability to mobilize, and, sometimes, their ethnic origins (Iraki and Tamim 2009). The greater the importance of their resources and assets, the more they were solicited by different political parties. As different parties sought to woo neighborhood association leaders, those leaders jumped from one to the next seeking a better position on the list or seeking a patron with better resources that he could deliver to his constituency (ibid.). In other words, neighborhood association leaders soon engaged in trans-humance, too.[105]

Thus, while the 1990s saw the rise of a new neighborhood association elite, it did not translate into a new way of doing politics. Being able to deliver on their promises to provide services meant that neighborhood association representatives had to engage in the same established forms of transhumance and corruption or lose their legitimacy. Without playing the game (or playing it poorly), neighborhood association elites could not deliver. Yet by engaging in transhumance they also lost their legitimacy. It is little wonder, as Iraki (2002a) notes, that neighborhood association elites were rarely reelected. When they were, it was often because of the "upward" linkages they had created—with the governor, for example.

Municipal Elites and Elite Capture

Morocco's decentralization reforms have done little to stop the corruption of political parties dominated by patron-clientelism, personal interests, and transhumance. As a consequence, they have done little to improve service delivery. The charters largely have maintained, if not encouraged, these practices and, as a result, have served to weaken political parties. Within this context, local councillors have taken advantage of the ample opportunities the charter provides to maintain and expand their networks of patrons and clients; most especially, they have taken advantage of the multiple mandates available to them under the charter and exploited the resources available under good governance and decentralization initiatives to further the abovementioned dynamics. The 2009 charter has institutionalized new channels by which councillors can enrich themselves. The charter elevates the role of civil society in municipal decision-making. At the same time, the charter elevates the role of councillors in the affairs of Morocco's civil society activists and, in particular, those involved in the field of development. Elected officials have taken advantage of the fact that they can wear multiple hats—as elected official (allowing the councillor to also vote on which CSOs obtain grants from the municipality), NGO founder and head, member of the local INDH committee, member of the equity and equal opportunities committee (perhaps simultaneously as the only civil society representative), civil society representative for the PCD, and, oftentimes, MP—to their electoral and personal benefit. All of this is further eased by the fact that the charter does not specify the degree to which civil society actors must be integrated into municipal committees. Quite simply, as a result of the charter, political parties—via the (legally mandated) multiple positions presidents and councillor may hold—can capture resources and power through new avenues and use these resources to maintain their networks of patron-clientelism; in this regard, decentralization stabilizes the authoritarian regime.

Opportunities abound for councillors to access greater resources and otherwise augment their wealth via the good governance and decentralization reforms. Most importantly, the PCD offers elected officials, particularly those with a close relationship to the governor or wali, to do so. Presidents and those to whom presidents have designated authority stand to make great wealth through the development projects targeted in the PCDs. With the complicity of the representatives of the central authorities, money is siphoned off as patrons and clients benefit from contracts and jobs. A client whose land is integrated into the PCD as a site for construction, for example, would see that land increase rapidly in price—to be sold shortly thereafter.[106] Or a councillor may benefit even more directly. In one example, the first vice-president of a municipal council is also the owner of a regional soccer team. Uncoincidently, one the municipality's projects, in conjunction with an association, is a 6 million dirham soccer stadium to be used in national competition, not by schoolchildren.[107]

Yet one of greatest means by which councillors have been able to take advantage of decentralization for their own political or economic use has been their exploitation of the opportunities and resources made available to civil society. To be sure, the INDH had already set into motion a process by which councillors sought to establish associations. The 2009 charter, however, made the option of establishing an association even more attractive to councillors as they can now also use the decision-making powers granted to CSOs to their advantage. As the former vice-president of one municipality stated: "Elected people only became interested in associations after 2009 because associations became *le pôle d'attraction de la population* [the center of attraction for the population]." The same vice-president bluntly stated: "Today, civil society helps the president get a majority."[108] He by no means stands alone in his assessment. The 2009 charter, one national-level politician explained, has given candidates a way to establish an association as a means of obtaining votes and then to use the municipality as a means to obtain a seat in parliament.[109] As one associational head exclaimed, "All political parties have NGOs that work for them, and this is how they receive votes."[110] A councillor in the same municipality echoed the same sentiment: "La société civile n'est pas innocente!" (civil society is not innocent).[111]

The 2009 charter thus furthered and deepened a process already begun with the INDH. By allowing (in fact, requiring) presidents and councillors to have multiple roles within the INDH and the INDH-selection procedure, the charter indirectly promotes the INDH as an attractive and easy route by which elected officials can access resources. While also chairing or sitting on the CLDHs, elected officials have established a large number of "INDH-inspired" associations. As I discussed in chapter 3, local activists have established a plethora of new associations as a result of the INDH. As the secretary-general of one association stated: "Since it is now easier to create an association, everybody does."[112] Yet many of the associations are created specifically for the purposes of submitting a project proposal or, as one NGO spokesperson stated, "for every new project they create a new NGO." Just as commonly, "one person creates ten associations," or he creates an association "in which the father is the president and the sons are the members."[113]

Councillors are no different and establish multiple associations.[114] In a typical example, a councillor is the president of two associations, one for children and one for seniors—both of which received INDH funding. However, councillors have easier access to INDH and other funding than other association heads do. In this case, the councillor is a member of the CPDH. The association for seniors also received grant money from the municipal council, which, of course, the councillor voted in support of, for the charter requires councils to support NGOs (without stipulating the criteria). A councillor who is also an association head can easily ensure that his or her association receives a grant. Oftentimes, a good relationship with the wali will suffice. One councillor whose association had received INDH funding said of himself: "beaucoup de casquettes, pas de casquettes [many caps, no caps]," which translates to "I wear a lot of caps but in the end it is just me" but can be interpreted as "I wear a lot of caps, but in the end there are just my interests."[115] By opening associations, councillors are able to access funds, ensure their respective clients are serviced, and through their position on the CLDH, potentially exclude any new civil society elites from funds.

Just as elected councillors sit in the stead of associations on the committees of equity and equal opportunities, they often dominate the quota designated for civil society on the INDH councils. They do so as presidents or members of associations "eager to influence the allocation of INDH resources to their associations which they then use in political competition" (Bergh 2012b: 417). They also often are appointed simultaneously as members of the CPDH—the provincial level for the INDH councils (see above). Although patron-clientelism has long been a feature of municipal politics in Morocco, since well before the INDH (130; Bergh 2009: 52), the INDH has done little to prevent it and indeed provides additional opportunities for it. So does the charter. It is little wonder that with the 2002 and 2009 charters, political parties have put far more energy into winning local elections ("Les véritables" 2003).

To be sure, some municipal councils do use INDH funds to benefit their citizens (in some cases, overtly encouraging a citizen to open an association with the end goal being some form of service provision, such as school buses, that the municipality cannot afford on its own).[116] However, thanks to good governance and decentralization initiatives, civil society has increasingly become the route through which politics is conducted. Councillors open multiple associations in order to distribute resources and gain votes at the expense of civil society activists. Decentralization has offered councillors greater opportunities for elite capture, and local councillors have taken advantage of these to maintain or expand their patron-client networks. Under decentralization, power has not fallen into the "wrong hands," which have subverted and distorted the reforms; rather, councillors have taken advantage of the opportunities that their multiple mandates have offered them to further their political agendas. Elite capture has been all but guaranteed with the charters.

The King to the Rescue

By weakening political parties on the one hand and providing opportunities for elite capture on the other, decentralization reforms have meant that Morocco has not witnessed the divisions and fracturing among and between pro-regime elites (at least not more than the system is intended to foster) as Jordan has. Nor do we witness the same perceived sense of begging among Morocco's councillors as we do in Jordan. Rather, as a result of their multiple mandates, decentralization has offered local councillors multiple avenues to power and resources. In this regard, while both centralization and decentralization are "undertaken by autocratic rulers to strengthen their power vis-à-vis potential internal and external opponents" (Hess 2013: 111), the impacts of centralization in Jordan and decentralization in Morocco are fundamentally different. Yet while decentralization works to the benefit of local political elites by maintaining and/or enhancing patron-clientelism and the personalization of politics, what of the general population that continues to endure unequal and inadequate services? Throughout Morocco, obstacles stand in the way of municipalities conducting their work in an efficient and effective manner while opportunities for corrupt behavior are readily available, and with the knowledge, and usually the complicity, of the representatives of the central authorities. It is a system that seems designed to fail. Corruption is exceedingly easy; in fact, most times it is technically not corruption. Because councillors are legally allowed to wear multiple hats, there is no conflict of interest. Councillors are mired in networks of patron-client ties and shifting alliances or in a financial and/or bureaucratic paralysis at best—all the while having been presumably given the tools and institutions by which to better help their constituencies by the king. In the end, as I argue below, the state swoops in to do what elected officials cannot or will not. In effect, the king comes to the rescue—saving citizens from their elected representatives by directly providing the services the citizens need via an equalization project, a PCD, or the INDH. Indeed, the only time corruption appears not to be tolerated is when it impedes one of king's equalization projects—in which case, the wali or governor reasserts his prerogatives discussed above.

Under decentralization, average citizens are frustrated and alienated.[117] They experience at best a municipal council where the members cater to their constituency's interests (or family's) and, at worst, a mud-slinging paralyzed council that achieves nothing for anyone. The latter scenario is not uncommon, for the 2009 charter, as noted above, did little to address the shortcomings in the 2002 charter, including the electoral system. As numerous councillors noted, it is extremely difficult for the council's executive bureau to agree on a budget or PCD if the bureau is governed by a coalition that is not relatively homogeneous. Exacerbating the ineffectiveness of many municipal councils is that governing coalitions are not required to include the party that won the majority of seats. As a consequence, it is common for coalitions forged following the elections to jointly hold the majority of seats and consequently take the presidency and the executive bureau from the party that actually won the majority of seats. The majority party is relegated to the "opposition." All municipal councils in Morocco comprise an executive bureau and what is referred to as the opposition— essentially the remaining seats on the council. The party or coalition that holds the majority of seats determines the presidency and makes up the executive bureau while the opposition only has four opportunities to voice its opinion. According to the charter, the council in its entirety (in other word the bureau and the opposition) is only required to hold four obligatory sessions (February, April, July, and October/November), largely related to the budget cycle. The opposition is effectively frozen out of any real input. As one councillor stated: the "so-called opposition are not opposition; they, too, represent the people, but they are on the outside."[118] Furthermore, the four obligatory sessions follow an *order de jour* (agenda) set by the president; no items may be added to the agenda without the support of one-third of the council. As another councillor complained, the four sessions are insufficient for the opposition to play any meaningful role: "If there is a majority, all you can do is survive."[119]

As a consequence, the system pits the bureau against the opposition. Even the choice of the term "opposition" reflects this antagonistic relationship. The so-called opposition may indeed support the decisions of the bureau; it simply is not in the bureau. It moreover sets the stage for the frustrated opposition to vote down the budget when proposed at one of the sessions and further hinders the bureau's ability to accomplish anything.[120] To be sure, the 2002 charter included provisions to help ensure greater stability within municipal councils. Prior to 2002, a president could be removed with two-thirds of the votes from council, leading not only to a high degree of turnover between elections but also to corruption as presidents used financial incentives to ensure that other council members voted in their favor (Catusse with Cattedra and Idrissi-Janati 2007: 124).[121] With the 2002 charter, the cessation of the president's function automatically results in the cessation of the entire council.[122] The 2009 charter reinforces the "obligation of stability." However, while this amendment encourages councils to negotiate and helps improve stability, a culture of "mudslinging" remains. The tension between the bureau and the opposition often creates a dynamic by which the opposition seeks to bring the governing coalition down. Opposition regularly report irregularities by the president or bureau members (real or fabricated) to the MoI, where an administrative court reviews all officially filed complaints.[123]

In the end, Morocco's municipalities continue to have inadequate and unequal services, with the source of the problem being the elected officials— divided, corrupt, and siphoning money from the municipality and from civil society alike. Quite simply, the charter exacerbates, if not facilitates, all of the above. In this context of failure—the terrible condition of roads and poor transportation systems, inadequate provision of water and electricity, and lack of cultural facilities, to name just a few—the state, representing the king, comes to the rescue. After a two-to-three-year delay, a wali "rescues" a municipality's citizens from their inept and/or corrupt council by imposing a PCD on the council that has proven itself to be too inept or too paralyzed to complete one or by taking over the management of a PCD project suffering from a lack of progress due to corruption within the municipality (commonly with much fanfare in the national press highlighting the incompetence of the elected officials and the need for the competent state). The king may also designate a variety of "equalization projects" to the municipality, ensuring that it receives necessary infrastructure (as opposed to councillors' pet projects). The problem, thus, is the elected officials; the solution is the (authoritarian) state—representatives of the central authorities or programs, such as INDH, sponsored by the king.

An example of an association for the protection of children that received funding from the INDH to establish a center for abandoned children demonstrates the process.[124] In 2005, the association applied directly to the governor and received INDH funding covering 75 percent of the total costs for the building of the center. The association was to be responsible for the costs of the center's equipment (25 percent). According to the association's founder, the elected municipal council began creating problems for the association shortly before the center's inauguration when the municipality approached the governor about building two additional centers—one for the elderly and one for youth—on the same land as the center for abandoned children. The governor agreed and decided that the children's center would now be subsumed under a larger project including all three centers. A new association, it was decided, would be created in order to manage the project (a "super association" as one councillor called it).[125] The governing board of this new association was decided at a meeting with— as the founder of the original association stated—the governor, the NGOs, elected councillors, and the rich people of the city. The founder of the association for the protection of children was elected vice-president of the new association, and the president of one of the eight municipalities involved was elected its treasurer. As a result of the creation of the new association, the original founder lost control over the children's center—including the INDH funding that was to be directed to the center for food. Similarly, all donations to the children's center now went to the newly enlarged association under leadership of the municipal president.

The founder of the children's center also lost direct control over the hiring process. She immediately witnessed changes that she felt were to the detriment of the center and ultimately the children. She was successful in preventing the councillors from replacing her trained staff with unqualified people associated with them. However, her staff suffered a theoretical reduction in pay—"theoretical" because the new association also froze their reduced salaries. Despite a healthy budget of 1 million euros, at the time of the interview, the staff had not been paid for one year. As the founder exclaimed, "The municipality is filling up their personal pockets!" Frustrated with the municipality's handling of the association and the corruption, she approached the Ministry of Social Development and received 30,000 euros. The founder's final conclusion was simple: "Ceux qui font la politique cassent le travail sociale" (Those who do politics break social work).[126]

Seen in this light, it is unsurprising that as one enters any town in Morocco, billboards announce the equalization projects under way and that INDH projects all have signs above their doors proclaiming the source of their funding. The imprint of the king cannot be ignored. The state's competence in providing these infrastructural projects (or in making other services happen) stands in contrast to the incompetence of many, if not most, elected municipal councils. Good governance and decentralization reforms have offered opportunities for elected officials to benefit their citizenry. However, these same opportunities more easily allow elected officials to benefit themselves. This was not unintentional. As long as elected councils continue to personally aggrandize themselves—despite having been technically provided with the institutions and tools to benefit their citizens—the appointed authorities, in the name of the king, can come to the rescue.

Conclusion

Under Morocco's decentralization process, walis use their vast discretionary powers to assist the municipal presidents with whom they see eye-to-eye either politically or personally, or they turn a blind eye to election regularities. Presidents amass powers at the expense of other councillors, all but ensuring the abuse of those powers in the name of a president's personal interests and/or those of his or her clients. Municipal staff—a staff that technically represents the MoI and as such is meant to ensure proper and legal procedures—is complicit in the corruption. New and old electoral candidates willingly embrace or succumb to transhumance. Within this politico-institutional context—one that the charters have maintained—elites representing the parties of the administration, or palace parties, and those of the former opposition, such as the Istiqlal, have successfully captured decision-making powers and resources targeted, at least in spirit, for civil society, and used them to further their own political and personal agendas.

Yet it is not as a result of power falling into the wrong hands that elite capture has occurred. Good governance initiatives and the charters have provided ample opportunities—seemingly intentionally so—for elites to further their interests and sustain the neo-patrimonial system on which the party system is built. Elected officials are able to—in fact, in some cases, required to—wear multiple hats, representing the council, the INDH, and CSOs. In this sense, the charter has provided more avenues and more resources for elected officials to access for their personal and political needs, and elected officials have taken advantage of these opportunities and used them to maintain and even expand their network of patrons and clients. The capturing of decision-making powers and resources largely intended for civil society representatives thus occurs under a "legal cover."

An examination of the 2002 and 2009 charters indicates that, to a large extent, this may have been the intention of the 2009 charter: to sustain the patron-clientelistic base of the pro-regime parties while providing an image of reform—an image intended to win over the country's newly empowered (and newly created) civil society elite. Even as, and precisely because, municipalities continue to fail in terms of their provision of services, the king maintains his image as a political reformer.[127] While elected officials sabotage opportunities for genuine civil society participation and prove to be too inept or corrupt to provide services to their constituencies, the representatives and/or the institutions of the monarchy provide the solution and come to the rescue. Thus, representatives of the central authorities impose an effective PCD and ensure its successful implementation. Or the municipality is bestowed with an equalization project and, for example, its roadways are upgraded. Even as the charter fails as an instrument of reform, the monarch remains a reformer.

In this regard, decentralization is far more stabilizing vis-à-vis the regime in Morocco than centralization is vis-à-vis the monarchy in Jordan. While in Jordan, elites have few to no new avenues for patronage and compete against each other for shrinking resources, decentralization in Morocco offers local elites new opportunities to access resources and maintain patron-client ties. At the same time, while the Jordanian monarch struggles to present himself as a reformer while centralizing, the Moroccan king can, even as the reforms fail, present himself as Morocco's only reformer.

To be sure, the parties of the opposition, namely the PJD, lying outside of these networks of patronage—at least during the period under study—provide a counter-narrative. The PJD, too, has recognized opportunities in the charter and taken advantage of them. Indeed, it has adapted its rationale for public action in line with the good governance discourse and has fulfilled the spirit of reform within the charter by, for example, facilitating civil society's entry into municipal decision-making. It has created coalitions with civil society activists and established genuine consultative committees. Partly as a result of doing so, the PJD successfully has been able to displace patrons from long-held positions in some municipal councils and to bring about effective and positive change in terms of service delivery. Yet, as I argue in the next chapter, while challenging the hegemony of the state, the PJD also serves to help stabilize the authoritarian regime by using and reinforcing the discourse of the monarchy.

CHAPTER VI

Morocco's Opposition Party, the PJD

A s we saw in the last chapter, the palace or administrative parties and the parties of the former opposition in Morocco have taken advantage of the opportunities in the charter to amass resources and decision-making powers ostensibly assigned to civil society activists largely in order to fuel their patron-client networks. Yet what about the opposition Parti de la Justice et du Développement (PJD)? Until very recently, the PJD had been considered the country's only real opposition party—"the only one remaining legal party with a potential to cause some headache to the palace" (Wegner and Pellicer 2009b: 3). In its internal democracy, upward mobility, and program, the PJD stands in contrast to both the palace parties—such as the Mouvement Populaire (MPP), Rassemblement National des Indépendants (RNI, National Rally of Independents), the Union Constitutionnel (UC), and, most recently, the Parti Authenticité et Modernité (PAM, Authenticity and Modernity Party, see below)—and the former opposition parties, such as the Istiqlal, and the Union Socialiste des Forces Populaires (USFP) (Pellicer and Wegner 2014: 6; Wegner 2011: 2–4). The PJD is, as Liddell (2008) states, "by any definition—the most modern political party in Morocco. It is the most internally democratic party, the only one with a constituent relations program, and the only one that draws votes based on the party's message and not the candidates' family names."[1] As a former RNI councillor stated when comparing the PJD to all other political parties, including his own: "Le PJD ça n'a rien à voir, c'est un parti politique."[2] Unlike other political parties, the PJD is a "real political party." The PJD thus stands outside of the patronage and the networks of patron-clientelism from which the above-mentioned parties benefit and promotes a political program as opposed to patrons. Standing as it does apart from these networks (at least during the period under study), does the PJD similarly engage in elite capture?

In this chapter, I argue that, unlike the palace and opposition parties, we do not see the PJD engage in elite capture; rather, in responding to the charters, the PJD has worked with civil society activists and helped them assume their designated place vis-à-vis the charter and in municipal governments. Yet this does not mean that the PJD is not taking advantage of opportunities in the charter to advance its political agenda and to come to power. Just as elite capture is not the result of power falling into the "wrong hands," the PJD's fulfillment of the charter is not the result of power falling into the "right hands." In municipalities throughout Morocco, the PJD has capitalized on the proliferation of civil society activists who seek to enter municipal politics as a result both of the monarchy's good governance discourse and initiatives and of the new decision-making roles assigned to civil society in the 2009 municipal charter. By becoming more active within civil society and reaching out to civil society activists, the PJD has been able to dispel lingering fears since the 2003 bombings regarding its dangerousness (see chapter 3), gain the support of the population, forge useful coalition agreements with civil society activists, and ultimately, in numerous municipalities, remove local patrons from power. Much of this would not have been possible without the charter, for it enables the PJD to forge ties with civil society activists based on the understanding that if elected to power, the party would fulfill the spirit and the letter of the charter by prioritizing civil society's concerns and integrating civil society activists in municipal decision-making. Thus, while remaining solidly within the monarchy's (and international) discourse, decentralization has offered the PJD the opportunity to successfully challenge some of the country's pro-regime parties, and thereby the hegemony of the state.

Following the 2003 Casablanca bombing and the PJD's consequent weak performance in the 2003 municipal elections, the PJD shifted its rationale for public action away from religion per se and toward the neoliberal values of managerial competence, technical know-how, and proximity to the citizens (Catusse with Cattedra and Idrissi-Janati 2007). It thus fell in line with the ideals of the state's good governance and decentralization programs. Having gained much of its support base as an "antisystem" party, the PJD saw a different set of opportunities in the charter than the palace and former opposition parties. By instructing its members to work in civil society organizations (CSOs), prioritizing civil society activists as candidates and as coalition partners, and, once in power, elevating civil society activists and their concerns as hallmarks of municipal politics, the PJD transformed itself into a party in service of civil society. With this strategy, PJD members were not only able to prove themselves as hard-working and competent to a broader segment of the population but demonstrate their common concerns with civil society activists and forge electoral coalitions with these activists based on these commonalities in order to capture political power at the municipal level. Once in power, the PJD fulfilled its commitment to civil society, and in keeping with the charter, it integrated civil society actors into the councils' decision-making processes.

Importantly, the CSOs to which the PJD reached out were largely technocratic or project-based in nature. As discussed in chapter 3, as a result of the monarch's good governance agenda and the Initiative Nationale du Développement Humain (INDH) in particular, there was a noticeable increase in the number of CSOs at the municipal level. Yet both as a result of the monarch's co-optation and depoliticization of civil society's discourse and as a result of the INDH, which promotes and funds apolitical CSOs, these activists were largely apolitical or technocratic, focusing on projects as opposed to the structures that underlie the authoritarian state. It is for this reason that I argue that while the PJD may be challenging the hegemony of the state at the municipal level, it is doing little to destabilize the authoritarian regime. While, as a result of the charter, the PJD has brought CSOs into local government and has indeed improved service delivery, it also has further legitimized the monarchy as a political reformer, both by rooting itself in and reinforcing the monarchy's discourse and by elevating project-based CSOs within municipalities.

The 2003 Casablanca Bombings

According to A. Maghraoui (2015), the PJD's evolution can be divided into two distinct evolutionary phases that reflect changing dynamics within the parliament, the government, the general public, and other political parties, as well as between the PJD and the Movement for Unity and Reform

(MUR, see chapter 3). The first is what Maghraoui labels its "moralist" phase, from 1997 to 2003; the second, what he calls its "legislative" phase, is from 2004 onward. The pivotal events marking the transition from one phase to another were the party's unexpected success in the 2002 elections and, most importantly, the 2003 Casablanca bombings. In the aftermath of the 2003 Casablanca bombings, for which the PJD was directly and indirectly blamed, we increasingly see the PJD and the MUR distance themselves from each other, with the PJD reorienting its rationale for public action away from religion and morality and toward good governance, technocracy, and decentralization. The PJD thus turned to the monarchy's discourse of good governance and presented itself as a nonideological, nondangerous, uncorrupt, and constructive force in municipal politics that can get things done.

The PJD's moralist phase includes its first two legislative elections: 1997 (as part of the Mouvement Populaire Democratique et Constitutionnel [MPDC]) and 2002. While the MPDC/PJD technically did not run in the 1997 municipal elections, party leader Abdelkrim al-Khatib allowed the Islamists to run as independents, with approximately 100 Islamists out of 24,000 candidates elected (three became municipal presidents) (Wegner 2011: 27; Willis 1999: 49–50, 2004: 57). At the same time, the Islamist leadership began investing in the organizational structure of the party, reinvigorating the MPDC's local and provincial units, and calling on its student leaders to open branches where there were no structures. Consequently, by the time the PJD was created, in 1998, it had developed party structures in fifty-one out of sixty-five prefectures and provinces with national, regional, provincial, and local (or branch) divisions (Wegner 2011: 35). It had also developed its party structure and formalized its nomination procedures for both party leaders and electoral candidates (35–44).

By the time of the 2002 parliamentary elections, the PJD had transitioned from a small- to a medium-sized party. However, in the context of the September 11, 2001 (in the aftermath of which, other political parties, particularly the Istiqlal, used the event to discredit the PJD) and with the Algerian civil war (triggered by Islamist victories at the polls) in mind, the PJD chose to contest fewer electoral districts in the 2002 parliamentary elections—fifty-five out of ninety-one (Willis 2004: 63).[3] Yet the fact that the MPDC/PJD was not associated with the disappointing performance of the government of *alternance* and that it consequently could credibly retain its title as an opposition party and declare itself "antisystem" (combined with its reputation for being a clean and hardworking party) served it well. In the final tally, despite that the MPDC/PJD had deliberately limited its campaign, it tripled its representation in parliament in 2002 (67). The party "that did not want to win" (67) became the third largest party in the Moroccan parliament (Wegner 2011: 63).

Emboldened by its results in the 2002 national elections, the PJD announced that it would "take over the cities" in the 2003 municipal elections (Catusse and Zaki 2010). The 2003 Casablanca bombings, however, forced the party to rethink not only its strategy but the entire rationale by which it justified its platforms, policies, and actions in politics. While all five of the suicide bombers were from a radical Islamist group, the monarchy and other political parties accused the PJD of having a moral responsibility for the attacks. Both the PJD and the MUR were put on the defensive as some parties, notably the USFP, called for their dissolution. Consequently, the PJD could no longer emphasize social conservatism and moral issues, which were associated with radical causes.

In both parliamentary elections of the moralist phase the party had run on electoral platforms that had called for the reinforcement of religion in Morocco. It demonstrated this same commitment to moral values, as opposed to substantive political problems or key economic or social politics, in its parliamentary performance between 1997 and 2002 (hence the labeling of the time period) (A. Maghraoui 2015). In 1997, the MPDC/PJD presented an electoral program called "For a Total Revival: Authenticity, Justice, Development," which focused on the "importance of attachments to religious identity, historical authenticity and what was seen as the cultural specificity of Moroccan society" (Willis 1999: 63).[4] In the 2002 elections, it similarly ran on a campaign, entitled "Toward a Better Morocco," that had centered on five axes: authenticity, sovereignty, democracy, justice, and development (with the authenticity axis containing the "Islam" part of the PJD message) (Wegner 2011: 104; Willis 2004: 65–66). As in 1997, the PJD called for a greater role for Islam in education and public life and for strengthening of Morocco's Islamic identity. To be sure, the 2002 parliamentary campaign saw the PJD place greater stress on economic and social development. For instance, it opposed the introduction of a microcredit scheme for the poor because the practice of usury is contrary to shari'a and the party felt the scheme was against the interests of the poor (Willis 1999: 58–59). Yet, overall, the party maintained that no meaningful reform could take place without reference to shari'a. In fact, by the time of the 2002 legislative elections, it was sensitive to criticisms that it was a radical Islamist party, and particularly that it was antiwomen (based on the party's opposition to proposed amendments to the Personal Status Law [PSL] banning polygamy and unilateral repudiation by husbands and raising the minimum age of marriage) (Cavatorta and Dalmasso 2009; Clark and Young 2008).

The party's stance vis-à-vis the role of shari'a was to change with the suicide bombings in Casablanca. Fearing for its survival, the PJD reacted "to the historic circumstances that it faced by . . . bring[ing] its program into line with the expectations of the palace" (Tozy 2008: 39). In response to the political and societal backlash against the party, it turned to the regime's discourse of good governance and began presenting itself as a non-ideological and nonthreatening but experienced, effective player. In the words of Wegner and Pellicer (2009a: 166), the 2003 bombings resulted in a change from opposition to technocracy as the PJD began to emphasize "the necessity of a 'culture of expertise and of figures' and feasible policy propositions that were 'scientifically valid.'"[5] In keeping with its transformation, it consequently discarded a sizeable portion of its leadership and brought locally trained young technocrats with Islamist leanings to the fore (Tozy 2008: 39).[6]

As A. Maghraoui (2015) summarizes, after 2003, the PJD parliamentary bloc "became diligent about the legislative process,. . . provid[ing] deputies with specialized staff members to help draft and propose bills and technical expertise on policy issues . . . [and] submit[ing] the largest number of oral and written questions to the government."[7] The party was vocal in its condemnation of terrorism as a means of silencing independent or opposition voices. It furthermore supported the above-mentioned PSL reforms, justifying its support based on the approval of the reforms by religious leaders, the benefits to women and children, and the fact that the reforms were the product of a democratic process involving widespread consultations with civil society, women's groups, and political parties (Clark and Young 2008; A. Maghraoui 2015).

The PJD's change in its rationale for public action and in its strategy was clearly reflected in its relationship to the MUR. While the MUR and PJD technically had been separate organizations with distinct mandates since 1996, after 2003 the PJD distanced itself from the MUR, vastly accelerating the institutional autonomy of the two entities (Tamam 2007: 111). When the PJD had become a party, its leadership (with exception of al-Khatib and his old guard) had been composed of historical MUR leaders, such as Abdelilah Benkirane, and its membership had largely come from the MUR. Between 1997 and 2002 virtually all of the PJD MPs had been MUR members. The PJD's organizational body furthermore had been based on MUR structures, and it had depended on MUR resources for mobilization, support, and human resources (Wegner 2011: 59). Following the MPDC's electoral success, the MUR released a document of complementarity that established the MUR's main functions as the dissemination of its beliefs, morals, and the general shaping of society, primarily via *da'wa* and education (Tamam 2007: 100). It defined the PJD as a political organization dealing with political issues and defending Islamic causes in state institutions (Wegner 2011: 57). The two organizations were specified as independent but linked by "consultation, cooperation, and coordination and their joint objectives and principles" (58). Yet while formally differentiated, the informal boundaries between the two organizations were "extremely porous" (58). While the PJD was not a mere politico-institutional branch of the MUR (60), it continued to depend on the MUR's structures and shared local offices with the MUR. The party had developed its own independent sources of financial and human resources, as well as its own newspaper and independent institutions, such as a youth and a women's organization. And certainly, in comparison to the 1997 parliamentary elections, a greater number of PJD candidates had no affiliation to the MUR in the 2002 parliamentary elections (61). Nevertheless, as Wegner (62) states, its relationship with the MUR remained crucial. During the 2002 elections, the MUR campaigned for the PJD; it also granted the party credibility through its endorsement and joint activities (62).

Amid the above-mentioned calls for the outlawing of the PJD following the bombings, the PJD sought distance from the MUR as the link between the two made the party more vulnerable to accusations that it was "nothing more than a Trojan horse for a radical Islamist movement" (Wegner 2011: 64). Some PJD members even partially blamed the MUR for helping give rise to terrorism (Tamam 2007: 100).[8] Consequently, the 2003 municipal elections saw even fewer MUR candidates (Wegner 2011: 65), and during the 2007 parliamentary elections, the MUR did not campaign on behalf of the PJD. The MUR furthermore refrained from officially endorsing the PJD and forbade its preachers from advocating the PJD in their sermons (69). Moreover, the legitimacy of the party leadership now rested on its election by party members in the National Congress and the

National Council, as well as on its accountability to party institutions, as opposed to its affiliation with the MUR (67).

Importantly, the differentiation enabled the PJD to devise public policies to find practical solutions to day-to-day problems while leaving discussion of how to consolidate religiosity within society to the MUR (Perekli 2012: 98). In the aftermath of the differentiation, PJD members began to utilize the terminology of human rights, democracy, civil state, pluralism, rule of law, and the peaceful rotation of power more frequently.[9]

A New Legitimizing Rationale

Beginning with the 2003 municipal elections, the PJD promoted a new rationale for public action, with candidates at the branch level presenting themselves as pragmatic local managers calling for good neoliberal governance. The PJD stressed religious references less and readjusted itself to the local level, employing watchwords such as "proximity," "integrity," and "morality" (Catusse and Zaki 2010). In a context of Morocco's limited decentralization on the one hand and competitive clientelism on the other, the PJD began to promote a "politics of doing." As noted in Catusse and Zaki's study of the 2003 electoral platforms (ibid.), three interrelated facets came to constitute the PJD's new approach at the local level: a managerial approach to governing; the "euphemization" of the party's relationship to Islam; and efforts to address the daily problems and social needs of the citizens. All three prongs went hand-in-hand with the king's neoliberal, technocratic discourse of reform.

At the heart of the PJD's legitimization strategies is its new managerial approach to governing. As Catusse and Zaki (2010) observe, the economic argument is omnipresent, taking precedence over social ones—clientelism in particular—and justifying the need to decrease staff and to outsource certain functions in order to respond more effectively to the needs of municipalities. Based on the level of education of its candidates, its moral work ethic and accountability (Catusse with Cattedra and Idrissi-Janati 2007: 128–29), the PJD promotes itself as a party with the knowledge and technical savvy to successfully negotiate and manage projects and get results (Catusse and Zaki 2010). During the 2003 election campaign, the PJD consequently stressed the qualifications and skills of their candidates. PJD candidates were (and continue to be) notably younger—intentionally so in order to demonstrate the party's "candor and dynamism" (ibid.)—and had higher levels of education than the candidates of other parties.[10] Based on their technical know-how, PJD leaders furthermore focused on disqualifying "their political opponents, locally elected officials, or decentralised authorities by questioning their abilities" (Catusse with Cattedra and Idrissi-Janati 2007: 128).

Closely related to good management is what Catusse and Zaki (2010) refer to as the "euphemization" of the party's relationship with Islam—the second facet of the PJD's new rationale and strategy during the 2003 municipal elections. The 2003 municipal elections were remarkably devoid of religious references, themes, or street protests. With only a very small number of municipalities as exceptions, topics such as prostitution and homosexuality were absent (ibid.). In their stead was a rationale for political action and, correspondingly, a campaign based on the "moralization of politics," or the need to "moralize the management of public affairs" (Wegner 2011: 111). Thus, the PJD began to argue that while religion may inform the identity of the party, it is not required to emerge clearly in the management of the municipality (Catusse and Zaki 2010). The needs of the citizenry and pragmatism, rooted in the rationale of good governance, take religion's place. In fact, between 2003 and 2009, the PJD reversed its opposition to the above-mentioned law regulating micro-credit, arguing that if it was good for humanity then it was good for the PJD (ibid.).

The third interrelated facet of the PJD's post-2003 rationale and strategy is its efforts to address the daily problems of citizens and their social needs. In this regard the PJD tries to implement "forms of personalized 'social and institutional mediation' with voters" (Catusse and Zaki 2010). PJD councillors thus stress their availability. This "politics of doing" is articulated around two main types of intermediation: "an institutional one, where the elected representatives play the role of translators of the administrative demands of voters, and a more political and social one, in which the elected representatives use the (scarce) local and political party resources which they have in order to reinforce the link with voters" (ibid.). The former, institutional intermediation, consists of facilitating processes for and requests of citizens (such as obtaining administrative documents). Toward this end, PJD representatives strive to personalize their relationships with the municipalities' *fonctionnaires*—the state bureaucrats working in the municipal halls (often referred to as the technical staff).

These same interrelated themes could be seen throughout 2003–2009 and during the 2009 elections. The PJD's electoral manifesto for the 2009 municipal elections did not refer to religious law; it stressed socioeconomic politics, such as establishing municipal hospitals, fighting illiteracy, encouraging institutions that deal with women's issues, increasing financial help for the needy, and improving public parks (Perekli 2012: 100). Rather than religion, the party focused on the "morality of political life" and on "getting things done." Thus, when I asked why the PJD won in the 2009 municipal elections in Erfoud, a rural municipality (redesignated as an urban municipality following the 2009 elections) in the Saharan province of Errachidia, the former first vice-president (PJD) stated that one of the primary reasons was "the morality of the political life. We put morality at the center of every activity; we are not corrupt. The population sees that when we propose something, we do it, we really implement it. We work strictly on the public sphere, not 'personal services.' "[11]

Similarly, when I asked the former PJD president of Erfoud (elected in 2009) what his campaign strategy would be in the next municipal elections, he was quick to say: "We just have to show our results!" He then pointed to a large poster listing the projects the PJD had accomplished as well as the future projects for which there was already funding and approval, and stated "Il n'y a que le travail!" (There is only work!): "The daily work is our strategy for the next elections, therefore we are always on the electoral campaign. The huge amount of daily work we do is our election campaign. If the population is not convinced by our daily work, they will not vote for us."[12]

Closely related to this theme of "getting things done" were the branch's efforts to demonstrate its managerial skills and to discredit those of the other parties. As the pasha of Erfoud observed: "The PJD conducted a very good electoral campaign—explaining to the people what the previous council has done and pointing out the previous flaws. They used the mistakes of the previous council in the right way; they made them a source of success."[13] Likewise, between 2003 and 2009, when the Kenitra branch of the PJD was in opposition, it sought to develop good working relationships with the municipality's bureaucrats in order to better understand municipal procedures for when they would be in the bureau and also to gain information regarding mismanagement by the ruling coalition in order to be able to raise these issues at the municipal government's quarterly sessions (see chapter 3).[14] A former PJD council member in Chefchaouen stated that the party's experience in opposition between 2003 and 2009 was extremely useful because it meant that in 2009 they had candidates with "practice at governing. They knew how things worked."[15] Although the PJD in Chefchaouen was in the opposition and therefore not in a position of "managing directly," its members could "watch from the inside and see what works well and what does not." As the councillor stated: "En 2009, on savait qu'est-ce-que il ne fallait pas faire."[16]

The various forms of mediation could also be seen in the 2009 election campaign. As noted above, the various types of mediation are not unrelated. When PJD members in Tiflet were asked about their electoral strategy, they quickly responded that it was twofold.[17] The first part was communicating with people and listening to their needs—not just at election time (when the PJD went door to door) but throughout the year. The second was to "keep an eye" on the municipal council and to watch what it does. Echoing PJD representatives in other municipalities, they argued that even though they were in the opposition, they were able to learn useful things regarding the council, its performance, and its procedures. Just as importantly, they strove to use their position in the opposition to address the issues they learned "in the field" by bringing issues to the council's attention. In other words, they sought to link their "ear to the ground" with their "eye on the mayor." Tiflet's PJD representatives thus proudly stated that they were able to bring the issue of a neighborhood that lacked electricity to the attention of the council and have it resolved.[18] Institutional and the political and social intermediation thus are interrelated. The one aids the other. Similarly, in Kenitra, between 2003 and 2009, when the party was in opposition, it opened a local headquarters with a full-time paid employee so that a party representative would be present at all times to receive the public and take their concerns to the council.[19]

Most importantly, the PJD further developed its various forms of mediation once elected to power. In Erfoud, for instance, the former PJD president and council members elected in 2009 personally dealt with citizens' complaints ranging from sewage to transportation.[20] It was not unusual for the president to visit a neighborhood association regarding the poor condition of the roads and then to personally relay these issues to the governor (demanding, for example, on behalf of the association that a transportation study be undertaken and the roads be paved).[21] On behalf of the grande taxi (large taxi) drivers, the Erfoud president went to the pasha with the complaint that the police were not enforcing the law.[22] On behalf of a citizen who called him with a complaint, the former first vice-president in Erfoud personally contacted the private electricity company (the National Society for Electricity), obtaining a speedy resolution of the citizen's problem.[23]

The PJD in Service of Civil Society

Having embraced the monarchy's good governance agenda, the charters offered the PJD a variety of opportunities to advance its political interests, namely to gain electoral power at the municipal level. As an opposition party that had historically run on, and maintained its base as, an antisystem party, the PJD not only lay outside the regime's networks of patronage but had based its credibility on rejecting them. Consequently, the PJD saw in the charters, and particularly the 2009 charter, the opportunity to prioritize civil society activism, and ultimately the concerns of civil society activists, in terms of the party's mandate and in terms of its selection of candidates and coalition partners. Local PJD branches thus have sought to prove the party's credibility and competence by encouraging individual members to work with and in nonpartisan NGOs, particularly those with a development focus. In this way, party members could prove their knowhow and effectiveness to a broader swath of the population and demonstrate their shared concerns with and capture the support of the country's new technocratic civil society activists—activists empowered by the monarch's good governance discourse and the INDH in particular.[24] The PJD thus gained supporters and coalition partners; what brings these coalition partners together is a shared bond not only over the prioritization of issues but the PJD promise, should it come to power, to fulfill the charter's specifications vis-à-vis civil society.

As discussed in chapter 3, at the core of Mohammed VI's reorientation of the monarchy's political management style are new ways of recruiting key elites (Tozy 2008: 37–38). Yet, as D. Maghraoui (2008: 194) states, while the regime has attempted to co-opt its new civil society elite and appropriated much of its discourse, it would be a mistake to assume that the role of civil society is merely artificial and manipulated by the state. Partnering with civil society actors has become part of the official discourse. This discourse, which both informs institutions and reforms such as the

INDH and the 2009 charter and is strengthened by these same institutions and reforms, has increased civil society's expectations for power and its desire to exercise control over public space—to implement its goals and demands (Wilcox 2009). Thus, as noted previously, we have seen the proliferation of CSOs and the entry of civil society activists into the political sphere where they seek to "transform their acquired managerial skills into political resources" (Eibl 2012: 52). Municipalities throughout the country consequently have witnessed the rise of technocratic civil society activists, largely as a result of the INDH, who see political problems as development issues. It is to these technocratic civil society activists— empowered by the king's discourse and initiatives yet frustrated by the politics and political parties of the traditional elites (see chapter 3)—that the PJD began to reach out following its disappointing performance in the 2003 municipal elections, when it won less than 10 percent of seats.[25]

The local branch of the PJD in Kenitra, a medium-sized urban municipality with approximately 430,000 inhabitants located 36 kilometers from Rabat, provides a good example of how the local party branches sought to reverse their fortunes in the 2009 municipal elections by reaching out to civil society. Beginning in 2003, the branch undertook several new initiatives.[26] The most important of these initiatives started to "work hard to create good relations between the PJD and the population."[27] The strategy seems to have worked. In 2009, the party raised the number of seats it won from twelve (2003) to twenty-nine out of fifty-nine seats, and it won the presidency. The initiative to which the first vice-president of Kenitra and other PJD members attribute the greatest credit for their 2009 success was their work with civil society. As Clark and Dalmasso (2015: 13–14) explain, between 2003 and 2009 the party undertook "three steps" vis-à-vis civil society that led to its success. Most importantly, it held numerous and regular open houses in neighborhoods throughout the city that were used to assist citizens in solving municipal-related issues. The party approached people well known in their neighborhoods—regardless of their political affiliation—asking if they would be willing to offer their homes for open houses during which time PJD representatives could hear citizens' issues, inform them of their rights, and direct them to the appropriate authorities.[28] Second, the PJD encouraged and assisted people in establishing neighborhood associations—legal associations, similar to those that arose in the 1990s (see chapter 5), created by citizens to address the immediate needs of their neighborhoods, such as sport activities. In addition, the party established small party committees to represent each of the areas and to work as intermediaries between the associations and the party.[29] The party's third step was to assist the neighborhood associations in creating a network to support the PJD (14). By the 2009 election, the Kenitra branch of the PJD had not only successfully mobilized civil society; it had substantially increased the number and size of PJD-sympathetic CSOs.

These three steps were supplemented by a strategy of encouraging PJD members to establish or join an association—regardless of its political affiliation—and of recruiting well-respected civil society activists to join the PJD. Thus, in response to a question by Clark and Dalmasso (2015) relating to the cooperation between Islamist and non-Islamists, a female PJD member active in Kenitra's associational life answered: "Yes they cooperate, in my women's association I am the only PJD member, but the other women are very happy, they said to me that we have transportation, meeting-rooms whenever we want. Our activities succeed thanks to our personal relations. . . . moreover our association has been included in the Muntada network [the PJD's women association national network]" (14). Similarly, when we asked one former PJD council member, who had been recruited by the president of Kenitra (Abdelaziz Rebbah) for the 2009 elections "as Real Madrid recruited Ronaldo" how he became involved in politics, he answered in the following way:

> Honestly I don't know, I had never thought about becoming involved in politics. I was involved in civil society and the former municipal council marginalized the civil society actors, we did not have the possibility to use the communal buildings, the gyms . . . in Kenitra there was a lack of infrastructures from the streets to the kindergartens, but then Rebbah arrived. I appreciate him a lot because he really wants to work for the city. . . . Rebbah knew me and came to me with a proposition because we share the same principles. First I refused to get involved but then Rebbah told me that if all the honest people refuse, things won't change because the same people will stay in power. Thus I participated in the 2009 elections and we won twenty-nine seats out of fifty-nine. Before Kenitra had two gyms and now four, and we are also building a cultural center. (15)

The example from the PJD in Kenitra demonstrates the local branches' focus on capturing civil society actors—the very actors who have been empowered by the king's focus on good governance and decentralization and whose role in municipal decision-making the charter had recently elevated—as candidates, supporters, and voters.[30] In terms of their election campaign and strategy, local PJD branches have a significant margin to maneuver vis-à-vis the central leadership.[31] According to representatives at the national level, the national party provides the "large orientations" of the election campaign—the discourse and the program in broad strokes; the local branches refine their own detailed programs, taking into account the particularities of their branch and municipality. The program provided by the national electoral committee—which includes values such as transparency, equity, efficiency, efficacy, and good governance—thus resembles a "skeleton" on which the branches add the meat.[32]

The selection of candidates for municipal elections also is left to the local branches, although the national level may interfere (Wegner 2011: 36–38). By the time of the 2003 municipal elections, the PJD had developed procedures specifying a series of committees—beginning with a committee of local members—for each stage of the selection process (38).[33] While the secretary-general technically has the authority to change the ranking of the candidates, to add candidates, and to withdraw the lists, in the majority of municipalities it appears that local-level choices are fully respected; local branches uniformly insisted that the selection of their candidates was "100 percent a local decision."[34]

In the context of the national party's broad strokes and of the opportunities granted to civil society in the charter, numerous local branches of the PJD encouraged and supported civil society activists as candidates in the 2009 municipal elections. In the municipality of Chefchaouen, an urban municipality and the main city of the province of Chefchaouen located in the Rif Mountains of northwest Morocco, for example, the PJD developed a "local strategy" of "mixing" with other associations.[35] When asked about the branch's strategy vis-à-vis civil society, a former PJD council member in Chefchaouen stated: "The PJD is in all sorts of associations, not just PJD-affiliated ones. We felt that it would be better to be all over, rather than isolated. We work in a professional manner in each association, and we chose this strategy. It is more useful to be spread out. The party only said that it is important to be active in civil society; the members have the liberty to join whatever they want. This is good for associations such as the ADL [Association de Développement Local de Chefchaouen (Association for Local Development of Chefchaouen)] and good for us."[36]

Another former PJD councilmember agreed: "The PJD is in almost all associations—they do not have to be PJD associations—and the PJD members talk to everyone and discuss issues with everyone."[37] As the PJD council member who spoke of the ADL stated: "We have done everything we could in order not to make the ADL be perceived as a PJD association; and it was a strategy."[38] In the end, according to the estimates of one civil society activist, 80–85 percent of people who work in NGOs in Chefchaouen supported the PJD in 2009; the majority of these were young professionals between the ages of 20 and 45.[39] The PJD raised the number of seats it won from eight in 2003 to thirteen in 2009 when it entered a coalition with the USFP (three seats) and the Parti Socialiste Unifié (PSU, United Socialist Party) (two seats) and took the presidency and bureau.[40]

Similar to the PJD in Chefchaouen and elsewhere, the PJD members in Erfoud individually have entered a broad spectrum of NGOs, founded "neither on politics nor religion."[41] To be sure, the PJD in Erfoud is "close" to five or six associations, the oldest having been created in 1989 and the most recent in 2011.[42] However, the party members work in a variety of neighborhood associations, including the union of neighborhood associations, charity associations, and youth associations, for example, which operate independently of any one political party.[43] The former PJD president was involved in the student union at university and has been the president or vice-president of numerous associations.[44] Another former PJD council member works in a village association dealing with development issues just outside Erfoud that created a center for literacy as well as a number of other associations in both the countryside and in Erfoud.[45]

Members of the PJD branch in Erfoud attribute much of their 2009 electoral success (during which they increased their number of seats to fourteen and gained the presidency) to their recent efforts in associational work. In the words of the 2009 PJD president: "Because the PJD has a 'direct relationship' with the people, the PJD understands people better than others."[46] As the president elaborated, in every neighborhood, the population knew the PJD candidates personally, knew them and their "good behavior from their work in associations. . . . The PJD made sure to select those members who were strong in associational life for the electoral list."[47]

As another former PJD bureau member stated: "The PJD won because of the individuals in it, less so its ideology, and because the population wanted change after being ruled for almost eighteen years by the same group of people. . . . Erfoud is a very small place, everyone knows everyone, and the PJD people are known for their good behavior, comportment. This is why we won." When asked what he meant by "good behavior," he explained, "Almost all PJD people who were elected work in associations, so the population knows their behavior. These NGOs cover all kinds of domains: youth, family, culture, sport, development, co-ops."[48]

Indeed, the former president attributes the "huge change in the mentality" of the local population vis-à-vis the PJD—and consequently, their 2009 electoral success—to PJD members' work in associational life. As the former first vice-president explained: "More people now know that the PJD is not dangerous. There has been a huge change in mentality. The population now knows that the PJD members are good and honest and do good work. This is because the PJD started serious work in the social field, in associations. In addition, members of the PJD studied at university and now have returned to Erfoud, so now everyone knows the PJD is educated and competent."[49]

This strategy of PJD members proving themselves via associational work was backed up by direct political activities via the neighborhood associations. Erfoud's seven neighborhood associations, were predominantly founded by or affiliated with PJD members.[50] Under the previous government, PJD members were also active in the Union of Neighborhood Associations (four of the most active members of the union then became members in the municipal bureau).[51] One NGO activist recounted how the union, working with the opposition members, became a force to counterbalance the ruling party. On one occasion, by raising complaints at one of the open quarterly session of the council, PJD members in the union were able to prevent the successful passing of three different initiatives of the previous bureau.[52]

It therefore is unsurprising that when I asked the former president of Erfoud and a PJD member of Erfoud's municipal council's previous bureau why the PJD won in 2009, they pointed to three reasons.[53] The first was the "daily communication with the population," the most important of which was the "face-to-face" contact in the streets, the souk, and the neighborhoods. "Daily communication" also included organized meetings with the public throughout the 2003–2009 period, as well as brochures documenting the PJD's program at election time.[54] Second, they stressed the "daily engagement" with the population that occurs year round in the associations in which PJD members are active. Third, they pointed to the "morality of the political life"—the fact that the PJD puts morality at the "center of everything" so that the population saw, according to them, that they were not corrupt in their various dealings and activities (that there were "no personal services").[55] In all of its activities, the PJD members are disciplined and organized: "Les gens du PJD sont des militaire." As the former president and bureau member elaborated, we train and act as if we are in the army, we are present everywhere, and we are very organized and very prepared.[56] Reflecting on why the PJD won in Erfoud and not in neighboring municipalities, the president added that it depends on how interconnected you are with the population.[57]

In Tiznit, a small urban municipality of approximately 50,000 inhabitants in the southern province of Tiznit, we also see PJD members working on an individual level within civil society—as elsewhere, these initiatives are neither in the name of the party nor affiliated with the MUR.[58] In 2003, the Tiznit branch of the PJD was one seat shy of winning the majority (it won thirteen out of a total of twenty-five seats), but as a result of the ensuing coalitions it was relegated to the opposition.[59] As a leading PJD representative stated, while the PJD in Tiznit had always worked with civil society, until 2003 it had only worked with those civil society organizations that were "close" to the party: in other words, with predominantly MUR associations. After 2003, there was an "enlargement" of this strategy, and the Tiznit branch started to work with all types of CSOs, especially those not affiliated with the MUR or with PJD members.[60] As she elaborated, beginning in 2003, party members focused on getting civil society involved in municipal work. Thus, this same representative is the president of an association (dealing with single mothers and abandoned children) in which there are only two other PJD members.[61] Her association works closely together with other associations, including leftist-leaning associations, dealing with similar issue areas in order that they may jointly collaborate on specific issues or host joint events such as on International Women's Day.[62]

To be sure, part of the attraction of working in civil society would have been that the PJD could build on experiences in and of the MUR. The MUR's years of experience no doubt aided PJD members. As one former PJD council member in Chefchaouen stated, the MUR was like "our school" where we learned things.[63] This same council member also likened the relationship between the MUR and the PJD to a "father and son."[64] There can be a high degree of cooperation between the party and the MUR at the local level. When, for example, we questioned a PJD councillor in Kenitra about the relations between the PJD and the MUR, he declared:

> There were political parties willing to integrate me, but no one was Islamist. There was only the MUR, which we call "the mother," and since 1989 I belong to it. . . . Now I am still a member, I participate in its activity but I do not have any official role. Here in Kenitra there are a dozen of MUR associations, they are at the origins of the party's success because it is thanks to its associations and its closeness to the people that the party won. . . . The PJD's associations and the MUR's ones work for the same project and when the PJD needs help to succeed in an activity, we ask for MUR's help. . . . PJD and MUR are more or less the same thing, last week we organized a joint activity. (Clark and Dalmasso 2015: 16)

The PJD's contribution to this joint activity involved it granting permission to the MUR association to use the public space in front of the municipal building. As another former councillor elaborated on the significance: "We considered that this kind of activity raises consciousness among the citizenry, makes the brain work in the good sense, promotes a cultural change. They deal with the family, the youth, the Sahara, the Palestine, the Arab Spring. . . . They talk about the Arab Spring in a positive way, how we [the PJD] get into power, how we do work at the governmental level and we also explain to citizens the current political [situation]" (ibid.).

The PJD in Chefchaouen also benefited from long-term local MUR strategies that came to fruition in 2009.[65] The RR/MUR-inspired magazine *Sa'ada Chefchaouen* (the magazine does not administratively belong to the party or movement, locally or nationally) was established in 1996.[66] The magazine covers political, cultural, and social issues of relevance to the municipality. A significant proportion of its distribution during its thirteen years of communication prior to the 2009 elections was to Moroccan emigrants. During the 2009 election, the local party made a strategic decision to target these émigrés, and by its own assessment much of its electoral success can be attributed to the votes of educated middle-class professionals who had left Chefchaouen for jobs elsewhere in Morocco or abroad: "These people really helped us. Someone in Rabat tells their family in Chefchaouen that change is possible [so they vote for us]. And these professionals also vote in Chefchaouen because they are still registered here.

And also some of these professionals came back just in order to help the PJD during election campaign because the PJD was not perceived as the PJD but as the party of Chefchaouen."[67] In one PJD representative's words, the journal became a "tool of communication" and a *force d'encouragement*.[68]

Yet while a MUR presence and activities certainly provide an important foundation on which the PJD bases its activities, following 2003, the PJD reached out to non-MUR CSOs. Its members engaged in CSO activities separate from those of the MUR. Furthermore, not all municipalities have a MUR presence. Tiflet, a small urban municipality—albeit one that the former president described as decidedly rural in nature—located 65 kilometers outside Rabat, provides an example of a municipality in which there is a weak MUR presence and where the PJD's approach vis-à-vis civil society (and hence, the charter) becomes particularly clear.[69] With the 2009 elections, the Tiflet PJD did not manage to secure any seats in the bureau. However, it did manage to increase the number of seats it won from two in 2003 to five—a significant increase in a municipality dominated for the last forty-odd years by the parties representing two dominant families (see chapter 5). As the former Mouvement Démocratique et Social (MDS, Democratic and Social Movement) affiliate president of the Tiflet stated, "five seats is a lot because they do not even come from Tiflet"—that is, the council members' origins are not from the municipality although they now live here.[70] In fact, following the 2009 elections, the PJD was on the cusp of attaining a seat in the bureau when it entered a coalition with the Parti Travailliste (Labor Party), the RNI, and the PAM. The deciding party was the Party of the Environment and Sustainable Development (Parti de l'Environnement et du Développement Durable). After being lured by the PJD and its coalition partners, it eventually joined a coalition with the president's party (MDS) and helped bring the latter to power.

While there is one MUR association in the municipality, PJD representatives argue that it "did not play the most important role in the [PJD's] success" in Tiflet.[71] Rather, they similarly attribute their success to their close contact to the population. As they pointed out, PJD activists are known throughout civil society. They are overwhelmingly in associations with no affiliation to the PJD (or ideological leanings in line with it), including a parents' association, sports association, children and youth associations, and the teachers' union. Most importantly, PJD representatives "upgraded" their field of intervention between 2003 and 2009 by going door to door in as many neighborhoods as their human resources would allow in an attempt both to decrease the number of nonvoters in general and to present the work they are doing on the council. It is to this strategy that the party representatives attribute the greatest source of their growing success. Echoing words elsewhere, one representative stated that it was their reputation and their personal relations that helped them secure more votes.[72] As in other municipalities with a PJD presence, the PJD in Tiflet attempted to create neighborhood associations. Yet it was unsuccessful in doing so, facing a population strongly divided by clientelistic ties to either the A'rchane or the Berkya family (see chapter 5) and a weak civil society that is not independent of the associated political parties.[73] Instead of neighborhood associations, the PJD in 2011 established a Neighborhood Committee, the purpose of which is to hold general meetings in the various neighborhoods, hear complaints, and bring them back to the council. While the committee also did not work as well as the PJD would have liked, as a result of the committee they were able to identify key people who "were very good at transferring information from the neighborhood to the council, and with time they became either members or sympathizers of the party."[74]

Working with civil society thus offers the PJD several advantages. As the PJD representative from Tiznit stated, PJD members work with civil society because it is open; there are no barriers to entry. Simply put, it is easy for the PJD to meet nonmembers and nonsympathizers via civil society.[75] Through their work in associational life, PJD members can demonstrate and prove their competence; they can, in other words, back up and reinforce their reputation as hard-working and effective managers. As the PSU member of the former Chefchaouen bureau stated, "Citizens voted for the PJD because they wanted change from Istiqlal but the PJD was also involved in civil society and people saw how well they worked in civil society organization." People saw how well the PJD worked in civil society and this was the main difference between the PJD and Istiqlal.[76] Representatives of the PJD in Tiflet agree—while being in the opposition may mean that a party has little to no access to real decision-making, an opposition party can work with civil society groups regardless of political affiliation.[77] The PJD can serve the citizenry better via civil society than it can being a political party in opposition—and in doing so, it can serve itself.[78] The PJD benefits from working with civil society as a conduit to the municipal council.[79] Just as importantly, the population, as the Tiznit representative stated, trusts civil society more than it trusts political parties.[80]

As the Tiznit representative put it, "PJD members work in civil society because politics is not enough to convince people."[81] Although the population does not trust political parties, individual PJD members can demonstrate that they are trustworthy and that they will bring the same level of competence to the council if elected. PJD members furthermore were able to reach out to civil society activists as fellow activists, not as party representatives per se. In this manner, they were able build ties with the very activists the charter sought to elevate in terms of decision-making. Representing a common sentiment among civil society activists, one head of an NGO stated: "We work with individuals who work well and support us, we do not work so much with parties per se. Civil society does not trust political parties—they come and go—it is far better to work with people."[82] One of the founders of Rif el-Andalous, an association focusing on the heritage and culture of Chefchaouen, agreed that the individual, not the party, matters, stating that "I do not care about the political color of the municipal council; I only care about the work and whether or not it is done, regardless of who does it."[83]

The Charter and the PJD's Coalition Strategies

The charter enabled the PJD to further its political interests by presenting it with an opportunity to gain the support of civil society activists, but it also enabled it to lay groundwork for electoral coalitions with those activists. The PJD branches reached out to the country's new technocrats—the largely middle-class urban professionals who engage in civil society activism—as coalition partners to help secure their electoral victories. In the municipalities under study, the PJD built their respective electoral lists based on the individual achievements of the potential candidates in civil society and chose their coalition partners based on the same criteria. Central to the PJD victories in Chefchaouen, for instance, was the success of the various individuals on the list—regardless of political stripe—in CSO work. These criteria also were reflected in its choice of coalition partners—with the local party prioritizing civil society activists over the allies of the national party. The PJD list in Chefchaouen was in fact a "mixed list" that included non-PJD members, all of whom were civil society activists (see below). The role of the charter in these coalitions was crucial, for at the heart of the coalition was the spoken or unspoken agreement that the PJD would prioritize civil society's concerns and fulfill the spirit and letter of the charter by bringing civil society into municipal decision-making.

As in the electoral campaigns, the PJD grants its branches significant freedom to determine its coalition partners.[84] In their study of PJD coalition building in the 2003 municipal elections, Wegner and Pellicer (2011: 303, 305, 309, 314, 321) found that the PJD had developed a highly pragmatic approach to coalition building—one that placed little importance on ideology in its selection of coalition partners. Following the Casablanca bombings, the PJD quite naturally sought as many municipal presidents as possible—this meant that it "could afford little to no consideration for differences in political agendas" (Pellicer and Wegner 2015: 40–41). Consequently, during the 2003 municipal elections, the general secretariat of the PJD decentralized the managing of the coalitions to the local levels and posed only two main criteria for the councillors when negotiating the coalitions (42–43): (1) the integrity and competence of the individual person proposed for mayor and (2) how a party had performed in terms of local management. As Wegner and Pellicer explain, what mattered the most was that the PJD forge coalitions only with people who had not been "completely delegitimized by their record of previous municipal management" (42), although this meant PJD councillors sometimes had to "close their eyes vis-à-vis some councillors or parties" (Wegner 2011: 113).

In 2009, PJD coalition building similarly was driven by largely strategic considerations when it faced stiff competition from the country's newest palace party (a decidedly anti-Islamist party), the PAM, which had won sweeping victories in the parliamentary elections in 2007.[85] As one former PJD councillor in Kenitra stated, "The secretary-general of the PJD at the national level gave permission to make any type of coalition, except not with those who had a reputation for illegal activities."[86] Tiflet PJD members concurred, stating that they had 100 percent freedom to make any coalition at the local level, that the national party does not impose anything at the local level "because at the local level it is a matter of offering services more than ideology or politics."[87]

For the research municipalities, this freedom was used to forge coalitions with civil society activists based on understandings that the PJD would fulfill the charter's commitment to civil society. Chefchaouen provides an excellent example. In the 2009 municipal elections in Chefchaouen, Mohamed Sefiani was put at the top of the PJD list and, based on the PJD victory, became president of the municipality. When asked about the role of civil society associations in the PJD list's 2009 victory in Chefchaouen, a former council member stated unequivocally that Sefiani was put at the top of the PJD list to send a clear message to civil society that the PJD would involve them more in the decision-making of the municipality should they win; they wanted to demonstrate that they were "open to civil society," which, until that point in time, had had no real experiences or dialogue with the municipality.[88] Sefiani is a well-known civil society activist in Chefchaouen. He is, however, neither a PJD member nor a sympathizer. According to Sefiani himself, he entered politics for the first time only two months prior to the 2009 elections with the encouragement of other civil society activists. While new to politics, Sefiani has been active and respected in civil society for most of his life; he was three times president of the ADL, one of the two largest and most active NGOs in the region. It was in the ADL that Sefiani, a political independent, forged ties with PJD members who were also working in the organization. In 2009, Sefiani created an independent list of candidates for the municipal elections; this independent list then decided to fuse with the PJD to create a stronger "mixed list."[89] It was this mixed list, under the banner of the PJD, that won thirteen of the municipal council's twenty-nine seats in 2009.

Following the elections, the PJD created a coalition government with the PSU and the USFP.[90] In doing so, it forced the Istiqlal, with an MP at the head of its list who had ruled the municipality since 1982 (with a brief exception of one term, 1994–1997), out of power.[91] Again, the coalition was made possible by the fact that PJD members worked with the USFP members in various associations.[92] The PJD's prioritization of civil society activism also was reflected in the 2009 bureau members. As one NGO founder pointed out, almost all of the council members, not just the PJD members, were involved in associational life, and most were "very active and dynamic."[93] The fifth vice-president and the PSU member on the municipal council, for example, had been active in associational work since secondary school. He was twice the vice-president for the Moroccan Association for Human Rights in Chefchaouen and the secretary-general for the Syndicate of Teachers of Chefchaouen. He was also active in his neighborhood association. Much like Sefiani, he did not enter political life directly until 2009, when various "comrades" asked him to participate in local politics; he subsequently joined the PSU. He attributed his decision to join to his previous civil society experiences; he had always had relations with the municipality and as a result became convinced that he needed to enter politics so he could better work in society. He understood that it was "good to be in politics to help civil society."[94]

Consequently, it was unsurprising when a former PJD councillor (and ADL member) attributed the PJD's success in 2009 in Chefchaouen to two reasons. The first was their accumulated experience since 2003—based on their experience in opposition between 2003 and 2009, the councillor stated that in 2009, "we knew what we shouldn't do!" ("En 2009, on savait qu'est-ce-que il ne fallait pas faire").[95] As an equally important reason, the councillor pointed to the PJD's list, arguing that it represented the entire city of Chefchaouen, not just the PJD. As he continued, the PJD needed a strong list so that the population would believe that change could happen; the population had wanted change for quite some time but needed a strong list to believe it was possible.[96] The PSU member of the bureau agreed, maintaining that the strength of the PJD list partly lay in the fact that it "reflected Chefchaouen society. Everyone saw someone. It was a strong list. It did not represent the PJD but the city of Chefchaouen."[97] This strong list meant a list of associational members, regardless of ideological persuasion, with proven track records in civil society.

Yet while having civil society activists on the list was crucial to the PJD electoral successes, not all activists are equal. When asked about their success, PJD members in Chefchaouen were quick to admit that there needed to be more to the list than civil society activists, regardless of their good reputation for activism. When one council member in Chefchaouen was asked about who voted for the PJD list, he answered: "Those who wanted change voted for us, but the problem was convincing them it was possible to vanquish a minister."[98] Indeed, one of the greatest challenges for the PJD was that "people understand that change is possible," and it is for this reason that the PJD "work[ed] so hard." As the council member elaborated: "The PJD had to have a strong list so that people would believe it could win against a minister, someone very powerful with lots of lands and who has support of other landowners. So [we] needed a strong list to convince people they could do it. People feared revenge . . . because, of course, if you fight against a minister, you better win."[99]

In Chefchaouen, the PJD list faced not only a mayor who was also an MP but a council largely made up of the municipality's economic elite, which, as discussed in chapter 5, had been dominating municipal politics in Chefchaouen since the mid-1970s. As one council member stated, "there is only one interest in Chefchaouen, and that is the land. And those who are interested in land vote for [the MP] Alami. Land is so important in Chefchaouen because there is so little that one meter makes a difference."[100] By placing Sefiani at the top of the list, the PJD not only demonstrated its commitment to civil society and the value they place on experience and education; they found a "social counterweight" to the previous president by capitalizing on the respect garnered by Sefiani's profession. When asked why Sefiani was put at the head of the PJD list, another council member referred to the fact that he is an engineer in a large well-respected international company: "First of all, he has an important job; he is considered someone important. And the PJD people knew him from working with him in the ADL. They knew that he is good, that he works hard and is very competent and has same values as the militants of the PJD. He is a serious person with lots of contacts and same values as the PJD. . . . If you want to substitute a minister you cannot do it with someone who is just a teacher."[101]

At the heart of the coalitions, however, lay the shared understanding that the PJD would fulfill the charter vis-à-vis civil society's role. In Chefchaouen, one of the PJD's first initiatives was to build and establish a Maison des Associations (a center for associations, functioning as of 2011).[102] The center is part of a larger project, entitled "Good Municipal Governance: The Reinforcement of Democracy and the Promotion of Civil Society Participation in Northern Morocco," funded by the Agence Andalouse pour la Coopération Internationale et Développement (AACID) and executed by ADL Chefchaouen and the Spanish NGO Prodiversa, in partnership with the municipality—to provide associations a space in which to meet and host activities.[103] The director of the association estimates that there are more than 100 active NGOs in Chefchaouen, seventy-five of which are registered with the center. The center also provides support to the associations, financial and otherwise. In addition, the municipality purchased three buses for the center so that associations, as well as the local football and basketball teams, may use them when needed.[104]

As part of the project on good municipal governance, the PJD-dominated municipal council also established a Commission du Dialogue avec la Société Civile, a consultative body comprising six "spaces of dialogue" (espaces de dialogues), or subcommittees, headed by a liaison from the municipal council (a bureau vice-president) and including the relevant associations. The spaces or subcommittees include, for example, culture and heritage, sustainable development, neighborhood associations, marketing and tourism, sports and youth, and *proximité sociale*, dealing with issues relating to equality for women, the physically challenged, and other human rights concerns.[105] These committees meet three times a year with the municipality, and the representatives of the project discuss the issues relating to their theme. The commission thus goes well beyond (and is supplementary to) the Committee of Equity and Equal Opportunities as stipulated in the 2009 charter.

While the PJD-dominated Chefchaouen council had no formal system for integrating civil society into its decision-making, it did invite organizations to participate in meetings regarding specific projects.[106] As the above-mentioned PSU member on the Chefchaouen council stated, there was a huge improvement in relations between the municipal council and civil society under the PJD—CSOs are involved in meetings to help determine projects, and there is now a fixed budget for annual grants for associations.[107] The Chefchaouen council involved approximately 100 CSOs in making its *plan communal de développement* (PCD, local development plan); CSO input was gathered via five or six meetings dealing specifically with the PCD.[108] The municipality's work with CSOs also extended into other forms of partnerships; the association Chefchaouen-on-Line (see below), for example, was put in charge of making an Internet portal for the city, managing its website, and training the administration.[109] As the head of one association dealing with tourism stated: "What Sefiani has done in three years, Istiqlal took thirty years."[110]

The PJD in Erfoud displayed the same strategy—seeking civil society activists as coalition partners. As in Chefchaouen, the PJD in Erfoud based its choice of coalition partners on those who were active in civil society and chose to forge its coalitions prior to the 2009 elections. The PJD ran in twenty-two out of Erfoud's twenty-three electoral districts; the PSU ran in seven. The PJD's 2009 list predominantly comprised well-known PJD party members as well as three to five new PJD members—those who had been considered "apolitical" and entered the list, on request of the local party, just prior to the elections.[111] Importantly, the PJD made a preelectoral coalition with one PSU candidate—a civil society activist—and agreed not to contest the electoral district in which he was running; if he were to win, he would be part of the majority.[112] As the then PJD president stated, the PSU member is the president of a charity association; thus the members of the PJD knew and respected him as a result of his associational work.[113] Having him as part of the coalition would not only "stop the local division" within the opposition vis-à-vis the previous government but also show, as the president stated, that the PJD is open to anyone who believes in the public good. Speaking in greater detail of the PJD's coalition with the PSU, the president stated:

> The PJD is open to anyone who has the same goals, the public good. Before the elections there was a coordination between all the actors who are against the lobbying of the criminals [*malfaiteurs*]. . . . We are open, we are not closed, to coordinating with other people and also [the PSU bureau member] is president of a charity associations to which members with different ideologies belong. The House for Elderly People, for example, exists thanks to [this type] of coordination. So people of different ideologies know each other and have been working together. Also, electoral pacts that were made before the election were respected afterward. There were twenty-three districts in Erfoud, the PJD presented candidates in twenty-two of them— everywhere except where the PSU candidate was running. . . . We were loyal to our accord [that if he won he would become part of the majority and not be in the opposition].[114]

The PSU member agreed: "The majority is made up of two parties which have heterogeneous ideologies but the same goals and good local management [*gestion locale*]. There are no problems because we have the same goal. The two parties are the PJD, which is Islamist and moderate, and the second is the Partie Socialist, which is extreme *gauche*. . . . The majority is made up of fifteen persons; fourteen are PJD, and one, myself, for the PSU."[115]

Significantly, and similar to Chefchaouen, the PJD in Erfoud granted its coalition partner an influential position in the bureau.[116] Much like the PJD made Sefiani president of the municipality in Chefchaouen, it made the elected PSU member in Erfoud vice-president for Planning and Finance (*planification et finances*), a portfolio of considerable responsibility and one that many would argue is the second most important in the bureau.[117]

The PSU member's assessment of the coalition and his reasons for being in it are very similar. When asked why he was asked to be in a coalition with the PJD when he was not needed for the PJD to win the majority of seats in the elections, he responded that the primary reason was his NGO and trade union experience, that he was well known and experienced. Second, he argued, is because he has good ideas—something the PJD members know from their joint work with him in NGOs. Third, he added, his presence helps demonstrate that the party is "not ideological."[118] In council, he added, they focus on "what they have in common": "They are honest, they want to work, and this is why I want to be with them. I do not care if they pray or not. . . . The PJD is by far the most democratic of all political parties."[119]

The PJD in Erfoud increased its number of seats from less than a handful in 2003 to fourteen out of a possible twenty-three seats in 2009; it furthermore won the presidency in 2009—the same PJD candidate who had run but not won the presidency in the 2003 elections won it in 2009. Once in power, the PJD-dominated municipal council bureau in Erfoud consulted a significant number of NGOs in the making of its PCD—between 80 and 100 civil society representatives attended a series of meetings at the Maison des Jeunes and at the municipality building in relation to the PCD. Following the integration of civil society inputs and the completion of the PCD, the municipality continued to hold ten meetings per year with civil society representatives—these were above and beyond the informal weekly meetings that occur.[120] It furthermore distributed approximately 350,000 dirham (US$26,000) per year to close to forty associations to help them with their activities.[121] Sending a strong signal as to the importance of civil society to the PJD and to the municipality, the former Erfoud president invited the minister of Civil Society, al-Habib al-Shobani, to hold a grande *rencontre*, a public meeting to discuss post–Arab Spring Morocco. Between 2,500 and 4,000 citizens attended the meeting at the municipality's Youth Center.[122]

As in the other PJD municipalities, the president of Kenitra, Rebbah, similarly involved CSOs in making the municipality's PCD. When Rebbah first became president, he established monthly meetings with the municipality's CSOs; these meetings were then reduced to meetings for specific projects and a once-per-year meeting for what is called a "day of study"—in other words an evaluation day of NGO work and the municipality's role in it.[123] Importantly, he created an entirely new administrative department within the municipality—a new department for social, cultural, sports, and educational activities that financially supports NGOs and assists them in carrying out their activities (such as helping NGOs locate and/or providing them with a space in which to host events). Of the approximately 1,300 NGOs in Kenitra in 2011, 180 applied for and received funding from the municipality; of these, forty were cultural associations, seventeen sports teams, seventy-four sport associations, and forty-nine social associations. In total, the municipality distributed 2,930,000 dirham, which amounted to 1.3 percent of the total municipal budget.[124]

Once in power, PJD branches generally live up to their promises to their civil society partners; PJD-dominated municipalities prioritize civil society's needs because the party is to a large extent beholden to civil society. This has not necessarily meant the establishment of a Committee for Equity and Equal Opportunities but a variety of other (and often, more significant) initiatives. However, in all cases, civil society was involved in making the PCD. These examples from PJD municipalities stand in contrast those discussed in chapter 5, or, for example, in the case of Tiflet, where according to NGO leaders, the council does not host any meetings with CSOs, and no CSOs were consulted in the making of the PCD (NGOs do contact the Tiflet president whenever they have a new idea or require funds).[125]

It is little wonder that in the opinion of civil activists in PJD-dominated municipalities, the charter has played a significant role in elevating the role and importance of civil society and that the PJD is largely equated with the positive effects of the charter. The charter grants municipal leaders the opportunity to include CSOs in decision-making and, by extension, the opportunity to reach out to civil society based on direct or indirect promises to fulfill the charter's sprit, if not letter. When asked about the role of the charter in the PJD's success in Chefchaouen, the president of the Neighborhood Association of Sebanine, one of the most active neighborhood associations in the city, argued that there was a "big change before and after 2009 as a result of the charter . . . the charter gives people the chance to manifest more for the neighborhood. And the commune listens more easily to the associations."[126] Similarly, one of the founders of ADL and Association Talassemtane pour l'Environnement et le Développement (ATED), one of the two largest associations in Chefchaouen, and of numerous other smaller associations stated: "2009 was a really big change at the local level!" Beginning in 2009, he continued, the municipality started to be increasingly willing to cooperate with associations.[127] The twenty-somethings who founded Chefchaouen-on-Line were emphatic when asked whether the 2009 charter had had any impact: "Yes! A huge change!"[128] With a well-worn copy of the charter with its germane sections highlighted on the main desk of their office, they argued that the main difference was the ability of NGOs to partner with the municipality on various projects and pointed to their own new partnership with the municipality: "There has been a big difference in practice. Now we have a partnership with commune to train the staff. . . . This type of partnership is in the new charter, Article 36. Now associations and the commune are doing a lot of work together."[129]

It is therefore unsurprising that the PJD and the charter are so closely associated with one another by civil society activists. The two are commonly treated as interchangeable. Thus, when I asked the former PSU bureau member in Chefchaouen about the relations between civil society and the municipal council, he responded: "There was a radical change in relations between civil society organizations and the commune after the PJD came to power—an opening, a dialogue between the two. . . . This opening or dialogue is only since 2009 with local elections . . . [and it is] due to the members of the council; they are all civil society militants. So the dialogue is not just due to the president or to the PJD. But of course, the charter played a role; it gives communes the choice to include civil society organizations."[130] The leader of one women's NGO concurred: "The tight relationship between civil society organizations and the commune is only since the last elections. It is much more, much better than before. This is because the president is also a civil society person . . . and also because the king has done a lot . . . for civil society organizations."[131]

Indeed, while the charter offered the opportunity to effect change at the local level, it was only PJD members that, in the words of Catusse with Cattedra and Idrissi-Janati (2007: 128), "inscribed themselves in a legal pattern that uses structures of representation, neglected by other partisan groups, to impose themselves on the political field." The PJD has used the charter to its advantage and consequently gained power at the municipal level. While not elite capture, as civil society activists also have benefited, the PJD has captured municipal power as a result of the charter. In doing so, it has not only fulfilled the monarchy's good governance agenda, and the charter in particular, but by all accounts it has improved service delivery. Yet the PJD demonstrates once again that under authoritarian regimes, such as in Morocco, elite capture or the lack of it is not a question of decentralized power falling into the wrong or right hands. Rather, both are the result of local political actors pursuing the most useful opportunities the municipal charters have to offer them in order to achieve their political goals.

PJD Relations with the Central Authorities

Politically, the significance of the change in the PJD's rationale for public action and strategy lies not only in its electoral successes but also in the manner in which it has challenged the rules of political competition and of local power. As Catusse with Cattedra and Idrissi-Janati (2007: 128) state, its emphasis on its expertise and technical savvy, its "capacity . . . to master technical projects," has become a "weapon or resource in political competition." The PJD thus has politicized the local arena by wielding technocracy in the face of politics based on patron-clientelism. The PJD's discourse of competence and clean management, backed up by its effective activism in civil society, stands in stark contrast to the clientelistic and corrupt practices of many pro-regime parties discussed in chapter 5. Moreover, by shifting the discourse to one of technical competence, the PJD also challenges the foundations on which the representatives of the central state rest. Operating within the blurred lines of jurisdiction between the elected representatives and the representatives of the central authorities (see chapter 5), the PJD undermines the justification for the prerogatives of the representatives of the central authorities and "pushes back" the jurisdictional boundaries that the appointed representatives of the central authorities have asserted for themselves. The PJD does not hesitate to challenge governors when political or personality differences stand in the way of technically sound good management decisions. In this manner, the PJD challenges the hegemony of the state, yet it is not challenging the stability of the authoritarian regime.

Chefchaouen provides an excellent example of how the PJD uses its technical skills as weapons vis-à-vis the technocrats representing the central authorities. Following its electoral win in 2009, the PJD in Chefchaouen renegotiated the municipality's contract for garbage collection. The bureau sought to end the existing contract with the public corporation and sign a seven-year contract with Tecmed, a private firm specializing in municipal waste collection and management. The new contract would cost the municipality significantly more money per year; however, the PJD government argued that Chefchaouen would receive far more benefits. While the previous contractual arrangement was limited to garbage collection, Tecmed would collect and treat waste and clean public spaces. In addition, Tecmed agreed to hire municipal employees, thus partly resolving the bloated number of municipal employees hired under previous governments;[132] Tecmed would reimburse the municipality for those workers and thereby reduce the municipality's *gaspillage* (waste).[133] For the PJD, the new contract was quite simply an issue of good management. The opposition (namely the Istiqlal) sought to turn, according to the PJD, a "technical issue into a political one" by informing the governor as well as other administrative bodies and the press of what it argued was a case of patronage.[134] The MoI in Rabat clearly agreed with the PJD. In anticipation of the governor's opposition to its proposal to bring in Tecmed for the provision of water, the PJD in Chefchaouen sent its budget, which included the allocation of funds to Tecmed, directly to the MoI in Rabat. The budget was approved without any reservations in Rabat. Only after it received approval in Rabat did the PJD send it to the governor for approval—a reversal of the established chain-of-command. When asked how this was possible, the PJD representative responded: "Do you know, this is a project ruled by the World Bank, the money that the MoI gave us is a grant from the World Bank because the World Bank has signed an agreement with the MoI in order to improve these kind of public policies in Morocco. So when we saw that the governor was against us, we went directly to Rabat; we went directly to the [Direction Générale des Collectivités Locales (DGCL, General Department for Local Communities)]."[135]

When asked if this was typical to bypass the governor, his response was simple: "Yes, of course, when you have problem with the governor, it is normal to go and try to find a solution in Rabat because you cannot stay waiting for the governor and do nothing; when you have a political problem, the only solution is make pressure in Rabat in order to solve it. It is not that everybody does it, only the active presidents do so because if the president wants to accomplish things then going to Rabat is the only possibility."[136]

By bypassing the governor, the PJD dismissed the competencies of the governor and asserted its own, confident of approval for the project. While not done on a regular basis, this was by no means the only occasion (or only PJD municipality) where I witnessed the PJD dismiss the local representatives of the central authorities in favor of Rabat.[137]

With the deconcentrated administrative structure of authority justified by the supposed need for the technical knowledge of the representatives of the central authority, the PJD thus undermines the rationale for the subservience of the decentralized structures of authority to the deconcentrated structures of authority. By asserting and demonstrating its technical competence, the PJD breaks "the false alternative between a representative legitimacy and a technological legitimacy" (Catusse with Cattedra and Idrissi-Janati 2007: 127). It challenges the foundations that justify the authoritarian administrative structure of authority. It effectively challenges the hegemony of the state.

Yet the PJD cannot be said to be challenging regime stability. Decentralization—and the PJD's strategic use of the rhetoric of good governance and decentralization, as well as of the 2009 charter itself—has contributed to the normalization of Moroccan authoritarianism. By adopting the regime's discourse, participating in elections, and winning in elections, the PJD contributes to the outward appearance of a politically liberal and democratic Morocco. Stated differently, it contributes to the legitimization of the regime by legitimizing its discourse and bringing technocratic civil society activists—the regime's new coalition partner—to the fore. The PJD thus normalizes both the INDH and the charter, and with them the legitimacy of the monarch. Moreover, this normalization is operationalized in PJD-dominated municipal councils once the PJD comes to power. PJD-dominated municipalities, as intended by the good governance agenda and the 2009 charter (see chapter 5), are largely depoliticized; as the councils work to fulfill civil society's needs and demonstrate their "politics of doing," politics in PJD-dominated municipalities becomes increasingly a technocratic exercise in development.

Conclusion

Good governance, decentralization, and the 2009 charter have empowered civil society by valorizing civil society's role in decision-making. By doing so, they also offer the PJD a political tool it can use to discredit traditional elites and broaden its support within civil society while remaining firmly within the king's discourse and "technocratic" path. Power, as a result of the charters, did not fall into the "right hands"; it fell into hands that viewed the empowerment of civil society as a result of the charter as working to their political advantage. The PJD's electoral successes in 2009, in terms of removing established elites or winning additional seats, were made possible by the fact that the party not only brought its legitimizing rationales and strategies in line with the king's good governance initiatives but that it embraced nonpartisan civil society work, selected its candidates based on their performance in civil society, and worked with and/or included in its coalitions and lists non-PJD members who had demonstrated their commitment to and success in civil society work. Civil society actors responded to the PJD, seeing that the party offered them new channels of participation to affect municipal decision-making.

The impact of decentralization on the local political arena in Morocco thus has been more profound—or least has resulted in some profound exceptional "enclaves"—than the many studies on decentralization under authoritarianism acknowledge. By legitimizing itself through the logics and principles of decentralization, the PJD has altered the rules of political competition and has forged a new type of relationship between parties and civil society. In contrast to the prevailing norms, according to which civil society is in the service of political parties (see chapter 3), the PJD has negotiated a new relationship according to which the PJD is in the service of civil society. The PJD furthermore has challenged the prevailing relationship between the representatives of the central authorities and elected local authorities by successfully asserting its jurisdictional claims.

At the same time, while the PJD may be changing the rules of local political competition, with its focus on moral clientelism, it remains to be seen if the PJD may simply be a new type of notable (Catusse and Zaki 2010). PJD councillors insist on the ethical dimension of their institutional and social mediation, that it is carried out in the interest of the citizens and not motivated by personal interest. They maintain that "moral clientelism" or "legitimate clientelism" is a form of better serving all citizens of the respective community, one in which services are better addressed to the needs of the population. In one municipality, the president made a point of demonstrating that he had two cell phones, one strictly for personal use and the other for municipal issues, in order to distinguish between traditional clientelism and the PJD's efforts to serve the citizenry. While, in essence, having two cell phones with different telephone numbers is meaningless in terms of clientelism, it was a symbolic gesture that the president sought in order to reinforce the "morality" of his party's tenure. The difference, the PJD insists, is that "the services they provide are not subject to favoritism, but are 'normal' services that citizens have the right to claim legitimately. Their actions aim at optimizing public services provided within the bounds of the law, contrary to other local political patrons who sometimes circumvent the law to satisfy their voters" (ibid.).

Yet despite the PJD's insistence that it shuns favoritism, PJD's mayors' personal involvement in citizens' cases indicates a strong possibility for a growing network of clients. Potential evidence of this can be seen in Kenitra, where civil society activists complain that Islamist CSOs are being giving preferential treatment (Clark and Dalmasso 2015).

Most importantly, however, the PJD's electoral victories as a result of the charters, serve in the long run to help stabilize the authoritarian regime. By capitalizing on good governance and decentralization reforms, the PJD has positioned itself with the authoritarian regime and with international (Western) economic agendas. It thereby promotes a discourse and a means of conducting politics that elevates the technocratic over the political—focusing on successful projects as opposed to challenging authoritarian structures.

Conclusion

In her article "Inside the Economy of Appearances," Tsing (2000) points to the "financial conjuring" that made the Canadian Bre-X gold prospecting company's meteoric rise in Indonesia possible. Financial conjuring, as she states (120), is intended to "call up a world more dreamlike and sweeter than anything that exists; magic, rather than strict description, calls capital." Thus, Canadian investors imagined a new frontier, one that shifted from mining in Canada to mining for Canada and one that would both make them rich and be a source of national pride. Most importantly, for the purposes of this book, successful conjuring the globe is only possible in "thick collaboration with regional and national conjurings" (121). Global projects come into being as articulations among partially hegemonic imagined different scales (143), global, national, and regional, and the links among them strengthen each project's ability to remake the world. In the case of Bre-X, financial conjuring in Canada "became linked with greedy elite dreams of an authoritarian nation-state supported by foreign funds and enterprises. . . . These in turn became linked with migrant dreams of a regional frontier culture in which the rights of previous rural residents could be wiped out entirely to create a Wild West scene of rapid and lawless resource extraction" (143). While intimately connected, each dream was pursued by independent actors with their own agency. Tsing's conceptualization thus helps us to better understand how global projects, such as the projects of international financial institutions, travel not only across the globe but from national to local levels. As an economic doctrine promoting the free circulation of goods, currencies, and labor across national and regional borders, neoliberalism is a set of scale-making projects. Decentralization also emanates from neoliberalism's program for global hegemony, and thinking in terms of conjuring across linked scale-making projects enables us to better visualize the practice of decentralization, the linked yet independent projects of agents at the international, national, and local levels. Decentralization is less imposed than it is negotiated.

This book demonstrates how the global project of decentralization links or crosses with the aspirations of authoritarian rulers to remain in power and then in turn with those of local political leaders intent on gaining or maintaining power. As in the case of Bre-X, where financial conjuring globally, specifically in Canada, was intimately linked to authoritarianism in Indonesia, the global decentralization project is linked to the maintenance, if not the strengthening, of authoritarianism and to elite capture in Morocco. With decentralization, the Moroccan monarchy has been able to pursue coalition strategies to keep it in power, pro-regime parties have been better able to develop patron-client ties, and opposition parties, namely the Parti de la Justice et du Développement (PJD), have been able to come to power. As the good governance and decentralization project unfolds, the Moroccan monarchy is able to present itself as a political reformer, both internationally and domestically, while forging coalition partners to help legitimate and sustain its rule, download responsibility for service delivery, and undermine local governments while simultaneously blaming them for all service-delivery failures and then using their failures as justification to "come to the rescue" of the citizens by bypassing elected officials and bringing services directly to the people. Rather than leading to improved service provision and local democracy, decentralization reforms consolidate the power of the existing regime, generate opportunities and resources that are more often than not captured by pro-regime political elites, enhancing clientelism and corruption, which the king and his representatives then use as justification to reassert central authority. Decentralization thus results in recentralization all but in name. To be sure, good governance and decentralization have produced some innovative success stories of effective local development. However, the Moroccan monarchy ensures that these success stories do not gain ground and remain isolated experiences. Decentralization enables the monarchy in Morocco to present itself as a political reformer and stabilize the authoritarian regime in ways that centralization in Jordan cannot. Rather than consolidating support for the regime, as has been the case with decentralization in Morocco, centralization in Jordan has fragmented regime support.

At the heart of the Moroccan monarchy's success in maintaining, if not deepening, authoritarianism as a result of—or, in fact, by using—good governance and decentralization lies the projection of the seemingly apolitical, technocratic discourse with which neoliberalism presents itself. As Khoo (2010) states, politics looks to technocracy "in order to embed the exercise of state power in many kinds of agendas, policies, decisions, and programs." The discourse of good governance and decentralization conjures a technical language that sees efficiency and procedural questions, not structural political issues, as the route to addressing Morocco's problems. Technocracy thus is an ideology that rests on the belief that it is nonideological, one that espouses the "use of value-free, objective criteria for making decisions, the creation of 'depoliticized solutions to all organizational environmental problems'" (Centeno 1993: 311). By projecting a "politically neutral" and "economically efficient" ideology, good governance and decentralization effectively de-ideologize and depoliticize fundamentally political issues.

We thus witness how the Moroccan monarchy has utilized good governance as a means of promoting itself as a political reformer while technocratizing civil society; basing itself on international norms of good governance, the regime has promoted and effectively created a civil society elite, the discourse of which it has appropriated for its own uses. What remains is a civil society with elite status both in terms of the regime's discourse and initiatives but one that is depoliticized and does not present a political threat to the regime. Likewise, the king's National Institute for Human Development (INDH) initiative acts to depoliticize civil society by not only 'filtering' which associations receive INDH funds—again those that present no political agenda or an agenda in line with that of the regime—but by funding technical projects. INDH rewards those civil society organizations (CSOs) that focus on projects that aim to address discreet social-welfare issues within the existing authoritarian political structures; with decentralization, this project-oriented civil society is then encouraged to enter politics—but it is a civil society that focuses on social welfare and service delivery as a technocratic exercise in getting the formula for the best project right.

We see the same phenomenon in Jordan. Jordan did not implement any form of overarching decentralization framework during most of the period under study; however, government in Jordan was significantly respatialized through the establishment of special economic zones, development zones, protected natural areas, and municipal restructuring. We thus consistently see democratic rights being removed or reduced in the name of economic development and growth. At the municipal level, this has translated into the central government repeatedly imposing municipal managers or executive directors who essentially usurp the powers of mayors and justifying their imposition in entirely economic rationale. Again, technocracy is promoted as distinct from and superior to politics. As in Morocco, it enables regime in Jordan to directly reinsert itself in local politics.

"Decentralized conjuring" lies in a discourse that not only identifies technocracy as apolitical and therefore more effective and efficient than the political but also identifies technocrats as superior to elected political representatives. Under the guise of decentralization, the Moroccan regime has not only maintained centralized political power by decentralizing authorities to the appointed governors but, as noted above, it has effectively ensured the undermining of elected municipal councils to its advantage. Morocco's municipal councils operate within vague, overlapping, and confusing jurisdictions that mean that municipal mayors and councillors often do not know whose authority is what and may easily have their authority usurped by a representative of the central government. Authorities and responsibilities that have been clearly granted to the municipalities invariably go to the councils' presidents; in other words, decentralization has increased presidential powers, not the councils' powers. This has created dissent and fragmentation in councils, which has been further exacerbated by a political system that also fosters instability as it pits the bureau against the so-called opposition. In this vein, decentralization has aided in fostering incompetent or corrupt municipal councils that the regime denounces as corrupt and particularistic as it calls for unelected representatives of the state to address the resultant poor service delivery. The authoritarian state saves citizens from their elected representatives; in doing so, it undermines democratic practice and even the concept of electoral democracy.

The success of decentralization as a tool for the authoritarian regime in Morocco lies in the fact that it links with the aspirations of local elites. The 1976 municipal charter downloaded decision-making responsibilities for the first time to the municipal level and, as a result, captured the attention of local, largely landowning elites, who now had means with which to protect and advance their interests. Decentralization in turn captured the attention of political parties, including opposition parties, who saw an opportunity to absorb these local elites and their votes and to gain power. Here we see how different project-making scales came together: bringing local elites into the political party system, opposition parties into the government, and ultimately co-opting both.

Elite capture thus cannot be isolated from regime coalition strategies. It is a fundamentally political project both on behalf of the regime and local actors. Municipal actors have their own agency, and elite capture, or the lack of it, is the result of these actors pursuing their interests. How local actors determine their political interests vis-à-vis good governance and decentralization reforms is determined largely by the extent to which they can benefit from and can take advantage of the patron-client ties that underpin the authoritarian regime. In the majority of municipalities throughout Morocco during the time period under study, pro-regime political elites were easily able to take advantage of good governance and decentralization reforms by capturing the resources and decision-making powers intended—at least in terms of discourse—for civil society. Exploiting the intentionally vague and overlapping powers—formal and informal—and jurisdictions of municipal councils and other bodies noted above, councillors who are simultaneously heads of nongovernmental associations open up new associations to try to grasp resources and decision-making authorities newly made available to CSOs. As councillors, associational leaders adjudicate on the INDH committees, the purpose of which are to grant funds to associations (and to which they also applied for funds). They furthermore serve as the civil society representative on the municipalities' local development plan (PCD) committees or other committees. All of this is with a blind eye or blessing of the representatives of the central authorities who "assist" in the election of pro-regime actors and parties, make appointments to INDH committees, and ultimately play the largest role in determining not only which associations receive funding from the INDH but which municipalities receive approval and funding for their PCDs. In this regard, decentralization offers multiple avenues for elite capture and serves to entrench local—pro-regime—political elites by enabling them to maintain and even expand their decision-making powers, their resources, and their client base.

Importantly, elite capture is conducted via legal means—it is state sanctioned, if not desired. Overlapping jurisdictions, a lack of separation of powers, conflicting interests, and a high degree of discretionary power on behalf of the representatives of the central authorities all but ensure elite capture and the political dominance of regime-loyal parties. As noted above, the corruption and consequent poor and inequitable service delivery these engender furthermore justify the existence of the administrative structure of authority—in other words, state intervention in municipal affairs. Elite capture thus is not a problem of power going to the "wrong people," one that can be alleviated or eliminated via greater regulation and accountability. As a political problem, elite capture requires a political solution, one that begins at the national level.

Because it is situated outside the regime's networks of patronage, the PJD takes advantage of a different set of opportunities within the good governance and decentralization reforms: the opportunity to capitalize on the growing urban middle class, particularly its civil society actors empowered by the king's good governance discourse and seeking avenues to enter the political realm to better conduct their associational work. Rather than capturing the resources and powers of civil society, the PJD has embraced the values of good governance and decentralization and has changed its rationale for public action and its strategies accordingly. In contrast to other parties, which employ the discourse of good governance but little else, the PJD seeks to uphold these values by prioritizing civil society activists as candidates (or civil society activism as essential to PJD candidacy) and coalition partners and by bringing the mandate of the party in line with the development goals of civil society activists. At the local level, the PJD has transformed itself into a party in service of civil society; this has enabled it to present its candidates as qualified and "efficient managers who use local funds responsibly" (Englecke 2015; see also Bennani 2015) and to gain power in municipal elections.

Certainly the 2015 municipal elections reflect this bipolar Moroccan landscape (Mezran 2015), one that confirms the options or opportunities good governance and decentralization reforms present to local party branches to gain power. The two parties that were the clear winners of the elections were the Parti Authenticité et Modernité (PAM, Authenticity and Modernity Party), which came in first and won approximately 21 percent of the votes, and the PJD, which won just under 16 percent of the votes and, importantly, the position of mayor in all the big cities—Casablanca, Rabat, and Agadir (Engelcke 2015).[1] This bipolarity is reflected ideologically and geographically, with the Islamist PJD dominating the majority of the urban centers and the secular PAM dominating the countryside. More accurately, I would argue the landscape is polarized between the technocratic party of the PJD and the newest (and premier) palace party of the PAM, which gains much of its electoral strength based on patron-clientelism and the promise of services based on the party's leadership's closeness to the monarchy. The PJD's breakthrough in the major urban centers of Morocco and its ability to win over voters who were not a part of its rank-and-file in 2015 was made possible by its pragmatic political rhetoric, the fact that its competitors were mired in corruption allegations, and the moderate image of Benkirane (ACRPS 2015).[2] The PJD was less ideological or Islamist than it was technocratic, presenting itself as an honest, hardworking party that got things done. The research results presented throughout this book indicate that the PJD's change in its rationale for public action, its embrace of the values of good governance as a legitimization strategy, would not be as successful in the voting booths if it had not also directed its members to redirect their efforts in civil society and transformed itself into a party in service of civil society. It was only through its civil society activism that the PJD was able to prove its technocratic skills and its commitment to the values of good governance and through its partnerships with civil society activists that it came to power.

Good governance and political decentralization thus have indeed raised the profile and importance of civil society in local politics, yet not as envisioned by the international good governance project. Civil society has become an important arena, if not the most important arena, of political competition with political parties, all political parties, pursuing their goals via civil society. Pro-regime party leaders establish CSOs to exploit their resources and gain votes. The PJD works through and with civil society to gain power. For all parties alike, civil society activism is the route to power. To a large extent, this is not new. Political competition historically has been related to civil society activism in Morocco; however, with good governance and decentralization, civil society activism is the dominant method, and increasingly the only method, by which politics is conducted at the local level. Yet it serves to undermine the political and, in most cases, neither fosters increased participation or democratization nor improves services and service delivery.

While economic reforms have disaggregated the state—granting greater powers to governors, to the INDH, and to private actors in Morocco, for example—they have not lessened central state power; more to the point, they have strengthened the power of the *makhzen*. Similarly, in Jordan, where public services also have been NGO-ized, the royal family has increased its powers through RONGOs and their public-private partnerships with service-delivery NGOs. While the two states have withdrawn, their disaggregation has allowed a more direct route by which each monarch may engage in coalition strategies. The Moroccan king brings an INDH dialysis center to a municipality. Jordan's King Abdullah Foundation provides the investors or the infrastructure for a local development project. In both cases, economic reforms ensure that the kings remain the central referent.

Yet while Morocco and Jordan share certain aspects of economic reform, decentralization has contributed toward stabilizing and sustaining the authoritarian regime in Morocco while centralization in Jordan has not. In Morocco, decentralization enables the king to be perceived as a significant political reformer, downloading powers and responsibilities to municipalities and, importantly, providing municipalities with the tools to help themselves. Even as municipalities fail in their service delivery tasks, the king retains the image of a political reformer as he is "forced" to step in and rescue citizens from their municipal plight. Ironically, the king maintains this image even as he undermines elected representatives and the concept of electoral democracy. Elite capture contributes toward the undermining and discrediting of democratically elected bodies so that representatives of the central state, newly empowered by the transferal of decision-making powers, new jurisdictions of power, and vast discretionary and informal powers, must come to the aid of citizens facing poor and inadequate services with much-needed resources and projects. Yom's words in regard to Jordan's parliament could easily apply to Morocco's municipalities. Referring to how members of parliament fight over reputation and patronage, Yom (2013: 16) aptly summarizes: "The circus that the . . . public sees . . . plays right into the palace's strategy. . . . How could anyone want power to devolve from the monarchy into the hands of such petty squabblers?"[3]

The PJD, the country's only opposition party during most of the period under study, also acts to reinforce the image of the king as a political reformer, even as it challenges, and in fact changes, the rules of the game in municipal politics. In a system underpinned by patron–clientelism and corruption, the PJD uses good governance and technical expertise as strategic tools with which to gain power and challenge the hegemony of the state. By seeking to ensure the sound management of municipal budgets, projects, and affairs, the PJD undermines the foundations on which the representatives of the central authorities justify state interference in municipal affairs. It chips away at the hegemony of the state as it challenges the "technocratic" legitimacy of the representatives of the central authorities. By upholding the king's good governance discourse and putting it into action, the PJD furthermore highlights the distance between the monarch's discourse and the practice of palace and administrative parties and also the distance between these parties and the PJD. As a consequence, the PJD is slowly and steadily undercutting the parties that help to sustain the regime. Yet the PJD remains solidly within the king's discourse and moreover contributes to the technocratization of politics with the inclusion of CSOs in municipal decision-making. By transforming itself into a party in service of civil society, local politics under the PJD have become an exercise in seeking and implementing technical service-delivery projects. The PJD thus serves to politically elevate a depoliticized civil society (and in the process, itself), one that presents no threat to the power structures that stabilize the national political system, and to contribute to the depoliticization of political issues.

Whereas decentralization reinforces the legitimacy of the political system and the monarchy in Morocco, centralization in Jordan serves to undermine the political system, specifically political parties, and reinforce tribalism while simultaneously making the latter less effective as a source of regime stability. In contrast to Morocco, where the regime uses decentralization to expand its coalition partners and thereby rejuvenate and legitimize a political system that works to its advantage, the regime in Jordan uses centralization as a tool to further privilege its coalition partner—the Transjordanian population, and its tribal elite in particular—in order to maintain its bedrock of support. Yet in a context of shrinking resources and a crisis in municipal service provision, particularly in the rural Transjordanian-dominated municipalities, the regime's strategy of centralization has exacerbated the competition between tribes and fragmented them along clan and family lines. To be sure, the regime historically has relied on competition between tribes, mediating their competition for state resources for stability, yet the increased competition and fragmentation at the local level reveals a growing sense of inequality between tribes/clans with even powerful tribes/clans perceiving themselves as have-nots. Furthermore, while centralization does not enable the monarchy to effectively present itself as politically reformist, any attempts to address the crisis with political decentralization reforms work against the interests of the very societal groups it seeks to privilege. That the regime grants patronage along tribal lines serves to continuously revitalize the institutions of tribalism; however, it is a tribalism that is increasingly divided along clan and family lines and that is entailing a growing alienation from the regime. At the municipal level, Transjordanian tribal leaders are frustrated not only with the dire economic situation of the municipalities but with the perceived begging they must engage in to address these economic challenges, the administrative obstacles they face in attempting to rectify the economic problems on their own, and the lack of recognition they as local leaders receive from the center. While for now many tribal leaders continue to call for economic restitution as opposed to demanding democratic reform, as witnessed by 2001 municipal protests against amalgamation, these frustrations and the consequent alienation are contributing, as Yom (2014: 229) states, to the "tectonic drifting" of the regime's social foundation.

As a result of Jordan's hyper-centralization, rural municipalities face high levels of unemployment (due largely, but by no means strictly, to the kingdom's reform policies) and growing pressures to raise their own revenues, but few if any viable means by which to do so. Municipal councils are unable to undertake even the most basic projects, such as building a tourist center, without essentially calling on favors from ministers or the king when he visits. Municipalities' dependence on the center thus goes well beyond simply onerous layers of red tape. It involves the financial support of the center, luck, and, commonly, the good mood of a minister. If Jordan can be called the Oliver Twist of the Middle East, as it needs aid money and cannot survive without continually asking for "more," the same can be said of Jordan's municipalities (Yom 2013: 137). Frustrated and despondent mayors—oftentimes even more so those who have had some success in establishing a revenue-generating project—are cognizant of this luck and dependency, sick of begging, and acutely aware of the differences between municipalities in terms of funding and services despite their efforts to raise the revenues and standards of their own municipality. In many cases, this frustration is further exacerbated by their knowledge of the undeveloped potential in terms of material and human resources that lies in the municipality. Mayors cite the rising education levels of the citizens in the same breath that they talk about high unemployment rates. Mayors and councillors are frustrated not just with the economic situation but with the political causes that exacerbate the economic situation. In some cases, these political frustrations have been further exacerbated by the treatment of the periphery by the center—as if the Transjordanian mayors throughout the rural areas "[do] not exist."[4]

Moreover, without strong political parties, it will be difficult for the king to decentralize powers to the municipal level in order to address the *wasta*-driven service delivery crisis and financial bankruptcy in the country's municipalities, particularly its tribally dominated rural municipalities. Jordan's electoral system ensures that tribal independents have a far greater chance of winning power than political parties. Tribal MPs thus fight and win elections based on the resources and services they can secure via wasta—via their connections to the center and those that hold the reins of decision-making, including municipal decision-making. With no party structure to establish party cells in municipalities outside of where their tribe/clan dominates, they cannot take advantage of any powers downloaded to the municipal level. It is for this reason, that Jordan's so-called decentralization law downloaded decentralized responsibilities to the (appointed) governors but also centralized powers from the municipalities. At the issue was the ability of the regime to continue to be able to control and direct resources. Political decentralization may be of interest to Jordan's mayors, who would benefit from it, but not to the tribal elites in Amman who rely on the networks of wasta that centralization makes possible both for their own prestige and for service delivery to their constituencies.

To be sure, King Abdullah has sought to create a new elite base of urban support: the ascendant businessmen and bourgeoisie who benefited from neoliberal market-oriented policies (Yom 2014: 231). Yet, while in the long run the monarchy may envision "shifting its base of support from the countryside to the city" (Yom 2013: 132), the new decentralization and municipalities laws indicate that the long run is still a very long way off. In the context of a Jordan that is more ethnically divided than ever before, the monarchy clearly perceives the maintenance of the coalition with the Transjordanian tribal elites as more important than ever. The ethnic demography of Jordan has dramatically changed in the last few years as a result of warfare and refugees. Without any precise data on ethnic or religious diversity in the kingdom, it is generally believed that Transjordanians do not constitute the majority in Jordan.[5] It is little wonder that the king increasingly has begun to personally visit municipalities granting municipal councils and individual citizens money, hospitals, schools, and the like ever since the onset of the Arab Spring protests in Jordan and beyond, much as his father, King Hussein, did before him (Bouziane and Lenner 2011). Yet while the king is increasingly seen as the solution, this comes with the further weakening of state institutions.

In this context, regime sustainability continues to depend on respecting the coalition that helped build the state. Indeed, it goes a long way to explaining why the decentralization law in Jordan continues the historical trend of greater centralization, even if it is labeled decentralization. Jordan's recent reforms have created neither new avenues for participation nor those to enhance municipalities' abilities to independently generate revenues. At the same time, with the restructuring of administrative bodies and the consequent further reduction in the number of "points of access" at the municipal level, competition for access to patron–client networks can only intensify with the reforms.

Tribalism in Jordan is changing. Tribal ties have broken down among the rural youth, and particularly those who have moved to Amman, and with the growth of an urban, cosmopolitan middle class. In some cases, meritocracy is beginning to replace tribalism in terms of political allegiance; as discussed in chapter 4, while mayoral candidates must have tribal support to win, some tribes are choosing those with the highest level of merit for their candidates. Most importantly, as witnessed by the growing number of electoral alliances dividing clans, tribal shaykhs increasingly cannot automatically deliver the votes of their fellow tribesmen and women. With tribal identities breaking down in a social sense, ongoing centralization and the patronage it allows is an attempt to ensure that they do not do so politically. Yet, as witnessed in 1989, the 2001 municipal protests, and the Arab Spring protests, the greatest beneficiaries of wasta often are the first to complain.

Morocco and Jordan are both monarchies, yet the relevance of my findings travels beyond these two specific case studies and includes those states whose regimes are similarly based on coalition strategies—whether along tribal, ethnic, sectarian, or other lines—and commonly were fostered by former colonial powers to legitimate their rule. The issue thus is less that Jordan and Morocco are monarchies than it is one of regime and elite survival, and it extends to authoritarian regimes and even democracies, particularly those with contested political systems, throughout the region. Decentralization is an inherently political tool, and decisions to decentralize are embedded within issues of power and political conflicts (Harb and Atallah 2015: 3). International financial institutions must be aware that under these conditions, decentralization will be a tool to strengthen authoritarianism. Furthermore, while it may also produce examples of good governance and improved service delivery at the municipal level, this, too, will be the result of political decisions the end goal of which may or may not be good governance for its own sake. As a political tool, the valorization of good governance may be temporary, contingent on changing political conditions.

Indeed, rather than being the driver of democratization, good governance and decentralization appear to be contingent on democratization. The findings in this book indicate that external donors must pay greater attention to the incentives that underlie the electoral system. Elite capture relies on voters who cast their ballots based on clientele ties and the promise of rewards to come, political actors who establish or join parties based on similar clientelistic incentives, and regimes that base their rule on coalition strategies that foster these clientelistic ties and incentives. Only a strong party system—one in which political parties are both independent and based on meaningful, ideologically based platforms and policies and differentiate themselves accordingly—can change the incentives for voters and political actors alike. For the incentive structures to change, political change must first come from the top, and this can only happen with greater democratization.

Notes

Introduction

1. Some studies of decentralization equate the creation or restoration of locally elected subnational governments with political decentralization (see Burki et al. 1999: 3). This book considers this equation insufficient to be considered political decentralization: local governments may be established or revived without any devolution of powers or authority. Political decentralization includes, at a minimum, "measures that seek to strengthen the political autonomy of subnational polities" (Falleti 2010: 38).

2. States rarely engage in only one type of decentralization; they commonly engage in all four types of decentralization simultaneously or in overlapping sequence.

3. For a more in-depth discussion of clientelism, see Fox 1994.

4. See also Rondinelli 1981.

5. For research on elite capture, see Bardhan and Mookherjee 2000, 2006b; Chowdhury and Yamauchi 2010; Park and Wang 2010; Hussain and Hussain 2009; La Ferrara 2002; and Prud'homme 1995.

6. Examining community-based or participatory aid projects, Platteau (2004) is one of a few studies to provide a detailed empirical analysis of the process of elite capture. He focuses on the reasons why the biases of power are tolerated by the poor and on the benefits both the poor and the elites receive from elite capture.

7. The World Bank makes community participation an explicit criterion for funding approval for a growing list of projects.

8. Harders (2003) provides an excellent discussion of clientelism as a result of Egypt's structural adjustment program in the 1990s. She does not look at decentralization.

9. There are several works on the effects of neoliberal reforms on national and local power configurations in general; few cover the Middle East (Bergh 2012a: 304). Examining Morocco, Hoffman (2013) looks directly at the issue of political decentralization and its impact on the rural municipality of Luant. She focuses on how the citizens of Luant experience the state and traces how decentralization transposes authoritarian rule to the local scale.

10. I included both Chefachaouen and Khemisset in the survey in order that I could build on existing literature (see Iraki 2002a).

11. Within this smaller sample, the PJD is overrepresented in order to better understand the relationship between opposition parties and elite capture. In the 2009 municipal elections, the PJD won only 5.5 percent of the seats.

12. In both Jordan and Morocco it was relatively easy to obtain a list of municipalities from MoMA and the Ministry of Interior, respectively. However, whereas the Jordanian list included mayors' names and personal telephone numbers, in Morocco, the list included municipalities' election results. It consequently was more difficult in Morocco to ascertain who the mayor and what the winning coalition were. At least in one case, my research assistant and I found that while one party had won the most seats in the elections, it had not secured a majority of seats and had failed in its quest to find a coalition partner and lead the executive bureau of the council. In this case, we unexpectedly found ourselves in a "PJD municipality" when in fact the PJD had not won the majority of seats, according to the election results.

1. Coalition Building and the Social Relations That Support Authoritarian Regimes

1. The term "Hashemite Compact" is used by Tell to refer to the monarchical pact developed under the British and in the first decades of the independent state of Jordan. Tell (2013: 12) describes the compact in the following manner: "Composed of a nexus of formal organizations and informal institutions, ranging from a militarized welfare regime to dynastic patronage networks, this compact exchanged loyalty for economic security, and sustained the East Bankers who formed the regime's core of 'social support.'"

2. Abdullah formed his first government in April 1921. With the exception of one minister of Transjordanian origin, the ministerial team was composed of Istiqlal (Independence Party) members who had fled Greater Syria following Faysal's ouster. Abdullah needed the Syrian nationalists for their administrative skills and to legitimate his claim to Greater Syria. He may also have needed them as a bargaining chip vis-à-vis any future negotiations with the French (Alon 2007: 40; Tell 2013: 62, 63; Vatiliotis 1967: 44).

3. The law had little to say about municipalities per se. Towns were subsumed under other district divisions. The 1871 revision of law distinguished between municipal and village affairs but failed to clarify the administrative or legal demarcation between urban and rural in the provinces. Reimer (2005: 193) notes that the first evidence of administrative councils for the *kaza* (juridical district) of Ajlun, centered on Irbid, dates from 1872. These councils may have been the first to have been elected by popular vote, but evidence is murky.

4. Reimer (2005: 193) states that the first municipal administration was in Irbid, sometime before 1883. The town's council, however, was not elected by the populace, as was mandated by the 1877 code. Rather it was elected by the district's (*kaza*) administrative council. Until 1921, municipalities (as well as other local authorities) had complete authority within their territories (Center for Strategic Studies 2004: 14–16).

5. The twenty-one-man Legislative Council had fourteen elected members, two appointed tribal representatives, the chief minister, and four other members appointed from the Executive Council (Abdullah's cabinet). The Legislative Council had mainly advisory duties (Wilson 1987: 96–97).

6. The old Arab Legion remained a police force.

7. Glubb brought back the *surra*—a money pouch the Ottomans originally gave to Bedouins to prevent them from attacking pilgrimage caravans; the British later emulated the practice to aid their efforts during the Arab Revolt (Massad 2001: 107).

8. Transjordanians are Jordanians who trace their origins to the east bank of the Jordan River before 1948. They are also known in the literature as East Bankers. Jordanians of Palestinian descent are referred to Palestinians. These definitions are not intended to oversimplify the reality in Jordan today. Prior to 1948, the population on the east bank of the Jordan River included Circassians, Syrians, Lebanese, and Palestinians who had settled in the area as early as the 1880s (Layne 1994: 18–19). Furthermore, there are some leading families historically from the West Bank who, for social and political purposes, are considered Transjordanian.

9. Jordan's Organic Law of 1928 included the right to form political parties.

10. Talal, Abdullah's son, briefly came to power after the assassination of Abdullah. As Talal had been mentally ill from a young age, Hussein became king

upon coming of age. Hussein dismissed Glubb to placate the opposition and also because he was frustrated with Glubb and shared some of the nationalists' sentiments vis-à-vis Glubb and his leadership of the army. Hussein also viewed Glubb as a rival (Massad 2001: 178–89).

11. For details, see Anderson 2005: 182–84.

12. Abu Nuwwar, who allegedly planned the plot, left Jordan for Syria; he was followed later by other leaders of the deposed cabinet who perceived signs of a "Palace coup" (Aruri 1972: 141).

13. Other than a brief period from 1963 to 1967, martial law was not lifted until the 1990s. The assembly was briefly reconvened in 1976 in order to postpone national elections indefinitely (Schwedler 2006: 44). Under the Eisenhower Doctrine, countries in the Middle East could request American economic assistance or aid from U.S. military forces if they were being threatened by armed aggression from another state, the Soviet Union in particular.

14. It also was an attempt to prevent the reemergence of a separate Palestinian political leadership.

15. During this time period there were also several coup attempts against King Hussein.

16. Palestinians (and others) have been known to "Jordanize" their names so that they reflect a tribal origin in order to cement their ties and alliances with top state officials.

17. These lines are not clear cut (Brand 1995: 54).

18. For other subsidies and benefits, see Baylouny 2010: 54.

19. Oil prices declined from their peak of US$36 per barrel to below US$15 per barrel in 1986 (Brynen 1992: 84).

20. Unemployment went from almost zero in the 1980s to 28 percent in the late 1990s (Baylouny 2010: 82).

21. For similar reasons, it was reluctant to increase domestic taxation

22. See http://www.economywatch.com/economic-statistics/economic-indicators /External_Debt_Percentage_GDP/1989/, accessed January 29, 2017.

23. The reforms were implemented in a piecemeal fashion. In 1995, Jordan signed the Euro-Mediterranean Partnership and, in 1998, the Greater Arab Free Trade Area. In 1998, it established the country's Qualified Trade Zones (QTZs). In 1999–2000, Jordan entered the World Trade Organization (WTO). In 2001, it signed the Free Trade Act with the United States and, in 2002, the EU-Jordan agreement.

24. In 1996, riots in Jordan's Transjordanian-dominated areas occurred again. Triggered by the removal of wheat subsidies that tripled the price of bread, the riots began in al-Karak (Baylouny 2010: 55).

25. The king remained the head of state; appointing the PM, members and the president of senate (House of Notables), and convening and adjourning the (elected) House of Representatives. Among other powers, the king could order elections and postpone elections to the House of Representatives, dissolve parliament at his discretion, declare martial law (thereby suspending the provisions of the constitution and ruling by decree), and approve and proclaim laws. Finally, he continued to be the commander-in-chief of the armed forces, with the sole responsibility for declaring war and signing treaties.

26. The 1912 Treaty of Fez made Morocco a protectorate of France. Spain was granted a protectorate in northern and southern Morocco in a second treaty signed in the same year.

27. The "oath of fealty" was used by sultans prior to the protectorate. When a new sultan came to power, the notables would gather to discuss terms for the bay'a, such as taxes. The bay'a (or its lack) determined the frontier between Bled al-Makhzen and Bled as-Siba, the latter being where the makhzen's authority was not recognized. See Waterbury 1970: 19.

28. Morocco's urban elites historically have been drawn predominantly from the royal cities of Rabat, Meknès, Marrakech and, most importantly, Fès. While the political elites expanded considerably following independence, the families from Fès dominated the leadership of the nationalist movement and are still considered the bedrock of today's elite (Pargeter 2009: 1034).

29. The creation of the UNFP weakened the Istiqlal and fragmented the entire party system. Consequently, several members of parliament, including the prime minister, abandoned their previous political platforms and shifted their allegiances to the UNFP, the perceived favorite party of the king. This left the king in a powerful position. See Storm 2007: 16–17 and Waterbury 1970: 217–19.

30. In 1957, the newly created Ministry of the Interior appointed a commission to set up rural municipalities. In 1959, a law was established regarding the election of municipal councils. The 23 June 1960 Municipal Charter (Charte Communale) then established the administrative autonomy of municipalities granting them limited consultative powers (Bergh 2007: 87, 91). Morocco's 1962 constitution gave status to the authorities representing the central state and fixed the number of councillors to be elected in each commune.

31. Abouhani (2006b: 63–64) agrees, the expansion of local administration was organized and financed by the central authorities in order to integrate rural and urban elites into the makhzenian system. The establishment of municipalities and the first municipal elections in 1960 largely were driven by the regime's need to bring the country administratively under its control, specifically under that of the Ministry of the Interior, and by an attempt to break

the power of the tribes and establish closer ties between the administration and local elites or notables.

32. Willis (2012) casts doubt on this second hypothesis.

33. The 1972 constitution maintained extensive powers for the monarchy and the one-house parliament and indirectly elected members. However, it stipulated the number of MPs to be directly and indirectly elected, making it "marginally more complicated" for the monarchy to manipulate the composition of parliament. It also increased the number of parliamentarians to be directly elected (now two-thirds). The period of elections was changed from six years back to four years (as in 1962) (Storm 2007: 31–32).

34. In 1983, the external debt as a percentage of GDP was significantly lower in the rest of Africa and the Middle East. It stood at 23.023 percent for the Middle East; 23.773 percent for the Middle East, North Africa, Afghanistan, and Pakistan; 30.889 percent for sub-Saharan Africa; and 29.633 percent for the Emerging and Developing Economies. See http://www.economywatch.com /economic-statistics/economic-indicators/External_Debt_Percentage_GDP /1989/, accessed January 29, 2017.

35. For additional details, see Catusse 2009b: 192.

36. In 1976, decentralization exacerbated these disparities as municipalities acquired the responsibility for rural infrastructure and social services without adequate finances for these services (Harrigan and El-Said 2009b: 113–14).

37. While technically prior to the IMF reforms, the 1981 riots also were in response to some limited cutbacks attempted by the state.

2. Centralization and "Decentralization" in Jordan

1. In 2016, partly as a result of this ethnic divide within the Muslim Brotherhood, the MB split into three organizations. A reorganized IAF was one of three Islamist organizations that ran in the 2016 national elections.

2. Today, the IAF is one of three parties representing the original MB. In 2013, a group of MB activists launched the ZamZam movement; it ran in the 2016 elections as the National Congress Party. In 2015, forty MB members officially registered the Muslim Brotherhood Society (MBS). The government rescinded the "original" MB's license, banned it from holding internal elections, and closed its offices in 2016. It ran in the elections as the MBS. In preparation for the 2016 elections, the IAF established the National Alliance for Reform (Al-Islah), which encompassed candidates from across the political spectrum, including minorities. In the elections it embraced a new

strategy of inclusion, tolerance, and moderation (see Wehler-Schoeck 2016: 5–6). These three parties joined the Centrist Islamist Party, which was founded by MB members who split from the MB in 2001. The IAF won the greatest number of seats of any party in the 2016 elections (although the vast majority of seats went to tribal independents). For more on the Islamist parties in the 2016 elections, see Sowell 2016.

3. This section is based on Clark 2006.

4. The government also continued the practice of reserved seats in parliament for religious and ethnic minorities (also dating back to the first Jordanian representative assembly in 1928). With the 2016 election law, the districts remain gerrymandered. Amman's Second District and al-Zarqa's First District respectively contain 9.71 percent and 10.92 percent of the total voting population but only 5.20 percent and 6.20 percent of seats. In contrast, al-Karak and Ma'an respectively have 4.05 percent and 1.43 percent of voters and 8.60 percent and 8.60 percent of seats (Wehler-Schoek 2016: 3). See also Sowell 2016.

5. In addition to its ties to society through its charity, the Islamic Center Charity Society, and other activities, several factors worked in the MB's favor in 1989. The very short campaign period of twenty-five days—a period too short for other candidates to fill the gap and successfully compete against the MB—gave an advantage to the long-organized MB. Furthermore, the Palestine Liberation Organization did not run in the Palestinian camps. The strong MB position in defense of the liberation of all of Palestine garnered it votes in the refugee camps. The MB also only fielded thirty candidates and consequently was more organized and disciplined than many of the secular parties, which fielded as many as 700 candidates. See Adams 1996: 511; Boulby 1999: 73, 104; Freij and Robinson 1996; Mufti 1999: 110; and Tal 1995.

6. Press and other forms of restrictions also were reinstated.

7. The IAF demanded that the electoral laws, for example, be changed to one-person-two-votes (Ryan 2002: 33).

8. The Jordanian branch of the MB was established in 1945 by Abdul Latif Abu Qura, a merchant from Salt, who met Egyptian Brotherhood members when visiting Palestine in the late 1930s. In the 1940s, Abu Qura wrote to the founder of the Muslim Brotherhood in Egypt, Hassan al-Banna, and asked to visit him. He did so and returned to Jordan with two Egyptian MBs to assist him in establishing the MB in Jordan. As the newly established monarchy sought to secure its legitimacy through the promotion of its religious credentials as descendant from the family of the Prophet Muhammad, it supported the early MB.

9. The early MB focused on religious education, with its activities taking place in schools; in the 1950s, it opened its own school.

10. The MB shared the regime's "anticommunist" tendencies (Schwedler 2006: 42–43).

11. By legalizing the organization, the regime was able to bring the MB above ground and monitor it (Boulby 1999: 46).

12. Throughout the1980s, the MB was active in the only free and fair elections at the time: local NGO elections, student council elections, and the elections of the country's professional associations and labor unions.

13. The blacklists proved to be a turning point for many centrists, liberals, and much of the public. Not only were many centrists and liberals on the lists, but the lists essentially criminalized all dealings with Israel when they were in fact accepted under law. The lists also were a direct attack on the legality of the regime, not just the government—something that discomforted many people (Kornbluth 2002: 100).

14. See http://www.jordanembassyus.org/new/aboutjordan/erl.shtml.

15. A heated public debate over Palestinian-Jordanian citizenship rights ensued with, for example, Palestinian critics viewing Jordan First as meaning Jordanians First (Lynch 2002: 47). See also Ryan 2002: 126–31.

16. Scholarships to study abroad for graduate studies similarly go overwhelmingly Transjordanians (Reiter 2002: 149).

17. Officially, these privileges are justified as being necessary to address the country's economically "weak areas," those in which the government cannot invest due to the economic crisis. The system of university admission refers to the quotas in terms of affirmative action (Reiter 2002: 155). While some of the Transjordanian–dominated governorates have the highest rates of poverty, Prince Ghazi b. Muhammad revealed the political motives of the quotas and the scholarships when he stated that the tribes demand equity because they live in the arid desert, have made sacrifices for the Arab Revolt and for Palestine, and serve in the army (154).

18. The government recently expanded social insurance provision to companies with fewer than five workers; previously it was only extended to the public sector and larger businesses.

19. Technically, RONGOs are called national intermediary NGOs. Members of the royal family establish RONGOs out of their personal interest in an area, the desire to increase their profile, or the "ambitions and rivalries among members of the royal family" (Brand 1998: 170).

20. In 2003, LDUs were created at the governorate level. In 2008, the PM's office transferred ninety-two functions from the line ministries to the governorates. As Hallaj et al. state (2015: 20–21), the intention was to make public services more accessible, but these services were limited in scope. Furthermore, neither the governors, the LDUs, nor the local authorities were sufficiently empowered to adopt a more proactive role. Until the 2015, the

LDUs primarily focused on reporting on the implementation of the projects by other government authorities at the level of the governorate to the center. LDUs thus have not acted as a catalyst for local development and participation.

21. Importantly, however, it did not receive separate fiscal authority.

22. From 1955 to 2001, Jordan had "village councils" to administer any tribal locality or village with fewer than 2,500 people. The governor designated the mayors of village councils and all their members (between three and eleven) and approved their decisions. These councils were abolished in 2001.

23. The PM in Jordan is also the minister of defense. Historically, Jordan has not had a Ministry of Defense. In 2014, however, the Ministry of Defense was activated.

24. It also provided for the formation of municipal councils, with mayors appointed by the Ottoman government. Mayors were to prepare the budget, collect and disburse revenue, and report to the council regarding municipal finance. Councils' duties included approving the budget, superintending accounts, acquiring and disposing of municipal property, sanctioning contracts, and appointing and dismissing municipal officials.

25. Municipalities' failure to do their jobs was due to a variety of factors, including increased tribal tensions. See Reimer 2005: 197.

26. In 1976, it became the Ministry of Municipal Affairs (MoMA). In 1980, the name was again changed to the Ministry of Municipal, Rural and Environmental Affairs. In 2002, it was renamed the Ministry of Municipal Affairs and remains such today.

27. According to a World Bank report (2005b: 13), the 1955 law did not provide sufficient municipal autonomy for the municipalities to respond to specific local needs or to make a policy of local development.

28. In 1994, King Hussein also announced the creation of four governorates centered around the cities of Madaba, Jerash, Ajloun, and Aqaba. The governorates were to develop their respective strengths: agriculture and industry in the case of Madaba; tourism in Jerash and Ajloun; and the port in Aqaba (Ababsa 2015).

29. The government argued that the appointed councils would implement the elections in a nonpartisan fashion and would not use their position on local council for campaigning purposes. However, the opposition claimed that the dismissals hindered the ability of the formerly elected council members to campaign on past achievements. In the weeks preceding the elections, several articles in the main newspapers reported on the strong performance of the appointed councils—indirect critiques of "representative government." The appointed council that replaced the Islamist-dominated elected council in al-Zarqa' received particular praise (NDI 1995: 9).

30. The 1995 elections law also had measures that worked to ensure the regime's preferred electoral outcome.
31. This section is based on Clark 2012: 362. See also Ababsa 2015.
32. Municipalities with tourist sites receive inadequate additional finances to pay for additional expenses.
33. The 2007 law also introduced the above-mentioned managers or executive directors to work "in conjunction" with the mayor and oversee the day-to-day administration of the respective municipalities.
34. Ababsa (2015) points out that even the Joint Services Councils, created in 1983 so that municipalities could work together to improve the efficiency and effectiveness of service delivery, were excessively restricted.
35. According to the 2007 law, the mayor is directly elected using a majoritarian (first-past-the-post) method whereas the councillors are elected via a single-nontransferable-vote system. The 2007 law included a quota for women in municipal council seats.
36. Municipal elections have a very short campaigning period, which makes it difficult for candidates to effectively campaign on policy-related issues. The short campaign period thus indirectly encourages voters to vote for their clan or tribal candidates.
37. In 2013, tribal candidates and businessmen loyal to the regime took the majority of seats.
38. Amman and Irbid have twenty-seven and twenty-three districts, respectively.
39. Of the thirty-three seats held by parties in the 110-seat elected House of Representatives, seventeen were held by the IAF. The rest were held by independents, most of whom were pro-regime tribal figures (Hourani, Abu Rumman, and Kamel 2004: 114).
40. The turnover of candidates is also high. As Lust-Okar (2006: 463) observes, it is much easier to promise patronage than to deliver it.
41. In 2003, only nine of Jordan's thirty-one parties fielded candidates (sixty-four in total) (Hourani, Abu Rumman, and Kamel 2004: 114). Five parties won parliamentary seats.
42. Consequently, voting turnout is highest where people believe that their candidates have the wasta to government officials (Lust-Okar 2006: 462). Nonvoters—largely Palestinians in urban areas—are those less connected to the regime. This remained the same in the 2016 parliamentary elections, for which the lowest voter turnout was in Palestinian-dominated al-Zarqa' and the highest voter turnout was in Transjordanian-dominated al-Mafraq (Lorentzen 2016, based on the Independent Elections Commission of Jordan, http://iec.jo).
43. Ratified in 2007, the Political Parties Law (replacing the 1992 Political Parties Law) stipulated that for a party to be legal it had to have a minimum of

500 founding members; the 1992 law had stipulated only fifty. Furthermore, there had to be a 10 percent minimum representation from at least five of the country's governorates (Köprülü 2014: 79). The king argued that strong political parties were necessary to carry democratization forward and, as a consequence, that Jordan's numerous small parties should unite into larger parties. As the tribes have the greatest ease in amassing 500 founders from across several governorates, the law made it difficult for new parties to establish and for already existing parties to reregister (*Map of Political Parties* n.d.: 17).

44. The gerrymandered districts were maintained.

45. As a Friedrich-Ebert-Stiftung report (Hussainy 2014: 9) states, the system does little to change the bias against parties. Out of the 150 seats in parliament, 123 went to independents in the 2013 elections; all are considered regime-loyalists. The vast majority of parties only won one seat. The highest number of seats won by a party (one party) was three; one other won two seats. While the number of parties has increased, with the exception of the IAF, they remain weak and ineffective and overwhelmingly concentrated in Amman. Of the twenty parties registered at the time of the Identity Center Report (*Map of Political Parties* n.d.: 34–57), seven had no tangible platform or vision for reform, two promoted reform but were supportive of the king's agenda, and three were inactive. The remaining eight fell along the spectrum of opposition parties and had a reformist agenda; some of these eight are active in the streets, and some rely on the media to get their message across.

46. In the 2016 national elections, only 18 percent of candidates participated in the elections as party members (Wehler-Schoeck 2016: 4). Furthermore, tribal alliances were the sole basis for 43.5 percent of the lists (5).

47. The UNDP missions were carried out in 1994 and 1996 (Clark 2012: 367). There were local advocates for amalgamation (see chapter 4); the UNDP and the World Bank also pushed for amalgamation in the mid-1990s (Hallaj et al. 2015: 18).

48. The government also established new local units called development clusters (groups of towns to facilitate local-level planning and coordination and to ensure greater regional homogeneity). But the populations of many cluster centers were below threshold levels for sustaining economic activity. As Doan (1991: 182–83) explains, the presence of so many small clusters was the "result of a political decision to preserve the autonomy of tribal settlements from the desert regions ensuring the political support of affiliated tribes, rather than to establish planning units with any measure of economic viability."

49. The governorate of Madaba was to have been the test case for the plan's rollout in 2010.

50. The plan did not explicitly state whether GAM would be independent or part of one of the three regions.

51. Mayors were supportive of the plan because they sought the increased funding and resources they would accrue.

52. Many in the central government also complained that decentralization would have limited benefits while adding the costs of creating a new level of bureaucracy.

53. Successive governments buried the plan deep in their lists of priorities because they viewed its implementation as too difficult and too controversial politically.

54. This would include the "We Are Jordan" initiative, announced one day prior to the launch of the National Agenda (which the king did not attend).

55. In 2008, the PM's office issued an ordinance transferring ninety-two functions from the line ministries to the governorates. While the stated intention was to make public services more accessible to the population, these services were limited in scope and neither the governors, the LDUs, nor the municipal authorities were sufficiently empowered to adopt more proactive roles (Hallaj et al. 2015).

56. For details on ministerial rivalry in the development of this law, see Ababsa 2015.

57. As with the first plan, the government created new bodies without any relinquishment of central control. The central authorities retained the ability to appoint members to the new councils and determine councils' compositions. The draft plan envisioned each governorate having four bodies: a local council (parliament for the governorate); an executive council; a consultation council (comprising the heads of municipalities); and the existing municipal councils. One-third of the local councils was to have been appointed. While the draft plan was unclear, there was some discussion that some mayors would also be appointed (presumably by the governors) to the councils—potentially pitting mayors in competition for these positions. In terms of duties, the local councils were to give recommendations to the governor and input into the budget. The executive councils of the governorates would have been entirely appointed and headed by the MoI-appointed governor. No change was anticipated to take place at this level. At the municipal level, the central government would have appointed an executive secretary responsible for all major tasks in municipalities.

58. Despite its extensive supervisory role, MoMA is a relatively weak ministry with a small budget. It played a very limited role in the overhaul of the municipalities law in 2010. According to an EU report on decentralization in Jordan: "MoMA should have been in the driving seat for the overhaul of the Municipal Law. However none of its staff, including the Directors, except

the legal advisor had been informed as to what this reform meant and what the consequences would be" (European Union n.d.).

59. As of 2013, 65 percent of Syrian refuges had settled in urban areas across Jordan. Some municipalities have experienced unsustainable population increases: al-Mafraq—128 percent; Ramtha—47 percent; al-Serhan—45 percent (Hallaj et al. 2015: 23). These municipalities have experienced heightened pressure on municipal and social services and housing shortages, leading to increased tensions between host and refugee communities. Hallaj et al. note that by 2013, the presence of Syrian refugees outside of the refugee camps in northern governorates had incurred an additional cost for municipal finances of approximately US$40.5 million annually,

60. Among other responsibilities, the executive council now prepares the strategic and executive plans for the governorate and harmonizes them with the strategic plans prepared by the municipal councils and other bodies. The role of the elected governorate council is predominantly to ratify the plans, projects, and budgets of the executive council and to propose recommendations and projects. When the two councils do not agree, the PM makes the final decision.

61. Municipalities are now divided into three categories instead of four, as previously.

62. Article 9.B–C of the Municipalities Law, https://iec.jo/sites/default/files /5MunicipalitiesLaw2015EN.doc%20%281%29_0.pdf.

63. Financially, municipalities continue to rely on the central government for the vast bulk of their finances. Article 23.B–C gives a free hand to the PM's council to transfer money collected in Palestinian-dominated al-Zarqa', for example, to Transjordanian municipalities such as al-Karak. Municipal governments have gained no new means for raising their own revenues, and their budgets continue to depend on MoMA approval. The central government furthermore retains the right to postpone or cancel municipal elections and may remove council responsibilities by simply informing councils.

3. Decentralization, Co-optation, and Regime Legitimation in Morocco

1. The de-concentration reforms of 1960 were implemented with the overt objective of extending central state control.

2. Morocco also was under increasing international pressure to democratize. In 1991, the European Parliament denied Morocco an aid package as a consequence of its poor human rights record (Ottaway and Riley 2006: 5; Zemni and Bogaert 2006: 105).

3. An important aspect of this new intellectual climate was that the associational activity was largely devoid of political party involvement; party affiliations did not cease to exist, but they became less important (Sater 2002b: 108, 116).
4. Several events explain why the monarch was keen to reconcile with the Koutla. The first of these was the 1990 Gulf War—the monarchy's decision to send troops to Saudi Arabia triggered demonstrations. Shared opposition to the Gulf War also strengthened the unity of the new Koutla. In addition, Morocco had been experiencing an Islamist resurgence; an increasing number of Moroccans were joining the banned al-Adl wal-Ihsan (Justice and Charity), the oppositional stream over which the monarchy had the least control (Storm 2007: 54–55).
5. In the lead-up to both elections, the number of "administrative parties" (centrist or right-wing parties) had increased significantly. Electoral districts had been highly gerrymandered in favor of rural constituencies where regime support is at its highest (Storm 2007: 45–47, 50–51).
6. As many studies have demonstrated, a small (non-rotating) group often makes decisions in place of various committees. See Pellicer and Wegner 2015: 37.
7. Under King Hassan II, royal sisters and daughters were married into key elite families in order to cement personal and family loyalties (Willis 2012: 62).
8. This worked to the advantage of administrative parties as well (Willis 2002: 14–15).
9. Dates for the foundation of the IY range from 1969 to 1972. For in-depth discussions of the roots of the PJD, see A. Maghraoui 2015; Wegner 2011: 21–27; Willis 1999.
10. The RR first approached the Istiqlal but rejected the conditions placed on it for entry (Wegner 2011: 26; Willis 1999: 47).
11. The exact number of other groups ranges from one (Rally for the Islamic Future) to three.
12. Khatib's party participated in the 1977 elections, winning three seats for the first and last time; the party boycotted subsequent elections to protest electoral manipulation (Willis 1999: 48). In 1997, a total of 140 MPDC members ran as independent candidates. Seeking not to be perceived as a threat by the regime and to avoid the "Algerian syndrome," the Islamists ran in a limited number of districts. See Wegner 2011: 27; Willis 1999: 45, 52–53, 2004: 56.
13. Eibl's discussion of the "politicization thesis" is based on Catusse 2002.
14. The INDH has been implemented in two phases (2006–2010 and 2011–2015). The budget for the second phase is 17 billion dirham (approximately 1.5 billion euros).
15. See, for instance, Fonds d'Equipement Communal, http://www.fec.org.ma, accessed June 20, 2014.

16. The charter also fixed the time period during which the MoI approved the disbursement of municipal funds following a council decision (Catusse with Cattedra and Idrissi-Janati 2007: 123).

17. Arrondissements are not legally recognized independent entities, but they are given certain autonomy over defined local matters.

18. In 2010, Morocco proposed reducing the number of regions from sixteen to twelve; this was put into effect in 2015.

19. For an overview of the constitutional changes, see Harsi and El Yaagoubi 2006: 31–36.

20. Catusse and Zaki (2009, 2010) refer to the 2002 charter as "ambiguous decentralization." See also "Plus de 160 clauses" 2008.

21. The MoI launched a grand strategy for decentralization in 2008, called Plan Horizon 2015. It was designed to help in the implementation of the 2009 charter. See http://www.pncl.gov.ma/fr/Decentrsalisation/Pages/Commune -l'Horizon-2015.aspx.

22. Bergh (2007: 421) notes that prior to this, municipalities were supposed to have their own plans as part of the national 2000–2004 Five-Year Plans. In practice, however, these did not amount to much more than a few separate project files, many of which were not implemented.

4. The Destabilizing Effects of Centralization

1. It is very challenging for parliamentarians to challenge legislation from the regime. The lower house is limited to amending what was sent to it; if it wants to reject a law, a joint session of both houses is held and it takes two-thirds vote of both houses to enforce a modification of the law. In practice, this has happened very few times in the parliament's history (Kao 2016).

2. Group interview, Farthakh, Ma'an, March 19, 2012.

3. Interview, Mohammed al-Masri, Center for Strategic Studies, University of Jordan, Amman, March 24, 2012.

4. Interview, former mayor, January 25, 2010.

5. Interview, LDU director, March 7, 2012.

6. Interview, al-Zarqa', March 7, 2012. Voters vote for MPs in order to receive personal favors and may mobilize votes for an MP. In one case, following the elections that brought him to power, an MP employed two nephews of the individual who mobilized significant votes; he obtained grants for two of the man's nephews to go on the pilgrimage to Mecca. Interview, former councillor, March 9, 2012.

7. Ibid.

8. Interview, al-Zarqa', March 7, 2012.

9. Interview, former mayor, January 25, 2010.

10. Interview, al-Zarqa', March 7, 2012.

11. Interview, former mayor, Ail, February 24, 2012.

12. Interview, civil society activist, Jerash, February 26, 2012.

13. Interview, Amman, March 20, 2012.

14. Interview, LDU director, March 7, 2012.

15. Interview, former mayor, Ail, February 24, 2012.

16. Group interview, February 13, 2012.

17. Interview, civil society activist, Jerash, February 26, 2012.

18. Interview, former councillor, March 9, 2012.

19. Interview, civil society activist, Jerash, February 26, 2012.

20. Interview, former councillor, al-Mazar al-Jadida, February 27, 2012.

21. Group interview, Jerash, February 13, 2012.

22. Group interview, Rihaba, al-Mazar al-Jadida, February 27, 2012.

23. Interview, former mayor, Ail, February 24, 2012

24. Interview, former mayor, al-Zarqa', March 7, 2012.

25. Ibid.

26. Group interview, Jerash, February 13, 2012.

27. Ibid.

28. Ibid.

29. Group interview, Rihaba, al-Mazar al-Jadida, February 27, 2012.

30. Interview, Amman, March 18, 2012.

31. Interview, civil society activist, Amman, February 9, 2012.

32. Interview, former mayor, Birayn, January 26, 2010.

33. Interview, former mayor, al-Zarqa', March 7, 2012.

34. Interview, civil society activist, Jerash, February 26, 2012.

35. Interview, former councillor, al-Mazar al-Jadida, March 9, 2012; interview, al-Zarqa', March 7, 2012.

36. Interview, former councillor, al-Mazar Al-Jadida, February 27, 2012.

37. Interview, former councillor, al-Mazar al-Jadida, March 9, 2012, paraphrased.

38. Ibid.

39. Ibid.

40. Interview, LDU director, al-Zarqa', March 7, 2012.

41. Group interview, Rihaba, al-Mazar al-Jadida, February 27, 2012.

42. Interview, Amman, March 18, 2012, paraphrased.

43. Ibid.

44. Ibid.

45. Ibid.

46. Ibid.

47. Interview, Amman, March 19, 2012.

48. Interview, former mayor, Ajloun, March 20, 2010.

49. Interview, former mayor, Amman, January 25 2010.

50. Interview, former mayor, Shoaleh, February 1, 2010.

51. Interview, municipal general manager, Jerash, March 29, 2010, paraphrased.

52. Interview, civil society activist, Amman, February 9, 2012.

53. At the municipal level, there are two ballot sheets. Mayors are elected via the majoritarian system while council members are elected via the single non-transferable vote system (SNTV) in which the top n vote-getters fill the number of seats in the council. There is also a women's quota where 20 percent of all council seats are allocated to females. These seats are awarded to the n women who win the greatest percentage of votes in their electoral district but do not win competitively where n is the number of quota seats (Gao 2012).

54. The 2012 elections law partially removed the one-man-one-vote system by granting voters two votes in the 2013 parliamentary elections: one for a candidate at the district level and another for a closed proportional list that competed at the national level.

55. Interview, Musa Shteiwi, Center for Strategic Studies, University of Jordan, Amman, March 21, 2012. While the previous block-voting system enabled large tribes or clans to make pacts between themselves and essentially to rotate positions of power in the council (freezing out smaller tribes and/or clans), the one-person-one-vote system does not as readily allow for such pacts (Hourani et al. 2010: 36–37).

56. Interview, civil society activist, Jerash, February 26, 2012.

57. Group interview, Jerash, February 13, 2012.

58. Interview, civil society activist, Jerash, February 26, 2012, paraphrased.

59. Interview, state employee, Jerash, March 17, 2012; interview, civil society activist, Jerash, February 26, 2012.

60. Interview, former mayor, al-Zarqa', March 7, 2012.

61. Interview, former mayor, Ail, February 24, 2012.

62. Interview, civil society activist, Amman, February 9, 2012.

63. Interview, civil society activist, Jerash February 26, 2012.

64. Group interview, Jerash, February 13, 2012.

65. Interview, al-Zarqa', March 7, 2012.

66. Group interview, Farthakh, Ma'an, March 19, 2012.

67. Group interview, Rihaba, al-Mazar al-Jadida, February 27, 2012.

68. Interview, former councillor, al-Mazar al-Jadida, February 27, 2012.

69. Interview, former mayor, Ail, February 24, 2012.

70. Interview, civil society activist, Jerash, February 26, 2012.

71. Interview, former councillor, al-Mazar al-Jadida, February 27, 2012.

72. Interview, former councillor, al-Mazar al-Jadida, March 9, 2012.

73. Interview, former councillor, al-Mazar al-Jadida, February 27, 2012.
74. Interview, former mayor, Amman, March 11, 2010.
75. Group interview, Jerash, February 13, 2012; group interview, Rihaba, al-Mazar al-Jadida, February 27, 2012.
76. Interview, former mayor, Ail, February 24, 2012.
77. Interview, civil society activist, Jerash, February 26, 2012.
78. Interview, LDU director, al-Zarqa', March 7, 2012.
79. As of 2012, mayors must have a high school education. Amman city council is the only one to require a minimum of a bachelor's degree.
80. This section is based on Clark 2012.
81. Interview, Abdul Razak Tubaishat, former minister of municipal affairs, Amman, January 19, 2010.
82. Interview, civil society activist, Amman, February 9, 2012.
83. Interview, MoMA Legal Department, Amman, March 21, 2012; interview, former mayor, al-Zarqa', March 7, 2012. In some cases, amalgamation affected the price of land. Interview, civil society activist, Amman, February 9, 2012.
84. Interview, LDU director, al-Zarqa', March 7, 2012, paraphrased.
85. Interview, former councillor, Mazar, February 27, 2012, paraphrased.
86. Interview, former councillor, Mazar, March 9, 2012.
87. Interview, MoMA Legal Department, Amman, March 21, 2012.
88. Interview, Amman, March 18, 2012.
89. Ibid.
90. Ibid.
91. Group interview, Jerash, February 13, 2012.
92. Interview, al-Zarqa', March 7, 2012, paraphrased.
93. Interview, MoMA Legal Department, Amman, March 21, 2012.
94. Ibid.
95. Interview, Ministry of Social Affairs, Amman, March 18, 2012.
96. A report by EuropeAid found no evidence that the MoMA advised municipalities on financial matters (or was capable of doing so) or that it trained municipal officials as the MoMA claims (European Union n.d.).
97. Interview, MoMA, Amman, January 20, 2010; interview, Cities and Villages Development Bank, Amman, January 21, 2010.
98. In 2005, the EU built upon the GIZ project and initiated its Poverty Alleviation and Local Development (PALD) program. Implemented in 2006–2008 and completed in December 2009, this program has since been continued and expanded under the name of Baladiyati (My Municipality). PALD was intended to help create LDUs and assist them in establishing appropriate development plans with input from civil society. The EU worked with eighteen municipalities plus the three GIZ municipalities. The EU chose its eighteen municipalities based primarily on poverty-related criteria but

also on the willingness and the state of the municipality. In contrast to the GIZ project, the EU project offered significant funding to municipalities that successfully completed the training and created viable developments plans in order that they could implement the latter. Interview, Omar Abu-Eid, European Union, Environment and Energy Focal Point, Amman, January 18, 2010.

MCC is a U.S. government corporation designed to work with some of the poorest countries. In 2007, MCC worked as part of a larger initiative in Jordan with USAID and embarked on a project for capacity building and strengthening at the municipal level. The two-year program provided technical assistance and training to empower local government and enhance citizen participation in local-level decision-making in nine municipalities. As in the EU and GIZ projects, the MCC projects involved close work with LDUs with a particular emphasis on public-private partnerships (PPPs).

99. For details, see Clark 2012: 371–72. The factory has now relocated.

100. Group interview, Rihaba, al-Mazar al-Jadida, February 27, 2012.

101. Interview, former mayor, Qreqra w Finan, March 25, 2010.

102. Interview, former mayor, Shoaleh, February 1, 2010.

103. Interview, former deputy mayor, Shobak, February 3, 2010. The factory began operating in 2009.

104. Group interview, Jerash, February 13, 2012.

105. The municipality rejected an earlier idea of establishing a sewing factory because investors could only offer what the municipality considered to be unacceptably low wages. Interview, former mayor, Wasatiyya, March 8, 2010. For details on Julfar, see Farawati 2010.

106. Administratively, Jordan's twelve governorates are divided into 100 municipalities that fall under the jurisdiction of the MoMA. Until 2015, the MoMA divided municipalities into four categories: (1) those that are the center of the governorate and any municipality that has a population over 100,000 inhabitants; (2) those that are the center of a subgovernorate (district) or any municipality that has a population between 15,000 and 100,000; 3) those that are the center of smaller administrative units and have populations between 5,000 and 15,000; (4) any other municipality (Ahmaro 2014: 68). Parallel to this is Jordan's hierarchy of territorial units—from largest to smallest, the *muhafazah* (governorate), *liwa'*, *qada'*, and the *nahia*—under the MoI. The there is no tidy hierarchy between the larger administrative units and municipalities. A municipal boundary may or may not overlap with the boundary of a liwa' or qada'.

107. Group interview, Jerash, February 13, 2012.

108. Interview, former mayor, al-Aghwar al-Janubiyya, January 31, 2010. These events were confirmed by MOMA representatives: interview, al-Aghwar al-Janubiyya, January 31, 2010.

109. In al-Mazar al-Jadida, the winds average 7.5 meters per second; the necessary threshold for a wind station is 4 meters per second. Two wind stations producing 1.78 megawatts of electricity already exist in the municipality; one was built in 1988 and the other in 1996. See http://www.wecsp.org.jo/about, accessed March 2, 2015.

110. According to the mayor, a wind farm could provide electricity for the entire north of Jordan.

111. Interview, former mayor, al-Aghwar al-Janubiyya, January 31, 2010.

112. Interview, former mayor, Shoaleh, February 1, 2010.

113. One study notes that, in 2008, of all the tourism in the governorate of Irbid, only 2.2 percent was to Birqish (Mustafa 2012: 53).

114. Interview, former mayor, Birqish, March 22, 2010.

115. The irony is that there is a royal palace in the hills overlooking the village of Birqish.

116. Interview, former mayor, Qreqra w Finan, March 25, 2010.

117. Ibid.

118. Interview, LDU member, al-Hashemiyya al-Jadida, March 6, 2010.

119. Interview, former mayor, Shoaleh, February 1, 2010.

120. Group interview, Ail, February 3, 2010; interview, former mayor, Ail, February 24, 2012.

121. Group interview, Jerash, February 13, 2012.

122. Interview, former mayor, Deir al-Kahaf al-Jadida, March 21, 2010.

123. Interview, University of Jordan, Amman, March 26, 2012.

124. Interview, former councillor, al-Mazar al-Jadida, March 9, 2012.

125. Ibid. Since coming to power, Abdullah II has established several of RONGOs, including the King Abdullah II Fund for Development (KAFD).

126. Interview, state employee, Jerash, March 17, 2012.

127. Interview, University of Jordan, Amman, March 26, 2012, paraphrased. People reach the royal diwan either directly or through ministers and MPs. Interview, former councillor, al-Mazar al-Jadida, March 9, 2012.

128. Interview, former councillor, al-Mazar al-Jadida, March 9, 2012.

129. Ibid.

130. Ibid.

131. Interview, former mayor, Qreqra w Finan, March 25, 2010.

132. Group interview, Farthakh, Ma'an, March 19, 2012, paraphrased.

133. Interview, al-Zarqa', March 7, 2012.

134. Interview, state employee, Jerash, March 17, 2012.

135. The municipality will however eventually see its wind-power capacities enhanced. In 2010, Jordan's National Energy Research Center (NERC) received a substantial boost of significant EU donor aid for its Renewable

Energy Strategy (2007–2020) for the installation of a wind-testing facility and a pilot solar power plant. The wind and solar plants will be installed in al-Shobak, in southern Jordan. The governorates of Ajloun and Irbid, including the municipality of al-Mazar al-Jadida, have been earmarked as eventual sites to which the project will be expanded.

136. The government facilitated the ease by which voters could vote for the 2013 municipal elections; otherwise, there were no reforms of note.

137. Interview, former mayor, al-Zarqa', March 7, 2012.

138. Interview, former mayor, al-Mazar al-Jadida, March 8, 2010.

139. Hourani et al. (2010: 20) note that there are no official reports showing the amount of tax evasion in municipalities, but sources from two municipalities indicate that there are a significant number of cases of tax evasion. For more details on tax evasion, see Gao 2012.

5. Elite Capture and Regime Stabilization in Morocco

1. There is only one other legal Islamist political party in Morocco, the Party of Renaissance and Virtue. It is a splinter party from the PJD and won one seat in the 2007 parliamentary elections but none in the 2011 elections. Other Islamist political parties, such as the Party of Liberation, and organizations, such as Justice and Spirituality (al-Adl wal Ihsane) are banned.

2. They are three categorizations (*encadrement du territoire*) (Madani, Maghraoui, and Zerhouni 2012).

3. The second house is the Chamber of Representatives, elected by direct universal suffrage.

4. Bergh (2012b: 421) documents that previously municipalities were supposed to have their own plans as part of the National 2000–2004 Five-Year Plans. These, however, did not amount to much more than a few separate project files, many of which were not implemented.

5. Municipalities must contribute toward all projects, including equalization projects; all available investment money goes to their contribution toward the costs of the major infrastructural projects.

6. Interview, Chefchaouen, March 21, 2011.

7. Interview, Chefchaouen, March 21, 2011.

8. Interview, Chefchaouen, March 22, 2011.

9. Statistics on municipalities, including funding, are published and available at the DGCL in Rabat.

10. Together, all local collectivities (regions, province/prefectures and municipalities) incur approximately 10 percent of total public expenditures and 2.44

percent of GDP. In 2006, this amounted to 14.064 million dirham (Ministère de l'Intérieur 2009a: 169).

11. To be sure, there are reformist elements with the DGCL.

12. Interview, Rabat, February 10, 2011.

13. Interview, Chefchaouen, March 21, 2011.

14. Projects of the four programs fall into three categories: (1) public works (ranging from schools to cultural centers and health clinics); (2) economic development projects (including income-generating activities and professional training); and (3) infrastructure projects. The overview of the INDH's structure is based on Bergh (2012b: 413–14). INDH donors include the Moroccan state, the World Bank, the European Union, and private donors, including the king of Saudi Arabia (Berriane 2010: 94).

15. Not all municipalities have INDH projects; of those that do, approximately half fall into the transversal program.

16. The CLDHs also are responsible for the implementation of and follow-up on the projects. There are also approximately 700 communal and neighborhood social mobilization teams (*les équips d'animation communale et de quartier*) designed to organize civil society (Bergh 2012b: 416).

17. The CPDL comprises municipal councillors, civil society representatives, and representatives of the ministries. Each group is granted one-third of the seats on the committee. There are twelve regional human development committees.

18. Given their powers, governors or DAS staff are easily able to personalize the INDH with clientelism determining the allocation of projects or procurement contracts. Berriane (2010: 104) notes that the INDH committees have allowed informal and indirect negotiations between NGO leaders, political actors, and representatives of the state.

19. Interview, political scientist, Rabat, February 7, 2012. See also Bergh 2012b: 415.

20. Interview, political scientist, Rabat, February 21, 2011.

21. Ibid.

22. Interview, Erfoud, March 28, 2011.

23. Interview, political scientist, Rabat, February 7, 2012.

24. Some walis are even more powerful based on their relationship to the king.

25. A January 2002 royal letter ordained the creation of RICs in order to centralize services for economic investors under the supervision of walis. See Catusse with Cattedra and Idrissi-Janati (2007: 125–27).

26. Interview, Erfoud, March 29, 2011.

27. During the regional workshops in preparation for the 2009 charter (see chapter 3), local elected officials identified approximately 160 unclear or ambiguous articles in the 2002 charter. Little has changed with the 2009 charter. See "Plus de 160 clauses" 2008.

28. Interview, Kenitra, March 3, 2011.

29. Interview, Chefchaouen, January 17, 2012.

30. A number of functions and powers granted to local institutions are not used by local officials because they are unaware of the relevant charters or legislation and do not know their powers (Filali-Ansary 2009).

31. Interview, Chefchaouen, January 17, 2012.

32. Interview, Oulad Ghanem, January 13, 2012.

33. Ibid.

34. "About Ramsar," http://www.ramsar.org/, accessed January 3, 2015.

35. Interview, Oulad Ghanem, January 9, 2012.

36. Interview, Oulad Ghanem, January 13, 2012.

37. Ibid.

38. Bergh (2012b: 419) notes a similar personalization of the INDH.

39. Interview, political consultant, Rabat, February 21, 2011.

40. Interview, Rabat, February 23, 2011, paraphrased.

41. Interviews, Chefchaouen, March 22–23, 2011.

42. Interview, Chefchaouen, March 22, 2011.

43. Interview, Khenifra, March 24, 2011.

44. Interview, Khenifra, March 25, 2011.

45. Interview, Oulad Ghanem, January 13, 2012.

46. Interview, Khenifra, March 25, 2011.

47. Many rural municipalities are dominated by generations of one family of notables; although with rural migration to many of the towns, this is changing.

48. Interview, Erfoud, March 28, 2011.

49. Ibid.

50. This discussion is based on Waterbury (1970), who bases his analysis on Fès. As he states, it can be applied to the Moroccan urban bourgeoisie in general. The makhzen families comprised those who served in the central administration and those who were local representatives of the makhzen—qaids, for example (95).

51. Conversely, mayors in Jordan commonly have little status or prestige, and elites work indirectly—through ministers, for example—to exert influence on municipal politics.

52. This led to the development of many private housing estates. The 1976 charter addressed these issues and provided municipal presidents with new powers related to property development.

53. As Iraki (2002a: 35–80) states, the local elite has remain closed due partly to the fact that there have been limited opportunities for outsiders to invest, few economic opportunities, and no real industry in the area. While there are some emerging elite, until recently, no real nouveau riche elite with

investments in new areas of economic activity and links to the central power able to displace the traditional elite.

54. Group interview with councilors and appointed officials, Khenifra, March 24, 2011. This was not the only municipality where I witnessed this formality. Group interview, Tiflet, April 12, 2011.

55. Group interview and lunch, Khenifra, March 24, 2011.

56. Interview, Khenifra, March 25, 2011.

57. Interview, Erfoud, March 29, 2011.

58. Interview, Chefchaouen, February 17, 2012.

59. Interview, Erfoud, March 29, 2011.

60. In the mid-1990s, Morocco had the highest proportion of the population living in shantytowns of all Maghrebi countries—a national average of 10 percent, with 14 percent in Casablanca and 22 percent in Meknès. A 1994 World Bank study found that only 14 percent of rural inhabitants had running water and electricity (compared to 90 percent of urban inhabitants) (Denoeux and Maghraoui 1998: 80).

61. Interview, Chefchaouen, February 14, 2012.

62. Group interview, Erfoud, March 29, 2011.

63. Interview, Tiflet, April 12, 2011.

64. See Iraki 2002a for details on how the family backgrounds and sources of wealth and legitimacy.

65. A'rchane was himself a senior civil servant in the Ministry of Interior for several years. Following that, he served as an MP.

66. Interview, Rabat, February 8, 2012.

67. Group interview, Tiflet, April 12, 2011.

68. Interview, association head, Chefchaouen, February 15, 2012. The case of Tiflet's industrial zone is similar. The debate over the zone revolved around personal interests. Even those who opposed it admitted it would be good for the city. Interview, Rabat February 7, 2012.

69. Abouhani (2006b: 63) argues that civil servants are often harassed to bend the law and are unable to refuse due to the imbalance in power.

70. Interview, Tiznit, April 1, 2012.

71. Interview, Kenitra, March 1, 2011.

72. Interview, Tiznit, April 1, 2011.

73. Ibid.

74. Interview, association head, Chefchaouen, February 16, 2012.

75. Interview, Rabat, February 8, 2012.

76. Ibid.

77. The 2009 charter strengthened the role of the secretary-general, who is charged with the oversight of all purely administrative functions. He is a senior civil servant who acts as a city manager.

78. Group interview, Tiflet, April 12, 2011.

79. Interview, Kenitra, March 1, 2011.

80. Interview, Chefchaouen, February 15, 2012.

81. Interview, Khenifra, March 25, 2011; group interview, Erfoud, March 29, 2011.

82. Interview with pasha, Erfoud, March 28, 2011.

83. Group interview, Erfoud, March 29, 2011; interview, Khenifra, March 25, 2011.

84. Interview, Khenifra, March 25, 2011.

85. Group interview, Erfoud, March 29, 2011.

86. Since 1983 there has only been one period (2003–2009) when neither was president.

87. Interview, Rabat, February 8, 2012.

88. Group interview, Erfoud, March 29, 2011.

89. Interview, association head, January 16, 2012.

90. Interview, Erfoud, February 21, 2012.

91. As Abouhani (2006b: 61) states, landowners accommodate thousands of households looking for home ownership at the lowest cost, making small lots of only 60 square meters. These sales are done entirely through private agreement— usually by installment and without any interest—and without any state mediation.

92. Interview, Erfoud, March 29, 2011. See Iraki and Tamim 2009.

93. Interview, Oulad Ghanem, January 13, 2012.

94. Group interview, Tiflet, April 12, 2011; interview, Khenifra, March 25, 2011.

95. Group interview, Erfoud, March 29, 2011.

96. Interview, Khenifra, March 25, 2011.

97. Interview, Rabat, January 9, 2012

98. Interview, Rabat, February 8, 2012.

99. Interview, association head, Erfoud, March 29, 2011.

100. The president argued that because his municipality was small, personalities count more: "Here we do not vote for the program especially because it will be the coalition that makes the program. So it is simply useless to make a program before because it will only be after the formation of the coalition that you know what you can do and what you cannot do." Interview, Khenifra, March 24, 2011.

101. Interview, Khenifra, March 25, 2011.

102. Group interview, Erfoud, March 28, 2011.

103. Interview, Erfoud, March 28, 2011.

104. Ibid.

105. Iraki (2002b) demonstrates that associational elites often lose their legitimacy once they are elected to either, due to their subsequent inability to deliver, their perceived corruption, or both.

106. Interview, Rabat, February 8, 2012.

107. Interview, Khenifra, March 24, 2011.

108. Group interview, Azrou, February 22, 2012.

109. Interview, Rabat, February 23, 2011.

110. Interview, Azrou, March 23, 2011.

111. Group interview, Azrou, February 22, 2012.

112. Group interview with association representatives, Tiflet, January 17, 2012.

113. Ibid.

114. This competition for funds has undermined associations' willingness and ability to work together and coordinate efforts, hurting service provision and their ability to mount a serious leadership challenge to pro-regime elites (Berriane 2010: 101, 102).

115. Group interview, Khenifra, March 24, 2011.

116. Interview, Oulad Ghanem, January 13, 2012.

117. Even with the fanfare of the new charter, voter turnout was only 52 percent of registered voters in the 2009 municipal elections.

118. Interview, Khenifra, March 25, 2011.

119. Interview, Khenifra, March 25, 2011.

120. Should a budget be voted down, the expenses required for the administration of the municipality as allotted in the previous budget carry over for one more year; however, no additional expenditures, such as on services and development projects, may be made. Interviews, DGCL, Rabat, February 28, 2011; March 1, 2011.

121. Interview, Kenitra, March 3, 2011.

122. Interview, DGCL, February 28, 2011.

123. There are two official systems of auditing municipalities. The first is the MoI's general inspection unit, which regularly goes to the municipalities and inspects for irregularities. The second is the administrative court, which reviews any concerns vis-à-vis a president or councillor based on an official complaint. If an irregularity is found, the president can be suspended or his/her position revoked upon approval of the prime minister. The majority of revocations are due to urban management issues such as substandard buildings, building in unapproved locations, or granting contracts to bids that do not meet the conditions of the tenders and to educational issues, specifically that the president does not have the required primary school certificate. According to the DGCL, the majority of complaints do not result in revocations of bureau members (and, presumably, were not legitimate accusations); however, they do contribute to the general negative public perception of elected officials. Interview, DGCL, February 28, 2011.

124. Interview, Azrou, March 23, 2011. The details of these events could not be verified by council members as they were hostile to all questions. Their

defensive attitudes seemed to lend credence to the founder's recounting of events. Group interview, Azrou, February 22, 2012.

125. Group interview, Azrou, February 22, 2012.

126. Ironically, one member of the council also ended the council's version of events by stating, "It is the politics that is against this center!" Ibid.

127. Sater (2016: 137) notes that an audit of the INDH was conducted in 2006 and made available to the public in 2007. The results revealed the lack of transparency, participation, and proper planning at the local level, all of which favored ready-made infrastructure projects often without the personnel to run them. Despite having been made public, the report received little media attention.

6. Morocco's Opposition Party, the PJD

1. See also Pellicer and Wegner 2015: 33, 37–40; Daadaoui 2010: 200.

2. Interview, Tiznit, April 1, 2011.

3. In both the 1997 and 2002 elections, the PJD ran in a limited number of districts. See Wegner 2011: 27; Wegner and Pellicer 2009a: 161; Willis 1999: 45, 52–53, 2004: 56.

4. For details, see Perekli 2012: 91–92; Willis 1999: 65.

5. For fuller discussion of PJD's move toward technocracy, see Hamzawy 2008.

6. The 2008 PJD national convention elected 'Abd al-Ilah Benkirane, considered a political dove but a cultural hawk, to the position of secretary-general of the PJD.

7. See also Sherif 2012: 665–69.

8. For the MUR's own reasons for seeking greater distance from the PJD, see Tamam 2007: 101–2.

9. See Perekli 2012: 100 for the 2007 electoral manifesto.

10. For details, see Pellicer and Wegner 2015: 39–40; Catusse 2010.

11. Interview, Erfoud, February 21, 2012.

12. Interview with president, Erfoud, February 21, 2012.

13. Group interview, Erfoud, March 28, 2011.

14. The party also encouraged the public to attend the sessions when they raised issues of mismanagement and ensured good coverage of these issues by releasing public statements (Clark and Dalmasso 2015: 13).

15. The PJD in Chefchaouen had two members who ran as independents and won in 1997; in 2003, eight members from the PJD list won. The independents took part in the bureau, and the PJD members were relegated to the opposition. Interview, PJD bureau member, Chefchaouen, February 14, 2012.

16. Interview, Chefchaouen, February 14, 2012. It also learned lessons from the municipalities of Temara and Ksar Kbir where the PJD had won elections in 2003.
17. Interview, Tiflet, April 28, 2015.
18. Ibid.
19. Interview, Rabat, April 14, 2011.
20. Interview, neighborhood association, Erfoud, February 21, 2012.
21. Ibid.
22. Interview, president and bureau member, February 21, 2012.
23. Ibid.
24. This is supported by Pellicer and Wegner 2014: 129.
25. Due both to the overall precarious situation in which it found itself and the pressure exerted on it by the MoI, the PJD contested far fewer candidates than it had planned to do. It ensured that it could not win a majority in the big- and medium-sized cities and did not allow any main party officials (with the exception of a very few PJD parliamentarians) to head the party lists (Catusse and Zaki 2010; Pellicer and Wegner 2015: 40; Wegner 2011: 8; Wegner and Pellicer 2009b: 35). For details on the results, see Catusse and Zaki 2010; Wegner 2011: 112–14; Wegner and Pellicer 2009b: 3.
26. The following discussion of the PJD and civil society in Kenitra is based on Clark and Dalmasso (2015) and supplemented with additional interviews.
27. Interview, PJD bureau member, Kenitra, April 14, 2011, paraphrased.
28. For details, see Clark and Dalmasso 2015: 13.
29. Interview, PJD councillor, Kenitra, February 10, 2012.
30. See also Catusse and Zaki 2010; Wegner 2011: 53.
31. Interview, president of the PJD Ethics Committee and PJD deputy for the region of Oujda, Rabat, August 5, 2014.
32. Ibid.
33. For details, see Wegner 2011: 41–42.
34. Group interview, PJD councillors, Tiflet, April 28, 2015; interview, PJD Tiznit MP, Rabat, April 14, 2015.
35. Interview, PJD councillor and ADL member, Chefchaouen, February 14, 2012. Chefchaouen's region of Morocco was formerly under Spanish colonial occupation.
36. Ibid.
37. Interview, PJD councillor, Chefchaouen, February 14, 2012.
38. Interview, PJD councillor and ADL member, Chefchaouen, February 14, 2012.
39. Interview, civil society representative, Chefchaouen, February 15, 2012.
40. One PJD seat switched to PAM following the elections. In total, the council has twenty-nine seats.

41. Group interview with elected PJD members, the pasha, and the secretary-general, Erfoud, March 28, 2011.

42. Interview, Erfoud president and first vice-president, Erfoud, February 21, 2012.

43. Interview, civil society representative, Erfoud, March 29, 2011.

44. Interview, Erfoud president, first vice-president, and the secretary-general of the municipality, Erfoud, March 29, 2011.

45. Group interview with elected PJD members, the pasha, and the secretary-general, Erfoud, March 28, 2011.

46. Interview, Erfoud president and first vice-president, Erfoud, February 21, 2012.

47. Group interview with elected PJD members, the pasha, and the secretary-general of the municipality, Erfoud, March 28, 2011, paraphrased.

48. Ibid.

49. Interview, Erfoud president and first vice-president, Erfoud, February 21, 2012.

50. Interview, civil society representative, Erfoud, March 29, 2011. The PJD recently added one more association for a neighborhood incorporated into the municipality (see chapter 5).

51. Ibid.

52. Ibid.

53. Erfoud was designated as a rural municipality at the time and used the first-past-the-post system.

54. Interview, Erfoud president and first vice-president, Erfoud, February 21, 2012. The Erfoud PJD does not have a regular newspaper; it distributes a magazine during the municipality's annual date festival with a list of PJD accomplishments. It attempted a website; however, it felt it was ineffective.

55. Ibid.

56. Interview, Erfoud president and first vice-president, Erfoud, March 29, 2011.

57. Interview, Erfoud president and first vice-president, Erfoud, February 21, 2012.

58. Tiznit is located 98 kilometers south of the major coastal city and tourist destination of Agadir and specializes in silver jewelry, trade, and, to a lesser extent, tourism.

59. Interview, PJD Tiznit MP, Rabat, April 14, 2015.

60. Telephone interview conducted via member of PJD's general secretariat, PJD Tiznit MP, Rabat, May 25, 2015.

61. Interview, PJD Tiznit MP, Rabat, April 14, 2015.

62. The PJD came in second place in the 2009 elections in Tiznit; it won eight out of thirty-five seats.

63. Interview, PJD bureau members, Chefchaouen, February 14, 2012.

64. Ibid.

65. Interview, civil society representative, Chefchaouen February 13, 2012.

66. Based on the experience in Chefchaouen, the PJD in Kenitra and Temara attempted to establish similar newspapers in their respective municipalities. Interview, PJD bureau members, Chefchaouen, February 14, 2012. It was unsuccessful in Kenitra.

67. Ibid.

68. Interview, PJD councillor and ADL member, Chefchaouen, February 14, 2012.

69. Tiflet is located east of Rabat and has a population of approximately 70,000.

70. Interview, president of Tiflet, Rabat, February 8, 2012.

71. Group Interview, PJD councillors, Tiflet, April 28, 2015.

72. Ibid.; interview, president of Tiflet, Rabat, February 8, 2012.

73. Group interview with president and civil society representatives, Tiflet, April 11, 2011.

74. Group interview, PJD councillors, Tiflet, April 28, 2015, paraphrased.

75. Interview, PJD Tiznit MP, Rabat, April 14, 2015.

76. Interview, PSU bureau member, Chefchaouen, March 22, 2011.

77. Group Interview, PJD Councillors, Tiflet, April 28, 2015, paraphrased.

78. Interview, PJD Tiznit MP, Rabat, April 14, 2015.

79. Ibid.

80. Ibid.

81. Ibid.

82. Interview, Chefchaouen, March 22, 2011.

83. Interview, Chefchaouen, September 15, 2012.

84. Decisions regarding coalitions are at the local branch level. Interview, president of the PJD Ethics Committee and PJD deputy for the region of Oujda, Rabat, August 5, 2014.

85. For details on the PAM, see Eibl 2012.

86. Interview, PJD, Kenitra, March 3, 2011, paraphrased.

87. Group interview, PJD councillors, Tiflet, April 28, 2015.

88. Interview, president, Chefchaouen, February 14, 2012.

89. Interview, president, Chefchaouen, March 21, 2011.

90. Despite strained relations between the PJD and the USFP at the national level, the Chefchaouen PJD deemed the USFP a suitable coalition partner as it had ended its alliance with the Istiqlal party, and with it, its position in the bureau, and had entered the opposition in 2008. The PJD, PSU, and USFP ensured that they would not compete against each other's candidates during the 2009 municipal elections. For discussion of hostility between PJD and USFP at the national level, see Willis 2004: 64–65.

91. Interview, president, Chefchaouen, March 21, 2011.

92. Interview, PJD, Chefchaouen, February 14, 2012.

93. Interview, Chefchaouen, February 13, 2012.

94. Interview, PSU, Chefchaouen, March 22, 2011.

95. Interview, PJD bureau member and ADL member, Chefchaouen, February 14, 2012.

96. Ibid., paraphrased.

97. Interview, PSU, Chefchaouen, March 22, 2011.

98. Interview, PJD bureau member and ADL member, Chefchaouen, February 14, 2012.

99. Interview, bureau member, Chefchaouen, February 14, 2012.

100. Ibid.

101. Interview, PJD bureau member, Chefchaouen, February 14, 2012.

102. Interview, director of the Center for Associations, Chefchaouen, February 15, 2012.

103. Ibid.; interview, PJD bureau member and ADL member, Chefchaouen, February 14, 2012.

104. Interview, director of the Center for Associations, Chefchaouen, February 15, 2012.

105. Interview, PJD bureau member and ADL member, Chefchaouen, February 14, 2012.

106. Interview, president, Chefchaouen, March 21, 2011.

107. Interview, PSU bureau member, Chefchaouen, March 22, 2011.

108. Interview, bureau member, Chefchaouen, February 14, 2012.

109. Interview, civil society representative, Chefchaouen, February 13, 2012.

110. Interview, civil society representative, Chefchaouen, February 15, 2012.

111. Group interview, PJD members, PSU member, pasha, and secretary-general of the municipality, Erfoud, March 28, 2011.

112. Ibid.; interview PSU bureau member, Erfoud, March 28, 2011.

113. Interview, president and first vice-president, Erfoud, March 29, 2011.

114. Ibid, paraphrased.

115. Group interview, PJD members, PSU member, pasha, and secretary-general of the municipality, Erfoud, March 28, 2011.

116. In total, seven PSU candidates ran in the elections; however, only one won: the PSU member with whom the PJD had made a coalition.

117. Interview, president and first vice-president, Erfoud, March 29, 2011. Catusse and Zaki (2010) similarly note that the PJD is loyal to its coalition partners.

118. Interview PSU bureau member, Erfoud, March 28, 2011.

119. Ibid.

120. Interview, president and first vice-president, Erfoud, February 21, 2012.

121. Ibid.

122. Ibid.

123. Interview, Ministry of Interior employees, Kenitra, January 12, 2012.

124. Ibid.

125. Group interview, civil society representatives, Tiflet, January 17, 2012.

126. Interview, president of the Neighborhood Association of Sebanine, Chefchaouen, February 13, 2012.

127. Interview, Chefchaouen, February 13, 2012.

128. Interview, Chefchaouen-on-Line, Chefchaouen February 13, 2012.

129. Ibid.

130. Interview, PSU bureau member, Chefchaouen, March 22, 2011.

131. Interview, civil society representative, Chefchaouen, March 22, 2011.

132. According to the PJD, there were 250 municipal employees in the municipality of Chefchaouen. At the time of the interview, the PJD had not hired a single employee since coming to power in 2009. Telephone interview, director of the Center for Associations, February 17, 2012.

133. Interview, PJD bureau member, Chefchaouen, March 23, 2011.

134. Ibid.; interview, Istiqlal councillor, Chefchaouen, March 22, 2011.

135. Interview, PJD bureau member, Chefchaouen, March 23, 2011, paraphrased.

136. Ibid.; interview PJD Bureau Member, Chefchaouen, February 14, 2012, paraphrased.

137. Group interview, president, first vice-president, and secretary-general of the municipality, Erfoud, March 28, 2011.

Conclusion

1. The PJD more than doubled the number of votes it received, increasing the number from 700,000 in 2009 to over 1.5 million (from both the middle class, particularly in urban areas, the poor) in 2015 (Engelcke 2015). The electoral turnout was approximately the same in 2009 and 2015. The leftist-leaning parties were the biggest losers as compared to their results in 2009. One of the PJD's biggest successes was in Kenitra, where Aziz Rabbah was again the head of the list. The PJD won 75 percent of the seats in Kenitra (Djama 2015).

2. The charismatic personality and positive track record of the Islamist prime minister, Benkirane, and the active role he played during the local elections, no doubt played a role in the Islamists' success.

3. Tribal frustrations with the king's economic policy as well as the gaps in infrastructure development between urban and rural Jordan were most obvious when land protests broke out in parts of the country throughout 2011. At the heart of these protests was the issue of state-owned *miri* lands that the tribes have been living on for generations, using them for pasture and/or agriculture, and regarding them as their own (Varulkar 2011). Headed by the

largest tribes, the Bani Sakher and the Bani Hassan, the protestors demanded by restoration of lands taken away from them as part of the king's economic policies and, they claimed, handed over to entrepreneurs and private developers. The tribes blocked key access roads and burned tires, demanding the restoration of the lands.

4. Through her research, Tobin (2012) finds that the demographic majority in Jordan are the Palestinians, constituting 50 percent of the population. Following the Palestinians are Transjordanian (30 to 35 percent), Iraqis (15 to 20 percent), and then smaller groups of Assyrians, Armenians, Chechens, Circassains, Mandeans, Syrians, and migrant workers from Egypt, Sri Lanka, and the Philippines.

5. There was tribal violence in the lead-up to the 2015 local elections.

Bibliography

Ababsa, Myriam. 2011. "Social Disparities and Public Policies in Amman." In Ababsa and Daher 2011, 205–32.

———, ed. 2013. *Atlas of Jordan: History, Territories and Society.* Beirut: Presses de l'IFPO.

———. 2015. "Country Report: Jordan." In Harb and Sami 2015a, 137–86. (In French.)

Ababsa, Myriam, and Rami Daher. 2011. *Cities, Urban Practices and Nation Building in Jordan.* Beirut: Presses de l'IFPO.

Abouhani, Abdelghani. 1999. *Pouvoirs, villes et notabilites locales: quand les notables font les villes.* Rabat: URBAMA.

———. 2006a. *Pouvoirs locaux et systèmes municipaux dans le Monde Arabe.* Rabat: Institut National d'Aménagement et d'Urbanisme.

———. 2006b. "Les nouvelles élites urbaines: Le rôle des notables et des cadres associatifs dans le système politico-administratif local." In Abouhani 2006a, 55–74.

———. 2011. *Gouverner les périphéries urbaines: de la gestion notabilaire à la gouvernance urbaine au Maroc.* Paris: L'Harmattan.

Abu Baker, Shaima. 2005. "Federalism in Multicultural and Multinational Polities." Paper presented for the Summer University of the Institute of Federalism, Amman.

Abu-Kharmeh, Suleiman S., and Jihad A. Abu-al Sondos. 2011. "Measurement of Resources Allocation Efficiency in the Jordanian Municipalities (Case Study: Greater Irbid Municipality)." *Journal of Geography and Regional Planning* 4, no. 2: 53–62.

Abu Libdeh, As'ad J., and Eman A. Fraihet. 2014. "Protest Movements in Trans-jordan from the End of the Ottoman Era Until the Establishment of the Emirate (1841–1921)." *University of Sussex Journal of Contemporary History* 15: 17–43.

Abu Rumman, Mohammad. 2007. *The Muslim Brotherhood in the Jordanian Parliamentarian Election 2007: A Passing "Political Setback" or Diminishing Popularity?* Amman: Friedrich-Ebert-Stiftung.

ACRPS. 2015. "Assessment Report: The September 2015 Municipal Elections in Morocco: The Performance of the Justice and Development Party." Arab Center for Research and Policy Studies—Policy Analysis Unit, September 17. http://english.dohainstitute.org/release/fcced191-e950-4b23-a664-3aabbe 24aef8.

Adams, Linda S. 1996. "Political Liberalization in Jordan." *Journal of Church and State* 38, no. 3: 507–28.

Aggestam, Karen, Laura Guazzone, Helena Lindholm Schulz, M. Christina Paciello, and Daniela Pioppi. 2009. "The Arab State and Neo-liberal Globalization." In Guazzone and Pioppi 2009a, 325–50.

Ahmaro, Ismail H. 2014. "Controlling the Financial Performance of Jordanian Municipalities by Improving Financial Regulations: An Analytical Study." *Journal of Business Studies Quarterly* 6, no. 2: 67–84.

Albert, Jean-Claude. 1997. "La régionalisation marocaine une réforme d'inspiration gaullienne." *Pouvoirs Locaux*, no. 33: 111–16.

Albrecht, Holger. 2005. "How Can Opposition Support Authoritarianism? Lessons from Egypt." *Democratization* 12, no. 3: 378–97.

Albrecht, Holger, and Oliver Schlumberger. 2004. " 'Waiting for Godot': Regime Change Without Democratization in the Middle East." *International Political Science Review* 25, no. 4: 371–92.

Albrecht, Holger, and Eva Wagner. 2006. "Autocrats and Islamists: Contenders and Containment in Egypt and Morocco." *Journal of North African Studies* 11, no. 2: 123–41.

Alfdeilat, Mohammed. 2014. "Jordan's Capital Split Between Rich and Poor." *Al-Monitor*, February 19. http://www.al-monitor.com/pulse/culture/2014/02 /amman-jordan-divided-capital-rich-poor.html.

Ali Mekouar, Mohamed. 1989. "Communes et environnement: localiser l'écologie." In *L'État et les collectivités locales* 1989: 119–31.

Allal, Amin. 2007. " 'Développement international' et 'promotion de la démocratie': à propos de la 'gouvernance locale' au Maroc." *L'Année du Maghreb*: 275–96.

Allam, Azzeddine. 2010. "La culture politique au Maroc aujourd'hui." In Centre d'Études Internationales 2009: 95–116.

Allen Matthew, and Zahid Hasnain. 2010. "Power, Pork and Patronage: Decentralisation and the Politicisation of the Development Budget of Papua New Guinea." *Commonwealth Journal of Local Governance* 6: 7–31.

"Almasry: Decentralization Law Will Increase the Participation of People in Decision Making." 2015. *Shihan News*, April 2. http://www.shihan-news.com. (In Arabic.)

Alon, Yoav. 2005. "The Tribal System in the Face of the State-Formation Process: Mandatory Transjordan, 1921–46." *International Journal of Middle East Studies* 37: 213–40.

——. 2007. *The Making of Jordan*. London: I. B. Tauris.

Alsondos, Jihad Abu, Khaled Awamleh, and Martin Beck, eds. 2011. *Decentralization and Local Development*. Amman: Konrad Adenauer Stiftung and Visions Center for Strategic and Development Studies. (In Arabic)

Amadouny, Vartan M. 1994. "Infrastructural Development Under the British Mandate." In Rogan and Tell 1994: 128–61.

Amar, Ali, Catherine Graciet, and Oumama Draoui. 2006. "Corruption, la gangrène du Maroc." *Le Journal Hebdomadaire*, no. 277 (November): 20–29.

Amawi, Abla M. 1994. "The Consolidation of the Merchant Class in Transjordan During the Second World War." In Rogan and Tell 1994: 162–86.

Amghar, Samir. 2007. "Political Islam in Morocco." CEPS Working Document no. 269, June 2007. http://aei.pitt.edu/11725/.

Amis, Jacob. 2013. "The Jordanian Brotherhood in the Arab Spring." *Current Trends in Islamist Ideologies* (Hudson Institute) 14: 38–57.

El Amrani, Issandr. 2009. "Security Policy and Democratic Reform in Morocco." In Guazzone and Pioppi 2009a: 299–324.

Anderson, Betty S. 1997. "The Status of 'Democracy' in Jordan." *Critique* 10: 59.

——. 2005. *Nationalist Voices in Jordan: The Street and the State*. Austin: University of Texas Press.

Antoun, Richard T. 1979. *Low-Key Politics*. Albany: State University of New York Press.

——. 2000. "Civil Society, Tribal Process, and Change in Jordan: An Anthropological View." *International Journal of Middle East Studies* 32, no. 4: 441–63.

Araujo, M. Caridad, Francisco H. G. Ferreira, Peter Lanjouw, and Berk Ozler. 2008. "Local Inequity and Project Choice: Theory and Evidence from Ecuador." *Journal of Public Economics* 92: 1022–46.

Aruri, Naseer H. 1972. *Jordan: A Study in Political Development (1921–1965)*. The Hague: Martinus Nijhoff.

Aswab, Mohamed. 2010. "Saïd Jafri: 'Les inconvénients de l'unité de la ville sont d'ordre politique.'" *Aujourd'hui le Maroc*, October 24. http://aujourdhui.ma /focus/said-jafri-les-inconvenients-de-lunite-de-la-ville-sont-dordre -politique-73559.

Atia, Mona. 2012. "'A Way to Paradise': Pious Neoliberalism, Islam and Faith-Based Development." *Annals of the Association of American Geographers* 102, no. 4: 808–27.

———. 2013. *Building a House in Heaven*. Minneapolis: University of Minnesota Press.

Auyero, Javier. 2000. "The Logic of Clientelism in Argentina: An Ethnographic Account." *Latin American Research Review* 35, no. 3: 55–81.

Ayoub, Ayman. 2010. *The State of Local Democracy in the Arab World: A Regional Report*. Stockholm: International Institute for Democracy and Electoral Assistance (International IDEA).

Baaklini, Abdo, Guilain Denoeux, and Robert Springborg. 1999. *Legislative Politics in the Arab World*. Boulder, Colo.: Lynne Rienner.

El Badaoui, Abderrahim. 2004. *Les rentiers du Maroc utile: partis politiques et non-développement économique*. N.p.: El Autor.

Bank, André. 2004. "Rents, Cooptation, and Economized Discourse: Three Dimensions of Political Rule in Jordan, Morocco and Syria." *Journal of Mediterranean Studies* 14, no. 1–2: 155–79.

Bar, Shmuel. 1998. *The Muslim Brotherhood in Jordan*. Tel Aviv: Tel Aviv University; Moshe Dayan Center for Middle Eastern and African Studies.

Barari, Hassan A. 2012. "Tribes and the Monarchy in Jordan." *Bitterlemons-international*. http://www.bitterlemons-international.org/inside.php?id=1503.

Barber, Benjamin R. 2013. *If Mayors Ruled the World*. New Haven: Yale University Press.

Bardhan, Pranab. n.d. "Notes of Decentralization." Initiative for Policy Change Working Paper Series, Columbia University, New York.

———. 2002. "Decentralization of Governance and Development." *Journal of Economic Perspectives* 16, no. 4: 185–205.

Bardhan, Pranab, and Dilip Mookherjee. 2000. "Capture and Governance at Local and National Levels." *Political Economy, Governance and Development* 90, no. 2: 135–39.

———, eds. 2006a. *Decentralization and Local Governance in Developing Countries*. Cambridge, Mass.: MIT Press.

———. 2006b. "Pro-Poor Targeting and Accountability of Local Governments in West Bengal." *Journal of Development Economics* 79: 303–27.

Barkey, Henri, ed. 1992. *The Politics of Economic Reform in the Middle East*. New York: St. Martin's.

Barnes-Darcy, J. 2012. "Europe and Jordan: Reform Before It's Too Late." *European Council on Foreign Relations*, no. 54.

Barnett, Andy, Bruce Yandle, and George Naufal. 2013. "Regulation, Trust and Cronyism in Middle Eastern Societies: The Simple Economics of 'Wasta.'" *Journal of Socio-economics* 44: 41–46.

Barter, Shane J. 2008. "The Dangers of Decentralization: Clientelism, the State and Nature in a Democratic Indonesia." Unpublished paper. http://www.soka.edu/files/documents/academics/shane-barter-syllabus/file.pdf.

Barwig, Andrew. 2012. "The 'New Palace Guards': Elections and Élites in Morocco and Jordan." *Middle East Journal* 66, no. 3: 425–39.

Bayart, Jean-François. 2004. *Global Subjects*. Translated by Andrew Brown. Cambridge: Polity.

——. 2009. *The State in Africa*. 2nd ed. Cambridge: Polity.

Baylouny, Anne Marie. 2005. "Jordan's New 'Political Development' Strategy." *Middle East Report* 236: 40–43.

——. 2008. "Militarizing Welfare: Neo-liberalism and Jordanian Policy." *Middle East Journal* 62, no. 2: 277–303.

——. 2010. *Privatizing Welfare in the Middle East*. Bloomington: Indiana University Press.

Bayraktar, S. Ulaş. 2007. "Turkish Municipalities: Reconsidering Local Democracy Beyond Administrative Autonomy." *European Journal of Turkish Studies*. http://ejts.revues.org/1103.

Bebcheich, Souleiman, and Myriem Khrouz. 2011. "Les fondations royales." *L'Express*, no. 3118 (April): 54–57.

Beblawi, Hazem, and Giacomo Luciani, eds. 1987. *The Rentier State*. London: Croom Helm.

Beinin, Joel, and Frédéric Vairel, eds. 2011. *Social Movements, Mobilization and Contestation in the Middle East and North Africa*. Stanford: Stanford University Press.

Belghazi, Saâd. 2003. "Local Governance, Development and Service Delivery." Thematic Paper for Workshop D, Arab States Local Governance Forum, Sana'a, Yemen, December 6–9.

Bellin, Eva. 2004. "The Political-Economic Conundrum: The Affinity of Economic and Political Reform in the Middle East and North Africa." Carnegie Papers, Middle East Series, no. 53.

Benabdallah, Mohammed Amine. 2003. "Propos sur la décentralisation territoriale au Maroc." *Revue marocaine d'administration locale et de développement*, no. 50: 9–24.

Bendourou, Omar. 2000. "Transition démocratique et réformes politiques et constitutionnelles au Maroc." *Annuaire de l'Afrique du Nord* 39: 233–53.

Benesrighe, Driss. 2008. "INDH: Initiative de Lutte contre la pauvreté et l'exclusion sociale ou politique pour le développement économique." *Revue marocaine des politiques publiques*, no. 2–3: 131–43.

Benhrimida, Mohamed. 2009. "La variable fiscale dans les finances des collectivités locales." *Massalik*, no. 11–12: 57–62.

Ben Mami, Skander. n.d. "La décentralisation et la déoncentration en Tunisie et au Maroc." Institut de Recherche et Débat sur la Gouvernance." http://www.institut-gouvernance.org/fr/analyse/fiche-analyse-366.html.

Benmansour, Abdelatif. 2009. "Gouvernance urbaine et démocratie locale au Maroc." *Massalik*, no. 11–12: 5–14.

Ben-Meir, Yossef. 2009a. "Morocco's Local Elections and Decentralisation." *Countercurrents.org*, July 16. http://www.countercurrents.org/benmeir160709.htm.

——. 2009b. "Opportunities for Decentralization in Morocco." *Dissident Voice*, October 30. http://dissidentvoice.org/2009/10/opportunities-for-decentraliza tion-in-morocco/.

——. 2011. "Morocco's Regionalization Roadmap and the Western Sahara." *International Journal of Sociology and Social Policy* 31, no. 1–2: 75–90.

Ben Nefissa, Sarah. 2009. "Cairo's City Government: The Crisis of Local Administration and the Refusal of Urban Citizenship." In Singerman 2009: 177–98.

Ben Nefissa, Sarah, Nabil Abd al-Fattah, Sari Hanafi, and Carlos Milani, eds. 2005. *NGOs and Governance in the Arab World*. Cairo: AUC Press.

Bennani, Hicham. 2015. "Pourquoi le PJD va gagner les élections communales 2015 (analyse)." *H24Info*, September 2. http://www.h24info.ma/maroc/poli tique/pourquoi-le-pjd-va-gagner-les-elections-communales-2015-analyse /35948. .

Bennani-Chraïbi, Mounia. 2008. " 'Businessman' Versus 'Professors': The Parliamentary 'Notabilisation' of a Party of Militants in Morocco." *Revue internationale de politique comparée* 15, no. 2: 205–19.

Bennani-Chraïbi, Mounia, Myriam Catusse, and Jean-Claude Santucci, eds. 2004. *Scènes et coulisses de l'élection au Maroc—les législatives 2002*. Paris: Karthala.

Bergh, Sylvia I. 2007. "Decentralization and Participatory Approaches to Rural Development: Assessing the Scope for State-Society Synergies in Morocco." PhD diss., Oxford University.

——. 2009. "Traditional Village Councils, Modern Associations, and the Emergence of Hybrid Political Orders in Rural Morocco." *Peace Review: A Journal of Social Justice* 21, no. 1: 45–53.

——. 2010a. "Assessing Local Governance Innovations in Morocco in Light of the Participatory Budgeting Experience in Brazil." *Journal of Economic and Social Research* 12, no. 1: 113–38.

——. 2010b. "Assessing the Scope for Partnerships Between Local Governments and Community-Based Organizations: Findings from Rural Morocco." *International Journal of Public Administration* 33, no. 12: 740–51.

——. 2010c. "Decentralisation and Local Governance in the MENA Region." *IEMed Mediterranean Yearbook*: 253–58.

——. 2012a. "Introduction: Researching the Effects of Neoliberal Reforms on Local Governance in the Southern Mediterranean." *Mediterranean Politics* 17, no. 3: 303–21.

——. 2012b. " 'Inclusive' Neoliberalism, Local Governance Reforms and the Redeployment of State Power." *Mediterranean Politics* 17, no. 3: 410–26.

——. 2017. *The Politics of Development in Morocco: Local Governance and Participation in North Africa*. London: I. B. Tauris.

Bergh, Sylvia I., and Daniele Rossi-Doria. 2015. "Plus ça change? Observing the Dynamics of Morocco's 'Arab Spring' in the High Atlas." *Mediterranean Politics* 20, no. 2: 198–216.

Berrahou, Salah Eddine. 2002. *L'État d'exception au Maroc: essai sur les rapports entre le pouvoir et les partis politiques de l'opposition.* Marrakech: Université Cadi Ayyad.

Berriane, Yasmine. 2010. "The Complexities of Inclusive Participatory Governance: The Case of Moroccan Associational Life in the Context of the INDH." *Journal of Economic and Social Research* 12, no. 1: 89–111.

Bertelsmann Stiftung. 2014. "BTI 2014 Jordan Country Report." http://www.bti -project.org/en/reports/country-reports/detail/itc/jor/ity/2014/itr/mena/.

Besley, Timothy. n.d. "Notes on Different Forms of Decentralization." Initiative for Policy Change Working Paper Series, Columbia University, New York.

Besley, Timothy, Jean-Paul Faguet, and Mariano Tommasi. 2003. "Synoptic Guide to Decentralization." Initiative for Policy Change Working Paper Series, Columbia University, New York.

"Bilan positif de trente années de mise en oeuvre de la charte communale." 2006. *Aujoud'hui le Maroc*, December 13.

bin Muhammad, Ghazi. 1999. *The Tribes of Jordan at the Beginning of the Twenty-First Century.* Hashemite Kingdom of Jordan: Jami'at Turath al-Urdun al-Baqi.

Bird, Richard M., and François Vaillancourt, eds. 1998. *Fiscal Decentralization in Developing Countries.* Cambridge: Cambridge University Press.

Blaydes, Lisa. 2006. "Who Votes in Authoritarian Elections and Why? Determinants of Voter Turnout in Contemporary Egypt." Paper presented at the 2006 Annual Meeting of the American Political Science Association, Philadelphia, August 31–September 3.

——. 2013. *Elections and Distributive Politics in Mubarak's Egypt.* Cambridge: Cambridge University Press.

Bocco, Riccardo, and Tariq M. M. Tell. 1994. "Pax Britannica in the Steppe." In Rogan and Tell 1994: 108–27.

Boerwinkel, Felia. 2011. "The First Lady Phenomenon in Jordan: Assessing the Effect of Queen Raina's NGO's of Jordanian Civil Society." Knowledge Programme Civil Society in West Asia Working Paper 19, University of Amsterdam.

Bogaert, Koenraad. 2011a. "The Problem of Slums: Shifting Methods of Neoliberal Urban Government in Morocco." *Development and Change* 42, no. 3: 709–31.

——. 2011b. "Uneven Development, Neoliberal Government and the Restructuring of State Power." PhD diss., Ghent University.

——. 2011c. "Urban Politics in Morocco." PhD diss., Ghent University.

Bono, Irene. 2010. "L'Activisme associatif comme marche du travail: normalisation sociale et politique par les 'activités génératrices de revenues' à El Hajeb." *Politique Africaine* 120: 25–44.

Bouabid, Ali, and Aziz Iraki. 2015. "Maroc: Tensions Centralisatrices." In Harb and Atallah 2015a: 47–90.

Bouachrine, Taoufik. 2012. "Jurisprudence 'sultanienne' et causeries hassaniennes." *Panoramaroc*, July. http://www.panoramaroc.ma/fr/jurisprudence-sulta nienne-et-causeries-hassaniennes-par-taoufik-bouachrine/.

Boubekeur, Amel. 2009. "Morocco: The Emergence of a New Palace Party." Carnegie Endowment for International Peace, July 28. http://carnegieendow ment.org/2009/07/28/morocco-emergence-of-new-palace-party/9jr.

Bouillon, Markus. 2002. "Walking the Tightrope." In *Jordan in Transition 1999–2000*, edited by George Joffé, 1–22. London: Hurst.

Boulby, Marion. 1999. *The Muslim Brotherhood and the Kings of Jordan, 1945–1993*. Atlanta: Scholars Press.

Boutouil, Ahmed. 2010. *De la régionalisation: préalables, voies et supports pour une croissance socio-économique équilibrée*. Rabat: Amok Graphic.

Bouziane, Malika. 2010. "The State from Below: Local Governance Practices in Jordan." *Journal of Economic and Social Research* 12, no. 1: 33–61.

——. 2016. "Jordan: Disquiet at the Island of Stability." *IEMed Mediterranean Yearbook 2016*: 214–17.

Bouziane, Malika, Cilja Harders, and Anja Hoffmann, eds. 2013. *Local Politics and Contemporary Transformations in the Arab World*. New York: Palgrave Macmillan.

Bouziane, Malika, and Katharina Lenner. 2011. "Protests in Jordan: Rumblings in the Kingdom of Dialogue." In *Protests, Revolutions and Transformation—The Arab World in a Period of Upheaval*. Working Paper no. 1: 148–61.

Brahimi, Mohamed. 1991. "Regard sur l'évolution de l'administration territoriale marocaine: organisation, fonctionnement, dysfonctions et projets pour l'avenir." *Revue de science administrative de la Méditerranée occidentale*, no. 34–35: 13–30.

——. 2006. "Appréciation de la régionalisation a l'ombre de la recomposition politique et institutionnelle." *Revue marocaine d'administration locale et de développement*, no. 52: 9–56.

Braizat, Fares. 2006. "Jordan: Why Political Reform Does Not Progress." *Arab Reform Bulletin* 4, no. 6. http://carnegieendowment.org/sada/20816.

Brand, Laurie A. 1994. *Jordan's Inter-Arab Relations*. New York: Columbia University Press.

——. 1995. "Palestinians and Jordanians: A Crisis of Identity." *Journal of Palestine Studies* 24, no. 4: 46–61.

——. 1998. *Women, the State, and Political Liberalization*. New York: Columbia University Press.

———. 1999. "The Effects of the Peace Process on Political Liberalization in Jordan." *Journal of Palestine Studies* 28: 52–67.

———. 2001a. "Development in Wadi Rum? State Bureaucracy, External Funders, and Civil Society." *International Journal of Middle East Studies* 33, no. 4: 571–90.

———. 2001b. "Displacement for Development? The Impact of Changing State-Society Relations." *World Development* 29, no. 6: 961–76.

Bratton, Michael, and Nicolas Van de Walle. 2004. "Neopatrimonial Regimes and Political Transitions in Africa." *World Politics* 46, no. 4: 453–89.

Brenner, Neil, Jamie Peck, and Nik Theodore. 2010. "Variegated Neoliberalization: Geographies, Modalities, Pathways." *Global Networks* 10, no. 2: 1–41.

Brenner, Neil, and Nik Theodore, eds. 2001. *Space of Neoliberalism*. Oxford: Blackwell.

———. 2002a. "Cities and the Geographies of 'Actually Existing Neoliberalism.' " *Antipode* 34, no. 3: 349–79.

———. 2002b. "Preface: From the 'New Localism' to the Spaces of Neoliberalism." *Antipode* 34, no. 3: 341–47.

Brinkerhoff, Derick W., and Arthur A. Goldsmith. 2004. "Good Governance, Clientelism and Patrimonialism: New Perspectives on Old Problems." *International Public Management Journal* 7, no. 2: 163–85.

Brosio, Giorgio, and Juan Pablo Jimenez, eds. 2010. *Decentralization and Reform in Latin America*. Cheltenham: Edward Elgar.

Brown, Nathan J., and Amr Hamzawy. 2010. *Between Religion and Politics*. Washington, D.C.: Carnegie Endowment for International Peace.

Brownlee, Jason. 2002. "And Yet They Persist: Explaining Survival and Transition in Neopatrimonial Regimes." *Studies in Comparative International Development* 37, no. 3: 35–63.

Brumberg, Daniel. 2002. "Democratization in the Arab World? The Trap of Liberalized Autocracy." *Journal of Democracy* 13, no. 4: 56–68.

Brusco, Valeria, Marcelo Nazareno, and Susan C. Stokes. 2004. "Vote Buying in Argentina." *Latin American Research Review* 39, no. 2: 66–88.

Brynen, Rex. 1992. "Economic Crisis and Post-Rentier Democratization in the Arab World: The Case of Jordan." *Canadian Journal of Political Science* 25, no. 1: 69–97.

Brynen, Rex, Bahgat Korany, and Paul Noble, eds. 1995. *Political Liberalization and Democratization in the Arab World, Vol. 1: Theoretical Perspectives*. Boulder, Colo.: Lynne Rienner.

Buehler, Matt. 2013a. "Safety-Valve Elections and the Arab Spring: The Weakening (and Resurgence) of Morocco's Islamist Opposition Party." *Terrorism and Political Violence* 25, no. 1: 137–56.

———. 2013b. "The Threat to 'Un-Moderate': Moroccan Islamists and the Arab Spring." *Middle East Law and Governance* 5: 231–57.

Burgess, Robin. n.d. "Notes on Empirical Evidence on the Impact of Decentralization." Initiative for Policy Change Working Paper Series, Columbia University, New York.

Burki, Shahid J., Guillermo Perry, William Dillinger, with Charles Griffin, Jeffrey Gutman, Fernando Rojas, Steven Webb, and Donald Winkler. 1999. *Beyond the Center: Decentralizing the State.* World Bank Latin American and Caribbean Studies, Viewpoint 19636. Washington, D.C.: World Bank.

Burnell, Peter, ed. 2000. *Democracy Assistance: International Cooperation for Democratization.* London: Frank Cass.

Burns, Danny, Robin Hambleton, and Paul Hoggett. 1994. *The Politics of Decentralisation.* Basingstoke: Macmillan.

Bush, Ray. 2004. "Poverty and Neo-liberal Bias in the Middle East and North Africa." *Development and Change* 35, no. 4: 673–95.

Cai, Hongbin, and Daniel Treisman. 2009. "Political Decentralization and Policy Experimentation." *Quarterly Journal of Political Science* 4, no. 1: 35-58. .

CAIMED (Centre for Administrative Innovation in the Euro-Mediterranean Region). 2002. "Administrative Reform in the Mediterranean Region: Summary of Jordan." Unpublished report. http://www.caimed.org.

Cammett, Melani. 2004. "Challenges to Networks of Privilege in Morocco." In Heydemann 2004a: 245–79.

Cantori, Louis J., and Iliya Harik, eds. 1984. *Local Politics and Development in the Middle East.* Boulder, Colo.: Westview.

Cattedra, Raffaele, and Myriam Cattuse. 2006. "Stratégies notabiliaires et recomposition du paysage urbain de Casablanca." In *Être notable au Maghreb: dynamique des configurations notabiliaires*, edited by Abdelhamid Hénia, 297–315. Paris: Maisonneuve et Larose.

Catusse, Myriam. 2000. "Économie des élections au Maroc." *Maghreb-Machrek* 168: 51–66.

——. 2002. "Le charme discret de la société civile. Ressorts politiques de la formation d'un groupe dans le Maroc 'ajusté.'" *Revue internationale de politique comparée* 9, no. 2: 297–318.

——. 2003. "Affaires, scandales et urnes dè verre à Casablanca: les ambiguïtés de la démocratie 'locale' à l'ère de la 'bonne gouvernance.'" In *L'Annuaire de l'Afrique du Nord*, edited by Eberhard Kienle, 279–306. Paris: CRNRS.

——. 2004. "À propos de 'l'entrée en politique' des 'entrepreneurs' marocains." *NADQ* 1, no. 19–20: 127–153.

——. 2007. "Les vraies fausses surprises du score PJD au Maroc—Législatives 2002." In *La surprise électorale: paradoxes du suffrage universel (Colombie, Équateur, France, Maroc, Suède, Turquie . . .)*, edited by Olivier Dabène, Michel Hastings, and Julie Massal, 151–82. Paris: Karthala.

——. 2009. "Morocco's Political Economy: Ambiguous Privatization and the Emerging Social Question." In Guazzone and Pioppi 2009a: 185–216.

——. 2010. *A Return to Partisan Politics? Partisan Logics and Political Transformations in the Arab World.* Beirut: Press de l'IFPO and the Lebanese Center for Policy Studies.

Catusse, Myriam, with Raffaele Cattedra and M'hammed Idrissi-Janati. 2007. "Decentralisation and Its Paradoxes." In Drieskens, Mermier, and Wimmen 2007: 113–35.

Catusse, Myriam, Raffaele Cattedra, and M'hammed Idrissi Janatti, with Olivier Toutain. 2005. "Municipaliser les villes? le gouvernement des villes marocaines a l'epreuve du politique et du territoire." In *Intégration à la ville et services urbains au Maroc*, edited by Claude de Miras, 313–61. Tanger: Institut National d'Aménagement et d'Urbanisme.

Catusse, Myriam, Blandine Destremau, and Éric Verdier, eds. 2008. *L'État face aux débordements du social au Maghreb.* Paris: Karthala.

Catusse, Myriam, and Karam Karam, eds. 2010. *A Return to Partisan Politics? Partisan Logics and Political Transformations in the Arab World.* Beirut: Press de l'IFPO and the Lebanese Center for Policy Studies. http://books.openedition.org/ifpo/1067.

Catusse, Myriam, and Frédéric Vairel. 2010. "Le Maroc de Mohammed VI: mobilisations et action publique." *Politique Africaine* 4, no. 120: 5–23.

Catusse, Myriam, and Lamia Zaki. 2009. "Gestion communale et clientèlisme moral au Maroc: les politiques du parti de la justice et du développement." *Critique Internationale* 1, no. 42: 73–91.

——. 2010. "The Transformations of the Justice and Development Party in Morocco in the Face of Urban Governance." In Catusse and Karam 2010.

Cavatorta, Francesco. 2006. "Civil Society, Islamism and Democratisation: The Case of Morocco." *Journal of Modern African Studies* 44, no. 2: 203–22.

——. 2009. *Civil Society Activism in Morocco: 'Much Ado About Nothing'?* Amsterdam: Knowledge Programme Civil Society in West Asia.

——. 2010. "The Convergence of Governance: Upgrading Authoritarianism in the Arab World and Downgrading Democracy Elsewhere?" *Middle East Critique* 19, no. 3: 217–32.

Cavatorta, Francesco, and Emanuela Dalmasso. 2009. "Liberal Outcomes Through Undemocratic Means: The Reform of the *Code de statut personnel* in Morocco." *Journal of Modern African Studies* 47, no. 4: 487–506.

"Ce que l'intérieur veut modifier dans la charte communale." 2008. *La Vie économique*, June 27. http://lavieeco.com/news/politique/ce-que-linterieur-veut -modifier-dans-la-charte-communale-5762.html

Centeno, Miguel Angel. 1993. "The New Leviathan: The Dynamics and Limits of Technocracy." *Theory and Society* 22: 307–35.

Center for Strategic Studies. 2004. *The Municipalities*. Amman: Center for Strategic Studies. (In Arabic.)

Center of Arab Women for Training and Research. 2014. *Gender and Decentralization in Jordan, Libya, Tunisia and Yemen*. Forum of Federations, Canada. Viewed January 10, 2015. http://www.forumfed.org/post/GenderandDecentralization_Forumfed.pdf.

Centre d'Études Internationales, ed. 2009. *Une décennie de réformes au Maroc (1999–2009)*. Paris: Karthala.

Chahir, Aziz. 2003. "Le Maroc est-il menacé par le séparatisme?" *Le Gazette du Maroc*, January 20. http://www.maghress.com/fr/lagazette/1814.

Charrad, Mounira M. 2011. "Central and Local Patrimonialism: State-Building in Kin-Based Societies." *ANNALS of the American Academy of Political and Social Science* 636: 49–68.

Charrad, Mounira M., and Julia Adams. 2011. "Introduction: Patrimonialism, Past and Present." *ANNALS of the American Academy of Political and Social Science* 636: 6–15.

Chatty, Dawn. 2006. *Nomadic Societies in the Middle East and North Africa: Entering the 21st Century*. Leiden: Brill.

Cheema, G. Shabbir, and Dennis A. Rondinelli, eds. 1983. *Decentralization and Development: Policy Implementation in Developing Countries*. Thousand Oaks, Calif.: Sage.

———. 2007. "From Government Decentralization to Decentralized Governance." In Rondinelli and Cheema 2007: 1–20.

Cheena, Ali, and Shandana K. Mohmand. 2006. "Bringing Electoral Politics to the Doorstep: Who Gains Who Loses?" Unpublished working draft.

Chmirou, Youssef. 2006. "Collectivités locales: cherche autonomie financière désespérément." *La Gazette du Maroc*, December 25. http://www.maghress.com/fr/lagazette/12152.

Choucair, Julia. 2006. "Illusive Reform: Jordan's Stubborn Stability." Carnegie Papers, Middle East Series, no. 76 (December). http://carnegieendowment.org/2006/12/04/illusive-reform-jordan-s-stubborn-stability-pub-18900.

Chowdhury, Shyamal, and Futoshi Yamauchi. 2010. "Has Decentralization in Indonesia Led to Elite Capture or Reflection of Majority Preference?" JICA Research Institute, Working Paper no. 14.

Christophersen, Mona. 2013a. *Jordan's 2013 Elections: A Further Boost for Tribes*. NOREF Norwegian Centre for Conflict Resolution, March 21. https://noref.no/Publications/Regions/Middle-East-and-North-Africa/Jordan-s-2013-elections-a-further-boost-for-tribes.

———. 2013b. *Protest and Reform in Jordan: Popular Demand and Government Response 2011 to 2012*. Fafo-rapport 2013:50. Oslo: FAFO, 50.

Claisse, Alain. 1987. "Makhzen Traditions and Administrative Channels." In Zartman 1987: 34–58.

Clapham, Christopher. 1982. *Private Patronage and Public Power.* London: Frances Pinter.

Clark, Janine A. 2004. *Islam, Charity and Activism: Middle-Class Networks and Social Welfare in Egypt, Jordan and Yemen.* Bloomington: Indiana University Press.

——. 2006. "The Conditions of Islamist Moderation: Unpacking Cross-Ideological Cooperation in Jordan." *International Journal of Middle East Studies* 38, no. 4: 539–60.

——. 2012. "Municipalities Go to Market." *Mediterranean Politics* 17, no. 3: 358–75.

——. 2015. "The 2009 Communal Charter and Local Service Delivery in Morocco." Yale Program on Governance and Local Development Working Paper no. 2, Yale University, New Haven, Conn.

Clark, Janine A., and Emanuela Dalmasso. 2015. "State Actor-Social Movement Coalitions and Policy-Making Under Authoritarianism." *Middle East Law and Governance* 7: 1–27.

Clark, Janine A., and Amy E. Young. 2008. "Islamism and Family Law Reform in Morocco and Jordan." *Mediterranean Politics* 13, no. 3: 333–52.

Cleveland, William L. 2000. *A History of the Modern Middle East.* 2nd ed. Boulder, Colo.: Westview.

Connerley, Ed, Kent Eaton, and Paul Smoke, eds. 2010. *Making Decentralization Work*, Boulder, Colo.: Lynne Rienner.

Conning, Jonathan, and Michael Kevane. 2002. "Community-Based Targeting Mechanisms for Social Safety Nets: A Critical Review." *World Development* 30, no. 3: 375–94.

"Consacrer la bonne gouvernance consultative." 2004. *La Gazette du Maroc*, February 23.

Conyers, Diana. 1983. "Decentralization: The Latest Fashion in Development Administration?" *Public Administration and Development* 3: 97–109.

Cornelius, Wayne A., Todd A. Eisenstadt, and Jane Hindley, eds. 1999. *Subnational Politics and Democratization in Mexico.* Boulder, Colo.: Lynne Rienner.

Coyne et Bellier. 2011. *Socio-Economic Report: Prepared by Econconsult Under Subcontract to Coyne et Bellier.* Draft final feasibility study report 12-147 RP 04: Red Sea–Dead Sea Water Conveyance Study Program.

Craig, Daniel, and Doug Porter. 2006. *Development Beyond Neoliberalism? Governance, Poverty Reduction and Political Economy.* New York: Routledge.

Crook, Richard C., and James Manor. 1998. *Democracy and Decentralization in South Asia and West Africa,* Cambridge: Cambridge University Press.

Cunningham, Robert B., and Yasin K. Sarayrah. 1993. *Wasta: The Hidden Force in Middle Eastern Societies.* London: Praeger.

Daadaoui, Mohamed. 2010a. "Party Politics and Elections in Morocco." *Middle East Institute Policy Brief* 29: 1–9.

——. 2010b. "Rituals of Power and Political Parties in Morocco: Limited Elections as Positional Strategies." *Middle Eastern Studies* 46, no. 2: 195–219.

Dabène, Olivier, Vincent Geisser, and Gilles Massardier, eds. 2008. *Autoritarismes démocratiques et démocraties autoritaires au XXIème siècle.* Paris: La Découverte.

Daher, Rami Farouk. 1999. "Gentrification and the Politics of Power, Capital and Culture in an Emerging Jordanian Heritage Industry." *Traditional Dwellings and Settlements Review* 10, no. 2: 33–45.

——. 2005. "Urban Regeneration / Heritage Tourism Endeavours: The Case of Salt, Jordan 'Local Actors, International Donors and the State.'" *International Journal of Heritage Studies* 11, no. 4: 289–308.

——. 2007. *Tourism in the Middle East: Continuity, Change and Transformation.* North York, Canada: Channel View.

——. 2010. *Urban Landscapes of Neoliberalism: Cranes, Craters and an Exclusive Urbanity.* Amman: Jordan Business.

Daher, Rami, and Irene Maffi. 2000. *Patrimony and Heritage Conservation in Jordan.* Document du CERMOC no. 10. Beirut: CERMOC.

Dalil, Mustapha. 2011. *Démocratie participative et développement local au Maroc.* Rabat: Revue Marocaine d'Administration Locale et de Développement.

——. 2008. "Le cloisonnement des collectivités communales, un écueil à la réforme." *Revue marocaine d'administration locale et de développement,* no. 80: 27–45.

Dalmasso, Emanuela. 2012. "Surfing the Democratic Tsunami in Morocco: Apolitical Society and the Reconfiguration of a Sustainable Authoritarian Regime." *Mediterranean Politics* 17, no. 2: 217–32.

Dalmasso, Emanuela, and Francesco Cavatorta. 2010. "Reforming the Family Code in Tunisia and Morocco—the Struggle Between Religion, Globalisation and Democracy." *Totalitarian Movements and Political Religions* 11, no. 2: 213–28.

Dann, Uriel. 1984. *Studies in the History of Transjordan, 1920–1949.* Boulder, Colo.: Westview.

——. 1989. *King Hussein and the Challenge of Arab Radicalism: Jordan 1955–1967.* New York: Oxford University Press.

Darif, Mohamed. 2003. "La décentralisation avortée." *La Gazette du Maroc,* January 20. http://www.maghress.com/fr/lagazette/1809.

David, Assaf, and Stefanie Nanes. 2011. "The Women's Quota in Jordan's Municipal Councils: International and Domestic Dimensions." *Journal of Women, Politics and Policy* 32: 275–304.

Dawisha, Adeed, and William Zartman, eds. 1988. *Beyond Coercion: The Durability of the Arab State.* London: Croom Helm.

Day, Ramsey. 2015. "New Governance Laws A Step Backwards for Jordan's Democracy?" *Democracy Speaks*, July 15. http://www.democracyspeaks.org/blog /new-governance-laws-step-backwards-jordan%E2%80%99s-democracy.

"Décentralisation: l'Intérieur veut reformer la charte communal." 2007. *Le Matin*, November 23. http://lematin.ma/journal/2007/Decentralisation_L-Interieur -veut-reformer-la-charte-communale/3410.html.

Demirtas-Milz, Neslihan. 2013. "The Regime of Informality in Neoliberal Times in Turkey: The Case of the Kadifekale Urban Transformation Project." *International Journal of Urban and Regional Research* 37, no. 2: 689–714.

Democracy Reporting International and Al-Urdun Al-Jadid Research Center. 2007. *Final Report: Assessment of the Electoral Framework—The Hashemite Kingdom of Jordan*. Berlin: Democracy Reporting International.

Denoeux, Guilain P., and Abdeslam Maghraoui. 1998. "The Political Economy of Structural Adjustment in Morocco." In Layachi 1998a: 55–87.

Dethier, Jean-Jacques, ed. 2000. *Governance, Decentralization and Reform in China, India and Russia*. Boston: Kluwer Academic.

Diamond, Larry. 1999. *Developing Democracy*. Baltimore: Johns Hopkins University Press.

Diamond, Larry, Juan Linz, and Seymour M. Lipset, eds. 1988. *Democracy in Developing Countries, Vol. 2*. Boulder, Colo.: Lynne Rienner.

Dickovick, J. Tyler. 2011. *Decentralization and Recentralization in the Developing World*. University Park: Penn State University Press.

Dimitrovova, Bohdana. 2010. "Re-shaping Civil Society in Morocco." *Journal of European Integration* 32, no. 5: 523–39.

Doan, Petra L. 1991. "Changing Administrative Regions in Jordan: Regional Development Strategy of Distraction?" *Tijdschrift voor Economische en Sociale / Journal for Economic and Social Geography* 82, no. 3: 177–84.

Doan, Petra L., and W. Adas. 2001. "Dilemmas of Top-Down Decentralization in Jordan." *Third World Planning Review* 23, no. 3: 273–88.

Doner, Richard F., and Eric Hershberg. 1999. "Flexible Production and Political Decentralization in the Developing World: Elective Affinities in the Pursuit of Competitiveness?" *Studies in Comparative International Development*: 45–82.

Doughan, Yazan. 2012. "Discrepancies in Value(s): Some Reflections on the Category of 'Corruption' in the Discursive Production of Reform and Revolution in Jordan." *Jadaliyya*, April 23. http://www.jadaliyya.com/pages/TME1 /5242/discrepancies-in-value(s)_discrepancies-in-value(s.

Douichi, K. 2005. "Charte communale: la réforme un an après." *La Vie économique*, January 28. http://lavieeco.com/news/politique/charte-communale-la-reforme -un-an-apres-5435.html.

Drieskens, Barbara, Franck Mermier, and Heiko Wimmen, eds. 2007. *Cities of the South: Citizenship and Exclusion in the Twenty-First Century*. Lebanon: Saqi Books, in association with Heinrich Boell Foundation and Institut Français du Proche-Orient.

Droz-Vincent, Philippe. 2011. "Cities, Urban Notables and the State in Jordan." In Ababsa and Daher 2011: 103–26.

Duclos, Louis-Jean. 1998. "The November 1997 Parliamentary Elections." *Jordanies*, Special Issue 5–6: 210–35.

Eaton, Kent. 2004. *Politics Beyond the Capital: The Design of Subnational Institutions in Latin America*. Palo Alto: Stanford University Press.

Eaton, Kent, Kai-Alexander Kaiser, and Paul Smoke. 2010. *The Political Economy of Decentralization Reforms*. Washington, D.C.: International Bank for Reconstruction and Development / World Bank.

Echeverri-Gent, John. 1992. "Public Participation and Poverty Alleviation: The Experience of Reform Communists in India's West Bengal." *World Development* 20, no. 10: 1401–22.

ECSWA (Economic and Social Commission for Western Asia). 2001. *Decentralization and the Emerging Role of Municipalities in the ESCWA Region*. New York: United Nations.

Egel, Daniel. 2011. "Tribal Diversity, Political Patronage and the Yemeni Decentralization Experiment." *Topics in Middle Eastern and North African Economies* 13. http://meea.sites.luc.edu/volume13/meea13.html.

Ehteshami, Anoushiravan, and Emma C. Murphy. 1996. "Transformation of the Corporatist State in the Middle East." *Third World Quarterly* 17, no. 4: 753–72.

Eibl, Ferdinand. 2012. "The Party of Authenticity and Modernity (PAM): Trajectory of a Political *deus ex machina*." *Journal of North African Studies* 17, no. 1: 45–66.

Eisenstadt, Shmuel N., and Rene Lemarchand, eds., 1981. *Political Clientelism, Patronage and Development*, Beverly Hills: Sage.

Eisenstadt, Shmuel N., and Luiz Roniger. 1984. *Patrons Clients and Friends*. Cambridge: Cambridge University Press.

Elahmadi, Mohsine. 2010. "Modernisation du champ religieux au Maroc." In Centre d'Études Internationales 2009: 117–40.

Elmoumni, Nadir. 2008. "Le découpage électoral et les résultats des élections législatives du 7 septembre 2007: éléments d'impact." In *Élections législatives, 7 septembre 2007: jeu et enjeux d'un scrutiny*, edited by Abdelmoughit B. Trédano, 15–25. Casablanca: CRESS.

Elsheshtawy, Yasser. 2008. *The Evolving Arab City: Tradition, Modernity and Urban Development*. New York: Routledge.

Elyachar, Julia. 2002. "Empowerment Money: The World Bank, Nongovernmental Organizations, and the Value of Culture in Egypt." *Political Culture* 14, no. 3: 493–513.

——. 2005. *Markets of Dispossession*. Durham: Duke University Press.

Engelcke, Dörthe. 2015. "The Ongoing, Steady Gains of Morocco's Islamist Party." *Jadaliyya*, September 29. http://www.jadaliyya.com/pages/index/22789 /the-ongoing-steady-gains-of-moroccos-islamist-part.

Entelis, John P. 1997. *Islam Democracy and the State in North Africa*. Bloomington: Indiana University Press.

———. 2007. "Multipartyism: Rubber Stamp or Robust Challenger." *Middle East Policy* 14, no. 4: 35–37.

L'État et les collectivités locales au Maroc. 1989. Casablanca: Presses de l'IEP de Toulouse & Sochepress.

European Neighbourhood and Partnership Instrument. 2007. *Jordan Strategy Paper 2007–2013 & National Indicative Programme 2007–2010*. https://ec.europa.eu /europeaid/sites/devco/files/csp-nip-jordan-2007-2013_en.pdf.

European Union. n.d. *Building Development Capacities of Jordanian Municipalities— Baladiaty. The Question for Decentralization Government in the Hashemite Kingdom of Jordan: Some Preliminary Findings of a Situation Analysis*. EuropeAid/129887/C /SER/JO. Viewed January 7, 2015. http://data.unhcr.org/syrianrefugees /admin/download.php?id=4229.

Eury, Pascaline. 1991. *Jordanie: les élections législatives du 8 novembre 1989*. Beirut: Presses de l'IFPO.

"Évolution de la décentralisation au Maroc." 2008. *Jeunes du Maroc*, February 25. http://www.maghress.com/fr/jeunesdumaroc/3059.

Ezzine, Abdelfattah. 2008. *Actes du cercle de citoyenneté*. Rabat: Institut Universitaire de la Recherche Scientifique, Université Mohamed V, Souissi.

Faculté des Sciences Juridiques, Économiques et Sociales d'Agadir. 2011. *Colloque international sur le développement local: résumés des actes du colloque*. Agadir: Faculté des Sciences Juridiques, Économiques et Sociales d'Agadir. (In French and Arabic.)

Faguet, Jean-Paul. n.d. "The Role of Civil Society in the Local Government Process." Initiative for Policy Change Working Paper Series, Columbia University, New York.

Faguet, Jean-Paul, and Fabio Sanchez. 2006. "Decentralization's Effects on Educational Outcomes in Bolivia and Colombia." Crisis States Research Centre Working Paper no. 62, London School of Economics.

Falleti, Tulia G. 2005. "A Sequential Theory of Decentralization: Latin American Cases in Comparative Perspective." *APSR* 3: 327–46.

———. 2010. *Decentralization and Subnational Politics in Latin America*. New York: Cambridge University Press.

Farawati, O. 2010. "Business with a Heart." *Venture Magazine* (May), 43–45.

Fathi, Schirin. 1994. *Jordan: An Invented Nation? Tribe-State Dynamics and the Formation of National Identity*. Hamburg: Deutsches Orient-Institute.

Faughnan, Brian M., Jonathan T. Hiskey, and Scott D. Revey. 2014. "Subnational Electoral Contexts and Corruption in Mexico." *Journal of Politics in Latin America* 6, no. 1: 45–81.

Ferguson, James. 2009. "The Uses of Neoliberalism." *Antipode* 41, no. S1: 166–84.

Ferreira, Francisco H. G. n.d. "Some Notes on Decentralization and Service Delivery." Initiative for Policy Change Working Paper Series, Columbia University, New York.

Ferrié, Jean-Noël. 1999. "La gifle sur la mise en place d'un espace public 'municipal' au Maroc." *Politique africaine*, no. 74 (June): 76–83.

Filali-Ansary, Abdou. 2009. "Walis, présidents de communes, régions, préfectures, qui fait quoi?" *La Vie économique*, September 28. http://lavieeco.com/news /politique/walis-presidents-de-communes-regions-prefectures-qui-fait -quoia-14685.html.

Fischbach, Michael R. 1994. "British Land Policy in Transjordan." In Rogan and Tell 1994: 80–107.

———. 2000. *State, Society, and Land in Jordan.* Leiden: Brill.

Fjeldstad, Odd-Helge. 2003. "Decentralization and Corruption: A Review of the Literature." CMI Working Papers, Chr. Michelsen Institute, Bergen. https:// www.cmi.no/publications/file/1860-decentralisation-and-corruption.pdf

Food and Agriculture Organization of the United Nations. 2006. "Part Two: Analyzing Decentralization Processes." In *Understand, Analyse and Manage a Decentralization Process: The RED-IFO Model and Its Use*, 59–97. Rome: Food and Agriculture Organization of the United Nations.

Foster, Kenneth W. 2007. "Associations in the Embrace of an Authoritarian State: State Domination of Society?" *Studies in Comparative International Development* 35, no. 4: 84–109.

Fox, Jonathan. 1994. "The Difficult Transition from Clientelism to Citizenship Lessons from Mexico." *World Politics* 46, no. 2: 151–84.

Fox, William F., and Tami Gurley. 2006. "Will Consolidation Improve Subnational Governments?" World Bank Research Working Paper 3913, World Bank, Washington, D.C.

Fraihat, Eman A. 2016. "The Historical Development of Municipality Laws in Jordan (1925-2014)." *International Journal of Humanities and Social Science Studies* 3, no. 3: 27–81. http://oaji.net/articles/2016/1115-1480921200.pdf.

Freij, Hanna Y., and Leonard C. Robinson. 1996. "Liberalization, the Islamists and the Stability of the Arab State." *Muslim World* 136, no. 1: 1–32.

Fritzen, Scott A., and Patrick W. O. Lim. 2006. "Problems and Prospects of Decentralization in Developing Countries." Unpublished paper. http://lkyspp.nus .edu.sg/wp-content/uploads/2013/04/wp16_06.pdf.

Furr, Anna, and Muwafaq Al-Serhan. 2008. "Tribal Customary Law in Jordan." *South Carolina Journal of International Law and Business* 4, no. 2: 17–34.

Gabbay, Shaul M. 2014. "The Status of Palestinians in Jordan and the Anomaly of Holding a Jordanian Passport." *Political Science and Public Affairs* 2, no. 1: 1–6.

Galasso, Emanuela, and Martin Ravallion. 2005. "Decentralized Targeting of an Antipoverty Program." *Journal of Public Economics* 89: 705–27.

Galloui, Mohamed. 2010. "La transition politique au Maroc." In Centre d'Études Internationales 2009: 35–54.

Gandhi, Jennifer, and Adam Przeworski. 2007. "Authoritarian Institutions and the Survival of Autocrats." *Comparative Political Studies* 40, no. 11: 1279–1301.

Gao, Eleanor X. 2012. "Diverse but Not Divisive: Tribal Diversity and Public Goods Provision in Jordan." PhD diss., University of Michigan.

——. 2016. "Tribal Mobilization, Fragmented Groups, and Public Goods Provision in Jordan." *Comparative Political Studies* 49, no. 10: 1372–1403.

García, Raquel Ojeda. 2003. "Les politiques de décentralisation au Maroc: où en sommes-nous?" *Revue marocaine d'administration locale et de développement*, no. 51–52: 9–28.

García, Raquel Ojeda, and Angela Suarez Collado. 2015. "The Project of Advanced Regionalisation in Morocco." *British Journal of Middle Eastern Studies* 42, no. 1: 46–58.

Gellner, Ernest, and John Waterbury, eds. 1977. *Patrons and Clients in Mediterranean Societies*. London: Gerald Duckworth.

"Gestion communale déléguée ou l'anarchie déclarée." 2012. *Panoramaroc*, July. http://www.panoramaroc.ma/fr/gestion-communale-deleguee-ou-lanarchie-declaree/.

"Gestion communale: le système de l'unité de la ville est-il une source de blocage?" 2010. *Aujourd'hui le Maroc*, October 22.

El-Ghobashy, Mona. 2008. "Constitutionalist Contention in Contemporary Egypt." *New American Behavioral Scientist* 51, no. 11: 1590–1610.

Ghomari, Mohamed. 1993. "La problématique de la démocratie locale au Maroc." *Revue marocaine d'administration locale et de développement*, no. 2–3: 7–16.

——. 1996. "Prédominance du pouvoir central et tolérance des pouvoirs locaux au Maroc." *Revue Franco-Maghrébine de droit*, no. 4: 51–61.

Gibson, Edward L., ed. 2004. *Federalism and Democracy in Latin America*. Baltimore: Johns Hopkins University Press.

——. 2005. "Boundary Control: Subnational Authoritarianism in Democratic Countries." *World Politics* 58, no. 1: 101–32.

Gilley, Bruce. 2010. "Democratic Enclaves in Authoritarian Regimes." *Democratization* 17, no. 3: 389–415.

Goldberg, Jeffrey. 2013. "The Modern King in the Arab Spring." *Atlantic*, April. https://www.theatlantic.com/magazine/archive/2013/04/monarch-in-the-middle/309270/.

Goldfarb, Benjamin. 2007. "The Politics of Deepening Local Democracy: Decentralization, Party Institutionalization, and Participation." *Comparative Politics* 39, no. 2: 147–68.

Goodwin, Jeff, and Theda Skocpol. 1989. "Explaining Revolutions in the Contemporary Third World." *Politics and Society* 17, no. 4: 489–509.

Gould, Roger V. 1996. "Patron-Client Ties, State Centralization, and the Whiskey Rebellion." *American Journal of Sociology* 102, no. 2: 400–429.

Greene, Kenneth F. 2010. "The Political Economy of Authoritarian Single-Party Dominance." *Comparative Political Studies* 43, no. 7: 807–34.

Greenwood, Scott. 2003. "Jordan's 'New Bargain': The Political Economy of Regime Security." *Middle East Journal* 57: 248–68.

——. 2008. "Bad for Business?: Entrepreneurs and Democracy in the Arab World." *Comparative Political Studies* 41, no. 6: 837–60.

Grindle, Merilee S. 1977. "Expertise and the 'Tecnico': Suggestions from a Mexican Case Study." *Journal of Politics* 39, no. 2 (May): 399–426.

——. 2000. *Audacious Reforms*. Baltimore: Johns Hopkins University Press.

——. 2007. *Going Local: Decentralization, Democratization, and the Promise of Good Governance*. Princeton: Princeton University Press.

Grossman, Guy., and Janet L. Lewis. 2014. "Administrative Unit Proliferation." *American Political Science Review* 108, no. 1: 196–217.

Grzymala-Busse, Anna. 2008. "Beyond Clientelism: Incumbent State Capture and State Formation." *Comparative Political Studies* 41, no. 4–5: 638–73.

Guazzone, Laura, and Daniela Pioppi, eds. 2009a. *The Arab State and Neo-liberal Globalization: The Restructuring of State Power in the Middle East*. Reading: Ithaca.

——. 2009b. "Interpreting Change in the Arab World." In Guazzone and Pioppi 2009a: 1–15.

Gubser, P., 1973. *Politics and Change in al-Karak, Jordan*. London: Oxford University Press.

——. 1983. *Jordan: Crossroads of Middle Eastern Events*. Boulder, Colo.: Westview.

Guibbert, Jean-Jacques. 2005. "Les services urbains comme enjeux de la participation et de la démocratisation de la vie locale au Maroc." In *Intégration à la ville et services urbains au Maroc*, edited by Claude de Miras, 287–312. Tangier: Institut National d'Aménagement et d'Urbanisme.

Haddad, Mohanna. 1992. " 'Detribalizing' and 'Retribalizing': The Double Role of Churches Among Christian Arabs in Jordan: A Study in the Anthropology of Religion." *Muslim World* 89, no. 1–2: 67–89.

Hallaj, Omar Abdulaziz, Myriam Ababsa, Karam Karam, and Ryan Knox. 2015. "Decentralization in the Mashrek Region: Challenges and Opportunities." Prepared for Platforma and SKL International. http://www.commed-cglu.org/wp-content/uploads/2014/04/Mashrek-Decentralisation-in-the-Mashrek-region.pdf.

Hamid, Shadi. 2010. "Civil Society in the Arab World and the Dilemma of Funding." Brookings Institution, October 21. http://www.brookings.edu/research
/articles/2010/10/middle-east-hamid.
——. 2014. "Political Party Development Before and After the Arab Spring." In
Kamrava 2014: 131–50.
Hamid, Shadi, and Courtney Freer. 2011. "How Stable Is Jordan? King Abdullah's Half-Hearted Reforms and the Challenge of the Arab Spring." Brookings Doha Center Policy Briefing.
Hamimaz, Mériem. 2003. *Élections et communication politique dans le Maroc rural: une
investigation dans une région du moyen atlas.* Rabat: Konrad-Adenauer-Stiftung.
Hammoudi, Abdellah. 1977. *Master and Disciple: The Cultural Foundations of Moroccan Authoritarianism.* Chicago: University of Chicago Press.
Hamrouch, M'Hamed. 2008. "La charte communale a-t-elle subi une réforme
profonde ou juste un léger lifting?" *Aujourd'hui le Maroc,* July 18. http://www
.maghress.com/fr/aujourdhui/62924.
Hamzawy, Amr. 2008. "Party for Justice and Development in Morocco: Participation and Its Discontents." Carnegie Papers, Middle East Series, no. 93, July.
http://carnegieendowment.org/files/cp93_hamzawy_pjd_final.pdf.
Harb, Mona, and Sami Attalah, eds. 2015a. *Local Governments and Public Goods:
Assessing Decentralization in the Arab World.* Beirut: LCPS and OSI.
——. 2015b. "Introduction: A New Framework for Assessing Decentralization in
the Arab World." In Harb and Atallah 2015a: 1–10.
Harders, Cijla. 2003. "The Informal Social Pact: The State and the Urban Poor
in Cairo." In Kienle 2003a: 191–213.
Harrigan, Jane, and Hamed El-Said. 2009a. *Aid and Power in the Arab World.* Basingstoke: Palgrave Macmillan.
——. 2009b. *Economic Liberalisation, Social Capital and Islamic Welfare Provision.* Basingstoke: Palgrave Macmillan.
——. 2011. *Globalisation, Democratisation and Radicalisation in the Arab World.* Houndmills: Palgrave Macmillan.
Harsi, Abdallah. 2009. "La réforme de la charte communale et les exigences d'une
meilleure gouvernance locale." *Revue marocaine d'administration locale et de développement,* no. 84–85: 17–27.
——. 2010. "Administration territoriale: bilan et perspectives." In Centre d'Études
Internationales 2009: 143–66.
Harsi, Abdallah, and Mohammed El Yaagoubi. 2006. "Rapport sur le cadre con-
ceptuel, législatif et réglementaire des processus de décentralisation et de régionalisation au Maroc." *50 ans de développement humain au Maroc et perspectives pour
2025 REMALD* 25: 31–36.
Harvey, David. 2003. *The New Imperialism.* New York: Oxford University Press.
——. 2006. *Spaces of Global Capitalism.* London: Verso.

Hattabi, Jamal, ed. 2010. *Le Maroc politique en 2009*. N.p.: Revue Marocaine des Politiques Publiques.

Hayajneh, Adnan M. 2008. *UCLG Country Profiles: The Hashemite Kingdom of Jordan*. United Cities and Local Government, United Nations.

Helmke, Gretchen, and Steven Levitsky. 2004. "Informal Institutions and Comparative Politics: A Research Agenda." *Perspectives on Politics* 2, no. 4: 725–40.

———, eds. 2006. *Informal Institutions and Democracy*. Baltimore: Johns Hopkins University Press.

Hen, Christian. 1989. "Le regroupement communal." In *L'État et les collectivités locales* 1989: 43–51.

Herb, Mona, and Sami Atallah. 2014. *Decentralization in the Arab World must be Strengthened to Provide Better Services*. *Jadaliyya*, May 30. http://www.jadaliyya.com/pages/index/17930/decentralization-in-the-arab-world-must-be-strengt.

Herbert, Steve. 2005. "The Trapdoor of Community." *Annals of the Association of American Geographers* 95, no. 4: 850–65.

Hermann, Katja. 2000. *Aufbruch Von Unten*. Hamburg: LIT Verlag.

Hess, Steve. 2013. *Authoritarian Landscapes: Popular Mobilization and the Institutional Sources of Resilience in Nondemocracies*. New York: Springer.

Heydemann, Steven. 2000. *War, Institutions, and Social Change in the Middle East*. Berkeley: University of California Press.

———. 2004a. *Networks of Privilege in the Middle East*. New York: Palgrave Macmillan.

———. 2004b. "Introduction: Networks of Privilege: Rethinking the Politics of Economic Reform in the Middle East." In Heydemann 2004a: 1–34.

———. 2007. "Upgrading Authoritarianism in the Arab World." Saban Center for Middle East Policy at the Brookings Institution Analysis Paper no. 13, Washington, D.C.

Hiatt, Joseph M. 1984. "State Formation and Encapsulation of Nomads: Local Change and Continuity Among Recently Sedentarized Bedouin in Jordan." *Nomadic Peoples*, no. 15 : 1–11.

Hibou, Béatrice, ed. 1999a. *La privatisation des états*. Paris: Karthala.

———. 1999b. "De la privatisation des économies à la privatisation des états." In Hibou 1999a: 11–67.

———. 2004. *Privatizing the State*. Translated by Jonathan Derrick. London: Hurst.

———. 2011. *The Force of Obedience*. English edition. Cambridge: Policy Press.

Hicks, Ursula K. 1961. *Development from Below*. Oxford: Clarendon.

Hilali, Minoun. 2002. "Réflexions sur les élites traditionnelles au Maroc: s'ouvrir ou périr!" In *L'Annuaire de la Méditerranée 2001*, edited by Vasconcelo de Alvaro, 67–91. Rabat: Groupement d'études et de recherches sur la Méditerranée.

Hilgers, Tina, ed. 2012. *Clientelism in Everyday Latin American Politics*. Houndmills: Palgrave Macmillan.

Hirchi, Mohammed. 2007. "Political Islam in Morocco: The Case of the Party of Justice and Development (PJD)." In *ACAS Bulletin 77: North Africa and the Horn in the Vortex of the US War on Terror*, edited by Jesse Benjamin and Fouzi Slisli. http://concernedafricascholars.org/bulletin/issue77/.

Hoffman, Anja. 2013. "Morocco Between Decentralization and Recentralization." In Bouziane, Harders, and Hoffman 2013: 158–77.

Hoffman, Katherine E. 2000. "Administering Identities: State Decentralization and Local Identification in Morocco." *Journal of North African Studies* 5, no. 3: 85–100.

Honey, Rex, Stephen Nichols, Suleiman Abu Kharma, Musa Khamis, and Petra Doan. 1986. "Planning Regions for Regional Planning in Jordan's 1986–1990 Plan." *Papers and Proceedings of Applied Geographers Conferences* 9: 1–12.

Houdaïfa, Hicham, and Fédoua Tounassi. 2006. "Les limites de la Fondation Mohammed V." *Le Journal Hebdomadaire*, no. 276 (November): 20–25.

Houdret, Annabelle, and Astrid Harnisch. 2017. "Decentralisation in Morocco: The Current Reform and Its Possible Contribution to Political Liberalisation." Deutsches Institut für Entwicklungspolitik Discussion Paper 11/2017, Bonn.

Hourani, Hani, Hussein Abu Rumman, and Nasser Ahmad Kamel. 2004. *Who's Who in the Jordanian Parliament, 2003–2007*. Amman: Al Urdun Al Jadid Research Center, UJRC.

Hourani, Hani, Basem Al-Tweisi, May Taher, and Hussein Abu Rumman. 2010. *State of Local Democracy in Jordan*. Amman: Institute for Democracy and Electoral Assistance (International IDEA), Al Urdun Al Jadid Research Center, and Sindibad Publishing House.

Hourani, Hani, Taleb Awad, Hamed Dabbas, and Sa'eda Kilani. 1993. *Islamic Action Front Party*. 1st ed. Translated by Sa'eda Kilani. Amman: Al-Urdun al-Jadid Research Center.

Huntington, Samuel. 1984. "Will More Countries Become Democratic?' *Political Science Quarterly* 99, no. 2: 193–218.

Huque, Ahmed S. 1986. "The Illusion of Decentralization: Local Administration in Bangladesh." *International Review of Administrative Sciences* 52: 79–95.

Hussain, Akmal, and Savail Hussain. 2009. "Poverty, Power and Local Government in Pakistan." In Wignaraja, Sirivardana, and Hussain 2009: 291–314.

Hussainy, Mohammed. 2014. *The Social Impact of Jordan's Electoral System*. Amman: Friedrich-Ebert-Stiftung Jordan and Iraq.

Hutchcroft, Paul D. 1997. "The Politics of Privilege: Assessing the Impact of Rents, Corruption and Clientelism on Third World Development." *Political Studies* 45: 639–58.

Ilahiane, Hsain. 2001. "The Social Mobility of the Haratine and the Re-working of Bourdieu's Habitus on the Saharan Frontier, Morocco." *American Anthropologist* 103, no. 2: 380–394.

International Bank for Reconstruction and Development. 1957. *The Economic Development of Jordan*. Baltimore: Johns Hopkins Press.

International Crisis Group. 2003. *Red Alert in Jordan: Recurrent Unrest in Maan*. Middle East Briefing no. 5. Amman: International Crisis Group.

——. 2012. *Popular Protest in North Africa and the Middle East (IX): Dallying with reform in a Divided Jordan*. Middle East/North Africa Report no. 118. Amman: International Crisis Group. http://old.crisisgroup.org/_/media/Files/Middle%20East%20North%20Africa/Iran%20Gulf/Jordan/118-popular-protest-in-north-africa-and-the-middle-east-ix-dallying-with-reform-in-a-divided-jordan-2.pdf.

International IDEA. 2012. *Local Democracy Assessment in Morocco*. Stockholm: International IDEA. http://www.idea.int/sites/default/files/pictures/SoD-Country-Report-Morrocco.pdf.

International Labour Organization. 2001. *The Impact of Decentralization and Privatization on Municipal Services*. Geneva: International Labour Organization.

Iraki, Aziz El Maoula. 2002a. *Des notables du Makhzen à l'épreuve de la 'gouvernance': élites locales, territoires, gestion urbaine et développement au Maroc*. Inau: L'Harmattan.

——. 2002b. "Élites locales et territoires: de l'élite cooptée à l'élite de proximité, nouvelles dynamiques sociales et/ou nouveau regard sur le système politique local au Maroc." In *L'Annuaire de la Méditerranée 2001*, edited by Vasconcelo de Alvaro, 93–116. Rabat: Groupement d'études et de recherches sur la Méditerranée.

——. 2003. "Du renouvellement des élites urbaines au Maroc: élites urbaines, territoire et système politique local." In *Annuaire de l'Afrique du Nord*, edited by Eberhard Kienle, 81–95. Paris: CRNRS.

——. 2006. "Élites locales et territoires: de l'élite cooptée à l'élite de proximité au Maroc." In Abouhani 2006a.

Iraki, Aziz, and Mohamed Tamim. 2009. "Réformes institutionnelles récentes, refontes politico-administrative des territoires et nouvelles formes de gouvernance urbaine." *Les Cahiers d'EMAM* 17: 85–114.

Iraqi, Fahd, and Youssef Zeghari. 2008. "Villes: où va l'argent des communes?" *Le Journal Hebdomadaire*, no. 375 (December 13–19): 20–27.

Ito, Takeshi. 2011. "Historicizing the Power of Civil Society: A Perspective from Decentralization in Indonesia." *Journal of Peasant Studies* 38, no. 2: 413–33.

Jabbra, Joseph G. 1989. "Bureaucracy and Development in the Arab World." *Journal of Asian and African Studies* 24: 1–11.

Jaber, Hana. 1998. "Typology of the Slogans in Amman's Second and Fourth Electoral Constituencies." *Jordanies* 5–6: 253–60.

Jamaïl, Aboubakr, Taïb Chadi, and Mouaad Rhandi. 2005. "Villes Islamistes: le pragmatisme des maires PJD." *Le Journal Hebdomadaire*, no. 234 (December 10–16): 22–29.

Jamal, Amaney. 2007. *Barriers to Democracy*. Princeton: Princeton University Press.

Jandari, Drisse. 2012. "The Political Party Experience in Morocco: Obscurity and Obfuscation." Case Analysis. Arab Center for Research and Policy Studies, Doha, Qatar.

Jari, Mostafa. 2010. "Local Governance in the MENA Region." *Journal of Economic and Social Research* 12, no. 1: 9–32.

Jay, Cleo. 2013. "Acting Up: Performance and the Politics of Womanhood in Contemporary Morocco." *Journal of African Cultural Studies* 25, no. 3: 305–18.

Joffé, George. 1988. "Morocco: Monarchy, Legitimacy and Succession." *Third World Quarterly* 10, no. 1: 201–28.

——, ed. 2002. *Jordan in Transition*. New York: Palgrave.

Johnson, Craig, Priya Deshingkar, and Daniel Start. 2003. "Grounding the State: Poverty, Inequality and the Politics of Governance in India's Panchayats." Overseas Development Institute Working Paper 226, London.

Jordan Center for Social Research. 2007. *The 2007 Municipal Elections in Jordan: An Exit Poll Conducted in Six Electoral Districts, Located in Six Municipalities*. Amman: Jordan Center for Social Research. http://jcsr-jordan.org/Registrationforms /633246675648146428.pdf.

"Jordan's Municipal Mess." 2011. *The Black Iris*. http://black-iris.com/2011/10/13 /jordans-municipal-mess/.

"Jordan Parliament Endorses Decentralization Law: It Introduces Election of New Government and Municipal Councils." 2015. *ANSAMed*, August 24. http:// www5.ansa.it/ansamed/en/news/nations/jordan/2015/08/24/jordan -parliament-endorses-decentralization-law_000bd992-bef2–4732-a1df -cffaef934e45.html.

Jreisat, Jamil E. 1989. "Bureaucracy and Development in Jordan." *Journal of Asian and African Studies* 24, no. 1–2: 94–105.

Jureidini, Paul A., and Ronald McLaurin. 1984. *Jordan: The Impact of Social Change on the Role of the Tribes*. New York: Praeger; Washington, D.C.: Center for Strategic and International Studies, Georgetown University.

Kaboub, Fadhel. 2011. "The Middle East's Neo-liberalism–Corruption Nexus." *Dollars and Sense*, May/June. http://personal.denison.edu/~kaboubf/Pub/Media /2011-May-DS-NeoliberalismCorruptionNexus.pdf.

Kadirbeyoğlu, Zeynep, and Bilgesu Sümer. 2012. "The Neoliberal Transformation of Local Government in Turkey and the Contracting Out of Municipal Services: Implications for Public Accountability." *Mediterranean Politics* 17, no. 3: 340–57.

Kamrava, Mehran, ed. 2014. *Beyond the Arab Spring: The Evolving Ruling Bargain in the Middle East*. Oxford: Oxford University Press.

Kao, Kristen. 2016. "How Jordan's Election Revealed Enduring Weaknesses in Its Political System." *Monkey Cage* (blog), *Washington Post*, October 3. https://www.washingtonpost.com/news/monkey-cage/wp/2016/10/03/how-jordans-election-revealed-enduring-weaknesses-in-its-political-system.

Karshanas, Massoud, and Valentine M. Moghadam, eds. 2006. *Social Policy in the Middle East*. Houndmills: Palgrave Macmillan.

Al-Kayed, Zuhair. 2004. "Public Administration in the Euro-Mediterranean Region: Case of Jordan." Presented to the Experts Meeting for the Reform of Governances and Public Administration in the Mediterranean Region, Naples, Italy, May 17–20.

Kendall, Frances, and Leon Louw. 1987. *After Apartheid*. San Francisco: ICS Press.

Khader, Bichara, and Adnan Badran, eds. 1987. *The Economic Development of Jordan*. London: Croom Helm.

Al-Khalfi, Mustapha. 2008. "Morocco: The PJD Between Inclusion and Cooptation." *Arab Reform Bulletin* 6, no. 2: 4–5.

Khamliche, Aziz. 2002. "Les vents de la réforme arrivent aux communes." *Aujourd'hui Le Maroc*, June 19. http://www.maghress.com/fr/aujourdhui/18224.

Al-Khatahtbeh, Amani. 2013. "Jordan: A Model for Reform or a Black Hole?" *MENASource*, November 20. http://www.atlanticcouncil.org/blogs/menasource/jordan-a-model-for-reform-or-a-black-hole.

Al-Khateeb, Jamal. 2010. *Decentralization and Enhancing the Local Governance: Minutes of the Workshops*. Amman: Al-Badeel Center for Studies and Research.

Khatib, Lina, and Ellen Lust, eds. 2014. *Taking to the Streets: The Transformation of Arab Activism*. Baltimore: Johns Hopkins University Press.

Khattabi, Mustapha. 1996. "Traits caractéristiques de la politique de décentralisation et de régionalisation au Maroc." *Revue Franco-Maghrébine de droit*, no. 4: 9–27.

Khemani, Stuti. 2009. "Gerrymandering Decentralization: Political Selection of Grants-Financed Local Jurisdictions." Development Research Group, World Bank, Washington, D.C.

Khoo, Boo Teik. 2010. "No Insulation: Politics and Technocracy's Troubled Trajectory." IDE Discussion Paper no. 236 (May).

Khrouz, Driss. 2008. "A Dynamic Civil Society." *Journal of Democracy* 19, no. 1: 42–49.

"The Kids Are Not Alright." 2013. *Jordan Business* (June).

Kienle, Eberhard, ed. 2003a. *Politics from Above, Politics from Below*. London: Saqi Books.

——. 2003b. Introduction to Kienle 2003a: 9–20.

Kilani, Sa'eda, and Basem Sakijha. 2002. *Wasta: The Declared Secret*. Amman: Arab Archives Institute in Amman.

Kinana, Essaid, and Mohamen Aziz. 1996. "Régionalisation et démocratie locale au Maroc." *Revue Franco-Maghrébine de droit*, no. 4: 85–111.

King, Stephen J. 2007. "Sustaining Authoritarianism in the Middle East and North Africa." *Political Science Quarterly* 122, no. 3: 433–59.

Kiser, Edgar and Audrey Sacks. 2011. "African Patrimonialism in Historical Perspective: Assessing Decentralized and Privatized Tax Administration." *ANNALS of the American Academy of Political and Social Science* 636: 129–49.

Kitschelt, Herbert. 2000. "Linkages Between Citizens and Politicians in Democratic Politics." *Comparative Political Studies* 33, no. 6–7: 845–79.

Kjellberg, Francesco. 1995. "The Changing Values of Local Government." *ANNALS of the American Academy of Political and Social Science* 540: 40–50.

Knowles, Warwick. 2005. *Jordan Since 1989: A Study in Political Economy*. London: I. B. Tauris.

Köprülü, Nur. 2009. "Trapped Between De-liberalization, Politics of Identity and Regional Predicaments: 'Lessons from the Hashemite Kingdom of Jordan.'" *Perceptions*, Autumn/Winter: 57–84.

——. 2014a. "Consolidated Monarchies in the Post-'Arab Spring' Era: The Case of Jordan." *Israel Affairs* 20, no. 3: 318–27.

——. 2014b. "Jordan Since the Uprising." *Middle East Policy* 21, no. 2: 111–26.

Kornbluth, Danishai. 2002. "Jordan and the Anti-normalization Campaign, 1994–2001." *Terrorism and Political Violence* 14, no. 3: 80–108.

Künkel, Jenny, and Margit Mayer, eds. 2012. *Neoliberal Urbanism and Its Contestations*. Houndmills: Palgrave Macmillan.

Laâbi, Abdellatif. 2011. *Maroc: quel projet démocratique?* Casablanca: Croisée des Chemins.

Laâbi, Chafik. 2004. "La charte communale bloque le fonctionnement des villes." *La Vie économique*, April 30. http://archive.fo/17mnW.

Laabid, Mohamed. 2008. "Laâyoune: La réforme de la charte communale en débat." *Le Maroc Aujourd'hui*, March 17. http://aujourdhui.ma/regions/laayoune-la-reforme-de-la-charte-communale-en-debat-55494.

La Ferrara, Eliana. 2002. "Inequality and Group Participation: Theory and Evidence from Rural Tanzania." *Journal of Public Economics* 85: 235–73.

Labonte, Melissa T. 2011. "From Patronage to Peacebuilding? Elite Capture and Governance from Below in Sierra Leone." *African Affairs* 111, no. 422: 90–115.

Lahlou, Kamal. 2008a. "Décentralisation désastreuse." *La Gazette du Maroc*, October 17. http://www.maghress.com/fr/lagazette/18373.

——. 2008b. "Le rôle central." *La Gazette du Maroc*, July 25. http://www.maghress.com/fr/lagazette/18039.

Landé, Carl H. 1983. "Political Clientelism in Political Studies: Retrospect and Prospects." *International Political Science Review* 4, no. 4: 435–54.

Landry, Pierre F. 2008. *Decentralized Authoritarianism in China.* New York: Cambridge University Press.

Lapidus, Ira M. 1969. *Middle Eastern Cities.* Berkeley: University of California Press.

Larner, Wendy. 2000. "Neo-liberalism: Policy, Ideology, Governmentality." *Studies in Political Economy* 63: 5–25.

Lawless, Richard, ed. 1987. *The Middle Eastern Village.* London: Croom Helm.

"The Laws of Decentralization and Municipalities Are Discussed in Mafraq." 2015. *Almejhar News.* http://www.almejharnews.com/index.php?page=article &id=103996. (In Arabic.)

Layachi, Azzedine. 1998a. *Economic Crisis and Political Change in North Africa.* Westport, Conn.: Praeger.

——. 1998b. *State, Society and Democracy in Morocco.* Washington, D.C.: Center for Contemporary Arab Studies.

Layne, Linda L. 1987. " 'Tribalism': National Representations of Tribal Life in Jordan." *Urban Anthropology and Studies of Cultural Systems and World Economic Development* 16, no. 2: 183–203.

——. 1989. "The Dialogics of Tribal Self-Representation in Jordan." *American Ethnologists* 16, no. 1: 24–39.

——. 1994. *Home and Homeland.* Princeton: Princeton University Press.

Leitner, Helga, Jamie Peck, and Eric S. Sheppard. 2007. *Contesting Neoliberalism: Urban Frontiers.* New York: Guilford.

Leitner, Helga, Eric S. Sheppard, Kristin Sziarto, and Anant Maringanti. 2007. "Contesting Urban Futures: Decentering Neoliberalism." In Leitner, Peck, and Sheppard 2007: 1–25.

Lemarchand, René. 1972. "Political Clientelism and Ethnicity in Tropical Africa." *American Political Science Review* 66, no. 1: 68–90.

Lenner, Katharina. 2013. "Poverty and Poverty Reduction Policies in Jordan." In Ababsa 2013: 335–43.

Leuvrey, Bruno, and Bertrand Riffiod. 2005. *Décentralisation et bonne gouvernance locale: étude sur la ville de Meknès.* Paris: AIMF.

Leveau, Remy. 2000. "The Moroccan Monarchy: A Political System in Quest of a New Equilibrium." In *Middle East Monarchies: The Challenge of Modernity,* edited by Joseph Kostiner, 87–129. Boulder, Colo.: Lynne Rienner.

Lewis, Norman N. 1987. *Nomads and Settlers in Syria and Jordan, 1800–1980.* Cambridge: Cambridge University Press.

Liddell, James. 2008. "Morocco: Modern Politics of the Politics of Modernity?" *Sada,* December 2. http://carnegieendowment.org/sada/?fa=22476.

——. 2010. "Notables, Clientelism and the Politics of Change in Morocco." *Journal of North African Studies* 15, no. 3: 315–31.

Lin, Justin Y. n.d. "Fiscal Decentralization in China." Initiative for Policy Change Working Paper Series, Columbia University, New York.

Litvack, Jennie, Junaid Ahmad, and Richard Bird. 1998. *Rethinking Decentralization in Developing Countries.* Washington, D.C.: World Bank.

Loewe, Markus, Jonas Blume, and Johanna Speer. 2008. "How Favoritism Affects the Business Climate: Empirical Evidence from Jordan." *Middle East Journal* 62, no. 2: 259–76.

Lorentzen, Maren. 2016. "Policy Brief on Jordan's 2016 Parliamentary Elections." *ARRD Legal Aid.* http://ardd-jo.org/sites/default/files/resource-files/ policy_ brief_on_jordans_2016_parliamentary_elections.pdf.

Lowenhaupt, Anna. 2000. "Inside the Economy of Appearances." *Public Culture* 12, no. 1 (Winter): 115–44.

Lucas, Russell E. 2003a. "Press Laws as a Survival Strategy in Jordan, 1989–99." *Middle Eastern Studies* 39, no. 4: 81–98.

——. 2003b. "Deliberalization in Jordan." *Journal of Democracy* 14, no. 1: 137–44.

——. 2004. "Monarchical Authoritarianism: Survival and Political Liberalization in a Middle Eastern Regime Type." *International Journal of Middle East Studies* 36, no. 1: 103–19.

——. 2005. *Institutions and the Politics of Survival in Jordan.* Albany: State University of New York Press.

Lust, Ellen. 2009. "Competitive Clientelism in the Middle East." *Journal of Democracy* 20, no. 3: 122–35.

——. 2011. "Why Now? Micro-Transitions and the Arab Uprisings." *Comparative Politics-Democratization Newsletter.* Reposted at *The Monkey Cage*, October 24. http://themonkeycage.org/blog/2011/10/24/why-now-micro-transitions-and -the-arab-uprisings/.

Lust, Ellen, Sami Hourani, and Mohammad el-Momani. 2011. "Jordan Votes: Election or Selection?" *Journal of Democracy* 22, no. 2: 119–29.

Lust-Okar, Ellen. 2001. "The Decline of Jordanian Political Parties: Myth or Reality?" *International Journal of Middle East Studies* 33, no. 4: 545–69.

——. 2004. "Divided They Rule: The Management and Manipulation of Political Opposition." *Comparative Politics* 36, no. 2: 159–79.

——. 2005. *Structuring Conflict in the Arab World.* Cambridge: Cambridge University Press.

——. 2006. "Elections Under Authoritarianism: Preliminary Lessons from Jordan." *Democratization* 13, no. 3: 456–71.

——. 2009 "Reinforcing Informal Institutions Through Authoritarian Elections: Insights from Jordan." *Middle East Law and Governance* 1: 3–37.

Lust-Okar, Ellen, and Amaney A. Jamal. 2002. "Rulers and Rules: Reassessing the Influence of Regime Type on Electoral Law Formation." *Comparative Political Studies* 35, no. 3: 337–66.

Lust-Okar, Ellen, and Saloua Zerhouni, eds. 2008. *Political Participation in the Middle East.* Boulder, Colo.: Lynne Rienner.

Lynch, Marc. 2002. "Jordan's Identity and Interests." In Telhami and Barnett 2002: 26–57.

El-Maarouf, Moulay D., Mourad el Fahil, and Jerome Kuchejda. 2009. "Morocco." KAS Democracy Report. http://www.kas.de/wf/doc/kas_29579-1522-3-30 .pdf?111201114833.

Madani, Mohamed, Driss Maghraoui, and Saloua Zerhouni. 2012. *The 2011 Moroccan Constitiution: A Critical Analysis*. Stockholm: IDEA. http://www.idea.int /sites/default/files/publications/the-2011-moroccan-constitution-critical -analysis.pdf.

Madani, Mohammed. 2006. *Le paysage politique marocain*. Rabat: Dar Al Qalam.

Maddy-Weitzman, Bruce. 2003. "Islamism, Moroccan-Style: The Ideas of Sheikh Yassine." *Middle East Quarterly*, Winter: 43–51.

Magaloni, Beatriz. 2008. "Credible Power-Sharing and the Longevity of Authoritarian Rule." *Comparative Political Studies* 41, no. 4–5: 715–41.

Maghraoui, Abdeslam. 2002. "Depoliticization in Morocco." *Journal of Democracy* 13, no. 4: 24–32.

——. 2004. "Démocratisation de la corruption au Maroc: réformes politiques dans une culture du pouvoir immuable." *NAQD* 1, no. 19–20: 105–26.

——. 2012. "The Perverse Effect of Good Governance: Lessons from Morocco." *Middle East Policy* 19, no. 2: 49–65.

——. 2015. "Morocco: The King's Islamists." Wilson Center, August 27. https:// www.wilsoncenter.org/article/morocco-the-kings-islamists.

Maghraoui, Driss. 2008. "The Dynamics of Civil Society in Morocco." In Lust-Okar and Zerhouni 2008: 193–216.

——. 2011. "Constitutional Reforms in Morocco: Between Consensus and Subaltern Politics." *Journal of North African Studies* 16, no. 4: 679–99.

Magno, Francisco A. 1989. "State, Patronage and Local Elites." *Kasarinlan Philippine Journal of Third World Studies* 4, no. 3: 10–18.

Makky, A., 2005. "Decentralization: Definition and Experiences in Developing Countries." Arab Media Internet Network, January 19. http://www.amin.org /look/amin/en.tpl?IdLanguage=1&IdPublication=7&NrArticle=1458.

Malkawi, Fuad K. 1996. "Hidden Structures: An Ethnographic Account of the Planning of Greater Amman." PhD diss., University of Pennsylvania.

——. 2001. "Democracy, Metropolitan Areas and the Problem of Local Governance in Jordan." In *Forum on Urbanizing World and Human Habitat II—Columbia University, New York—Conference Proceedings Theme 8: Metropolitan Governance and Urban Political Culture*, 1–12. New York: International Research Foundation for Development.

——. 2002. "Amalgamation Is a Solution in Jordan." Presented at Empowering Local Government Institutions in the MENA Region, Beirut, January 22–23. http://www.mafhoum.com/press4/118S30.pdf.

Mango, Tamam, and Ahlam Shabaneh. 2016. "Service Delivery, Legitimacy, Stability and Social Cohesion in Jordan: An Analytical Literature Review." Leading Point Management Advisory Services and UKAid.

Manor, James. 1999. *The Political Economy of Democratic Decentralization*. Washington, D.C.: World Bank.

Mansuri, Ghazala, and Vijayendra Rao. 2004. "Community-Based and Driven Development: A Critical Review." *World Bank Observer* 19, no. 1: 1–39.

Manzetti, Luigi, and Carole J. Wilson. 2007. "Why Do Corrupt Governments Maintain Public Support?" *Comparative Political Studies* 40, no. 8: 949–70.

Map of Political Parties and Movements in Jordan 2013/14. n.d. Amman: Identity Center. http://identity-center.org/en/node/260.

Martinez, Jose C. 2014. "Bread Is Life: The Intersection of Welfare Politics and Emergency Aid in Jordan." *Middle East Report* 44, no. 272. http://www.merip.org/mer/mer272/bread-life.

Masbah, Mohammed. 2014. "Islamist and Secular Forces in Morocco." *SWP Comments* 51: 1–8.

El Maslouhi, Abderrahim. 2010. "La voie marocaine de la démocratisation." In Centre d'Études Internationales 2009: 15–34.

Al-Masri, Walid Masri al-Din. 2010. "Imad al-Azzam: Engineer." *Al-Sijil*, January 6: 78. (In Arabic)

Massad, Joseph A. 2001. *Colonial Effects*. New York: Columbia University Press.

Massadeh, Abdel-Mahdi. 1992. "A Comparison of Jordanian Governorate Councils and Local Government Councils: Constitutional Perspectives and Legal Implications." *Arab Law Quarterly* 7, no. 2: 99–115.

——. 1999. "The Structure of Public Administration in Jordan: A Constitutional and Administrative Law Perspective." *Arab Law Quarterly* 14, no. 2: 91–111.

Mazur, Michael P. 1979. *Economic Growth and Development in Jordan*. Boulder, Colo.: Westview.

MCC (Millennium Challenge Corporation). 2008. "Forming a Union of Jordanian Municipalities: Final Report." Local Governance Development Program, MCC, Washington, D.C.

McCarney, Patricia, and Richard Stren, eds. 2003. *Governance on the Ground*. Washington, D.C.: Woodrow Wilson Center Press; Baltimore: Johns Hopkins University Press.

McFaul, Michael, and Tamara Cofman Wittes. 2008. "The Limits of Limited Reforms." *Journal of Democracy* 19, no. 1: 19–33.

McLure, Charles E., Jr. 1995. "Comment on 'The Dangers of Decentralization' by Prud'homme." *World Bank Research Group* 10, no. 2: 221–27.

Mecham, Quinn, and Julie Chernov Hwang. 2014. *Islamist Parties and Political Normalization in the Muslim World*. Philadelphia: University of Pennsylvania Press.

El Mehdi, Rachida, and Christian M. Hafner. 2013. "Local Government Efficiency: The Case of Moroccan Municipalities." Institut de Statistique Biostatistique et Sciences Actuarielles (ISBA) Discussion Paper 2013-01, Université Catholique de Louvain.

Menza, Mohamed M. 2012. "Neoliberal Reform and Socio-structural Reconfiguration in Cairo's Popular Quarters: The Rise of the Lesser Notables in Misr Al Qadima." *Mediterranean Politics* 17, no. 3: 322–39.

El Messaoudi, Amina. 2011. "Gouvernance et réalités électorales au Maroc: les législatives 2007." In *Le mouvement de la réforme du droit et de l'économie*, edited by Mohammed Jalal Essaid, 153–78. N.p.: N.p.

Mezran, Karim. 2015. "Morocco's Local Elections: A Polarized Political Landscape." *MENASource*, September 9. http://www.atlanticcouncil.org/blogs/menasource/morocco-s-local-elections-a-bipolar-political-landscape.

Mhammed, Echkoundi. 2006. "Du rôle de la gouvernance locale dans la réalisation de l'initiative nationale du développement humain au Maroc." *Revue marocaine d'audit et de développement* 22: 113–30.

Ministère de l'Intérieur, Direction générale des collectivités locales. 2004a. *Collectivités locales en chiffres 2004*. Rabat: Ministère de l'Intérieur.

———. 2004b. *Organisation de la région*. Rabat: Centre de Documentation des Collectivités Locales.

———. 2004c. *Organisation des collectivités préfectorales et provinciales*. Rabat: Centre de Documentation des Collectivités Locales. (In French and Arabic)

———. 2009a. *Collectivités locales en chiffres*. Rabat: Ministère de l'Intérieur.

———. 2009b. *Organisation des finances locales*. Rabat: Centre de Documentation des Collectivités Locales.

———. 2010. *Réforme de la charte communale—actes des séminaires organisés en 2008–2009*. Casablanca: Konrad Adenauer Stiftung.

Ministry of Municipal and Rural Affairs. 1995. *The Municipalities—Law Number 29, Year 1955*. Jordan. (In Arabic)

Mitchell, Timothy. 2002. *Rule of Experts*. Berkeley: University of California Press.

Mohan, Giles, and Kristian Stokke. 2000. "Participatory Development and Empowerment: The Dangers of Localism." *Third World Quarterly* 21, no. 2: 247–68.

Ba Mohammed, Najib. 2002. "Notables ou élites au Maroc?" In *L'Annuaire de la Méditerranée 2001*, edited by Vasconcelo de Alvaro, 53–65. Rabat: Groupement d'études et de recherches sur la Méditerranée.

Monjib, Maati. 2009. "Morocco: Local Elections Bring Victory to Voter-Buyers and a Royal Friend." Brookings Institution, June 19. http://www.brookings.edu/research/opinions/2009/06/19-morocco-monjib.

———. 2014. "Winners and Losers in a New Political Climate." *Qantara*, September 17. https://en.qantara.de/content/democratic-change-in-morocco-winners-and-losers-in-a-new-political-climate.

Moore, Pete W. 2001. "What Makes Successful Business Lobbies? Business Associations and the Rentier State in Jordan and Kuwait." *Comparative Politics* 33, no. 2: 127–48.

———. 2004. *Doing Business in the Middle East.* Cambridge: Cambridge University Press.

Moore, Pete W., and Bassel F. Salloukh. 2007. "Struggles Under Authoritarianism: Regimes, States, and Professional Associations in the Arab World." *International Journal of Middle East Studies* 39: 53–76.

El-Mossadeq, Rkia. 1987. "Political Parties and Power-Sharing." In Zartman 1987: 59–83.

El Mouchtaray, Mohammed. 2000. *Le rôle des collectivités locales dans le développement économique et social au Maroc.* Rabat: Revue Marocaine d'Administration Locale et de Développement.

Mourji, Amal. 1989. "La tutelle de l'état sur les communes." In *L'État et les collectivités locales* 1989: 133–69.

Moustafa, Tamir. 2002. "The Dilemmas of Decentralization and Community Development in Authoritarian Contexts." *Journal of Public and International Affairs* 13: 123–44.

Mufti, Malik. 1999. "Elite Bargains and the Onset of Political Liberalization in Jordan." *Comparative Political Studies* 32, no. 1: 100–129.

Mundy, Martha, and Bassim Musallam, eds. 2000. *The Transformation of Nomadic Society in the Arab East.* Cambridge: Cambridge University Press.

Muno, Wolfgang. 2010. "Conceptualizing and Measuring Clientelism." Presented at the German Institute of Global and Area Studies, Hamburg, August 23.

Murphy, Emma C. 2006. "The Tunisian Mise à Niveau Programme and the Political Economy of Reform." *New Political Economy* 11, no. 4: 519–40.

Mustafa, Mairna H. 2012. "Improving the Contribution of Domestic Tourism to the Economy of Jordan." *Asian Social Science* 8, no. 2: 49–61.

Nachatti, Amhem. 2002. "Gestion, unité de la ville et monopole de l'intérieur." *Le Gazette du Maroc,* June 24. http://www.maghress.com/fr/lagazette/775.

———. 2003. "Les grandes réformes de la nouvelle charte communale." *La Gazette du Maroc,* 20 January. http://www.maghress.com/fr/lagazette/1811.

Nadeem, Malik. 2016. "Analyzing Good Governance and Decentralization in Developing Countries." *Journal of Political Sciences and Public Affairs* 3, no. 3: 1–8.

Naima, Aba. 2009. "Fiscalité locale: quel apport de la nouvelle réforme fiscale pour le développement local." *Massalik,* no. 11–12: 21–32.

Nasser, Djama. 2015. "Élections locales au Maroc: le PJD du chef du gouvernement Benkirane va diriger la plupart des grandes villes du royaume." *L'Usine Nouvelle,* September 8. http://www.usinenouvelle.com/article/elections-locales
-au-maroc-le-pjd-du-chef-du-gouvernement-benkirane-va-diriger-la
-plupart-des-grandes-villes-du-royaume.N348415.

Ncube, Mthuli, John Anyanwu, and Kjell Hausken. 2013. "Inequality, Economic Growth and Poverty in the Middle East and North Africa (MENA)." African Development Bank Group Working Paper Series no. 195: 5–27.

NDI (National Democratic Institute for International Affairs). 1995. *Democracy and Local Government in Jordan: 1995 Municipal Elections.* Amman: NDI.

——. 2007. *Final Report on the Moroccan Legislative Elections—September 7, 2007.* Washington, D.C.: NDI.

Nellis, John R. 1984. "Decentralization, Regional Development, and Local Public Finance in Tunisia." Occasional Paper no. 79, Metropolitan Studies Program, International Series, Maxwell School of Citizenship and Public Affairs, Syracuse University, Syracuse, N.Y.

Nevo, Joseph. 2003. "Changing Identities in Jordan." *Israel Affairs* 9, no. 3: 187–208.

Nichter, Simeon. 2011. "Electoral Clientelism or Relational Clientelism? Healthcare and Sterilization in Brazil." Presented at the American Political Science Association, Seattle, Wash., September 1–4. http://ssrn.com/abstract=1919567.

Nickson, R. Andrew. 1995. *Local Government in Latin America.* Boulder, Colo.: Lynne Rienner.

Norton, Augustus R. 1998. "Reflections on the Dilemma of Reform in the Middle East." *Critique* 13: 32–44.

Nygaard, Ivan. 2008. "External Support to Local Institutions." *European Journal of Development Research* 20, no. 4: 649–65.

Oi, Jean C. 1985. "Communism and Clientelism: Rural Politics in China." *World Politics* 37, no. 2: 238–66.

O'Neill, Kathleen. 2001. "Decentralization: The Latin American Experience." Initiative for Policy Change Working Paper Series, Columbia University, New York.

——. 2003. "Decentralization as an Electoral Strategy." *Comparative Political Studies* 36, no. 9: 1068–91.

——. 2005. *Decentralizing the State: Elections, Parties, and Local Power in the Andes.* New York: Cambridge University Press.

Ottaway, David. 2012. "Morocco's Islamists: In Power Without Power." Viewpoints no. 5, Woodrow Wilson International Center for Scholars, Washington, D.C. https://www.wilsoncenter.org/sites/default/files/moroccos_islamists_in_power_without_power_1.pdf.

Ottaway, Marina. 2013. "Morocco: 'Advanced Decentralization' Meets the Sahara Autonomy Initiative." Viewpoints no. 27, Woodrow Wilson International Center for Scholars, Washington, D.C.

Ottaway, Marina, and Meredith Riley. 2006. "Morocco: From Top-Down Reform to Democratic Transition?" Carnegie Papers, Middle East Series, no. 71: 3–20.

Oxhorn, Philip, Joseph S. Tulchin, and Andrew D. Selee. 2004. *Decentralization, Democratic Governance, and Civil Society in Comparative Perspective: Africa, Asia, and Latin America*. Washington, D.C: Woodrow Wilson Center Press; Baltimore: Johns Hopkins University Press.

PAD Maroc (Programme d'Appui à la Décentralisation au Maroc). 2010. *Présentation du processus de décentralisation marocain*. http://padmaroc.org/article.php3?id_article=11.

Pan, Lei, and Luc Christiaensen. 2012. "Who Is Vouching for the Input Voucher? Decentralized Targeting and Elite Capture in Tanzania." *World Development* 40, no. 8: 1619–33.

Pande, Rohini. 2001. "Overview of Decentralization in India." Initiative for Policy Change Working Paper Series, Columbia University, New York.

Pargeter, Alison. 2009. "Localism and Radicalization in North Africa: Local Factors and the Development of Political Islam in Morocco, Tunisia and Libya." *International Affairs* 85, no. 5: 1031–44.

Park, Albert, and Sangui Wang. 2010. "Community-Based Development and Poverty Alleviation: An Evaluation of China's Poor Village Investment Program." *Journal of Public Economics* 94: 790–99.

Parker, Christopher. 2009. "Tunnel-Bypasses and Minarets of Capitalism: Amman as Neoliberal Assemblage." *Political Geography* 28: 110–20.

Parker, Christopher, and Pascal Debruyne. 2011. "Reassembling the Political Life of Community." In Künkel and Meyer 2011: 155–72.

Peck, Jamie, and Adam Tickell. 2002. "Neoliberalizing Space." *Antipode* 34, no. 4: 380–404.

Pelham, Nicolas. 2011a. "Jordan Starts to Shake." *New York Review of Books*, December 8. http://www.nybooks.com/articles/2011/12/08/jordan-starts-shake/.

——. 2011b. "King Abdullah of Jordan and the Arab Spring." NOREF Norwegian Centre for Conflict Resolution, December 21. https://noref.no/Publications/Regions/Middle-East-and-North-Africa/King-Abdullah-of-Jordan-and-the-Arab-Spring/(language)/eng-US.

Pellicer, Miquel, and Eva Wegner. 2012. "Electoral Rules and Clientelistic Parties: A Regression Discontinuity Approach." IDEAS Working Paper Series, St. Louis, Mo.

——. 2014. "Socio-Economic Voter Profile and Motives for Islamist Support in Morocco." *Party Politics* 20, no. 1: 116–33.

——. 2015. "The Justice and Development Party in Moroccan Local Politics." *Middle East Journal* 69, no. 1: 32–50.

Pennell, C. R. 2000. *Morocco since 1830: A History*. New York: New York University Press.

Perekli, Feriha. 2012. "The Applicability of the "Turkish Model' to Morocco: The Case of the Parti de la Justice et du Développement (PJD)." *Insight Turkey* 14, no. 3: 85–108.

Persha, Lauren, and Krister Anderson. 2014. "Elite Capture Risk and Mitigation in Decentralized Forest Governance Regimes." *Global Environmental Change* 24: 265–76.

Perthes, Volker, ed. 2004. *Arab Elites.* Boulder, Colo.: Lynne Rienner.

Philifert, Pascale, and M. Jolé. 2005. "La décentralisation au Maroc: une nouvelle dynamique pour les acteurs et les métiers de l'aménagement urbain ?" In *Intégration à la ville et services urbains au Maroc,* edited by C. D. Miras, 363–401. Rabat: Institut National d'Aménagement et d'Urbanisme.

Piro, Timothy J. 1998. *The Political Economy of Market Reform in Jordan.* Lanham, Md.: Rowman and Littlefield.

Platteau, Jean-Philippe. 2004. "Monitoring Elite Capture in Community-Driven Development." *Development and Change* 35, no. 2: 223–46.

"Plus de 160 clauses imprécises." 2008. *Le Matin,* December 3.

Policy Paper: Building Grassroots Participation for Decentralization. n.d. Amman: Identity Center. http://identity-center.org/en/node/240.

Posusney, Marsha P. 2002. "Multi-Party Elections in the Arab World: Institutional Engineering and Oppositional Strategies." *Studies in Comparative International Development* 36, no. 4: 34–62.

Prospective Maroc 2030. n.d. *Actes du Forum II: La société marocaine: permanences, changements et enjeux pour l'avenir.* Casablanca: Haut-Commissariat au Plan du Maroc.

Prud'homme, Rémy. 1992. "Informal Local Taxation in Developing Countries." *Environment and Planning C: Government and Policy* 10, no. 1: 1–17.

——. 1995. "The Dangers of Decentralization." *World Bank Research Observer* 10, no. 2: 201–20.

Pruzan-Jørgensen, Julie E. 2010a. "Analyzing Authoritarian Regime Legitimation: Findings from Morocco." *Middle East Critique* 19, no. 3: 269–86.

——. 2010b. "The Islamist Movement in Morocco: Main Actors and Regime Responses." Report 2010:5, Danish Institute for International Studies.

Quintal, Magalie, and Catherine Trudelle. 2013. "Maroc: les associations locales dans la Vallée du Ziz. Une nouvelle gouvernance territoriale." *Économie rurale,* no. 334: 39–53.

Al-Ramahi, Aseel. 2008. "*Wasta* in Jordan: A Distinct Feature of (and Benefit for) Middle Eastern Society." *Arab Law Quarterly* 22: 35–62.

Raounak, Abdelhadi. 2010. "Aménagement du territoire et développement régional." In Centre d'Études Internationales 2009: 167–85.

RASED. n.d. *Analysis of the Expected Democratic Impact of the 2014 Draft Decentralization Law.* Amman: Al Hayat Center for Civil Society Development.

Razzaz, Omar M. 1991. "Law, Urban Land Tenure and Property Disputes in Contested Settlements: The Case of Jordan." PhD diss., University of Michigan.

———. 1993a. "Examining Property Rights and Investments in Informal Settlements: The Case of Jordan." *Land Economics* 69, no. 4: 341–55.

———. 1993b. "Contested Space: Urban Settlement Around Amman." *Middle East Report*, no. 181: 10–14.

———. 1994. "Contestation and Mutual Adjustment: The Process of Controlling Land in Yajouz, Jordan." *Law and Society Review* 28, no. 1: 7–40.

———. 1996. "Land Conflicts, Property Rights and Urbanization East of Amman." In *Amman: The City and Its Society*, edited by Jean Hannoyer and Seteney Shami, 499–526. Beirut: CERMOC.

Reimer, Michael J. 2005. "Becoming Urban: Town Administrations in Transjordan." *International Journal of Middle East Studies* 37: 189–211.

Reiter, Yitzhak. 2002. "Higher Education and Sociopolitical Transformation in Jordan." *British Journal of Middle East Studies* 29, no. 2: 137–64.

———. 2004. "The Palestinian-Transjordanian Rift." *Middle East Journal* 58, no. 1: 72–92.

Ribot, Jesse C. 2002. "African Decentralization: Local Actors, Powers and Accountability." Democracy, Governance and Human Rights Paper no. 8, UNRISD and IDRC. www.unrisd.org/unrisd/website/document.nsf/O/3345ac67e6875754c1256d12003e6c95/$FILE/ribot.pdf

———. 2009. "Authority Over Forests: Empowerment and Subordination in Senegal's Democratic Decentralization." *Development and Change* 40, no. 1: 105–29.

Richards, Alan, and John Waterbury.1990. *A Political Economy of the Middle East.* Boulder, Colo.: Westview.

Rifi, Omar. 2003. "De l'état centralisé à l'état polycentrique." *La Gazette du Maroc*, January 20. http://www.maghress.com/fr/lagazette/1812.

Robinson, Glenn. 1998. "Defensive Democratization in Jordan." *International Journal of Middle East Studies* 30: 387–410.

Rogan, Eugene L. 2002. *Frontiers of the State in the Late Ottoman Empire.* Cambridge: Cambridge University Press.

Rogan, Eugene L., and Tariq Tell., eds. 1994. *Village, Steppe and State.* London: British Academic Press.

Romeo, Leonardo G. 2003. "The Role of External Assistance in Supporting Decentralisation Reform." *Public Administration and Development* 23: 89–96.

Rondinelli, Dennis A. 1981. "Government Decentralization in Comparative Perspective: Theory and Practice in Developing Countries." *International Review of Administrative Science* 67: 133–45.

Rondinelli, Dennis A., and Shabbir G. Cheema, eds. 2007. *Decentralizing Governance: Emerging Concepts and Practices.* Washington, D.C.: Brookings Institution Press.

Rondinelli, Dennis A. John R. Nellis, and G. Shabbir Cheema. 1984. "Decentralization in Developing Countries: A Review of Recent Experience." World Bank Staff Working Papers no. 581, Management and Development Series no. 8, World Bank, Washington, D.C.

Roniger, Luis, and Ayse Gunes-Ayata. 1994. *Democracy, Clientelism and Civil Society*. Boulder, Colo.: Lynne Rienner.

Ronsin, Caroline. 2010. "Wasta and State-Society Relations: The Case of Jordan." *Revue Averroés*, no. 3: 1–7

Rosenbaum, Allan. 2013. "Decentralization and Local Governance: Comparing US and Global Perspectives." *Halduskultuur—Administrative Culture* 14, no. 1: 11–17.

Roumate, Fatima. 2013. "Islamisation of Democracy or Democratization of Political Islam? The Future of Morocco After the Arab Spring." In *Faith in Civil Society: Religious Actors as Drivers of Change*, edited by Heidi Moksnes and Mia Melin, 118–21. Uppsala: Uppsala University.

Rousset, Michel. 1989. "La décentralisation marocaine: réflexions pour un bilan." In *L'État et les collectivités locales* 1989: 173–86.

——. 1994. "La déconcentration: mythe et réalité." *Revue marocaine d'administration locale et de développement*, no. 9: 43–52.

——. 2003. "Constantes et évolution de la notion de contrôle sur les élus." *La Gazette du Maroc*, April 21. https://www.maghress.com/fr/lagazette/2403.

——. 2005. *Démocratie locale au Maroc*. Rabat: Confluences.

——. 2009a. "Actualité de la démocratie locale au Maroc." *Revue marocaine d'administration locale et de développement*, no. 87–88: 17–33.

——. 2009b. "Le nouveau concept de l'autorité et la modernisation de l'administration marocaine." In Centre d'Études Internationales 2009: 55–72.

Rumman, Hussein Aby. 2009. "The Development Governorates." *Al-Sijil*, October 4: 16–19. (In Arabic.)

Ryan, Curtis. 2002. *Jordan in Transition: From Hussein to Abdullah*. Boulder, Colo.: Lynne Rienner.

——. 2004. "'Jordan First': Jordan's Inter-Arab Relations and Foreign Policy Under King Abdullah II." *Arab Studies Quarterly* 26, no. 3: 43–62.

——. 2010. "Civil Society and Democratization in Jordan." Knowledge Programme Civil Society in West Asia Working Paper no. 7, University of Amsterdam.

——. 2011. "Political Opposition and Reform Coalitions in Jordan." *British Journal of Middle Eastern Studies* 38, no. 3: 367–90.

——. 2012a. "The Armed Forces and the Arab Uprisings: The Case of Jordan." *Middle East Law and Governance* 4: 153–67.

——. 2012b. "The Implications of Jordan's New Electoral Law." *Foreign Policy*, April 13. http://foreignpolicy.com/2012/04/13/the-implications-of-jordans-new-electoral-law/.

Saadi, Mohamed Said. 2012. "Water Privatization Dynamics in Morocco: A Critical Assessment of the Casablanca Case." *Mediterranean Politics* 17, no. 3: 376–93.

Sadanandan, Anoop. 2012, "Patronage and Decentralization: The Politics of Poverty in India." *Comparative Politics* 44, no. 2: 211–28.

Sadiqi, Fatima. 2008. "The Central Role of the Family Law in the Moroccan Feminist Movement." *British Journal of Middle Eastern Studies* 35, no. 3: 325–37.

———. 2015. "Morocco's Emerging Democracy: The 2015 Local and Regional Elections." Viewpoints no. 83, Woodrow Wilson International Center for Scholars, Washington, D.C.

El-Said, Hamed, and Jane Harrigan. 2009. " 'You Reap What You Plant': Social Networks in the Arab World—The Hashemite Kingdom of Jordan." *World Development* 37, no. 7: 1235–49.

Saif, Ibrahim. n.d. "Employment Poverty Linkages and Policies for Pro-Poor Growth in Jordan (1990–2003)." Unpublished paper.

———. 2005. "Changing the Rules of the Game: Understanding the Reform Process in Jordan." Unpublished paper, Center for Strategic Studies, University of Jordan, September.

———. 2007. "The Political Economy of Governance in the Euro-Mediterranean Partnership." Process of Economic Reform in Jordan 1990–2005 Working Paper 0709, University of Jordan.

Saito, Fumihiko, ed. 2008. *Foundations for Local Governance.* Heidelberg: Physica-Verlag.

Salame, Ghassan, ed. 1994. *Democracy Without Democrats?* London: I. B. Taurus.

Sansour, Maxim. 2011. "Jordan—Between Tribes and Political Parties." *Majalla*, February 4. http://eng.majalla.com/2011/02/article2038/jordan-between-tribes-and-political-parties.

Sarker, Abu E. 2003. "The Illusion of Decentralization: Evidence from Bangladesh." *International Journal of Public Sector Management* 16, no. 7: 523–48.

Sarrouh, Elissar. 2003. "Decentralized Governance for Development in the Arab States: A Background Paper on Decentralization and Local Governance Policies, Legal Frameworks, Programmes, Lessons Learned and Good Practices." Presented at Local Governance Forum in the Arab Region, Sana'a, Yemen, December 6–9.

Sater, James N. 2002a. "Civil Society, Political Change and the Private Sector in Morocco: The Case of the Employers' Federation' *Confédération Générale des Enterprises du Maroc (CGEM).*" *Mediterranean Politics* 7, no. 2: 13–29.

———. 2002b. "The Dynamics of State and Civil Society in Morocco." *Journal of North African Studies* 7, no. 3: 101–18.

———. 2007. *Civil Society and Political Change in Morocco.* London: Routledge.

———. 2010. *Morocco: Challenges to Tradition and Modernity.* London: Routledge.

———. 2016. *Morocco: Challenges to Tradition and Modernity*. 2nd ed. London: Routledge.

Satloff, Robert. 1994. *From Abdullah to Hussein*. New York: Oxford University Press.

———. 2005. "A Reform Initiative in Jordan: Trying to Keep Pace with Iraqi and Palestinian Elections." Policywatch 953, Washington Institute, Washington, D.C.

———. 2013. "Political Instability in Jordan." Contingency Planning Memorandum no. 19, Council on Foreign Relations, Washington, D.C. http://www.cfr.org/jordan/political-instability-jordan/p30698.

Saunders, Doug. 2013. "Suddenly, All Politics Is Municipal." *Globe and Mail*, July 20. http://www.theglobeandmail.com/globe-debate/suddenly-all-politics-is-municipal/article13319338/.

Scham, Paul L., and Russell E. Lucas. 2001 "'Normalization' and 'Anti-Normalization' in Jordan." *MERIA* 5, no. 3: 54–70.

Schenker, David. 2013. "Down and Out in Amman: The Rise and Fall of the Jordanian Muslim Brotherhood." *Foreign Affairs*, October 3. https://www.foreignaffairs.com/articles/middle-east/2013-10-03/down-and-out-amman.

Schlumberger, Oliver, ed. 2006. "Rents, Reform and Authoritarianism in the Middle East." *Internationale Politik und Gesellschaft (IPG)* 2: 43–57.

———. 2007. *Debating Arab Authoritarianism: Dynamics and Durability in Nondemocratic Regimes*. Stanford: Stanford University Press.

Schmidt, Steffan W., Laura Guasti, Carl H. Landé, and James C. Scott. 1977. *Friends, Followers and Factions*. Berkeley: University of California Press.

Schneider, Aaron, and Rebeca Zuniga-Hamlin. 2005. "A Strategic Approach to Rights: Lessons from Clientelism in Rural Peru." *Development Policy Review* 23, no. 5: 567–84.

Schoenwaelder, Gerd. 1997. "New Democratic Spaces at the Grassroots? Popular Participation in Latin American Local Governments." *Development and Change* 28: 753–70.

Schwedler, Jillian. 2006. *Faith in Moderation: Islamist Parties in Jordan and Yemen*. Cambridge: Cambridge University Press.

———. 2010. "Jordan's Risky Business as Usual." Middle East Research and Information Project, June 30. http://www.merip.org/mero/mero063010.

———. 2015. "Jordan: The Quiescent Opposition." Wilson Center, August 27. https://www.wilsoncenter.org/article/jordan-the-quiescent-opposition.

———. 2016. "Jordan Drops the Pretense of Democratic Reform." Middle East Research and Information Project, April 28. http://merip.org/jordan-drops-pretense-democratic-reform.

Schwedler, Jillian, and Janine A. Clark. 2006. "Islamist-Leftist Cooperation in the Arab World." *International Institute for the Study of Islam in the Modern World (ISIM) Review* 18: 10–11.

Scott, James C. 1972. "Patron-Client Politics and Political Change in Southeast Asia." *American Political Science Review* 66, no. 1: 91–113.

Scott, John. 2008. "Modes of Power and the Re-conceptualization of Elites." *Sociological Review* 56, no. 1: 25–43.

Scott, Tim. 2006. "Decentralization and National Human Development Reports." NHDR Occasional Paper 6, United Nations Development Programme, New York.

Seabright, Paul. 1996. "Accountability and Decentralisation in Government: An Incomplete Contracts Model." *European Economic Review* 40: 61–89.

Sedjari, Ali. 2004. "Le renouveau municipal au Maroc et la philosophie du retour à l'unité de la ville." Centre National de Documentation, Rabat. http://www .abhatoo.net.ma/maalama-textuelle/developpement-economique-et-social /developpement-social/etat-politique/decentralisation-et-deconcentration/le -renouveau-municipal-au-maroc-et-la-philosophie-du-retour-a-l-unite-de -la-ville.

Seijaparova, Dinara, and Jack W. van Holst Pellekaan. 2004. *Jordan: An Evaluation of World Bank Assistance for Poverty Reduction, Health and Education*. Washington, D.C.: World Bank.

Sekeris, Petros G. 2010. "Endogenous Elites: Power Structure and Patron Client Relationships." Center for Research in the Economics of Development Working Paper 2010/08, University of Namur.

Selee, Andrew. 2011. *Decentralization, Democratization, and Informal Power in Mexico*. University Park: Penn State University Press.

Serraj, Karim. 2003. "Proximité et pouvoirs du président du conseil communal." *La Gazette du Maroc*, June 16. http://www.maghress.com/fr/lagazette /2914.

Serrar, Alae Eddin. 2008. "Morocco Dabbles with Devolution as Means to Quel Discontent." *Federations* 7, no. 3: 17–18, 32. http://www.uquebec.ca/observgo /fichiers/68792_2.pdf.

Shami, Seteney, ed. 2001. *Capital Cities: Ethnographies of Urban Governance in the Middle East*. Toronto: University of Toronto Press.

Sewell, David O. 1996. "'The Danger of Decentralization' According to Prud'homme: Some Further Aspects." *World Bank Research Observer* 11, no. 1: 143–50.

——. 2004. "Decentralization: Lessons from Other Middle Eastern Countries for Iraq." World Bank, Washington, D.C.

Shahateet, Mohammed I. 2006. "How Serious Regional Economic Inequality in Jordan? Evidence from Two National Household Surveys." *American Journal of Applied Sciences* 3, no. 2: 1735–44.

Al-Shalabi, Jamal, and Yahya Ali. 2013. "The Crisis of the Center with the Peripheries in Jordan." *Confluences méditerranée* 85, no. 2: 75–86.

Shalaby, Abdallah, Salah a. al-Jurshi, Mostafa El-Nabarawy, Moheb Zaki, Qays J. Azzawi, and Antoine N. Messara, eds. 2010. *Towards a Better Life: How to Improve the Status of Democracy in the Middle East and North Africa*. Istanbul: Global Politics and Trends.

Sharp, Jeremy M. 2012. "Jordan: Background and U.S. Relations." CRC Report for Congress, Congressional Research Service 7-5700, Washington, D.C. http://www.crs.gov RL33546.

Sheba Center for Strategic Studies. n.d. "Decentralization, Democratization and Local Governance in the Arab Region." http://www.shebacss.com/ndsp.

Shefter, Martin. 1977. "Party and Patronage: Germany, England and Italy." *Politics and Society* 7, no. 4: 403–51.

El Sherif, Ashraf N. 2012. "Institutional and Ideological Re-construction of the Justice and Development Party (PJD): The Question of Democratic Islamism in Morocco." *Middle East Journal* 66, no. 4: 660–82.

Shryock, Andrew. 1997. "Bedouin in Suburbia Redrawing the Boundaries of Urbanity and Tribalism in Amman, Jordan." *Arab Studies Journal* 5, no. 1: 40–56.

Shunnaq, Mohammed. 1997. "Political and Economic Conflict Within Extended Kin Groups and Its Effects on the Household in a North Jordanian Village." *Journal of Comparative Family Studies* 28, no. 2: 136–50.

Shunnaq, Mohammed S., and William A. Schwab. 2000. "Continuity and Change in a Middle Eastern City: The Social Ecology of Irbid City, Jordan." *Urban Anthropology* 29, no. 1: 69–96.

Siegle, Joseph, and Patrick O'Mahoney. 2006. *Assessing the Merits of Decentralization as a Conflict Mitigation Strategy*. Washington, D.C.: USAID Office of Democracy and Governance.

——. 2010. "Decentralization and Internal Conflict." In Connerley, Eaton, and Smoke 2010: 135–66.

Signoles, Aude. 2010. *Local Government in Palestine*. Paris: Agence Française de Développement. http://www.afd.fr/webdav/site/afd/shared/PUBLICATIONS /RECHERCHE/Scientifiques/Focales/02-VA-Focales.pdf.

Silva, Patricia. 1991. "Technocrats and Politics in Chile: From Chicago Boys to the CIEPLAN Monks." *Journal of Latin America Studies* 23, no. 2: 385–410.

——. 2004. "Doing Politics in a Depoliticised Society: Social Change and Political Deactivation in Chile." *Bulletin of Latin American Research* 23, no. 1: 63–78.

Singerman, Diane, ed. 2009. *Cairo Contested: Governance, Urban Space and Global Modernity*. Cairo: American University in Cairo Press.

Slater, David. 1989a. "Territorial Power and the Peripheral State: The Issue of Decentralization." *Development and Change* 20: 501–31.

——. 1989b. *Territory and State Power in Latin America: The Peruvian Case*. New York: St. Martin's.

Slater, Richard, and John Watson. 1989. "Democratic Decentralization or Political Consolidation: The Case of Local Government Reform in Karnataka." *Public Administration and Development* 9: 147–57.

Sluglett, Peter. 2008. *The Urban Social History of the Middle East, 1750–1950.* Syracuse: Syracuse University Press.

Smaoui, Sélim. 2009. "La probité comme argument politique: la campagne du Parti de la Justice et du Développement à Hay Hassani (Casablanca)." In Zaki 2009: 265–97.

Smires, M'Faddel. 2001. *Centralisation et décentralisation territoriale au Maroc.* Fez: Faculté des Sciences Juridiques, Économiques et Sociales.

Smith, Andrew R., and Fadous Loudiy. 2005. "Testing the Red Lines: On the Liberation of Speech in Morocco." *Human Rights Quarterly* 27, no. 3: 1069–19.

Smouni, Rachid. 2009. "La gestion déléguée des services publics urbains." *Massalik,* no. 11–12: 41–56.

Soumadi, Mustafa M., Bassam F. al-Theabat, and Ziyad M. al-Shwiyat. 2014. "Workers Attitudes in the Municipalities and Provinces Towards the Decentralized and Regional Projects in Jordan." *Journal of Economics and Sustainable Development* 5, no. 28: 119–37.

Sowell, Kirk H. 2016. "Jordan's Elections and the Divided Islamists." *Sada,* September 15. http://carnegieendowment.org/sada/?fa=64589.

Springer, Simon. 2011. "Violence Sits in Places? Cultural Practice, Neoliberal Rationalism and Virulent Imaginative Geographies." *Political Geography* 30: 90–98.

——. 2012. "Neoliberalism as Discourse: Between Foucauldian Political Economy and Marxian Poststructuralism." *Critical Discourse Studies* 9, no. 2: 133–47.

Stacher, Joshua. 2012. *Adaptable Autocrats.* Stanford: Stanford University Press.

Storm, Lise. 2007. *Democratization in Morocco.* London: Routledge.

Strachan, Anna Louise, 2014. "Conflict Analysis of Morocco." GSDRC Applied Knowledge Services. http://www.gsdrc.org/wp-content/uploads/2015/07/GSDRC_ConflAnal_Morocco.pdf.

Stren, Richard, with Judith Kjellberg Bell. 1995. *Urban Research in the Developing World—Volume 4: Perspectives on the City.* Toronto: Centre for Urban and Community Studies.

Susser, Asher. 2008. "Jordan: Preserving Domestic Order in a Setting of Regional Turmoil." *Crown Center for Middle East Studies,* no. 27: 1–7.

——. 2011. "Jordan 2011: Uneasy Lies the Head." *Middle East Brief,* no. 52: 1–9.

Sweis, Rana F. 2016. *Policy Paper: Familiar Slogans, A Skeptical Public: The 2016 Parliamentary Elections.* Amman: Friedrich-Ebert-Stiftung.

Taamneh, Mohammad. 2007. "Local Governance and Decentralization Process: The Case of Jordan." Presented at the European Group of Public Administration (EGPA) Conference, Madrid, September 19–22.

Tajbakhsh, Kian. 2000. "Political Decentralization and the Creation of Local Government in Orna: Consolidation or Transformation of the Theocratic State?" *Social Research* 67, no. 2: 377–404.

——. 2003. "Decentralization and Governance in Iran: The Impact of Fiscal and Political Reforms." Presented at the World Bank Regional Meeting, Amman, n.d.

Tal, Lawrence. 1995. "Dealing with Radical Islam: The Case of Jordan." *Survival* 37, no. 3: 139–56.

Tamam, Hussam. 2007. "Separating Islam from Political Islam: The Case of Morocco." *WSI Arab Insight*, no. 1: 99–112. http://www.ikhwanweb.com/arti cle.php?id=14283.

Tarik, Richard. 2008. "Réforme de la Charte communale: Les associations réclament un Cadre Légal." *Le Matin*, October 13. http://lematin.ma/journal/2008 /Reforme-de-la-Charte-communale_Les-associations-reclament-un-cadre -legal/99874.html.

Tarrad, Mohannad. 2014. "Urban Planning Response to Population Growth in Jordanian Cities (Irbid City as Case Study)." *Research Journal of Applied Sciences, Engineering and Technology* 7, no. 20: 4275–80.

Teichman, Judith. 1996. "Neoliberalism and the Transformation of Mexican Authoritarianism." CERLAC Working Paper Series no. 6, York University.

Telhami, Shibley, and Michael Barnett, eds. 2002. *Identity and Foreign Policy in the Middle East*. Ithaca: Cornell University Press.

Tell, Tariq. 2000. "Guns, Gold, and Grain." In Heydemann 2000: 33–58.

——. 2013. *The Social and Economic Origins of Monarchy in Jordan*. New York: Palgrave Macmillan.

Tendler, Judith. 1997. *Good Government in the Tropics*. Baltimore: Johns Hopkins University Press.

Tendler, Judith, and Sarah Freedheim. 1994. "Trust in a Rent-Seeking World: Health and Government Transformed in Northeast Brazil." *World Development* 22, no. 12: 1771–91.

Terris, Robert, and Vera Inoue-Terris. 2012. "A Case Study of Third World Jurisprudence—Palestine: Conflict Resolution and Customary Law in a Neopatrimonial Society." *Berkeley Journal of International Law* 20, no. 2: 462–95.

Teti, Andrea. 2012. "Beyond Lies the *Wub*: The Challenges of (Post) Democratization." *Middle East Critique* 21, no. 1: 5–24.

Theobald, Robin. 1982. "Patrimonialism." *World Politics* 34, no. 4: 548–59.

Tobin, Sarah A. 2012. "Jordan's Arab Spring: The Middle Class and Anti-Revolution." *Middle East Policy* 19, no. 1: 96–109.

Tosun, Mehmet, and Serdar Yilmaz. 2008a. "Centralization, Decentralization and Conflict in the Middle East and North Africa." Presented at Equity and Economic Development ERF 15th Annual Conference, Cairo, November 23–25.

———. 2008b. "Centralization, Decentralization and Conflict in the Middle East and North Africa." Policy Research Working Paper no. 4774, Sustainable Development Network, Social Development Department, World Bank, Washington, D.C.

Touhtou, Rashid. 2014. "Research Paper: Civil Society in Morocco Under the New 2011 Constitution: Issues, Stakes and Challenges." Arab Center for Research and Policy Studies, September. http://english.dohainstitute.org /release/23b7ebd3-367c-427e-8f33-f125d410d6e2.

Tozy, Mohamed. 2008. "Islamists, Technocrats, and the Palace." *Journal of Democracy* 19, no. 1: 34–41.

———. 2009. "Reorganisaton of the Moroccan Political Landscape." In *IEMed Mediterranean Yearbook 2009*, 190–96. Barcelona: European Institute of the Mediterranean.

Twal, Malek. 2007. "Decentralization Versus Deconcentration: Political Implications of Local Government in Jordan." Presented at "Municipi D'Oriente" Convegno Studi, Scuola Superiore Della Pubblica Administrazione Locale, Rome, December 5–7.

Tweissi, Basim. 2014. "Municipality Councils and Local Media Study on the Right of Access to Information in Jordan." *Journal of Media and Communication Studies* 6, no. 1: 11–22.

UNDP (United Nations Development Programme). 2004. *Jordan Human Development Report: Building Sustainable Livelihoods*. United Nations Development Report. Amman: Ministry of Planning and International Cooperation; UNDP; JUHUD/Queen Zein Al Sharaf Institute for Development.

———. 2013. "Jordan Poverty Reduction Strategy Final Report." January 23. http:// www.jo.undp.org/content/dam/jordan/docs/Poverty/Jordanpovertyreduc tionstrategy.pdf.

———. 2014. "Municipal Needs Assessment Report: Mitigating the Impact of the Syrian Refugee Crisis on Jordanian Vulnerable Host Communities." http:// www.undp.org/content/dam/jordan/docs/Poverty/needs%20assessment%20 report.pdf.

UNDP (United Nations Development Programme) and German Federal Ministry for Economic Cooperation and Development. 2000. *The UNDP Role in Decentralization and Local Governance: A Joint UNDP–Government of Germany Evaluation*. New York: United Nations Development Programme.

Valbjørn, Morten. 2013. "The 2013 Parliamentary Elections in Jordan: Three Stories and Some General Lessons." *Mediterranean Politics* 18, no. 2: 311–17.

Valbjørn, Morten, and André Bank. 2010. "Examining the 'Post' in Post-democratization: The Future of Middle Eastern Political Rule Through Lenses of the Past." *Middle East Critique* 19, no. 3: 183–200.

Vallianatos, Stefanos. 2013. "Arab Civil Society at the Crossroad of Democratization: The Arab Spring Impact." Neighbourhood Policy Paper, Center for International and European Studies. http://www.khas.edu.tr/cms/cies/dosya lar/files/NeighbourhoodPolicyPaper(10)(3).pdf.

Van der Steen, Eveline J. 2006. "Tribes and Power Structures in Palestine and the Transjordan." *Near Eastern Archaeology* 69, no. 1: 27–36.

Varulkar, H. 2011. "The Arab Spring in Jordan: King Compelled to make Concession to Protest Movement." Inquiry and Analysis Series Report no. 771, Middle East Media Research Institute, Washington, D.C. http://www.memri .org/report/en/0/0/0/0/0/0/5906.htm.

Vatiliotis, Panayiotis J. 1967. *Politics and the Military in Jordan.* London: Frank Cass.

Vengroff, Richard, and Hatem Ben Salem. 1992. "Assessing the Impact of Decentralization on Governance: A Comparative Methodological Approach and Application to Tunisia." *Public Administration and Development* 12: 473–92.

"Les véritables enjeux des prochaines élections." 2003. *La Vie économique,* August 8. http://lavieeco.com/news/politique/les-veritables-enjeux-des-prochaines -elections-5265.html.

Wallace, Jeremy. 2013. "Cities, Redistribution, and Authoritarian Regime Survival." *Journal of Politics* 75, no. 3: 632–45.

Waterbury, John. 1970. *The Commander of the Faithful.* New York: Columbia University Press.

Wegner, Eva. 2011. *Islamist Opposition in Authoritarian Regimes: The Party of Justice and Development in Morocco.* Syracuse: Syracuse University Press.

Wegner Eva, and Miquel Pellicer. 2009a. "Islamist Moderation Without Democratization: The Coming of Age of the Moroccan Party of Justice and Development?" *Democratization* 16, no. 1: 157–75.

——. 2009b. "Morocco's Local Elections: With a Little Help from my Friend." *Notes Internacionals,* no. 3: 1–5. https://www.cidob.org/publicaciones/serie_ de_publicacion/notes_internacionals/n1_03/morocco_s_local_elections_ with_a_little_help_from_my_friend.

——. 2011. "Left–Islamist Opposition Cooperation in Morocco." *British Journal of Middle Eastern Studies* 38, no. 3: 303–22.

Wehler-Schoeck, Anja. 2016. *Parliamentary Elections in Jordan: A Competition of Mixed Messages.* Amman: Friedrich-Ebert-Stiftung.

Weingast, Barry R. n.d. "A Political Approach to the Assignment of Powers in a Federal System." Initiative for Policy Change Working Paper Series, Columbia University, New York.

———. 2007. "Second Generation Fiscal Federalism: Implications for Decentralized Democratic Governance and Economic Development." Working draft.

Weingrod, Alex. 1968. "Patrons, Patronage, and Political Parties." *Society for Comparative Studies in Society and History* 10, no. 4: 377–400.

Weitz-Shaprio, Rebecca. 2012. "What Wins Votes: Why Some Politicians Opt Out of Clientelism." *American Journal of Political Science* 56, no. 3: 568–83.

Wignaraja, Ponna, Susil Sirivardana, and Akmal Hussain. 2009. *Economic Democracy Through Pro-Poor Growth*. New Delhi: SAGE.

WikiLeaks. 2003. "Pillars of the Regime Part II of IV: The East Bank Tribes." February 12. Wikileaks, n.d. https://wikileaks.org/plusd/cables/03AMMAN967_a .html.

———. 2004. "King Back Decentralization, Pushes Reluctant Governors." February 6. Wikileaks, August 30, 2011. http://wikileaks.1wise.es/cable/2004/07 /04AMMAN5939

———. 2005. "Royal Commission on Decentralization Appointed; Parliament Moves to Restore Election of Municipal Councils." February 6. WikiLeaks, August 30, 2011. https://wikileaks.org/plusd/cables/05AMMAN981.html.

———. 2007. "Casablanca: Post-Election Talk of the Town." October 26. Wikileaks, n.d. https://www.wikileaks.org/plusd/cables/07CASABLANCA207_a.html.

———. 2008. "Municipal Government Accountability Improves but Development Remains Challenging." September 15. Wikileaks, n.d. https://wikileaks.org /plusd/cables/08AMMAN2672_a.html.

———. 2009. "King Renews Calls for Decentralization, Government Stalls for Time." April 15. Wikileaks, n.d. https://wikileaks.org/plusd/cables /09AMMAN886_a.html.

Wiktorowicz, Quintan. 1999a. "State Power and the Regulation of Islam in Jordan." *Journal of Church and State* 41, no. 4: 677–95.

———. 1999b. "The Limits of Democracy in the Middle East: The Case of Jordan." *Middle East Journal* 53, no. 4: 606–20.

———. 2000. "Civil Society as Social Control: State Power in Jordan." *Comparative Politics* 33, no. 1: 43–62.

———. 2001. *The Management of Islamic Activism*. Albany: State University of New York Press.

———. 2002. "The Political Limits of Nongovernmental Organizations in Jordan." *World Development* 30, no. 1: 77–93.

Wilcox, Luke. 2009. "Reshaping Civil Society through a Truth Commission: Human Rights in Morocco's Process of Political Reform." *International Journal of Transitional Justice* 3, no. 1: 49–68.

Willis, Eliza, Christopher da C.B. Garman, and Stephan Haggard. 1999. "The Political of Decentralization in Latin America." *Latin American Research Review* 34, no. 1: 7–55.

Willis, Michael. J. 1999. "Between Alternance and the Makhzen: At-Tawhid wa Al-Islah's Entry into Moroccan Politics." *Journal of North African Studies* 4, no. 3: 45–80. DOI:10.1080/13629389908718373.

——. 2002. "Political Parties in the Maghrib: The Illusion of Significance?" *Journal of North African Studies* 7, no. 2: 1–22.

——. 2004. "Morocco's Islamists and the Legislative Elections of 2002: The Strange Case of the Party That Did Not Want to Win." *Mediterranean Politics* 9, no. 1: 53–81.

——. 2009. "Conclusion: The Dynamics of Reform in Morocco." *Mediterranean Politics* 14, no. 2: 229–37. DOI:10.1080/13629390902990851.

——. 2012. *Politics and Power the Maghreb.* London: Hurst.

Wils, Oliver. 2004. "From Negotiation to Rent-Seeking, and Back?" In Heydemann 2004a: 133–55.

Wilson, Mary. 1987. *King Abdullah, Britain and the Making of Jordan.* Cambridge: Cambridge University Press.

Wong, Sam. 2010. "Elite Capture or Capture Elites? Lessons from the 'Counter-elite' and 'Co-opted-Elite' Approaches in Bangladesh and Ghana." United Nations University–World Institute for Development Economic Research (UNU-WIDER) Working Paper no. 2010/82, Helsinki.

——. 2013. "Challenges to the Elite Exclusion-Inclusion Dichotomy— Reconsidering Elite Capture in Community-Based Natural Resource Management." *South African Journal of International Affairs* 20, no. 3: 379–91.

Work, Robertson. n.d. *The Role of Participation and Partnership in Decentralised Governance: A Brief Synthesis of Policy Lessons and Recommendations of Nine Country Case Studies on Service Delivery for the Poor.* New York: United Nations Development Programme.

——. 2002. *Overview of Decentralization Worldwide: A Steeping Stone to Improved Governance and Human Development.* New York: United Nations Development Programme.

World Bank. 1984. *The World Development Report.* Washington, D.C.: World Bank; New York: Oxford University Press.

——. 1995. *Fiscal Decentralization in the Hashemite Kingdom of Jordan.* World Bank Groups.

——. 1999. *World Development Report 1999/2000: Entering the 21st Century.* Washington, D.C.: World Bank; New York: Oxford University Press.

——. 2003. *World Development Report 2004: Making Services Work for Poor People.* Washington, D.C.: World Bank; New York: Oxford University Press.

——. 2005a. "Legal Framework, Suggested Best Practices: Annex A." In *The Hashemite Kingdom of Jordan Ministry of Tourism and Antiquities, Third Tourism Development Project: Secondary Cities Revitalization Study.* Washington, D.C.: World Bank.

——. 2005b. "General Analysis of the Municipal Sector: Annex B." In *The Hashemite Kingdom of Jordan Ministry of Tourism and Antiquities, Third Tourism Development Project: Secondary Cities Revitalization Study*. Washington, D.C.: World Bank.

——. 2007. "Decentralization and Local Governance in MENA: A Survey of Policies, Institutions and Practices—A Review of Decentralization Experience in Eight Middle East and North Africa Countries." World Bank, Sustainable Development Department, no. 36516. http://documents.worldbank.org/curated/en/940531468275089510/Decentralization-and-local-governance-in-MENA-a-survey-of-policies-institutions-and-practices-a-review-of-decentralization-experience-in-eight-Middle-East-and-North-Africa-countries.

——. 2009. "Decentralization and Deconcentration in Morocco: A Cross-Sectoral Status Review." Washington, D.C.: World Bank. http://www-wds.worldbank.org/external/default/WDSContentServer/WDSP/IB/2012/06/15/000425962_20120615115517/Rendered/PDF/697060ESW0P1020n0StatusReview0Final.pdf.

Wright, J. W., and Laura Drake, eds. 2000. *Economic and Political Impediments to Middle East Peace: Critical Questions and Alternative Scenarios*. New York: Macmillan.

El Yaagoubi, Mohammed. 2001. *Les grandes contradictions de la réforme administrative au Maroc*. Rabat: Revue Marocaine d'Administration Locale et de Développement.

——. 2003a. "Les cours régionales des comptes et la démocratie locale au Maroc." *Revue de droit et d'économie*, no. 20: 255–64.

——. 2003b. "Décentralisation et développement social au Maroc." *Revue marocaine d'administration locale et de développement*, no. 50: 25–38.

——. 2006. "La région en tant que nouvelle collectivité locale au Maroc." *Revue marocaine d'administration locale et de développement*, no. 52: 57–81.

Yacoubian, Mona. 2005. "Promoting Middle East Democracy II: Arab Initiatives." USIP Special Report 136. United States Institute of Peace, Washington, D.C.

Yaghi, Mohammad. 2012. "Jordan's Election Law: Reform or Perish?" *Fikra Forum*, Washington Institute, October 4. http://www.washingtoninstitute.org/policy-analysis/view/jordans-election-law-reform-or-perish.

Yaghi, Mohammed, and Janine A. Clark. 2014. "Jordan: Evolving Activism in a Divided Society." In Khatib and Lust 2014: 236–67.

Yilmaz, Serdar. 2002. "Intergovernmental Fiscal Relations and Municipal Finance in Jordan (Module 4 Decentralization)." Presented at the World Bank Institute Capacity Building Workshop on Rural Development Policies and Institutional Reform, Beirut, June 3–6.

Yilmaz, Serdar, and Varsha Venugopal. 2013. "Local Government Discretion and Accountability in Philippines." *Journal of International Development* 25: 227–50.

Yom, Sean. 2013. "Jordan: The Ruse of Reform." *Journal of Democracy* 24, no. 3: 127–39.

——. 2014. "Tribal Politics in Contemporary Jordan: The Case of the Hirak Movement." *Middle East Journal* 68, no. 2: 229–47.

Yom, Sean L., and F. Gregory Gause III. 2012. "Resilient Royals: How Arab Monarchies Hang On." *Journal of Democracy* 23, no. 4: 74–88.

Zahran, Mudar. 2012. "Jordan Is Palestinian." *Middle East Quarterly* 19, no. 1: 3–12.

Zaki, Lamia. 2007. "Séduction électorale au Bidonville: jouer de l'opulence, de la jeunesse ou du handicap à Casablanca." *Politique Africaine* 3, no. 107: 42–61.

——. 2008. "Le clientélisme, vecteur de politisation en régime autoritaire?" In Dabène, Geisser, and Massardier 2008: 157–80.

——. 2009. *Terrains de campagne au Maroc: les élections législatives de 2007.* Paris: IRMC-Karthala.

Zaki, Moheb. 2010. "The Status of Political Parties in the Arab World." In Shalaby et al. 2010: 79–122.

Zartman, I. William. 1964. *Problems of New Power Morocco.* New York: Atherton.

——, ed. 1987. *The Political Economy of Morocco.* London: Praeger.

Zartman, I. William, Mark Tessler, John P. Entelis, Russel A. Stone, Raymond Hinnebusch, and Shahrough Akhavi, eds. 1982. *Political Elites in Arab North Africa.* New York: Longman.

Zeghal, Malika. 2009. *Islamism in Morocco.* Translated by George Holoch. Princeton: Markus Wienner.

Zemni, Sami, and Koenraad Bogaert. 2006. "Morocco and the Mirages of Democracy and Good Governance." *UNISCI Discussion Papers*, no. 12: 103–20.

——. 2011. "Urban Renewal and Social Development in Morocco in an Age of Neoliberal Government." *Review of African Political Economy* 38, no. 129: 403–17.

Zidouri, Fatima. 2008. "Développement humain et gouvernance locale au Maroc." *Revue marocaine d'administration locale et de développement*, no. 80: 69–76.

——.2009. "La gestion participative des ressources financières locales." *Massalik*, no. 11–12: 15–20.

Zyani, Brahim. 2002. *Décentralisation et réforme administrative au Maroc.* Presented at Fourth Mediterranean Forum on Development, Amman, April.

Regularly Consulted English-, Arabic- and French-Language News Sources

Al-Arabiya News
Aujourd'hui le Maroc

Al Doustour
La Gazette du Maroc
Al-Ghad
Jeune Afrique
Jordan Times
Maroc Hebdo
Le Matin
Al-Rai
Telquel
La Vie économique

Index

associations (Morocco): municipalities and, 231–33, 236–37, 265–66, 268–70, 280; neighborhood associations, 228–29, 250, 252–53, 256, 313n105, 317n50; PJD and, 252–56, 263–66, 268–69, 317n50. *See also* civil society actors (Morocco); NGOs (Morocco)

Atallah, Sami, 5, 23

authoritarian regimes: and decentralization, 3–5, 23–24, 199, 277, 287 (*see also* "decentralization" in Jordan; decentralization in Morocco); fall of (1980s–90s), 13. *See also* Jordanian monarchy; Moroccan monarchy

Azzam, Imad al, 182

Ba'ath Party, 48–49, 111

baladiyyas. See municipal governments (Jordan)

al-Balqa', Jordan (city), 57, 92

al-Balqa' governorate, Jordan, 95

al-Balqa' movement, 43

Bani Hassan tribe, 34, 170–72, 320–21n3

Bani Sakhr tribes, 41–43, 320–21n3

al-Banna, Hassan, 295n8. *See also* Muslim Brotherhood

Bardhan, Pranab, 25

Basri, Driss, 221

bay'a (Moroccan oath of allegiance), 64, 293n27

Bedouin Control Law (1936), 45–46

Bedouin tribes: Glubb's policies toward, 44–46, 291n7; and the Jordanian army, 50–51; monarchy supported by, 49–50, 75; shaykhs and state-building in Jordan, 38–47, 75. *See also* Jordan; Transjordanians; tribalism in Jordan

Benkirane, Abdelilah, 34, 136–37, 315n6, 320n2

Ben-Meir, Yosseff, 149

Ben Nefissa, Sarah, 29–30, 31

Berber tribes (Morocco): elites, 20, 37–38, 58–59, 62, 65–69, 75–76, 216; under the French protectorate, 37, 61, 65–66, 216; Moroccan monarchy's coalition with, 20, 37–38, 58–59, 62, 65–69, 75–76. *See also* PMP

Bergh, Sylvia I.: on the 2002 municipal charter, 25, 138, 145; on decentralization and economic expansion, 131; on development funding/grants, 206–7, 232; on the INDH, 30–31, 310n14, 311n38; on Mohammed VI's "new concept of authority," 138–39; on municipal councils under the 1976 charter, 147, 217; on municipal planning, 303n22, 309n4; on neoliberal ideology, 10, 14; on PCDs, 204; on regional associations, 140

Berkya family, 221–23, 227, 260

Berriane, Yasmine, 31, 206, 310n18

bidonvilles (Moroccan shantytowns), 64, 74, 312n60

Birayn, Jordan, 176–77, 179, 191

Birqish, Jordan, 184–85, 308n115

Black September (1970), 52

Bled al-Makhzen, 65, 293n27

Bled as-Siba, 65–66, 75, 293n27. *See also* Berber tribes (Morocco)

Bocco, Riccardo, 44, 45

Boerwinkel, Felia, 91

Bogaert, Koenraad, 31, 128, 140, 206

Bono, Irene, 30–31

Bouziane, Malika, 90

Brand, Laurie A., 51–54

bread riots (Morocco), 74, 294n37

Brenner, Neil, 9–10

Bre-X company, 276

British colonial powers, in Jordan, 37, 39–49, 54, 95. *See also* Jordan; nationalist movement (Jordan); Transjordan

Brynen, Rex, 56–57

Buehler, Matt, 214

Cairo, Egypt, 27–28, 31. *See also* Egypt

Cammett, Melani, 70–71

Canada, 276

Casablanca, Morocco: 2015 election results, 281–82; bombings, 138, 142–43, 149, 244 (*see also* PJD: strategy and rationale shifted); municipal council and privatization, 30; riots, 64, 136; shantytown population, 312n60; urban municipalities in, 146–47

Cattedra, Raffaele, 205, 209, 214, 270–71, 273

Catusse, Myriam: on the 2002 charter, 303n20; on Casablanca's territorial configurations, 146; on councils' proposals, 205; on the INDH, 144; on jurisdictional confusion, 209; on the king's reference to walis, 150; on maps and censorship, 214; on the PJD, 247–48, 270–71, 273, 319n117; on privatization in Morocco, 73–74; on state disengagement, 143; on walis, 150

Cavatorta, Francesco, 141, 207

CDT (Democratic Confederation of Labor; Confédération Démocratique du Travail), 126, 127

Centeno, Miguel Angel, 278

centralization (generally): in the Global South, 11–12; in the MENA region, 4; neoliberalism opposed to, 13 (*see*

also neoliberalism). *See also* centralization in Jordan

centralization in Jordan, 2, 5, 7–8; access to resources reduced by, 196; amalgamation of municipalities, 79, 114–15, 157, 173–78, 191, 194–95, 299nn47–48, 306n83; clawback of municipal responsibilities, 99–106, 119–21, 286; coalition incentives for, 18–20, 284; hyper-centralized system, 80, 93, 96, 103, 178, 194, 285; Jordanian monarchy and, 32, 79 (*see also* Jordanian monarchy); MPs pitted against mayors by, 112, 116; and municipal politics, 2, 194; political system undermined by, 284; reasons for choosing, 6; red tape, 182–84; regionalization and regional development, 96–99; tribes divided/ fractured by, 156–58, 167, 173, 175–78, 194–95, 284–85; and wasta, 121 (*see also* wasta). *See also* "decentralization" in Jordan; governorates (Jordan); Jordanian government; Jordanian monarchy; Jordanian parliament; mayors (Jordan); municipalities (Jordan)

Centrist Islamist Party, 294–95n2

Cheema, G. Shabbir, 14–16

Chefchaouen, Morocco: elite domination and property development in, 217–18, 311n52, 311–12n53; municipal employees, 224, 320n132; PJD in, 36, 250, 254–55, 258–66, 269–72, 315n15, 316n40, 318n90, 320n132; under Spanish occupation, 316n35; tourism in, 222

China, 23

Christiaensen, Luc, 26

Churchill, Winston, 41

Cities and Villages Development Bank. *See* CVDB

Cities Without Slums. *See* Villes sans Bidonvilles program

civil service (Jordan), 53. *See also* municipalities (Jordan): employees

civil society (generally), 11, 14, 16–17, 282. *See also* civil society actors (Morocco); civil society organizations; NGOs (Jordan); NGOs (Morocco)

civil society actors (Morocco): 2002 charter and, 146; 2009 charter and, 76, 123–24, 153–54, 269–70, 274; increase in CSOs, 139, 140; INDH and, 207, 242, 278, 280 (*see also* INDH); monarchy's attempt to co-opt/integrate, 20, 76, 139–44, 146–48, 153–54, 251–52 (*see also* 2002 Municipal Charter; municipal charters); and municipal councils, 202, 230–31, 280; PJD and, 7, 28, 241–42, 250–66, 268–70, 274–75, 281; and planning and development, 203–4, 207, 280; and political parties, 139–40; politics conducted through civil society, 230–33; restrictions on, 140–41. *See also* civil society organizations; NGOs (Morocco)

civil society organizations (CSOs; Morocco): charters and, 122, 153; and elite capture, 7; increase of, 139–40, 144, 242, 253; INDH and, 30–31 (*see also* INDH); PJD and, 7, 242, 266; political parties and, 139–40, 282; restrictions on, 140–41. *See also* civil society actors (Morocco); NGOs (Morocco)

Clark, Janine A., 27–28, 252–53

CLDH (Local Committee for Human Development), 206–7, 310n16

clientelism. *See* moral clientelism; *and headings beginning with* patron-clientelism

coalition incentives, 18, 19, 20–21

coalition strategies, 6, 20–21. *See also* Jordanian monarchy; Moroccan monarchy; PJD; political parties (Morocco)

Committee(s) for Equity and Equal Opportunities, 153, 202–4, 230, 232, 266, 269

Communist Party, Jordanian, 111

Communist Party, Moroccan (PCM), 64

Confédération Démocratique du Travail, 126, 127

Conning, Jonathan, 26

Consultative Councils (Jordan), 94. *See also* governorates (Jordan): councils

Conyers, Diana, 23

corruption (generally), 25

corruption (Jordan), 1, 105, 193. *See also* patron-clientelism (Jordan); wasta

corruption (Morocco), 1, 199; administrative structure of authority justified by, 281; civil servants and, 222–25, 237, 312n69; coup attempts provoked by, 69; ease of, 233–34; electoral fraud, 224–25, 226–27; municipal councils and, 199, 229–33; parties seen as corrupt, 135; PJD seen as not corrupt, 249, 256–57; presidents and, 199, 222–27. *See also* patron-clientelism (Morocco)

councils. *See* executive councils (Jordan); municipal councils (Morocco); municipal governments (Jordan)

CPDH (Provincial Committee for Human Development), 206–7, 232, 310n17

Craig, Daniel, 14–15
CSOs. *See* civil society organizations
CVDB (Cities and Villages Development Bank), 107, 113, 165–66

Dalmasso, Emanuela, 141, 207, 252–53
DAS. *See under* Ministry of the Interior (Morocco)
Decent Housing for Decent Living, 90
decentralization (generally): authoritarian regimes and, 3–5, 23–24, 199, 277, 287; central government strengthened by, 30–31; and coalition strategy, 6, 20–21; deconcentration, 15, 200–202 (*see also under* municipalities [Morocco]); democratization and, 13, 287; elite capture and, 3–4, 6–7, 23–29, 197–98, 280 (*see also* elite capture); forms (types), 15–17, 289n2; global project of, 277; and good governance, 2, 13–17 (*see also* good governance); incentives and disincentives to, 4–6, 17–23; inclusion of civil society in reforms, 11 (*see also* civil society); literature on, 4–5, 8–9; neoliberalism as process of creative destruction, 11 (*see also* neoliberalism); policy vs. practice, 2–3, 8; and regime stability/power, 3–4, 7, 29–32; "regions" plan, 115–17, 299n48, 300nn50–57; rural development and, 12–13; trends leading to, 11–14. *See also* "decentralization" in Jordan; decentralization in Morocco
"decentralization" in Jordan, 2, 279; 2005–present, 115–20; 2015 municipalities and decentralization laws, 118–20; administrative decentralization, 96; disincentives for, 39, 77; electoral incentives and, 22–23; elite capture resulting from,

3–4; Inter-Ministerial Committee on, 117; Jordan First campaign, 85–86; monarchy's balancing act, 3, 78–81; National Agenda, 78, 86, 115, 300n54; potential impact on patron-clientelism, 18–19, 287; powers removed from municipal councils, 33, 286; pressure for political decentralization, 57–58; regionalization and regional development, 96–99; Transjordanian resistance to, 80–81. *See also* centralization in Jordan; Jordan; mayors (Jordan); municipal governments (Jordan); municipalities (Jordan)
decentralization in Morocco, 2, 3; administrative reforms, 145 (*see also* 2002 Municipal Charter; 2009 Municipal Charter); central state powers increased, 30–31, 200; as coalition-expansion strategy, 6, 38, 154; "decentralized conjuring," 279; deconcentrated/decentralized structures of authority, 200–207, 273 (*see also* governors [Morocco]; walis); elite capture resulting from, 3–4, 6–7, 279–80 (*see also* elite capture [Morocco]); goals of reforms, 200; impact on local politics, 274; and the monarchy as political reformer, 7, 29, 32, 74, 76, 123, 146, 153–54, 199, 238, 242, 277–78, 283; monarchy/regime strengthened and stabilized, 7, 29, 32, 199, 236, 237, 273, 277–79, 283; most extensive in MENA region, 33; patron-clientelism and personalization of politics maintained, 233; phases, 122; political parties' institutional strength and, 6, 123 (*see also* political parties

[Morocco]); and regionalization, 149–51, 303n18; as way to deal with debt, 130–31. *See also* Morocco; municipal charters; municipal councils (Morocco); municipalities (Morocco); political reforms (Morocco); presidents; *and specific charters by year*

deconcentration, 15, 200–202. *See also* municipalities (Morocco): deconcentrated structure of authority

découpage administratif, 213–14

delegation (defined), 15

Democratic and Social Movement (MDS), 221

Democratic Confederation of Labor, 126–27

Democratic Party of Independence (PDI), 67

democratization and decentralization, 13, 287

Denoeux, Guilain P., 73

Desert Force (Desert Patrol), 44–45

Deshingkar, Priya, 25–26

development, 14. *See also* local development (Jordan); local development (Morocco); *and specific organizations and programs*

devolution (defined), 15

DGCL (Direction Générale des Collectivités Locales; General Department for Local Communities), 201

Doan, Petra L., 95–99, 299n48

Droz-Vincent, Philippe, 111

East Bank, 291n8. *See also* Palestinians

Eaton, Kent, 17–19, 21–22, 37

Economic Consultative Council (Jordan), 88

economic decentralization (defined), 15

economic reforms: first-, second-, and third-generation literature, 8–9; in Jordan, 54, 56, 86–92, 292n23; in the MENA region, 29–30, 290n9; in Morocco, 72–75, 142; and the politics of elite capture, 17 (*see also* elite capture); regime stability strengthened by, 29–30. *See also* privatization; SAPs

education: in Jordan, 90, 102, 161, 188–89, 296nn16–17; in Morocco, 66, 83, 148, 152, 216, 295n9

Egypt, 29–30, 31, 49, 295n8

Eisenhower Doctrine, 50

electoral incentives, 18, 22–23

electoral system (Jordan): 1989–1993, 57–58, 81, 293n25; 1993 electoral law, 81–83, 110–11, 295nn6–7; 2013 electoral law, 112–13, 309n136; biased against political parties, 79, 80, 82–83, 110–11; block voting system, 82, 168, 305n55; elections and patronage/wasta, 158–59, 303n6; electoral districts, 105–6, 175–76, 177; municipal elections, 102–6, 168–73, 298n30, 298n33, 298nn35–36, 305nn53–55; one-person-one-vote system, 83, 112, 168, 305nn54–55; Political Parties Laws, 298–99n43; tribally based, 81, 110–12, 168–73, 175–76, 286. *See also* Jordanian parliament

electoral system (Morocco): 1970 reforms intended to consolidate monarchy's power, 64–65; 2007 and 2008 electoral laws, 132, 214; constitutions and, 128, 294n32; electoral fraud, 224–25, 226–27; at municipal level, 198–99, 214, 216, 234–35, 314n120 (*see also* municipalities [Morocco]). *See also* Moroccan parliament elite capture (generally), 23–29; analyses of, 5, 24–28; civil society actors and, 17; decentralization and, 3–4, 6–7, 23–29, 197–98, 280; defined, 3, 28–29; literature on, 9; processes of, 24–25; strong party system key to avoiding, 287

elite capture (Jordan): monarchy's coalition with tribes and tribal elites, 19–20, 42–43, 46–47, 49–51, 54, 75, 77, 86–92, 284–85; municipal amalgamation and, 173–78; wasta, municipalities, and tribalism, 156–73, 194–96. *See also* Jordanian monarchy; patron-clientelism (Jordan); wasta

elite capture (Morocco): 1976 charter and, 19–20, 38, 59, 132–33, 217–18, 279–80; 2002 and 2009 charters and, 20–21, 25, 38, 229–33; author's methodology for studying, 36; municipal elites and, 198, 229–33, 236–38; opportunities provided by charters generally, 32, 196, 269–70; PJD not engaged in, 241; PJD's exploitation of reforms, 24, 197, 269–70 (*see also* PJD); pro-regime parties' exploitation of reforms, 24, 197–98; regime strengthened through, 283; state-sanctioned, 281. *See also* civil society actors (Morocco); Moroccan elites; political parties (Morocco); *and specific organizations and parties*

elites. *See* Bedouin tribes; Berber tribes; Moroccan elites; wasta; *and headings beginning with* elite capture *and* patron-clientelism

Erfoud, Morocco, 249–51, 255–57, 266–68, 317n53, 317n54

Euro-Mediterranean Partnership, 292n23

European Union (EU): aid projects in Jordan, 179–81, 306–7n98, 308–9n135; EU-Jordan agreement (2002), 292n23; Morocco's INDH supported, 310n14; relations with Morocco, 74, 301n2

executive councils (Jordan), 94, 118, 300n57, 301n60. *See also* governorates (Jordan): councils

FAR (Royal Armed Forces), 68. *See also* military, Moroccan

Farhan, Izhaq, 83

Faysal bin Husayn, Sharif, 39–40

Fès (Fez), Morocco, 61, 65, 150, 293n28

field research, 34–36, 290nn10–12

fiscal decentralization (defined), 15

Fjeldstad, Odd-Helge, 24, 25

France, 145, 215. *See also* French protectorate

French protectorate (Morocco), 58–62, 66, 216, 293n26

fuel tax transfer (Jordan), 107

GAM. *See* Greater Amman Municipality

GATT (General Agreement on Trades and Tariffs), 74

General Department for Local Communities (DGCL), 201

General Union of Moroccan Workers, 127

Ghazi b. Muhammad, Prince, 296n17

El-Ghobashy, Mona, 4–5

GIZ (German Development Corporation; also GTZ), 179, 187, 306–7n98

Global South, 11–14, 18. *See also* Latin America; MENA region; *and specific countries*

Glubb, John, Capt., 44–46, 48–49,
291n7, 292n10
good governance: decentralization
reforms at heart of, 2, 13–17;
democratization and, 13, 287;
discourse of, in Morocco, 142–45,
278 (see also 2002 Municipal Charter;
2009 Municipal Charter; civil
society actors [Morocco]); as "softer"
neoliberalism, 14, 278. See also
decentralization in Morocco;
economic reforms; and headings
beginning with civil society
"Good Municipal Governance: The
Reinforcement of Democracy and
the Promotion of Civil Society
Participation in Northern Morocco"
(project), 265–66
governorates (Jordan): 2015
municipalities and decentralization
laws and, 118–20, 301n60;
administrative structure (present),
118; budgets and funding, 93–94,
106, 107; councils, 94, 118, 300n57,
301n60; creation of, 92–93, 98–99,
297n28; divided into 100
municipalities, 307n106; governors'
roles and responsibilities, 93–94, 118,
182, 286; place in administrative
structure, 93–95; and the proposed
"regions" plan, 115–17, 300n55;
reduction and restructuring, under
National Agenda, 78; Syrian refugees
in, 118, 301n59. See also specific
governorates
governors (Morocco), 200–201;
appointed by king, 206; bypassed by
PJD, 272; discretionary powers,
207–10, 212–15; and local planning
and development, 207, 310n18; and
the making of PCDs, 203–4; powers

and responsibilities, 202, 204, 206–8;
presidents' relations with, 224. See
also walis
Great Britain. See British colonial
powers
Greater Amman Municipality (GAM):
creation of, 98; funding and
expenditures, 106, 109; under PM's
authority, 36, 94, 98, 119–20; and the
"regions" plan, 300n50
Green March, 59, 71, 73, 130
Grindle, Merilee S., 25
GTZ. See GIZ
Gubser, P., 96, 97
Gulf War (1990–1991), 84, 302n4

HACCP (hazard analysis and critical
control point) systems, 193
Hallaj, Omar Abdulaziz, et al., 117,
296–97n20
Hammoudi, Abdellah, 67–68
Harakat al-Tawhid wal-Islah. See MUR
Harb, Mona, 5, 23
Harders, Cijla, 4, 290n8
Harrigan, Jane, 52, 53, 71, 143, 146
Hashemite Compact, 37, 47, 50, 75,
290n1. See also Transjordan;
Transjordanians
al-Hashemiyya al-Jadida, Jordan, 187
Hassan II, king of Morocco: assumption
and consolidation of power by,
63–64; constitutional revisions, 128;
coup attempts against, 68–70,
294n32; and human rights, 125;
loyalist parties encouraged, 72; and
the Moroccan military, 68–70;
nationalist parties wooed/coopted,
69–72; opposition parties wooed/
co-opted, 125–29, 302n4; party
institutional strength reinforced, 132;
patronage used to create loyal parties,

Hassan II, king of Morocco (*cont.*)
65; political liberalization by, 73–75,
125–29 (*see also under* political
reforms [Morocco]); populist
policies, 70–71, 143; privatized
companies acquired, 134; royal
females married off for political
reasons, 302n7. *See also* Moroccan
monarchy

Hejaya, Rana, 167

Hess, Steve, 4, 12–13, 233

Heydemann, Steven, 8–11

Hibou, Béatrice, 60

Hoffman, Anja, 60, 290n9

Hourani, Hani, et al., 105, 309n139

humane imperialism policy, 44–45,
291n7

Husayn ibn Ali, Sharif, 39–40

Hussein, king of Jordan: and the 1993
electoral law amendments, 82–83;
accession to throne, 291–92n10;
coalition with the tribes, 50–51; coup
attempts against, 292n15; Glubb
dismissed, 49, 292n10; governorates
created, 297n28; and the MB, 83;
and the nationalist movement
(1950s), 47–48, 49–50; policies
toward Palestinians, 51, 52, 292n14;
political liberalization under, 81–83;
and Qreqra w Finan's land, 185;
reforms in response to 1989 riots,
57–58, 293n25; and regional
development, 97

IAF (Islamic Action Front): and the 1989
elections, 82; and the 2007 and 2013
municipal elections, 105; and the
2016 elections, 294n1, 294–95n2;
capacity of, 80; formation of, 82;
increasing prominence, 111;
monarchy's efforts to control, 79; and

the National Alliance for Reform,
294–95n2; power of, 21; protests
over 1993 electoral law, 83;
replacement of mayors not protested,
194; seats held in 2005, 298n39; and
tribal politics, 169–70

Ibn Saud, 45

ibn Zayid, Shakir, 42, 44

Idrissi Janati, M'hammed, 205, 209, 214,
270–71, 273

IFIs. *See* IMF; international financial
institutions; World Bank

IG (Islamic Group; al-Jama'a
al-Islamiyya), 136–37. *See also* RR

IMF (International Monetary Fund), 54,
56, 73. *See also* SAPs

INDH (Initiative Nationale du
Développement Humain; National
Initiative for Human
Development): audit of, 315n127;
center for abandoned children
funded, 236; and civil society
actors/CSOs, 207, 242, 278, 280;
clientelism, 310n18; distribution of
grants by, 207; donors, 310n14; and
elite capture, 231–32; good
governance and, 142–45, 278;
impact on municipalities,
population, 141–42, 207;
implementation and budget,
302n14; INDH-inspired
associations, 231–32; monarchy
legitimized by, 207; normalized by
PJD's practices, 273; origins and
role, 142–43, 199; programs, 205–6,
310n14; and the rise of civil society
activists, 251–52 (*see also* civil
society actors [Morocco]); top-
down approach, 30–31, 202–3, 205;
transversal program, 30, 205–6,
310n15. *See also* CPDH

international financial institutions (IFIs), 2, 11–13. *See also* IMF; World Bank

International Monetary Fund. *See* IMF

Iraki, Aziz El Maoula, 217–18, 220–21, 229, 311n53, 313n105

Irbid, Jordan (city/municipality), 42, 48, 91–92, 109, 291nn3–4, 298n38

Irbid governorate, Jordan, 95, 98–99, 181, 309n135

Islam: Islamist parties and groups in Jordan, 103–4, 169–70 (*see also* IAF; MBS; Muslim Brotherhood); Islamist parties and groups in Morocco, 126–27, 135–38, 243, 302nn9–12, 309n1 (*see also* MUR; PJD; political parties [Morocco]; *and other specific organizations*); MB and religious education, 83, 295n9; Moroccan monarchy's religious authority, 60, 64, 136; PJD stance on shari'a, 244–45. *See also* Islamist extremism

Islamic Action Front. *See* IAF

Islamic Center Charity Society, 295n5

Islamic Group. *See* IG

Islamist extremism (Morocco), 138, 142–43, 145, 149, 244, 246

Israel, 48, 51–52, 81, 84

Istiqlal (Independence) Party (Jordan), 291n2

Istiqlal (Independence) Party (Morocco): and the 2002 charter, 152; associated organizations, 132; co-opted by monarchy, 38, 69, 71–72, 123–24; divisions within, 67, 293n29 (*see also* UNFP); establishment of, 61–62; and independence, 75; institutional strength, 76–77, 131–32; local notables enlisted, 133; monarchy's

power struggle against, 20, 37, 59, 66–67; and municipal politics in Tiflet, 221–22; as part of Koutla, 127; vs. the PJD, 240, 243, 272; structure and leadership, 66, 76–77. *See also* political parties (Morocco)

IY (Islamic Youth; al-Shabiba al-Islamiyya), 135, 136–37, 302n9. *See also* PJD

al-Jama'a al-Islamiyya. *See* IG

Jerash, Jordan, 105–6–7, 109, 167, 171, 183, 186

La Jeunesse Istiqlalienne (The Istiqlal Youth), 132

JNM (Jordanian Nationalist Movement), 48, 49, 83

Johnson, Craig, 25–26

Jordan: anti-normalization movement, 84–85, 296n13; Arab Spring protests, 117–18, 177, 191; author's field research in, 34–36, 290n12; author's reasons for studying, 32–33; British colonial legacy, 37, 39–47, 75, 95 (*see also* British colonial powers); debt, 55–56; demographics, 286–87, 321n4; economic reforms, 54, 56, 86–92, 292n23; health and education spending, 53; independence, 47, 48; industrial development, 55, 87; Jordanization programs, 51–54, 86 (*see also* Jordan First campaign); martial law imposed (1957–1990s), 50, 292n13; military, 50–53, 89–90, 296n17 (*see also* Arab Legion); nationalist movement, 47–50, 83, 292n10, 292n12; patron-clientelism in (*see* patron-clientelism [Jordan]; wasta); poverty in, 91–92, 107, 109; regionalization and regional

Law of Municipalities No. 29 (Jordan, 1955), 101
Legislative Council (Transjordan), 43, 291n5
Liddell, James, 66, 133, 240
LIHDs (local initiatives for human development), 206. *See also* local development (Morocco)
Local Committee for Human Development. *See* CLDH
local councils (Jordan), 78, 118–19
local development (Jordan): land for, 162, 180–82, 185–87, 320–21n3; LDUs, 93, 178–82, 195–96, 296–97n20, 306–7n98; municipalities, wasta, bureaucracy and, 178–88, 191–92
local development (Morocco): under the 1976 charter, 311n52; civil society actors and, 144, 206; emphasized in 2002, 2009 municipal charters, 122–23, 153; equalization projects, 236, 237; INDH and, 205–7, 310nn14–16 (*see also* INDH); by landowners, 217–18, 220–21, 226, 313n91 (*see also* landownership [Morocco]); prefectural and provincial councils and, 208; Ramsar Convention and, 211; rural development neglected, 67; walis and governors and, 205–7, 208. *See also* PCDs
local development units (LDUs). *See under* local development (Jordan)
local governments. *See* municipal councils (Morocco); municipal governments (Jordan)
Lust-Okar, Ellen, 125–26, 158–59, 191, 298n40
Lyautey, Louis-Huberet-Gonzales, Marshall, 61

Ma'an, Jordan (municipality): electoral districts and population, 105–6, 295n4; municipality established, 42; population, 95; poverty in, 92; public university, 90; riots in, 56, 85; Shobak clothing factory, 181; Transjordanians in, 57
Ma'an governorate, Jordan, 95
Madaba, Jordan (municipality), 42, 107
Madaba governorate, Jordan, 299n49
al-Mafraq, Jordan (municipality), 90, 92, 105–6, 107, 301n59
al-Mafraq governorate, Jordan, 98–99
Maghraoui, Abdeslam, 73, 242–43, 245
Maghraoui, Driss, 144
Majali tribe, 41
makhzen, the: Bled al-Makhzen and Bled as-Siba, 65–66, 293n27; defined, 59–60; elected officials and, 198, 216; French protectorate and, 66; makhzen families, 216, 311n50 (*see also* Moroccan elites; urban elites [Morocco]); Moroccan monarchy and, 67–68; political parties and, 132–36, 225–26; strengthened by economic reforms, 283. *See also* Moroccan monarchy; patron-clientelism (Morocco)
Manor, James, 13
Map of Political Parties and Movements in Jordan (report), 112–13
Marrakech, Morocco, 150, 293n28
Massad, Joseph A., 44, 52
mayors (Jordan): and amalgamation, 174; authority and powers of, 161–64, 172; challenges facing, 192–94, 285–86; vs. city managers, 102; elected mayors replaced by

appointed mayors, 192, 194; election of, 183, 305n53 (*see also* electoral system [Jordan]: municipal elections); vs. executive directors, 119; impact of amalgamation on, 115, 157; and local development, 179–80, 182–83, 187–88; low status/prestige of, 192, 311n51; nepotism by, 191; often appointed, 98, 104; under Ottoman and British rule, 297n24; pitted against MPs, 112, 116; qualifications, 172–73, 306n79; and red tape, 182–84; and the "regions" plan, 116, 117, 300n51, 300n57; and wasta, 110, 156–68, 195

mayors (Morocco). *See also* presidents

Mazar, Jordan, 162, 174–75

al-Mazar al-Jadida, Jordan, 174–75, 183–84, 192, 308nn109–110, 308–9n135

al-Mazar al-Shamaliyya, Jordan, 171

MB. *See* Muslim Brotherhood

MBS (Muslim Brotherhood Society), 169–70, 294n2

MCC (Millennium Challenge Corporation), 179, 184–86, 307n98

McLaurin, Ronald, 48

Meknès, Morocco, 65–66, 150, 293n28, 312n60

MENA region, 3–4, 5, 29–30, 294n34. *See also and specific countries*

Menza, Mohamed M., 27–28

methodology for this volume, 32–36, 290nn10–12

Middle East and North Africa. *See* MENA region

military, Jordanian, 50–53, 89–90, 296n17. *See also* Arab Legion

military, Moroccan, 68–70

Millennium Challenge Corporation. *See* MCC

ministries (Jordan), 102, 297n24. *See also* Jordanian government; *and specific ministries*

ministries (Morocco), 125, 209–10, 279. *See also* Moroccan government; *and specific ministries*

Ministry for Municipal and Rural Affairs (Jordan), 101, 297n26. *See also* Ministry of Municipal Affairs

Ministry of Human Rights (Morocco), 125

Ministry of Municipal Affairs (Jordan; MoMA): and the 2010 overhaul of the municipalities law, 300–301n58; and amalgamation, 173, 177–78; and local development, 93, 178–79, 182–83; municipal executive directors appointed, 119; and municipal funding, 107, 165–66; and municipalities, 94–95, 163, 165–67, 178–79, 182–84, 306n96, 307n106 (*see also* municipal governments [Jordan]; municipalities [Jordan]); role and responsibilities, 94–95; and wasta networks, 165–66

Ministry of Planning and International Cooperation (Jordan; MoPIC), 94

Ministry of the Interior (Jordan; MoI): authority over municipalities, 101, 103–4, 182–83; complaints about municipal councils audited, 235, 314n123; and governorates, 93, 94; role and responsibilities, 94, 102; territorial units under, 307n106

Ministry of the Interior (Morocco; MoI): and the creation of rural municipalities, 68, 293nn30–31; DAS (Social Action Division), 205–7, 310n18; and the determination of municipal boundaries, 213–14; elections administered by, 224–25;

Ministry of the Interior (Morocco;
MoI) (*cont.*)
and the INDH, 142, 205–6 (*see also*
INDH); and municipal decision-
making, 147; and municipal funding,
272, 303n16; municipalities under
authority of, 201, 203, 223–24; Plan
Horizon 2015, 303n21; types of local
collectivities under, 149–50 (*see also*
municipalities [Morocco]; regions in
Morocco); workshops conducted on
2002 charter problems, 151–52, 310n27
Ministry of Tourism (Jordan), 102–3,
102–3, 184–85, 187, 298n32
Mohammed V, king of Morocco, 63,
65, 143. *See also* Moroccan monarchy
Mohammed VI, king of Morocco: and
the 2002 and 2009 charters, 145–46,
153–55; and civil society actors/
CSOs, 139–43, 146, 153, 251–52;
political liberalization under, 138–42,
145–46, 153–54; regionalization plan,
149, 151 (*see also under*
decentralization in Morocco). *See also*
Moroccan monarchy
moral clientelism, 274–75. *See also* PJD
Moroccan elites: Berber elites, 20,
37–38, 58–59, 62, 65–69, 75–76, 216;
categories of, 216; and
landownership, 217–18, 220–21; and
municipal politics, 216–18;
neighborhood association elites,
228–29, 313n105; political parties'
relationships with, 132–34; politics as
priority for elite families, 220–21;
rural elites, 66–68, 227, 293–94n31;
urban elites, 65–66, 68, 217–18, 220,
293n28, 293–94n31, 311–12n53;
votes garnered through patron-
clientelism, 225–27. *See also* elite
capture (Morocco)

Moroccan government: 1977 national
elections, 71–72, 123; administrative
structure, 122, 200–202, 208–10;
constitution (1962), 63, 139, 293n30;
constitution (2011), 201; constitutions
(1970s), 64–65, 294n32; constitutions
(1990s), 125, 128; coup attempts
(early 1970s), 68–70, 292n15, 294n32;
electoral incentives and
decentralization, 23; good
governance reforms and state
control, 30–32 (*see also* INDH);
international pressure to
democratize, 301n); and
jurisdictional confusion, 209–10;
municipal system in major cities of,
36; public expenditures, 204–5,
309–10n10; regionalization plan, 149
(*see also under* political reforms
[Morocco]). *See also* corruption
(Morocco); electoral system
(Morocco); governors (Morocco);
Moroccan monarchy; Moroccan
parliament; municipal charters;
municipal councils (Morocco);
municipalities (Morocco); patron-
clientelism (Morocco); political
parties (Morocco); political reforms
(Morocco); presidents; walis; *and
specific ministries*
Moroccan monarchy: and the 2002 and
2009 charters, 145–46, 153–54;
administrative organization under,
67–68; Alawite dynasty, 60; bay'a
(oath of allegiance to king), 64,
293n27; and civil society actors, 20,
76, 139–44, 146–48, 153–54;
coalition strategy and
decentralization decision, 20–21, 38,
75–76, 123, 154; coalition strategy
reversed following coup attempts,

69, 76, 126; coalition with Berber elite, 37–38, 58–59, 62, 65–69, 75–76; constitutional powers, 63–65; coup attempts against (early 1970s), 68–70, 294n32; economy dominated by, 134; governors appointed by, 206; and independence, 62, 63; INDH and, 207; king as reformer, 7, 29, 32, 74, 76, 123, 146, 153–54, 199, 238, 242, 277–78, 283; king as "rescuer," 29, 234–38, 277; nationalist parties wooed/coopted, 59, 69–72; opposition parties wooed/coopted, 123–31; and palace/administrative parties, 62, 65, 67, 72, 76; parties integrated into makhzen system, 133, 302n7; and the PJD, 135; political liberalization in wake of riots, 73–75; power struggle against nationalists, Istiqlal, 20, 37, 59, 66–67; religious authority of, 60, 64, 136; Royal Armed Forces created, 68; rural development and land reform neglected, 67; services and infrastructure provided directly, 199, 234; strengthened by decentralization, 7, 29, 32, 199, 236–37, 273, 277–79. *See also* Hassan II; Mohammed V; Mohammed VI

Moroccan nationalist movement. *See* nationalist movement/parties (Morocco)

Moroccan parliament: under the 1970 and 1972 constitutions, 64–65, 294n32; 1977 national elections, 71–72, 123; 1980s reforms, 74; 1984 elections, 127, 302n5; under the 1996 constitution, 128; 1997 elections, 128–29, 137, 244, 315n3; 2002 elections, 243–44, 246, 315n3; dual mandates of some MPs, 215;

monarchy's use of, in securing dominance, 71–72, 76 (*see also* Moroccan monarchy); repressed and suspended (1960s), 63–64; two houses, 128, 201, 309n5. *See also* electoral system (Morocco); political parties (Morocco); *and specific parties*

Morocco: author's field research in, 35–36, 290nn10–12; author's reasons for studying, 32–33; bidonvilles, 64, 74; debt, 73, 294n34; economic reforms and SAPs, 72–75; elites (*see* elite capture [Morocco]; Moroccan elites); before the French, 59–60, 65–66; French protectorate and its political legacy, 37, 58–62, 293n26; and human rights, 125, 301n2; illegal settlements in, 214, 226; independence, 62–63; land reform, 67, 70; military, 68–70; "Moroccanization," 68, 70; nationalist movement in (*see* nationalist movement/parties [Morocco]); phosphate revenues, 70, 72–73; privatization in, 73–74, 134, 142, 147 (*see also* INDH); rural-urban disparities, 74, 294n36 (*see also under* municipalities [Morocco]); rural-urban migration, 67, 74; social/political unrest and riots, 74, 126, 135, 136, 294n37 (*see also* Green March); social welfare in (*see* social welfare [Morocco]); trade policy, 70–71; urbanization rate, 220, 312n60; Western Sahara (Green March) campaign, 71, 130 (*see also* Western Sahara). *See also* Berber tribes; decentralization in Morocco; makhzen, the; Moroccan government; Moroccan monarchy

Mouti, Abdelkrim, 136

Mouvement Populaire (MPP; PMP). *See* PMP

Movement for Unity and Reform. *See* MUR

MPDC (Mouvement Populaire Democratique et Constitutionnel; Popular Democratic and Constitutional Movement), 135, 137–38, 243–44, 302n12. *See also* PJD

MPP (Mouvement Populaire). *See* PMP

Mufti, Malik, 82

mukhabarat (General Intelligence Agency, Jordan), 182–83

municipal charters (Morocco): 1960 charter, 122, 293n30, 301n1; civil society actors included, 11; and patron-clientelism, 154 (*see also* political parties [Morocco]). *See also* *specific charters by year*

municipal councils (Morocco): 1960 elections, 216; 1976 elections, 71–72; 2002 charter and, 148–49, 151–53, 200, 202; 2009 charter and, 153, 155, 200, 202, 269; 2009 councils, 33–34; 2009 elections, 275; auditing of complaints about, 235, 314n123; autonomy and authority, 33, 147–48, 198–99, 217, 303n16; budgets, 234, 314n120; central representatives accused of tolerating corruption, 224–25; and civil society actors, 202, 230–31, 280; and corruption, 199, 229–33; councilors and elite capture, 198, 229–33, 236–38, 279–80; councilors' multiple hats, 230–34, 237; election of, 198–99, 201, 216; elites and, 216–18; and the INDH, 205–8, 310nn15–16; ineffectiveness

and incompetence, 233–37; jurisdictional confusion, 209–12, 279; lack of autonomy and authority, 200, 202–5, 208–10, 218–19, 279; PJD and (*see* PJD); planning by (PCDs), 202–5, 230–31, 234, 235–36, 303n22, 309n4; presidents' power and, 215–22 (*see also* presidents); role and responsibilities, 147–49, 153; and *transhumance*, 228, 237. *See also* municipalities (Morocco); presidents; *tutelle*

municipal governments (Jordan; councils), 103–4; 2007 and 2013 municipal elections, 105, 192, 298n37, 309n136; 2007 councils, 34; under the 2015 decentralization and municipalities laws, 118–19; and amalgamation, 175–76; budgets, 160, 165–67, 183–84, 193–94; challenges facing, 192–94, 285–86; city managers vs. mayors, 102, 279; and decentralization plans in the 2000s, 300n57; directly elected, 78; elected vs. appointed councils, 34, 98, 102, 104–5, 192, 297n29; electoral system and, 305nn53–55; fiscal mismanagement, 193–94; funding, 106–9, 301n63; and local development, 180–82, 285; low respect for, 192; mayors' relationships with, 161–65; municipal elections laws, 102–6, 298n30, 298n33, 298nn 35–36; under the Ottomans, 42, 100, 291nn3–4, 297n24; powers granted to, 101; powers removed from, 33, 78–79, 99–106; wasta, tribalism, and, 156–73, 303n6 (*see also* wasta). *See also* mayors (Jordan); municipalities (Jordan); municipal services (Jordan)

municipal governments, accountability of (generally), 16–17

municipalities (Jordan): 2015 municipalities and decentralization laws, 118–19, 301n61, 301n63; administrative structure (present-day), 118–19; amalgamation of, 79, 114–15, 157, 173–78, 191, 194–95, 299nn47–48, 306n83; Arab Spring protests in, 118; budgets, 1, 160, 165–67, 173–74, 183–84, 193–94; categories of, 307n106; centralization and municipal politics, 2, 194; clawback of municipal responsibilities, 99–106, 119, 120–21, 286; crisis, 78–80, 110–13, 285–86; and decentralization plans in the 2000s, 117, 300n57; dependent on royal patronage, 188–91; employees, 113, 163–64, 166–67, 191, 193; funding, 79, 106–9, 186–87, 301n63; governors' role vis-a-vis, 94; land use and ownership, 162, 180–82, 185–87; and local development (LDUs), 93, 178–88, 191–92 (*see also* local development [Jordan]); under MoMA's authority, 94–95, 165–67, 182–84, 307n106 (*see also* Ministry of Municipal Affairs); municipalities laws, 100, 101–4, 297n27; number of, 113–14, 178; Ottoman system, 42, 100, 291n3, 297n24; and the "regions" plan, 117; social unrest in, 172, 173; taxes, 186–87, 309n139; wasta, tribalism, and, 157–73, 194–96, 303n6. *See also* municipal governments (Jordan); municipal services (Jordan); *and specific cities and municipalities*

municipalities (Morocco), 2; 1976 elections, 123; 1983 elections, 127, 302n5; 1997 elections, 243, 244; 2003 elections, 244, 246–48, 252, 254, 262, 268, 316n25; 2009 elections, 249, 252–53, 254–57, 262–65, 314n120, 315n16, 316n40, 318n90; 2015 elections, 281; and associations and NGOs, 231–33, 236–37, 265–66, 268–70, 280 (*see also* associations, in Morocco); auditing of, 314n123; budgets and expenditures, 203–5, 209, 213, 234, 309n5, 309–10n10, 314n120; and civil society actors, 202, 252, 280 (*see also* civil society actors [Morocco]); creation and administrative structure of rural municipalities (1957–1960), 67–68, 293nn30–31; deconcentrated "bottom-up" structure of authority, 200–202, 208; determination of administrative boundaries, 213–15; electoral system, 214 (*see also* electoral system [Morocco]); employees (civil servants), 222–25, 237, 312n69; *fonctionnaires* (state bureaucrats, technical staff), 248; implementation delays, 210–11; increasing numbers of, 146–47; and INDH projects, 141–42, 205–8, 310nn15–16; jurisdictional confusion, 209–12; monarchy and the makhzenian system, 67–68; party presence in, 132 (*see also* PJD); place within top-down administrative structure, 200–201; planning by (PCDs), 202–5, 230–31, 234, 235–36, 303n22, 309n4; powers expanded under 1976 charter, 131; response to reforms based on own interests, 27–29, 280; secretaries-general, 223–24, 312n77; urban vs. rural, 35, 132, 201, 213–14 (*see also* rural municipalities; urban municipalities). *See also* municipal charters; municipal councils

municipalities (Morocco) (*cont.*)
(Morocco); municipal services
(Morocco); presidents; *and specific
municipalities; and specific charters by
year*

municipal services (Jordan): in the
1990s, 1; amalgamation and, 173–78;
municipal system bankrupt (1990s),
58; responsibility for (jurisdiction
over), 101–3, 183, 298n34; wasta and,
80, 110–13, 161–65, 195 (*see also*
wasta)

municipal services (Morocco): decaying
infrastructure, 1–2; inadequate and
unequal, 233, 235; jurisdiction over,
209–10; PJD and, 249–51, 271–72;
privatization's impact, 147; provided
directly by monarchy, 199 (*see also*
Moroccan monarchy: king as
rescuer); service delivery poor, 32,
199

MUR (Movement for Unity and
Reform; Harakat al-Tawhid
wal-Islah), 137, 242–47, 257–58. *See
also* RR

Muslim Brotherhood (MB): and the
1989 elections, 82, 295n5; and the
IAF, 111, 294n1, 294–95n2; in Jerash,
183; Jordanian branch established,
83, 295n8; monarchy's relations with,
83–84, 296n10–11; politicization of,
83–84, 296n12; and religious
education, 83, 295n9; and tribal
politics, 169–70

Muslim Brotherhood Society (MBS),
169–70, 294n2

al-Nabulsi, Sulayman, 49

NAC (National Action Bloc), 61–62. *See
also* Istiqlal Party (Morocco)

Naimat tribe (Jordan), 34, 170, 190

Nasser, Jamal Abdel, 47

National Aid Fund (NAF), 91

National Alliance for Reform
(Al-Islah), 169, 294–95n2. *See also*
IAF; MBS

National Bloc (al-Koutla
al-Watanniyya), 71. *See also* Istiqlal
Party (Morocco); UNFP

National Congress Party (Jordan),
294n2

National Constitutional Party (Jordan),
111

National Initiative for Human
Development. *See* INDH

nationalist movement (Jordan), 47–50,
83, 292n10, 292n12

nationalist movement/parties
(Morocco), 59, 61–63, 70–72, 139,
293n28. *See also* Istiqlal Party
(Morocco); National Bloc; PDI;
UNFP

National Rally of Independents (RNI),
72, 240

National Socialist Party (NSP; Jordan),
48–49

National Union of Popular Forces. *See*
UNFP

neighborhood associations (Morocco),
228–29, 250, 252–53, 256, 313n105,
317n50. *See also* associations, in
Morocco

Nellis, John R., 122, 154

neoliberalism, 9–11, 13–14, 29–30, 88,
247, 290n9. *See also* decentralization
(generally); good governance

Nevo, Joseph, 84

NGOs (Jordan), 87, 90. *See also* RONGOs

NGOs (Morocco): in Chefchaouen,
265–66; and development projects,
206–7; increase in, 139; and the
INDH, 143, 206, 310n18; and PCDs

Porter, Doug, 14–15
poverty: in Jordan, 91–92, 107, 109 (*see also* local development [Jordan]; social welfare [Jordan]); in Morocco, 312n60 (*see also* bidonvilles); poverty reduction programs in Morocco, 142–43, 153 (*see also* INDH; local development [Morocco])
PPPs. *See* public-private partnerships
PPS (Progress and Socialism Party; Partie du Progrès et du Socialisme), 127
prefectural and provincial councils (Morocco), 200–201, 208
presidents (Moroccan mayors): 2015 election results, 281–82; authority and powers of, 148–49, 153, 199, 215, 279, 311n52; central authority over, 147; and civil servants, 222–25, 237; and the concentration of power, 215–22, 237; connections and effectiveness of, 212–13; and corruption, 199, 222–27; education requirement, 148, 152; election of, 201; and electoral fraud, 224–25; family lineage of, 227; and governors and walis, 205, 212–13, 224, 237; and INDH-inspired associations, 231–32; landowner-developers as, 226; opportunities to make wealth, 230; personality over program, 228, 313n100; PJD and, 274–75 (*see also* PJD); removal by councilors, 235; role and responsibilities, 122, 131. *See also* Sefiani, Mohamed
prime minister (Jordan): GAM under control of, 94, 98, 119–20; and Qreqra w Finan's development, 186; and regionalization, 96; role and authority, 93, 297n24, 301n60

prime minister (Morocco), 124, 128–29, 135. *See also* Moroccan government
privatization: and central state control, 29–30; in Jordan, 86–89 (*see also* Jordan: SAP and privatization in); and loss of accountability, 29–30; in Morocco, 73–74, 134, 142, 147 (*see also* INDH)
Professional Syndicates Association, 85, 296n13
Progress and Socialism Party (PPS), 127
Provincial Committee for Human Development. *See* CPDH
Prud'homme, Rémy, 25–27
PSU (Parti Socialiste Unifié; United Socialist Party), 255, 263–64, 266, 318n90, 319n116
public-private partnerships (PPPs; Jordan), 28, 87, 90–91, 134, 283. *See also* patron-clientelism (Jordan); privatization (Jordan)

Qreqra w Finan, Jordan, 180–81, 185–86

Rabat, Morocco, 61, 281–82, 293n28
Ramsar Convention, 211
Rania, Queen of Jordan, 91
Rassemblement National des Indépendants (RNI), 72, 240
Rebbah, Abdelaziz, 253, 268, 320n1
regional development groups (Jordan), 96–99
regional investment centers (RICs; Morocco), 150, 208, 310n25
regions (wilaya) in Morocco, 149–51, 303n18. *See also* walis
Reimer, Michael J., 42, 199, 291nn3–4
Reiter, Yitzhak, 84, 87–88
rentierism: in Jordan, 54–58, 88–89, 158 (*see also* oil); in Morocco, 70–71 (*see also* phosphates)

Riley, Meredith, 128–29

RNI (Rassemblement National des Indépendants; National Rally of Independents), 72, 240

Rondinelli, Dennis A., 14–16

RONGOs (royal NGOs; Jordan), 87, 90–91, 180–82, 189, 283, 296n19, 308n125

Royal Commission for Administrative Development, 97

Royal Commission of the Regions, 115

royal family of Jordan. *See* Jordanian monarchy; RONGOs

RR (Reform and Renewal; As-Islah was At-Tajdid), 136–37, 302n10. *See also* MUR

rural elites (Morocco), 66–68, 227, 293–94n31. *See also* Berber tribes

rural municipalities (Morocco), 35, 201, 213–15, 311n47. *See also* municipalities (Morocco); *and specific municipalities*

Rusaifa, Jordan, 105–6, 109

Ryan, Curtis, 86, 88

Saadi, Mohamed Said, 30

El-Said, Hamed, 52–53, 71, 143, 146

Salt, Jordan, 42, 48, 56, 109

San Remo Resolution (1920), 40

SAPs (structural adjustment programs), 13; and elite capture in Misr Al Qadima (Cairo), 27–28; in Jordan, 20, 33, 81, 86–92, 113 (*see also* municipalities [Jordan]: crisis); in Morocco, 33, 72–75, 139, 143–44; socioeconomic and political consequences, 14

Sater, James N., 64, 69, 72, 153, 315n127

Satloff, Robert, 78, 116

Saudi Arabia, 49, 310n14. *See also* Ibn Saud

Schwedler, Jillian, 57, 82

secretaries-general, municipal (Morocco), 223–24, 312n77. *See also* municipal councils (Morocco); municipalities (Morocco)

Sefiani, Mohamed, 262–63, 265

Al-Shalabi, Jamal, 120

shantytowns. *See* bidonvilles

shari'a, PJD stance on, 244–45

Shoaleh, Jordan, 166–67, 181, 187

Shobak, Jordan, 181, 186

al-Shobani, al-Habib, 268

Smoke, Paul, 18–19, 21–22, 37

Socialist Union of Popular Forces. *See* USFP

Social Priority Programme (Morocco), 146. *See also* social welfare and social services (Morocco)

Social Productivity Programme (Jordan), 91

social welfare (generally), 31

social welfare (Jordan): economic reforms and, 90–91; for military personnel, families, 89–90; monarchy's role, 188–89; NGOs, RONGOs and, 90–91, 283 (*see also* RONGOs); private-sector employees ineligible, 53; social insurance extended to small businesses, 296n18; Social Security Corporation (SSC), 87; Transjordanians benefitted disproportionately, 89–92, 296nn16–17

social welfare and social services (Morocco): 1970–1983, 71; center for abandoned children, 236–37; monarchy and, 143, 145, 146; privatization of, 142 (*see also* INDH); social security, 74